GLENCOE ENGLISH

Spectrum of English 9

Composition
Speech
Grammar

Yvonne Kuhlman
Joyce Bartky

CONSULTANTS
Donna M. Hughes
Louise K. Lowry
Richard W. Clark

Glencoe Publishing Co., Inc.
Encino, California

ACKNOWLEDGMENTS

Brandt & Brandt Literary Agents, Inc.: From *One Ordinary Day, With Peanuts* by Shirley Jackson. First published in *The Magazine of Fantasy and Science Fiction,* © 1955 by Shirley Jackson. Reprinted by permission of Brandt & Brandt Literary Agents, Inc.

Four Winds Press: From *The Natural Snack Cookbook* by Jill Pinkwater, © 1975. Used by permission of Four Winds Press, a division of Scholastic Magazines, Inc.

Harcourt Brace Jovanovich: From "My Name is Aram" by William Saroyan. Used by permission of Harcourt Brace Jovanovich.

Harcourt Brace Jovanovich: From "A Worn Path." From *A Curtain of Green and Other Stories* by Eudora Welty. Used by permission of Harcourt Brace Jovanovich.

Alfred A. Knopf, Inc.: From *Tell Freedom: Memories of Africa* by Peter Abrahams, © 1954. Used by permission of Alfred A. Knopf, Inc.

Little, Brown and Company: From *Mythology* by Edith Hamilton. Used by permission of Little, Brown and Company.

Harold Ober Associates, Inc.: From "The Old Demon." From *Today and Forever* by Pearl S. Buck, © 1939, copyright renewed 1966. Used by permission of Harold Ober Associates, Inc.

Oxford University Press: From *The Sea Around Us* by Rachel Carson. Used by permission of Oxford University Press.

Parents' Magazine Enterprises: From "Accident Prevention for Your Pet" by Jo and Paul Loeb. From *Parents'* Magazine, February, 1979. Reprinted by permission of Parents' Magazine Enterprises.

Laurence Pollinger Limited: From "My Name is Aram." From *Locomotive 38, The Ojibway* by William Saroyan. Used by permission of Laurence Pollinger Limited.

Random House, Inc.: From *The Complete Book of Running* by James F. Fixx. Used by permission of Random House, Inc.

Random House, Inc.: From "Miriam." From *Selected Writings of Truman Capote* by Truman Capote. Used by permission of Random House, Inc.

Alfred A. Knopf, Inc.: From *Out of Africa* by Isak Dinesen, © 1972. Used by permission of Alfred A. Knopf, Inc.

Russell & Volkening, Inc.: From "A Worn Path." From *A Curtain of Green and Other Stories* by Eudora Welty, © 1941, renewed 1969 by Eudora Welty. Reprinted by permission of Russell & Volkening, Inc. as agent for the author.

Sports Illustrated: From "They Crawl by Night" by Bil Gilbert. From *Sports Illustrated,* August 27, 1979, © 1979 Time Inc. Reprinted courtesy of *Sports Illustrated.*

Triangle Communications Inc.: "Movie of the Month" by Edwin Miller. From *Seventeen* Magazine, March, 1979. Reprinted from *Seventeen* Magazine, © 1979 by Triangle Communications Inc. All rights reserved.

Woman's Day Magazine: From "Drownproofing" by Carla Stephens. From *Woman's Day* Magazine. Reprinted by permission of *Woman's Day* Magazine, © 1976 by CBS Publications, Inc.

World Book-Childcraft International, Inc.: Adapted from articles from *The World Book Encyclopedia.* © 1979 World Book-Childcraft International, Inc. Used by permission of World Book-Childcraft International, Inc.

Ziff-Davis Publishing Co.: From "Stalking the IQ Quark" by Robert J. Sternberg. From *Psychology Today* Magazine, September, 1979. Reprinted by permission of *Psychology Today* Magazine, © 1979, Ziff-Davis Publishing Co.

Photography

All photography by Marshall Berman except page 271, left Nick Pavloff/Icon; right Gregg Mancuso/Jeroboam.

Illustration

Francis Livingston
Ed Taber

Design and Production

Design Office / Bruce Kortebein, Peter Martin, Cindy Croker, Ann Brennan

Cover Design: Glencoe staff.

Glencoe Publishing Co., Inc.
17337 Ventura Boulevard
Encino, California 91316
Collier Macmillan Canada, Ltd.
Printed in the United States of America

ISBN 0-02-656750-4 (Student Text)
ISBN 0-02-656760-1 (Teacher's Annotated Edition)

3 4 5 6 7 8 9 84 83 82

CONTENTS

Composition

CHAPTER 1   **The Writing Process**   1

    1. Finding a Subject   2
    2. Drafting   7
    3. Composing   10
    4. Revising: Words   12
    5. Revising: Sentences   15
    6. Proofreading   18

CHAPTER 2   **Descriptive Writing**   20

    1. Using a Topic Sentence and Supporting Details in a Descriptive Paragraph   21
    2. Using Sensory Details in a Descriptive Paragraph   24
    3. Developing a Descriptive Paragraph with an Unusual Comparison   27
    4. Using Spatial Organization in a Descriptive Paragraph   29
    5. Writing a Descriptive Essay   32

CHAPTER 3   **Narrative Writing**   34

    1. Describing a Story Character   35
    2. Using Actions to Develop Characters   39
    3. Using Dialogue to Develop Characters   43
    4. Developing a Story Plot   47
    5. Using Chronological Order in Stories   50
    6. Writing a Short Story   53

CHAPTER 4   **Expository Writing**   54

    1. Writing a Paragraph of Directions   55
    2. Using Comparison in an Expository Paragraph   58
    3. Using Contrast in an Expository Paragraph   61
    4. Using Examples in an Expository Paragraph   64
    5. Writing an Expository Essay   67

CHAPTER 5   **Research Reports**   68

    1. Planning a Research Report   69
    2. Taking Notes for a Research Report   72
    3. Outlining a Research Report   74
    4. Writing a Research Report   77

CHAPTER 6   **Persuasive Writing**   80
                 1. Writing Persuasive Slogans   81
                 2. Writing a Persuasive Paragraph   85
                 3. Writing a Persuasive Essay   88

CHAPTER 7   **Practical Writing**   90
                 1. Writing a Business Letter   91
                 2. Writing a Movie Review   94
                 3. Completing an Application Form   97

Composition Handbook

SENTENCES

1 Sentence Variety
1a. Variety of Sentence Length   102
1b. Variety of Sentence Beginnings   103
1c. Combining Sentences   104

**FORMS
AND
GUIDELINES**

2 Proofreading
2a. Proofreading Checklist   105

3 Note-Taking
3a. Summary Sentences   106
3b. Bibliography Cards   107
3c. Bibliography   108
3d. Note Cards   109
3e. Footnotes   110

4 Outlines
4a. Writing Outlines   111

5 Letters
5a. Friendly Letters   112
5b. Business Letters   113
5c. Envelopes   114

PARAGRAPHS

6 Paragraph Development
6a. Topic Sentences in Paragraphs   115
6b. Using Details to Develop Paragraphs   116
6c. Using Incidents to Develop Paragraphs   117
6d. Using Reasons to Develop Paragraphs   118

6e. Using Examples to Develop Paragraphs   119
6f. Using Comparison or Contrast to Develop Paragraphs   120

7 Paragraph Organization

7a. Using Chronological Organization in Paragraphs   121
7b. Using Spatial Organization in Paragraphs   122

Speech

CHAPTER 8   Narrative Speaking   124

                 1. Telling a Story   125
                 2. Making a Narrative Speech   128

CHAPTER 9   Expository Speaking   130

                 1. Presenting Information in a Conversation 131
                 2. Giving a Summary Speech   134
                 3. Using Visual Aids in a Speech   136
                 4. Presenting a Research Report   138

CHAPTER 10   Persuasive Speaking   140

                 1. Speaking Persuasively in Informal Meetings 141
                 2. Giving a Formal Persuasive Speech   144

CHAPTER 11   Listening   146

                 1. Listening in a Conversation   147
                 2. Listening in a Formal Meeting   149
                 3. Asking Questions in an Interview   151
                 4. Listening and Responding in an Interview 155

Speech Handbook

COMMUNICATION **1** The Communication Cycle

                   1a. Analyzing Communication   158

                   2 Using Your Voice

                   2a. Speaking Strongly and Clearly   160
                   2b. Speaking Distinctly   160
                   2c. Using Vocal Variety   162

3 Listening

    3a. Participating in a Conversation   163
    3b. Listening to a Speech   164

4 Using Your Body

    4a. Communicating Meaning and Emotions   166
    4b. Understanding Audience Response   166

5 Word Choice

    5a. Using Specific Words and Vivid Language   168
    5b. Using Appropriate Language   168
    5c. Using Direct Language   168

6 Attitudes

    6a. Attitudes toward Yourself   170
    6b. Attitudes toward Your Listeners   170
    6c. Attitudes toward Your Subject   170

FORMS AND GUIDELINES

7 Kinds of Speaking

    7a. Narrative Speaking   172
    7b. Expository Speaking   173
    7c. Persuasive Speaking   174
    7d. Interviewing   175

8 Special Speeches

    8a. Introducing a Speaker   176
    8b. Nominating a Candidate   176
    8c. Presenting an Award   177
    8d. Accepting an Award   177
    8e. Oral Book Reports   178

9 Group Speaking

    9a. Group Discussions   179
    9b. Panel Discussions   180
    9c. Parliamentary Procedure   182
    9d. Debates   184
    9e. Speaking in Debates   185

10 Diagnostic Checklists

    10a. Using Your Voice   186
    10b. Listening   186
    10c. Using Your Body   187
    10d. Word Choice   187
    10e. Attitudes   188
    10f. Speaking in Groups   188

Grammar Handbook

SENTENCES

1 Kinds of Sentences

1a. Declarative, Interrogative, and Imperative Sentences   190

2 Subjects and Predicates

2a. Subjects and Predicates in Most Declarative Sentences   191
2b. Subjects and Predicates in Declarative Sentences with Inverted Order   192
2c. Subjects and Predicates in Imperative Sentences   192
2d. Subjects and Predicates in Interrogative Sentences   193

Reviewing   **1** Kinds of Sentences and   **2** Subjects and Predicates   194

PARTS OF SPEECH

3 Verbs

3a. Recognizing and Using Verbs   196
3b. Past Tense Verb Forms   197
3c. Forms of **Be**   198
3d. **Be** as an Auxiliary   199
3e. **Have** as an Auxiliary   200
3f. Modals   201
3g. Separated Verb Phrase Words in Declarative Sentences   202
3h. Separated Verb Phrase Words in Interrogative Sentences   202
3i. **Do** as an Auxiliary   204
3j. Modals with the Auxiliary **Be**   205
3k. Modals with the Auxiliary **Have**   205
3l. The Auxiliary **Have** with the Auxiliary **Be**   206
3m. Modals with the Auxiliary **Have** and the Auxiliary **Be**   206
3n. Verb Tenses   208
3o. Progressive Verb Tenses   210
3p. Sentences with Passive Verb Phrases   212
3q. Subjunctive Form of **Be**   214

Reviewing   **3** Verbs   216

4 Nouns

4a. Recognizing and Using Nouns   218
4b. Proper Nouns and Common Nouns   219
4c. Gerunds   220
4d. Infinitives as Nouns   221

5 Pronouns

5a. Recognizing and Using Personal Pronouns   222

5b.	Possessive Pronoun Forms	224
5c.	Indefinite Pronouns	225
5d.	Reflexive Pronouns	226
5e.	Interrogative Pronouns	226
5f.	Demonstrative Pronouns	227
5g.	Relative Pronouns	227

Reviewing **4** Nouns and **5** Pronouns   228

6 Adjectives

6a.	Recognizing and Using Adjectives	230
6b.	Distinguishing between Adjectives, Indefinite Pronouns, and Demonstrative Pronouns	232
6c.	Proper Adjectives	233
6d.	Adjectives after the Nouns and Pronouns They Modify	234
6e.	Participles as Adjectives	235

7 Adverbs

7a.	Recognizing and Using Adverbs	236
7b.	Adverbs That Modify Adjectives	237
7c.	Adverbs That Modify Other Adverbs	238
7d.	Infinitives as Adverbs	239

8 Prepositions

8a.	Recognizing and Using Prepositions and Prepositional Phrases	240
8b.	Prepositional Phrases as Adjectives and as Adverbs	242

9 Conjunctions

9a.	Recognizing and Using Coordinating Conjunctions	243
9b.	Correlative Conjunctions	243
9c.	Subordinating Conjunctions	244

10 Interjections

10a.	Recognizing and Using Interjections	245

Reviewing **6** Adjectives **7** Adverbs **8** Prepositions
9 Conjunctions and **10** Interjections   246

SENTENCE PATTERNS

11 Sentences with Intransitive Verbs

11a.	Subject Nouns and Pronouns with Verbs and Verb Phrases	248
11b.	Modifiers in Sentences with Intransitive Verbs	249
11c.	Sentences with Compound Subjects	250

11d.	Sentences with Compound Predicates	250
11e.	Diagraming Sentences with Intransitive Verbs	252
11f.	Diagraming Sentences with Adjectives and Adverbs	253
11g.	Diagraming Sentences with Qualifying Adverbs	254
11h.	Diagraming Sentences with Prepositional Phrases	255
11i.	Diagraming Sentences with Compound Subjects	256
11j.	Diagraming Sentences with Compound Predicates	257

Reviewing **11** Sentences with Intransitive Verbs   258

12 Sentences with Direct Objects

12a.	Direct Object Nouns and Pronouns	260
12b.	Modifiers in Sentences with Direct Objects	261
12c.	Intransitive Verbs and Transitive Verbs	262
12d.	Sentences with Compound Direct Objects	263
12e.	Passive Verb Phrases from Sentences with Direct Objects	264
12f.	Diagraming Sentences with Direct Objects	265

13 Sentences with Indirect Objects

13a.	Indirect Object Nouns and Pronouns	266
13b.	Modifiers in Sentences with Indirect Objects	267
13c.	Sentences with Compound Indirect Objects	268
13d.	Passive Verb Phrases from Sentences with Indirect Objects	269
13e.	Diagraming Sentences with Indirect Objects	270

14 Sentences with Object Complements

14a.	Object Complement Nouns and Adjectives	271
14b.	Modifiers in Sentences with Object Complements	272
14c.	Diagraming Sentences with Object Complements	273

Reviewing **12** Sentences with Direct Objects **13** Sentences with Indirect Objects and **14** Sentences with Object Complements   274

15 Sentences with Linking Verbs

15a.	Sentences with Predicate Adjectives	276
15b.	Sentences with Predicate Nominatives	276
15c.	Modifiers in Sentences with Predicate Adjectives and Sentences with Predicate Nominatives	278
15d.	Sentences with Compound Predicate Adjectives	279
15e.	Sentences with Compound Predicate Nominatives	280
15f.	Sentences with Adverbs after Linking Verbs	281
15g.	Sentences with Prepositional Phrases after Linking Verbs	281
15h.	Diagraming Sentences with Linking Verbs	282
15i.	Simple Subjects and Simple Predicates	283

Reviewing **15** Sentences with Linking Verbs   284

ix

PHRASES AND CLAUSES

16 Phrases

16a.	Identifying and Using Prepositional Phrases	286
16b.	Gerund Phrases	287
16c.	Diagraming Gerund Phrases Used as Subjects	288
16d.	Diagraming Gerund Phrases Used as Direct Objects	289
16e.	Nonrestrictive Participial Phrases	290
16f.	Restrictive Participial Phrases	292
16g.	Diagraming Participial Phrases	293
16h.	Infinitive Phrases Used as Nouns	294
16i.	Infinitive Phrases Used as Adjectives	295
16j.	Infinitive Phrases Used as Adverbs	296
16k.	Diagraming Infinitive Phrases Used as Nouns	297
16l.	Diagraming Infinitive Phrases Used as Adjectives and as Adverbs	298
16m.	Appositive Phrases	299

Reviewing **16** Phrases — 300

17 Clauses

17a.	Identifying and Using Independent Clauses	302
17b.	Diagraming Compound Sentences	303
17c.	Adverb Clauses	304
17d.	Diagraming Adverb Clauses	305
17e.	Adjective Clauses with Relative Pronouns as Subjects	306
17f.	Adjective Clauses with Relative Pronouns as Direct Objects	308
17g.	Adjective Clauses Beginning with **When, Where,** or **Whose**	309
17h.	Restrictive and Nonrestrictive Adjective Clauses	310
17i.	Diagraming Adjective Clauses	312
17j.	Noun Clauses Used as Subjects	313
17k.	Noun Clauses Used as Predicate Nominatives	314
17l.	Noun Clauses Used as Direct Objects, as Indirect Objects, and as Objects of Prepositions	315
17m.	Diagraming Noun Clauses	316
17n.	Simple, Compound, Complex, and Compound-Complex Sentences	317

Reviewing **17** Clauses — 318

USAGE

18 Sentence Problems

18a.	Correcting Sentence Fragments	320
18b.	Correcting Run-on Sentences	321
18c.	Correcting Rambling Sentences	322
18d.	Avoiding Unnecessary Repetition in Sentences	324

19 Subject–Verb Agreement

19a.	Present Tense Verb Forms	325

19b.	Indefinite Pronoun Subjects	326
19c.	Collective Noun Subjects	327
19d.	Subject Noun or Pronoun Modified by a Prepositional Phrase	328
19e.	Compound Subject	329
19f.	Sentences Beginning with **Here** and **There**	330
19g.	Titles, Names of Organizations, and Names of Countries as Subjects	331
19h.	Expressions of Amount as Subjects	332
19i.	**Do** and **Does; Don't** and **Doesn't**	333

Reviewing   **18**   Sentence Problems and   **19**   Subject-Verb Agreement   334

20   Verb Usage

20a.	Irregular Verb Forms I	336
20b.	Irregular Verb Forms II	337
20c.	Irregular Verb Forms III	338
20d.	Irregular Verb Forms IV	339
20e.	Irregular Verb Forms V	340
20f.	Irregular Verb Forms VI	341
20g.	Irregular Verb Forms VII	342
20h.	Irregular Verb Forms VIII	343
20i.	**Lie** and **Lay**	344
20j.	**Rise** and **Raise**	345
20k.	**Sit** and **Set**	346
20l.	**Teach** and **Learn**	158
20m.	Avoiding Unnecessary Changes in Verb Tense	347

Reviewing   **20**   Verb Usage   348

21   Modifiers

21a.	Distinguishing between Adjectives and Adverbs	350
21b.	Distinguishing between **Good** and **Well**	351
21c.	Comparisons with Adjectives	352
21d.	Comparisons with **Good** and **Bad**	352
21e.	Comparisons with Adverbs	353
21f.	Comparisons with **Well**	353
21g.	**Other** and **Else** in Comparisons	354
21h.	Avoiding Misplaced Adjectives	355
21i.	Avoiding Dangling Modifiers	356
21j.	Avoiding Misplaced Adverbs	357
21k.	Avoiding Double Negatives	358
21l.	**Less** and **Fewer**	359

Reviewing   **21**   Modifiers   360

22   Pronouns

22a.	Subject and Object Form Pronouns	362
22b.	Avoiding Unclear Antecedents	363
22c.	Avoiding Missing Antecedents	364
22d.	Pronouns and Compound Antecedents	365

22e. **Who** and **Whom** as Interrogative Pronouns 366
22f. **Who** and **Whom** as Relative Pronouns 367
22g. Pronouns in Comparisons 368
22h. Possessive Pronouns before Gerunds 368

23 Prepositions
23a. **Between** and **Among** 369
23b. **Beside** and **Besides** 369
23c. **In** and **Into** 370
23d. **Of** 370
23e. **At** 370

24 Parallel Structure
24a. Parallel Structure: Nouns, Adjectives, and Adverbs 371
24b. Parallel Structure: Gerunds and Infinitives 372
24c. Parallel Structure with Correlative Conjunctions 373

Reviewing **22** Pronouns **23** Prepositions and
24 Parallel Structure 374

MECHANICS

25 Capital Letters
25a. Capital Letters at the Beginning of Sentences 376
25b. Capital Letters in Direct Quotations 377
25c. Capital Letters in Names of People 377
25d. Capitalizing the Personal Pronoun **I** 377
25e. Capital Letters in Titles of People 378
25f. Capital Letters in Titles of Relatives 378
25g. Capital Letters in Names of Days, Months, and
Holidays 379
25h. Capital Letters in Abbreviations of Days and Months 379
25i. Capital Letters in Names of Streets and Highways 380
25j. Capital Letters in Place Names 380
25k. Capital Letters in ZIP Code Abbreviations 381
25l. Capital Letters in Abbreviations of Academic Degrees 381
25m. Capital Letters in Abbreviations of Time 381
25n. Capital Letters in Names of Geographical Features 382
25o. Capital Letters in Names of Buildings and Other
Structures 383
25p. Capital Letters in Titles 384
25q. Capital Letters in Names of Organizations 385
25r. Capital Letters in Names of Historical References 385
25s. Capital Letters in Brand Names 386
25t. Capital Letters in Names of Ships, Planes, and Trains 386
25u. Capital Letters in Names of Monuments and Awards 387
25v. Capital Letters in Names of School Subjects 387
25w. Capital Letters in Proper Adjectives 388
25x. Capital Letters in Names of Languages and
Nationalities 389
25y. Capital Letters in Names Related to Religions 389

Reviewing **25** Capital Letters   390

26 Periods, Question Marks, and Exclamation Marks
  26a. End Punctuation   392
  26b. Periods in Abbreviations   392

27 Commas
  27a. Commas in Dates   393
  27b. Commas in Place Names and Addresses   393
  27c. Commas in Series   394
  27d. Commas between Adjectives   394
  27e. Commas with Nouns of Address   395
  27f. Commas with Interrupters   395
  27g. Commas with Introductory **Yes** and **No**   395
  27h. Commas with Interjections   395
  27i. Commas in Compound Sentences   396
  27j. Commas with Appositive Phrases   397
  27k. Commas with Introductory Adverbial Prepositional
       Phrases   398
  27l. Commas with Participial Phrases   399
  27m. Commas with Introductory Adverb Clauses   400
  27n. Commas with Nonrestrictive Adjective Clauses   401
  27o. Commas with Transitional Words and Phrases   402
  27p. Commas with Abbreviations   403

Reviewing **26** Periods, Question Marks, Exclamation Marks
         and   **27** Commas   404

28 Other Punctuation Marks
  28a. Quotation Marks with Titles   406
  28b. Underlines with Titles   406
  28c. Punctuation Marks with Direct Quotations   407
  28d. Quotation Marks within Quotations   408
  28e. Apostrophes in Possessive Nouns   409
  28f. Apostrophes in Contractions   409
  28g. Colons before Lists   410
  28h. Colons in Expressions of Time   410
  28i. Semicolons in Lists   411
  28j. Semicolons in Compound Sentences   412
  28k. Hyphens   413
  28l. Parentheses   413

Reviewing **28** Other Punctuation Marks   414

SPELLING AND VOCABULARY

29 Plural Forms of Nouns
  29a. Nouns That Add **-s**   416
  29b. Nouns That Add **-es**   416
  29c. Nouns That End in a Consonant and **y**   417

29d. Nouns That End in a Vowel and **y**   417
29e. Nouns That End in **f** or **fe**   418
29f. Nouns That End in a Consonant and **o**   419
29g. Nouns That End in a Vowel and **o**   419
29h. Compound Nouns   420
29i. Irregular Nouns   420
29j. Nouns That Do Not Change   420
29k. Greek and Latin Nouns   421

30 Prefixes

30a. The Prefixes **in-, il-, im-,** and **ir-**   422
30b. The Prefixes **non-, un-,** and **dis-**   422
30c. The Prefixes **mis-, over-, under-,** and **re-**   423
30d. The Prefixes **pre-, post-,** and **anti-**   423

31 Suffixes

31a. Spelling That Does Not Change   424
31b. Dropping Final **e**   424
31c. Keeping Final **e**   424
31d. Changing Final **y** to **i**   425
31e. Keeping Final **y**   425
31f. Doubling the Final Consonant in One-Syllable Words   426
31g. Doubling the Final Consonant in Words of More Than One Syllable   426

32 Spelling Rules

32a. Words That Are Spelled with **ie** or **ei**   427
32b. Words That End in **-cede, -ceed,** or **-sede**   427

33 Spelling Words Correctly

33a. Dividing Words into Syllables   428
33b. Pronouncing Words Distinctly   428
33c. Words That May Be Confused with Other Words   429
33d. A List of Commonly Misspelled Words   430

34 Defining Words

34a. Latin Prefixes and Roots   432
34b. Learning New Words   434
34c. Words That Have Multiple Meanings   434
34d. Words That Can Be Used as Different Parts of Speech   434

Index   435

Composition

The Writing Process   2

Descriptive Writing   20

Narrative Writing   34

Expository Writing   54

Research Reports   68

Persuasive Writing   80

Practical Writing   90

CHAPTER 1

The Writing Process

Successful writing involves a great deal more than recording words and sentences on paper. Writing is a process that follows a series of developmental stages.

All writers use the developmental stages of the writing process. Because experienced writers are so familiar with the stages of writing, they usually do not consider those stages individually. Student writers, however, need to consider each stage in the writing process individually and to practice developing the skills of each stage.

In the other composition chapters of this book, you will use all the stages of the writing process in completing each assignment. In this chapter, you will prepare for those assignments by discussing and using each stage. You will

- find topics to write about
- draft your ideas on those topics
- compose your ideas into paragraphs
- revise the words of your paragraphs
- revise the sentences of your paragraphs
- proofread your paragraphs

1 Finding a Subject

One of the most exciting aspects of writing is that you, as a writer, have an opportunity to express your own ideas. Before you are ready to express your ideas, however, you need to spend some time thinking about them. The first two stages in the writing process are devoted to that kind of thinking. These stages are sometimes called "prewriting activities," because they involve work that prepares you to actually write a paragraph, an essay, or a report. In the first stage of the writing process, you select a subject to write about. In the second stage, you develop your ideas about the subject and plan your presentation of those ideas.

You usually begin the writing process, then, by selecting a subject to write about. Occasionally, you may have in mind a single subject about which you want to write, or you may be assigned to write on a certain subject. In most of the lessons in this book, you will be given a suggested subject which you can use or adapt.

Frequently, however, you need to consider a variety of subjects, rejecting some, investigating others. Once you have selected a subject, you will develop your ideas on the subject and define your purpose for writing about it. In this first stage, however, your goal is to get started by finding a subject to write about.

There are many different ways to find subjects for writing. Sometimes you may be able to think of subjects by sitting alone, considering, and jotting down notes. At other times you may find interesting subjects by discussing ideas with other people. And sometimes you may find subjects while you are exploring other materials, such as books, articles, pictures, movies, or television shows. You may want to set aside a section of your notebook or create a special notebook for recording your various writing ideas.

DISCUSSING THE WRITING PROCESS

Even though you may sometimes be able to discuss possible writing subjects with other people, you should be able to think and plan by yourself. The best way to practice working alone is to sit quietly and let your mind go. Consider different writing subjects and let another new subject grow out of each possibility. If you concentrate, you can do this without taking notes. However, in order to improve your concentration and to keep track of the growth of your ideas, it is best to jot down each subject.

For example, you might start by thinking about your friend Sten Ryda, whom you met last summer. If you let your mind go from that point and consider other related ideas, you might write the following list of possible subjects:

Sten Ryda
summer
heat
air conditioning
energy conservation
possible new energy sources
political problems with nuclear energy
presidential elections
political conventions
television news coverage

A. Think about the sample list of subjects.

1. Explain how each subject might have grown out of the subjects before it on the list.

2. Imagine you were listing your own ideas for writing subjects. What subjects might have grown out of the subject "summer"? What other writing subjects might you have thought of?

B. Think about how you might develop your own list of possible writing subjects.

1. Choose one of the following subjects as a starting point.
   —fire
   —the solar system
   —newspapers
   —symphonies

2. Name at least four other possible writing subjects that you might develop from the subject you chose.

Sometimes you will be able to discuss possible writing subjects with other people. A good discussion will give you a chance to try out some of your ideas and to listen to the suggestions of others. As in any conversation, you should not spend all your time thinking about what you want to say. Listen to the ideas that others are expressing.

For example, you might begin a discussion by mentioning Sten Ryda to two other students who also met Sten last summer. One of the students might remember that Sten came from Sweden. Perhaps that student will recall in detail a story Sten told about life in the Swedish countryside. The other student might recall that Sten was an excellent soccer player. That student might describe the highlights of all the summer's soccer games.

4

C. Think about the sample discussion.

　　1. What possible writing subjects would the first student's remarks suggest to you?

　　2. What possible writing subjects would the second student's remarks suggest to you?

Another way to search for writing subjects is to consider the printed and visual materials that you see and read each day. Reading a magazine article, glancing through a newspaper, looking at a picture, or even watching television might help you think of possible subjects. Practice reading and looking critically. Think about the ideas communicated by various materials, and react to those ideas.

For example, you might see a color photograph of a large city, taken from the air. The picture might make you think about small airplanes, about smog, or about urban renewal. Any of those ideas might be developed as a subject for writing.

D. Think about the subjects suggested by a photograph of a city.

　　1. Why could the same photograph make different people think of different subjects?

　　2. What other writing subjects might that photograph make you think of?

E. Think of a magazine or newspaper article you have read recently.

　　1. What was the subject of the article?

　　2. Name three possible writing subjects the article suggests to you.

Making notes, talking with others, and using printed or visual materials are only three of the ways you might search for possible writing subjects. Of course, you will rarely use one of these methods by itself. You might start by listing possible subjects and continue by discussing some of your subjects with a friend. Or you might read a magazine article, jot down some of the possible subjects it suggests to you, and then list other subjects that grow out of your first ideas. You should practice gathering ideas for writing in as many ways as possible. As you gain experience, you will discover how to use each method, and you will find the method that works best for you.

USING THE WRITING PROCESS

■ Working alone, make a list of at least six possible writing subjects. You may start with the subject "school," or you may start with another subject of your own choice. Let each possible subject develop from the one before it.

■■ With two or three other students, briefly discuss the extracurricular activities available at your school. Express your own ideas, and listen and react to the ideas of the other students. After the discussion, make a list of at least three possible subjects for writing.

■■■ Look at the two pictures below. Choose one picture. List at least four possible writing subjects that the picture suggests to you.

EVALUATING THE WRITING PROCESS

Read the subjects on each of your lists.

—Which subject on each list is most interesting?
—Which subject would you most like to write about?

Compare your list of writing subjects suggested by the photograph with the list of another student who chose the same photograph.

—Which subjects on your list are also on the other student's list?
—Which subjects on your list are not on the other student's list?
—What new writing subjects are suggested to you by the subjects on the other student's list?

2 | Drafting

Once you have selected a subject, you are ready to begin the second stage in the writing process—drafting. A draft is a preliminary plan or version. In preparing a draft for your written work, you will develop your ideas on the subject you have chosen, organize your ideas, select special words and phrases to use, and sometimes even write complete sentences or passages for your paragraph, essay, or report. In the DRAFTING section of each composition lesson that follows, you will prepare such a draft.

An important step in drafting is deciding on a purpose for your writing. Usually your purpose will fall into one of four categories: to describe someone or something, to tell a story about someone or something, to explain something, to persuade people to believe or do something. These four kinds of purposes correspond to the four kinds of writing—descriptive, narrative, expository, and persuasive—that you will practice in other chapters of this book.

Knowing your purpose for writing will help you throughout the stages of the writing process. As you draft, knowing your purpose will help you select the ideas that should be presented in your paragraph, essay, or report.

DISCUSSING THE WRITING PROCESS

You may begin some writing assignments with a purpose firmly in mind. In those cases, you can start drafting by writing a sentence or a phrase that states the purpose of your writing. Then you can list the details or examples that will contribute to that purpose. These are the details or examples that you will present in your final composition.

For example, if you have chosen bicycles as your subject, you may know from the beginning that you want to describe how the bicycles of the nineteenth century looked. You would start drafting, then, by writing a statement of your purpose and a list of details that will help you achieve that purpose. You might make the following drafting notes:

describe appearance of bicycles used in late nineteenth century—

    huge front wheel—as high as 5 feet, or 1.5 meters
    small rear wheel
    seat over front wheel
    short set of handlebars
    appearance led to name, "high-wheeler"

A. Think about the drafting example.

1. How does each detail contribute to the purpose?
2. Read the following list of details. Which details would contribute to the purpose for writing? Which would not?
   —bicycles in early nineteenth century had no pedals
   —rear wheel of high-wheeler usually had about 24 thin spokes
   —traffic rules important for cyclists

After you have chosen a subject for writing, you may sometimes have a variety of ideas and no set purpose in mind. In those cases, it is best to list your ideas briefly. Then read your list, and think about the details and examples presented there. Look for a pattern in those details and examples, and try to develop a purpose from that pattern.

For example, you might begin with various ideas on the subject of bicycles, and then draft the following list of ideas:

—riding bikes saves fuel
—helps avoid air pollution
—horns and bells important on bikes
—riding good exercise, develops fitness and health

When you reread your list of ideas, you will see that most of them are about the advantages of riding bicycles instead of driving. On the basis of those ideas, you might decide that your purpose in writing would be to persuade people to ride bicycles instead of drive.

B. Think about the drafting example above.

1. Which details from the list would be included in a paragraph with the purpose of persuading people to ride bicycles?
2. Which idea in the list would not be included in a paragraph with that purpose?

Your statement of purpose will help you decide which details and examples to include in your writing. Those details and examples will form the basis of your composition. However, before you are ready to start writing, you still need to plan your organization.

There are many different ways to organize the details and examples presented in writing. For some kinds of writing, you may organize your details and examples according to their location in space or their occurrence in time. For other kinds of writing, you may organize your details and examples according to their importance. Whichever method of organizing you choose, it is important to plan that organization carefully. In the drafting stage of the writing process, you can consider different methods of organizing your ideas. When you have chosen one method to use, number each item on your list to show its position within your organization.

For example, you might consider your list of details about the appearance of bicycles used in the late nineteenth century. If you chose to organize the details of your writing according to their location in space, from front to back, you might number the details like this:

describe appearance of bicycles used in the late nineteenth century—

     1—huge front wheel—as high as 5 feet, or 1.5 meters
     5—small rear wheel
     4—seat over front wheel
     3—short set of handlebars
     2—appearance led to name, "high-wheeler"
     6—rear wheel usually had about 24 thin spokes

USING THE WRITING PROCESS

■ Choose three of the following subjects. Think of three different purposes for writing about each subject you choose. Write a sentence that states each purpose.

friends	news magazines	New York City	machinery
space exploration	poetry	dating	winter

■■ Choose one of your purposes for writing. List at least four details or examples that you would use in writing for that purpose.

■■■ Choose one of the writing topics suggested to you by the photographs in the previous lesson. List at least six details or examples that you might use in writing on that topic.

■■■■ Read your list of details or examples, and look for a pattern there. On the basis of the ideas in your list, write a sentence stating a purpose for writing on that topic.

■■■■■ Choose one of your purposes and the list that goes with it. Decide on an organization for the details or examples. Number each detail or example to show its position in your organization.

EVALUATING THE WRITING PROCESS

Read each statement of purpose for which you developed a list of details or examples. Think about the details or examples in the list.

—Which details or examples, if any, should not be included in the list?
—What other details or examples, if any, should be added?

Think about your organized list of details or examples.

—What method of organization did you use?
—What other methods of organization might you have chosen?

3 | Composing

Once you have selected a subject to write about and have developed and organized your ideas, you have completed most of the work of writing. You have already made a complete plan. In the next stage of the writing process—composing—you will use that plan to write your paragraph, essay, or report.

In composing, however, you should not be limited by the plan you have drafted. As you write, you may discover a new idea that should be included in your writing. You may also realize that one or more of your planned ideas should not be included. You should rely on your plan, but you should also be willing to make changes. In the COMPOS- ING section of each composition lesson that follows, you will use your draft to write your paragraph, essay, or report.

DISCUSSING THE WRITING PROCESS

The statement of purpose that you wrote and used while you were drafting will also help you as you compose. Unlike the details and examples of your list, your statement of purpose is not intended to be included in your final writing. Rather, it should be a guide that helps you decide what you should and should not present as you write.

When you compose, you present the details and examples from your list in complete sentences. Usually, you will add more information as you write. Some details or examples from your list may result in several complete sentences or even paragraphs. Others may be combined, so that two or three details are presented in a single sentence.

Read the following plan from the **Drafting** lesson. Then read the paragraph that was composed from the plan.

describe appearance of bicycles used in the late nineteenth century—
  huge front wheel, as high as 5 feet, or 1.5 meters
  appearance led to name, "high-wheeler"
  short set of handlebars
  seat over front wheel
  small rear wheel
  rear wheel usually had about 24 thin spokes

The bicycle of the late nineteenth century looked quite different from the bicycles of today. Instead of having two wheels of equal size, the nineteenth-century bicycle was dominated by one huge wheel in front. The front wheel was often a full 5 feet, or 1.5 meters, high. From that wheel the bicycle got its name, the "high-wheeler." The high-wheeler had a simple set of short, straight handlebars, and the small seat was set over the front wheel. Behind the seat was a very small rear wheel, which was usually supported by 24 thin spokes.

A. Think about how the paragraph was developed from the plan.

   1. How are the details organized in the plan and in the paragraph?

   2. Which detail is presented in more than one sentence?

   3. Which details are combined into one sentence?

USING THE WRITING PROCESS

■ Read the following plan for a paragraph about a gila monster. The plan presents the purpose for writing and an organized list of details. Following the plan, compose a paragraph that describes the appearance of a gila monster.

describe the appearance of a gila monster—

   large lizard—up to two feet long
   pebbly skin
   brown or black, with pink or orange splotches
   small, blunt head
   stout body
   four thin, short legs
   fat, long tail

■■ Reread the plan you wrote in the previous lesson. Use your statement of purpose and your list of details to write a paragraph.

EVALUATING THE WRITING PROCESS

Compare your paragraph about a gila monster with the paragraphs written by other students.

—In what ways is your paragraph like those of other students?

—In what ways is your paragraph different from those of other students?

Read the paragraph based on your own plan, and compare the paragraph with the plan.

—How is each detail or example from the plan presented in the paragraph?

—What information not included in the plan is presented in the paragraph?

4 | Revising: Words

As you have seen, composing—the actual writing of your paragraph, essay, or report—is not the first stage in the writing process. It is also not the last. Before you are ready to let anyone else read your work, you must read it yourself. You must read your work critically, and you must make changes to improve it. This stage in the writing process is called revising.

As you revise, you should concentrate on two aspects of your writing: the words and the sentences. In this lesson, you will practice revising the words in your writing. In the next lesson, you will practice revising the sentences. You will revise the words and sentences of your writing in the REVISING section of each composition lesson that follows.

When you are revising your own composition, it is best to read carefully and make notes in pencil. Make a check above any word you think should be changed. If another word comes to mind, write that word in pencil. Then go back and see how your changes will improve your writing. Decide whether each checked word should be changed. Consider whether each suggested new word will improve your composition. You may find that some of the changes you noted in pencil should not be made. In those cases, simply erase your penciled notes. You will probably find that some of your other changes should be incorporated into your composition. Erase the notes for those changes, and make the changes neatly in ink.

DISCUSSING THE WRITING PROCESS

You should revise the words of your composition with two guidelines in mind. Each word should be as specific as possible, and each word should be appropriate to your composition.

As you revise, watch for any word that is too general or vague to communicate your idea clearly. Such a word should be replaced with a more specific word. The first sentence below, for example, does not communicate a clear idea about the room, because the word *nice* is vague. The second and third sentences show how the vague word *nice* might be replaced with a more specific word.

> It was a nice room.
> It was a spacious room.
> It was a cozy room.

A. Think about the three sentences.

  1. What specific words replace *nice* in the second and third sentences?

  2. What other specific words might you use in place of *nice*?

B. Read the following pairs of sentences. In the second sentence in each pair, identify each specific word that has replaced a vague word.

> The dog walked toward the door.
> The setter loped toward the door.

> That furniture looks good.
> That sofa looks comfortable.

In addition to revising your writing to make the words specific, you should also revise to make the words appropriate. Words and expressions that do not fit the style of your composition are inappropriate; they may distract your reader from the ideas you wish to communicate.

As a rule, the style of your compositions will be formal. Informal or slang words and expressions are inappropriate in such compositions. They are usually also vague. As you revise your work, you should replace any inappropriate words or expressions with more formal, specific words.

In the first sentence below, for example, the expression *laid back* is inappropriate. The second and third sentences show how that inappropriate expression might be replaced with a more formal word.

> Ms. Young had been unusually laid back on that occasion.
>
> Ms. Young had been unusually relaxed on that occasion.
>
> Ms. Young had been unusually lenient on that occasion.

C. Think about the three sentences above.

  1. What more formal words replace *laid back* in the second and third sentences?

  2. If you were revising the first sentence, what other more formal words might you use in place of *laid back*?

D. Read the following pairs of sentences. In the second sentence in each pair, identify the more formal word that has replaced each inappropriate word or expression.

> She spent every free moment fooling around with that engine.
> She spent every free moment tinkering with that engine.

> Gordon presented a dilly of a plan to the other committee members.
> Gordon presented a workable plan to the other committee members.

USING THE WRITING PROCESS

■ Revise the following sentences. In each sentence, replace at least two vague words with specific words.

1. The performer walked off the stage.
2. A large insect landed on his clothing.
3. A vehicle went past us.
4. Those machines need fuel.
5. The seafood tasted funny.
6. The animals moved slowly.

■■ Revise the following sentences. In each sentence, replace the inappropriate word or expression with a more formal word.

1. The chairperson and a few other guys may have made inquiries into the situation.
2. A few of the suggestions seemed somewhat far-out for our consideration.
3. The students grasped the solution with no sweat at all.
4. Her assistant, wearing a stylish suit and a groovy tie, distributed the press release.
5. Most of the members of the Drama Club have been into acting for several years.
6. When he first suspected that someone had ripped off his briefcase, Mr. Hardwell telephoned the police.
7. Members of the press were invited to speak with the mayor and her pals.
8. George had prepared his campaign speech carefully, but he became so nervous that he messed up the presentation.

■■■ Revise the paragraph you wrote in the previous lesson. Replace any vague words with specific words. Replace or take out any inappropriate words or phrases.

EVALUATING THE WRITING PROCESS

Compare your revised paragraph with the original paragraph you composed.

—Which vague words were replaced with specific words?
—Which inappropriate words or expressions were replaced with more formal, specific words?
—How did each change improve the paragraph?
—What other changes, if any, should be made in the words of the paragraph?

14

5 Revising: Sentences

When you revise your composition, you should consider the sentences as well as the individual words in your paragraph, essay, or report. You should mark in pencil any possible changes in the sentences of your work. Then, after you have read through your work, you should reread it, considering each change. Select and reject the possible changes in your sentences just as you selected and rejected the possible changes in your words. Choose the changes that will improve your composition, and make those changes neatly in pen. Erase the notes for changes that you do not want to use. You will make these kinds of changes in the REVISING section of each composition lesson that follows.

After you have completely revised your composition, you may find that it has become messy or difficult to read. If that has happened, you should recopy the entire composition.

DISCUSSING THE WRITING PROCESS

As you revise the sentences of your composition, you should keep two guidelines in mind. The structure of the sentences should have variety, and the sentences should relate clearly to one another.

A composition in which all the sentences have the same structure is usually boring. The boring sentences may easily distract the reader from the ideas that are being expressed. As you read your own composition, be aware of the length of your sentences. Some should be short; others should be long. Be aware, too, of how each sentence begins. Repetitious beginnings soon become uninteresting. Consider which sentences might be divided to avoid a series of long, complicated sentences. Also consider which sentences might be reorganized to avoid repetitious beginnings. (See the lessons on **Sentence Variety,** pages 102–104.)

The following two paragraphs show how the sentences of a composition might be revised. Read the first paragraph, and think about the sentences in it. Then read the second, revised paragraph, and think about how the sentences have been changed.

Margaret Chase Smith had a long, active career in national politics. She became a member of the United States House of Representatives in 1940. She replaced her husband there. She served four full terms in the House of Representatives. She was elected to the United States Senate in 1948. She became a respected member of the Senate. She won reelection to the Senate in 1954. She won reelection again in 1960. She won reelection for the last time in 1966. She campaigned for the Republican presidential nomination in 1964. Her campaign was not successful.

Margaret Chase Smith had a long, active career in national politics. When her husband died in 1940, she replaced him as a member of the United States House of Representatives. Smith served four full terms in the House of Representatives before she was elected to the United States Senate in 1948. She became a respected member of the Senate, and she won reelection in 1954, 1960, and 1966. In 1964, Smith also campaigned for the Republican presidential nomination. Her campaign, however, was not successful.

A. Compare the first paragraph and the revised paragraph.
   1. Which sentences have been combined in the revised paragraph?
   2. Which sentences have been reorganized to avoid repetitious beginnings?
   3. How has each change improved the composition?

As you revise the structure of your sentences, you should also think about how the sentences work together. Each sentence should develop from the previous sentence and lead into the next sentence. As you read, you may notice a sudden break between the ideas expressed in two sentences. Perhaps you have left out a connecting idea. Now is the time to add a word, a phrase, or a sentence to express that connecting idea.

B. Compare the two example paragraphs again.
   1. What information about the beginning of Chase's political career is not included in the first paragraph?
   2. Where has that information been added in the second paragraph?

You may sometimes need to add a transitional word or phrase to show how the ideas expressed in sentences relate to one another. Some transitional words and phrases, such as *soon* and *in the following week,* show relationships of time. Some transitional words and phrases, such as *nearby* and *on the left,* show relationships of space. Still other transitional words and phrases, such as *therefore, however,* and *on the other hand,* show relationships of cause and effect or of contrast.

C. Think again about the two example paragraphs.
   1. What transitional word has been added to the revised paragraph?
   2. How does that addition improve the paragraph?

USING THE WRITING PROCESS

■ Revise the sentences of the following paragraph. Combine some sentences to avoid series of short, choppy sentences. Reorganize some sentences to avoid repetitious beginnings. You may also want to add a transitional word or phrase.

The body of a kangaroo is especially adapted to the kangaroo's unique way of moving quickly. A kangaroo hops or leaps on its two back feet. It does not run on two feet. The kangaroo's body is small and light on the top. It is large and strong on the bottom. The kangaroo has a delicate head. It has short, slender front legs. It uses these legs only when it is moving very slowly. It does not use its front legs at all to hop or leap. It has large, powerful hind legs. They enable the kangaroo to hop at speeds up to 40 miles, or 64 kilometers, per hour. They enable the kangaroo to leap as high as 6 feet, or 1.8 meters. The kangaroo also has a long tail. It may be 4 feet, or 1.2 meters, long. It is also quite thick. The kangaroo uses its tail for balance.

■■ Reread the paragraph which you wrote in the **Composing** lesson and which you revised in the **Revising: Words** lesson. Revise the sentences of that paragraph.

EVALUATING THE WRITING PROCESS

Compare the paragraph in the first activity with your revised version of that paragraph.
—Which sentences were combined?
—Which sentences were divided?
—Which sentences were reorganized?
—What transitional words or phrases were added?
—How did each change improve the paragraph?
—What other changes, if any, should be made in the sentences of the paragraph?

Compare your revised paragraph with the original paragraph you composed.
—Which sentences were combined?
—Which sentences were divided?
—Which sentences were reorganized?
—What transitional words or phrases were added?
—How did each change improve the paragraph?
—What other changes, if any, should be made in the sentences of the paragraph?

6 Proofreading

The final stage in the writing process is proofreading. This is your last effort before you give your writing to a reader. It is an opportunity to be sure your composition will make a good impression.

Proofreading involves reading your composition carefully and correcting any mistakes you have made in sentence structure, capitalization, punctuation, or spelling. It should involve, as well, any changes that are necessary to make your work neat and your handwriting easily legible. You will proofread your composition in the PROOFREADING section of each composition lesson that follows.

DISCUSSING THE WRITING PROCESS

When you proofread, you should look at your own writing as objectively and as critically as possible. You should read your composition slowly and carefully at least three times. First read to be sure your composition makes sense. Be sure, for example, that you have not crossed out a necessary word or phrase while you were revising your work. Then read your composition again, looking for specific mistakes in sentence structure, capitalization, punctuation, and spelling. Follow the guidelines presented in the PROOFREADING CHECKLIST on page 351. Correct each mistake as you find it. Once you have finished correcting your mistakes, read your composition once more, to be sure your proofreading corrections are accurate.

As you gain experience proofreading your own writing, you will discover which particular kinds of problems you must be most aware of. You may find, for example, that you have trouble spelling many words correctly. In that case, concentrate especially on the spelling of each word as you proofread. Or perhaps you will discover that you forget to use commas when you write. In that case, think especially carefully about commas as you proofread.

The following paragraph shows how you can make changes when you proofread your own writing.

Agatha christie, the author of nearly 100 mysteries is perhaps best remembered for the two famus detectives she created Christie introduced one of her famous detectives Hercule Poirot, in her first novel, The Mysterious Affaire at Styles. Poirot was a precise and sometimes pompous private instevigator from belgium. Who always thought each case through very ~~careful.~~ *carefully* Christie's other famous detective, Miss Jane Marple, was introduced in <u>Murder at the ⱽicarage</u>. Marple was an insightful woman who had spent a quiet life in the Ɛnglish countryside and was able to use her vast knowledge of ~~humin~~ *human* nature to solve dangerous mysteries.

A. Think about the proofread paragraph.

1. What mistakes were corrected?

2. How was each correction made?

USING THE WRITING PROCESS

■ Proofread the following paragraph. Write the paragraph, correcting each mistake in sentence structure, capitalization, punctuation, and spelling.

This cuntry's first convention for womens' rights was held in Seneca Falls New York, in July 1848. although the only formol anouncement of the convention was placed in a local newpaper less then a week in advance, more than 300 people. Attended the convention. The convention members adopted the Declaration of Sentiments, which persented a statement of the equality of men and women, The declaration insisted that women should emmediately be granted "all the rights and privileges which belong to them as citizens of the United States." the convention members also adopted a series of resolutions. Calling for specific changes. these changes included fairer laws regarding marrage and property and the right for woman to speak, teach, write, and engage in busness on an equal basis with men. The most unusual resolution adopted at seneca Falls stated that women should be granted the rite to vote.

■■ Proofread the paragraph you wrote and revised in the previous lessons of this chapter. Correct any mistakes you have made in sentence structure, capitalization, punctuation, or spelling.

EVALUATING THE WRITING PROCESS

Reread your proofread paragraph.

—What changes were made in the proofreading stage?

—How did proofreading improve the paragraph?

Descriptive Writing

Writing is generally divided by its purpose into four main categories—description, narration, exposition, and persuasion. The purpose of descriptive writing is to describe, "to transmit a mental image or impression with words." Description develops an image of how its subject looks, sounds, smells, feels, or even tastes. Usually, details are used to develop that image clearly and completely.

Certain essays consist entirely, or almost entirely, of descriptive writing. More often, descriptive writing is included in sections of stories, novels, explanations, or directions.

In this chapter, you will learn about paragraph development by writing descriptive paragraphs. You will

- use topic sentences in descriptive paragraphs
- use supporting details in descriptive paragraphs
- use sensory details in descriptive paragraphs
- use unusual comparisons in descriptive paragraphs
- use spatial organization in descriptive paragraphs
- write descriptive essays

1 Using a Topic Sentence and Supporting Details in a Descriptive Paragraph

The appearance of a specific person may be the subject of a descriptive paragraph. Such a paragraph should present a single main impression of the person. Usually, the main impression is stated in a single sentence. That sentence is the **topic sentence** of the paragraph.

A descriptive paragraph about a person should also include details of the person's appearance. Every detail should support the main impression stated in the topic sentence. The details should help create a clear picture for the reader.

WORKING
WITH
THE MODEL

Read the following descriptive paragraph.

In an armchair, with an elbow resting on the table and her head leaning on that hand, sat the strangest lady I have ever seen, or shall ever see. She was dressed in rich materials—satins and lace and silks—all of white. Her shoes were white. She had a long white veil dependent from her hair, and she had bridal flowers in her hair, but her hair was white. Some bright jewels sparkled on her neck and on her hands, and some other jewels lay sparkling on the table. She had not quite finished dressing, for she had but one shoe on—the other was on the table near her hand—her veil was but half arranged, her watch and chain were not put on, and some lace lay with those trinkets, and with her handkerchief and gloves, all confusedly heaped about the looking glass.

Charles Dickens
Great Expectations

A. 1. What is the topic sentence of the paragraph?

2. What main impression of the woman does the topic sentence state?

3. What specific details about the woman's face, body, and clothing are included in the description?

4. Identify the word or group of words that is used to state each specific detail.

B. Which of the following details could have been used in the paragraph to support the topic sentence? Which could not? Explain your answers.

—lined, wrinkled face
—ordinary blue eyes
—bouquet of wilted flowers
—the smile typical of a friendly older person
—the long train of her dress
—a bright green sash
—her lacy white gloves

C. Imagine that the following sentence had been the topic sentence of the paragraph:

> On the narrow bench, with her back straight and her gloved hands folded in her lap, sat the most formal-looking woman I have ever seen, or shall ever see.

The details included in the paragraph need to be changed to support the new topic sentence.

1. Which details about the woman's face need to be changed to support the new topic sentence?
2. Which details about her body need to be changed?
3. Which details about her clothing need to be changed?
4. What specific words would you use to state each new detail?

DRAFTING

■ Choose one person whose appearance you can describe. The person should be someone you know well or someone who has made a vivid impression on you. Write the name of the person you choose.

■■ Think carefully about the appearance of the person you have chosen to describe. Decide on a single main impression of that person to present in your description. Write a sentence that states your main impression.

■■■ Consider the details of the appearance of the person you will describe. Think about the person's face, body, and clothing. Select six details that support the main impression stated in your sentence. Using a short group of words for each detail, list those details below your sentence.

■■■■ Reread your sentence and list of supporting details. As you read, ask yourself the following questions:

—What main impression does the sentence state?
—What words in the sentence are vague? Which specific words could be used in place of the vague words to make the main impression more clear?
—Which details in the list support the main impression?
—Which details, if any, do not directly support the main impression?
—What other details might be added to the list of details that support the main impression?
—Which words in the list of details are vague? What specific words could be used in place of the vague words to make the details in the list more clear?

Then revise your sentence and list of supporting details. Replace any vague words with specific words. Take out of your list any details that do not support the main impression. Add to your list any other supporting details that you have remembered.

COMPOSING

Use your sentence and your list of details to write a descriptive paragraph.

The sentence you composed will become the topic sentence of your paragraph. Begin your paragraph with that topic sentence.

In the other sentences of your paragraph, include the supporting details from your list. You may need to change the wording of some details to compose clear and interesting sentences. As you compose those sentences, be careful not to include any other details that do not directly support your main impression.

REVISING

Read your paragraph carefully. As you read, ask yourself the following questions:

—What is the topic sentence of the paragraph?
—What main impression does the topic sentence state?
—Which details in the paragraph support the main impression stated in the topic sentence?
—Which details in the paragraph, if any, do not support the main impression stated in the topic sentence?
—What other details might be added to support the main impression stated in the topic sentence?
—Which sentences in the paragraph, if any, are not clear?
—What rewording or reorganizing would make those sentences more clear?
—Which words in the paragraph, if any, are vague?
—What specific words might be used in place of those vague words?

Make any changes that are necessary, so that your paragraph is as clear and well developed as possible. After you have made your changes, you may need to recopy the paragraph.

PROOFREADING

Proofread your paragraph. Follow the steps presented in the PROOFREADING CHECKLIST on page 105. Correct any mistakes you have made in sentence structure, capitalization, punctuation, or spelling.

2 Using Sensory Details in a Descriptive Paragraph

Details are an important part of any description. Specific, vivid details appeal effectively to the five senses. They can help the reader see, hear, feel, smell, and taste what is being described. Such details are called **sensory details.**

It is usually difficult to include details that appeal to all five senses in a single paragraph of description. However, using details that appeal to three or even four different senses is a good way to create a vivid description.

WORKING
WITH
THE MODEL

Read the following descriptive paragraph. Notice the sensory details that help make the description clear.

It was a lovely morning. The last stars withdrew while we were waiting, the sky was clear and serene but the world in which we walked was somber still, and profoundly silent. The grass was wet; down by the trees where the ground sloped it gleamed with the dew like dim silver. The air of the morning was cold; it had that twinge in it which in northern countries means that the frost is not far away. The grey mist lay upon the hills, strangely taking shape from them; it would be bitterly cold on the buffalo if they were about there now, grazing on the hillside, as in a cloud.

Isak Dinesen
Out of Africa

A. 1. What sensory details are included in the paragraph? To which sense does each of those details appeal? Identify the word or group of words that is used to state each sensory detail.
    2. Which sensory details in the description are most vivid?
    3. What main impression does the paragraph present?
    4. What is the topic sentence of the paragraph?

B. The following word groups state details that might have been included in the description. Which details are sensory details? Explain your answers.

    —a narrow path
    —the dry, cracked soil of the path
    —sweet fragrance of morning flowers
    —first sparkling lights of the rising sun
    —five-thirty in the morning
    —two friendly companions
    —the thudding footsteps of the companions
    —the soft, friendly voice of a companion
    —the tingling feeling of cool, fresh air

C. Imagine you are composing a paragraph similar to the model. However, instead of describing the lovely autumn morning in Africa, you are describing an unpleasant stormy morning in an area near your home. Think about what you would see, hear, feel, and smell. Consider whether you might also taste something.

1. What sensory details would you include in your description?
2. What words would you use to present each sensory detail?
3. What main impression would you present in the paragraph?
4. What topic sentence would you use to state that main impression?

DRAFTING

■ Look carefully at the photographs below. Choose one of the photographs, and imagine you are in the scene it shows. Think about what you would see, hear, feel, and smell there. Consider whether or not you might also taste something.

List eight sensory details you could use in a description of the scene you have chosen. Include details that appeal to at least three different senses.

■■ Think again about the pictured scene you have chosen to describe. Read your list of sensory details, and decide on a single main impression of that scene. Write a sentence that states your main impression.

■■■ Reread your list of sensory details and your statement of a main impression. As you read, ask yourself the following questions:

—To which sense does each detail appeal?
—Which words, if any, should be changed to make each sensory detail more vivid?
—Which details, if any, do not directly support the main impression?
—What other sensory details might be used to support the main impression?

Then revise your list of sensory details and your sentence.

COMPOSING

Use your list of sensory details and your statement of a main impression to write a descriptive paragraph. Begin your paragraph with the topic sentence that states your main impression. In the other sentences of your paragraph, include the sensory details from your list. As you develop the sentences of your paragraph, you may need to include other details about the scene. Be sure that each detail you include supports the main impression stated in the topic sentence.

REVISING

Read your paragraph carefully. As you read, ask yourself the following questions:

—To which senses do the details of the paragraph appeal?
—Which sensory details should be made more vivid? What words that state those details should be changed?
—What main impression does the paragraph present?
—Which sentence states that main impression?

Make any changes that are necessary, so that your paragraph presents as clear and vivid a description as possible. After you have made your changes, you may need to recopy the paragraph.

PROOFREADING

Proofread your paragraph. Follow the steps presented in the PROOF-READING CHECKLIST on page 105. Correct any mistakes you have made in sentence structure, capitalization, punctuation, or spelling.

3 Developing a Descriptive Paragraph with an Unusual Comparison

An unusual comparison can often be used to make a description more clear and interesting. A comparison can help the reader to recognize an unfamiliar object or to see a familiar object in a new way.

An unusual comparison may be used as the basis for a descriptive paragraph. In such a paragraph, the comparison is stated as the main impression in the topic sentence. All the details in the paragraph support the comparison presented in the topic sentence.

WORKING
WITH
THE MODEL

Read the following descriptive paragraph. Notice the comparison on which it is based.

The freeway system spreads across Los Angeles like a huge octopus stretching out on the floor of the sea. Its bulky body lurks near the center of the city, and its strong arms push out from there in all directions. One heavy tentacle circles the downtown area, clinging not to underwater boulders but to the sides of towering buildings. Another tentacle stretches directly from the central area to the beaches of the Pacific Ocean. The rest reach out to the city's various suburbs, seeking sources of life in ever more distant locations.

A. 1. What is the topic sentence of the paragraph? What comparison does the topic sentence present?

2. What details about the freeway are included in the paragraph? How does each detail support the comparison stated in the topic sentence? What specific words emphasize the comparison?

B. Read the following word groups. Which groups state details that could be included in the paragraph? Explain your answers.

—five lanes of traffic in each direction
—exit ramps like the suckers on an octopus' tentacle
—two eyes of an octopus
—freeways that, like tentacles, become more narrow at greater distances from the center
—three hearts of an octopus
—octopus' ability to change colors

C. Imagine you are composing a paragraph similar to the model. However, instead of comparing a freeway system to an octopus, you are comparing it to a maze.

1. What topic sentence would you use in the paragraph?

2. What details would you include in the description?

3. How would each of those details support the comparison stated in the topic sentence?

DRAFTING

■ Think of an unusual comparison to describe each of the following things. Write a sentence that presents each of your comparisons.

1. smoke from a fire
2. a particular roller coaster
3. a favorite pillow
4. a messy workroom
5. some other specific thing of your choice

■■ Read the sentences you have written. Choose one comparison to use as the basis of a descriptive paragraph. List at least five details you would include in the paragraph.

■■■ Reread your sentence and your list of supporting details. As you read, ask yourself the following questions:

—What two things are being compared?
—Which details, if any, do not directly support the comparison?
—What other details might be used to support the comparison?

If necessary, revise your sentence and your list of supporting details.

COMPOSING

Use your sentence and your list of supporting details to write a descriptive paragraph. Use the sentence that states your comparison as the topic sentence at the beginning of the paragraph. In the other sentences of the paragraph, include the supporting details from your list.

REVISING

Read your paragraph carefully, and ask yourself these questions:

—Which words, if any, in the statement of the comparison are vague? Which specific words could be used to replace those vague words?
—Which words, if any, in the statements of details should be changed to emphasize the comparison made in the topic sentence?

Make any changes that are necessary, so that your paragraph is as clear and interesting as possible. After you have made your changes, you may need to recopy the paragraph.

PROOFREADING

Proofread your paragraph. Follow the steps presented in the PROOF-READING CHECKLIST on page 105. Correct any mistakes you have made in sentence structure, capitalization, punctuation, or spelling.

4 | Using Spatial Organization in a Descriptive Paragraph

The details in a descriptive paragraph must be carefully chosen to support the topic sentence. However, even carefully chosen details may not develop a clear description if they are not clearly organized.

In many descriptions, the details can be most clearly organized according to their location. The details may be observed from right to left or from left to right. They may be observed from far to near or from near to far. They may be observed from top to bottom or from bottom to top. Details observed in one kind of order should be organized and presented in that order. Such organization of details is called **spatial organization.**

WORKING
WITH
THE MODEL

Read the following descriptive paragraph. Notice the spatial organization of the details.

In marching position, each team made a triangle. There were eight guitarists in a line. In front of them walked a line of banjoists. This was slightly shorter than the line of the guitarists. Next came two lines of bone-players. Each had an evenly shaped set of bones in each hand. They rattled these, producing a sound like that of castanets. Next came the tambourine-players. They completed the orchestra. In front of them were the dancers, in two lines. Each dancer carried a beribboned stick, which he twirled while pirouetting about the street. Finally, there was the leader at the apex of the triangle. He was the most elaborately made-up member of the team, the brightest in a galaxy of bright peacocks.

Peter Abrahams
Tell Freedom

A. Think about the marching team described in the paragraph.
   1. What is the shape of the team?
   2. Which details about the team are presented first in the paragraph?
   3. Which details about the team are presented second?
   4. Which details about the team are presented last?
B. Think about the spatial organization used in the paragraph.
   1. What are the different kinds of spatial organization that can be used in a paragraph? Which kind of spatial organization do the details of the paragraph follow?
   2. In the third sentence, the word group **in front of them** helps make the spatial organization of details clear. What other words and word groups in the paragraph help make the spatial organization clear?

C. Suppose that the writer had presented details about the leader of the team first rather than last.

   1. In what order would the other details of the paragraph have been presented?
   2. What different words or word groups might have been used to help make the spatial organization clear?

D. Imagine that you are composing a paragraph similar to the model. However, instead of describing a marching team, you are describing a fantastic carousel or merry-go-round. The following sentence might be the topic sentence of your paragraph:

Brightly colored animals of every shape paraded around the carousel, floating up and down in time to the music.

   1. What details would you include in the descriptive paragraph?
   2. What kind of spatial organization would you use in presenting those details?
   3. What words and word groups would you use to help make your spatial organization clear?

DRAFTING

■ Think of a familiar object or place to describe. You may choose one of the following:

—your classroom
—a room in your home
—an unfinished jigsaw puzzle
—the inside of a closet

—a specific park or yard
—the surface of a cluttered desk
—a section of your school library

Decide on a main impression of the object or place you have chosen to describe. Write one sentence which states that main impression.

■■ Think about the place or object you have chosen. List at least six details about its appearance. Be sure each detail supports the main impression stated in your sentence.

■■■ Read your list of supporting details, and choose a spatial organization that will present those details as clearly as possible. Number each detail to show its order in your spatial organization. After at least two details, write a word or group of words that will help make the location of that detail clear.

■■■■ Reread your sentence and your organized list of details. As you read, ask yourself the following questions:

—What main impression does the sentence present?
—Which details, if any, do not directly support that main impression?

—Which kind of spatial organization will you use to present the details?

—Which details, if any, are out of order for that kind of spatial organization?

COMPOSING

Use your sentence and your list of details to write a descriptive paragraph. Use your sentence as the topic sentence at the beginning of the paragraph. In the other sentences of the paragraph, present the supporting details according to the spatial organization you have planned.

REVISING

Read your paragraph carefully. As you read, ask yourself the following questions:

—In what kind of spatial organization are the details of the paragraph presented?

—Which details, if any, are not in the correct order for that spatial organization of the paragraph?

—Where should the misplaced details be presented?

—Which specific words and word groups help make the spatial organization of the details clear?

—What other words and word groups should be added to make the spatial organization more clear?

—What main impression is stated in the topic sentence of the paragraph?

—Which details, if any, do not directly support the main impression stated in the topic sentence?

—What other details, if any, should be added to support the main impression stated in the topic sentence?

—Where should those added details be presented?

Make any changes that are necessary, so that your paragraph develops as clear a description as possible. After you have made your changes, you may need to recopy the paragraph.

PROOFREADING

Proofread your paragraph. Follow the steps presented in the PROOF-READING CHECKLIST on page 105. Correct any mistakes you have made in sentence structure, capitalization, punctuation, or spelling.

Often, a complete description cannot be presented in a single paragraph. For example, two or more paragraphs may be needed to describe the appearance of one subject under different circumstances.

In a description of more than one paragraph, each paragraph should have a topic sentence that states a main impression. The other sentences of the paragraph should present supporting details. The details should be carefully chosen to support the main impression and carefully organized to develop a clear description.

DRAFTING

■ The two photographs below show the same park at two different times of day. Look at the photographs carefully. Think about the similarities and the differences between the two scenes in the photographs.

Decide on a main impression of each scene. Choose two main impressions that show either the similarities or the differences between the two scenes. Write two sentences that state your two main impressions. Plan to use these two sentences as the topic sentences in a two-paragraph description of the park.

■■ Look again at the two scenes in the photographs, and read your two topic sentences. For each topic sentence, list at least six supporting details. Include details that appeal to at least three different senses. Be sure that all the details in each list support the main impression stated in the topic sentence.

■■■ Reread your lists of details, and think about the kinds of spatial organization you might use in presenting the details. Select one kind of spatial organization to use in both paragraphs. Number the details in each list to show the order in which they will be presented. After at least two details in each list, write a word or word group you could use to help make its location clear.

COMPOSING

Write two paragraphs describing the park at two different times of day, as shown in the photographs. Begin each paragraph with the topic sentence you wrote in DRAFTING. In the other sentences of each paragraph, present the supporting details according to the spatial organization you have planned.

REVISING

Read your composition carefully. As you read, ask yourself the following questions:

—What is the topic sentence of each paragraph? What words, if any, should be changed to make the main impression stated in each topic sentence more clear?

—What details in each paragraph support the main impression stated in the topic sentence? What details, if any, do not support the main impression? What other details might be added to each paragraph?

—What kind of spatial organization is used in each paragraph? Which details, if any, are not presented in the correct order for that spatial organization? Where should those details be presented?

—What words, if any, in the presentation of the details are vague? What specific word might be used in place of each of those vague words?

Make any necessary changes in your composition, so that your paragraphs present as clear and interesting a composition as possible. After you have made your changes, you may need to recopy the paragraph.

PROOFREADING

Proofread your composition. Follow the steps presented in the PROOFREADING CHECKLIST on page 105. Correct any mistakes you have made in sentence structure, capitalization, punctuation, or spelling.

CHAPTER 3

Narrative Writing

1.

2.

3.

A narrative is a story. Narration, or narrative writing, is writing that tells a story. The story may be true or imaginary, or even partly true and partly imaginary.

Sections of narrative writing occur in many different works. Narration is the principal form of writing, however, in such works as stories, novels, biographies, and autobiographies.

In this chapter, you will develop your narrative skills by writing short stories. You will

- describe story characters
- use action to develop characters
- use dialogue to develop characters
- develop story plots
- organize events in chronological order
- write short stories

1 Describing a Story Character

A short story often focuses on one main character. That character is usually introduced in detail at the beginning of the story. The rest of the story develops the problems, events, and decisions that affect the main character.

Such a story usually opens with a descriptive paragraph that introduces the main character and presents the beginning of the story. The descriptive paragraph may include details about the appearance, actions, and attitudes of the main character. It may also include details about the setting or location of the story and about the kinds of problems the main character will face.

WORKING
WITH
THE MODEL

Read the following paragraph. It introduces the main character in a short story.

It was December—a bright frozen day in the early morning. Far out in the country there was an old woman with her head tied in a red rag, coming along a path through the pine woods. Her name was Phoenix Jackson. She was very old, and small, and she walked slowly in the dark pine shadows, moving a little from side to side in her steps, with the balanced heaviness and lightness of a pendulum in a grandfather clock. She carried a thin small cane made from an umbrella, and with this she kept tapping the frozen earth in front of her. This made a grave and persistent noise in the still air that seemed meditative, like the chirping of a solitary little bird.

Eudora Welty
"A Worn Path"

A. Think about the story character introduced in the paragraph.

1. What details about the appearance of the character are presented in the paragraph?

2. What specific words are used to make the details of her appearance clear?

3. What details about the actions of the characters are presented in the paragraph?

4. What specific words are used to make the details of her actions clear?

5. What details about the attitude of the character are presented in the paragraph?

6. What specific words are used to make the details of her attitude clear?

B. Think about the other aspects of the story that are introduced in the paragraph.

   1. What details about the setting of the story are presented in the paragraph?
   2. What specific words are used to make the details of the setting clear?
   3. What important problems might the main character of the story face?
   4. Which words and phrases in the paragraph indicate those kinds of problems for the main character?

C. Imagine you are composing a paragraph similar to the model. However, instead of introducing an old woman as the main character of the story, you are introducing a lively little girl. Like Phoenix Jackson, this little girl is walking along a path through the woods.

   1. How would you change the details about the character's appearance?
   2. What specific words would you use to make the details of her appearance clear?
   3. How would you change the details about the character's actions and attitude?
   4. What specific words would you use to make the details of her actions and attitude clear?
   5. What other details in the paragraph would you change?
   6. What specific words would you use to make those new details clear?

DRAFTING

■ Look at the three people pictured on the next page. Choose one of the people to use as the main character of a short story. Think about how you might introduce that character at the beginning of the story. Write one sentence that gives the name of your character and presents your main impression of the character.

■■ List at least three specific details about the appearance of the character you have chosen.

■■■ List at least two specific details about the actions of the character.

■■■■ List at least two specific details about the attitude of the character.

■■■■■ List at least two other story details. You may include details about the setting of the story or about the kinds of problems the story character will face.

■■■■■■ Read your statement of a main impression and your lists of details carefully. As you read, ask yourself the following questions:

—How do the details in each list support the main impression of the story character?
—Which details about the character's appearance, if any, do not support the main impression?
—What other details about the character's appearance, if any, should be added to the list?
—Which details about the character's actions, if any, do not support the main impression?
—What other details about the character's actions, if any, should be added to the list?
—Which details about the character's attitude, if any, do not support the main impression?
—What other details about the character's attitude, if any, should be added to the list?

—Which details about the story, if any, do not fit in with the main impression of the story character?
—What other story details, if any, should be added to the list?
—What specific words make the details in each list clear?
—Which words, if any, are vague?
—What specific words should be used in place of each vague word?

Then make any changes or additions that will improve your lists of details.

COMPOSING

Use your statement and your lists of details to write a paragraph about your story character. This paragraph will describe the character you have created and will introduce a story in which that character is the main figure.

REVISING

Read your paragraph carefully. As you read, ask yourself the following questions:

—What words in the paragraph present details about the character's appearance? Which words should be replaced with more specific words to make those details more clear?
—Which words in the paragraph present details about the character's actions? Which words should be replaced with more specific words to make those details more clear?
—What words in the paragraph present details about the character's attitude? Which words should be replaced with more specific words to make those details more clear?
—What words in the paragraph present other story details? Which words should be replaced with more specific words to make those details more clear?

Revise your paragraph to make it as clear and as specific as possible. After you have made your changes, you may have to recopy the paragraph.

PROOFREADING

Proofread your paragraph. Follow the steps presented in the PROOF-READING CHECKLIST on page 105. Correct any mistakes you have made in sentence structure, capitalization, punctuation, or spelling.

2 Using Actions to Develop Characters

Depicting the actions of characters is an essential part of narrative writing. Actions can show what is happening to a character and how the character responds. Actions can show, instead of simply describe, what a character thinks and feels.

A narrative paragraph may develop the main character of a story by showing that character's actions. A clear and detailed presentation of the actions contributes to the reader's understanding of the character.

WORKING
WITH
THE MODEL

Read the following narrative paragraph. Notice how the character's actions are presented.

Mr. John Philip Johnson shut his front door behind him and came down his front steps in the bright morning with a feeling that all was well with the world. Mr. Johnson radiated a feeling of well-being as he came down the steps and onto the dirty sidewalk. He smiled at people who passed him, and some of them even smiled back. He stopped at the newsstand on the corner and bought his paper, saying "*Good* morning" with real conviction to the man who sold him the paper and the two or three other people who were lucky enough to be buying papers when Mr. Johnson skipped up. He remembered to fill his pockets with candy and peanuts, and then he set out to get himself uptown. He stopped in a flower shop and bought himself a carnation for his buttonhole, and stopped almost immediately afterward to give the carnation to a small child in a carriage, who looked at him dumbly, and then smiled. Mr. Johnson smiled, and the child's mother looked at Mr. Johnson for a minute and then smiled too.

Shirley Jackson
"One Ordinary Day, with Peanuts"

A. Think about the character in the paragraph.

1. How does the character feel?
2. Which sentence makes a direct statement about his feelings?
3. What does the character do?
4. How does each action develop your image of the character and his feelings?
5. How do other people in the story react to the character's feelings and actions?
6. Which specific words in the paragraph make the character's actions clear and vivid?
7. Which details of the character's actions are most important in developing your image of the character?

B. Imagine that you are composing a narrative paragraph similar to the model. However, instead of feeling especially cheerful, the character in your paragraph feels very unhappy. Your paragraph might begin with the following sentence:

Ms. Lora Jane Loredson slammed her front door behind her and came down her front steps in the gloomy morning with a feeling that not one single thing was right today.

1. How would the actions of the character presented in this paragraph be different from the actions presented in the model paragraph?
2. Name at least three specific character actions that you would include in the paragraph.
3. What specific words would you use to present each action in as clear and detailed a way as possible?
4. How would each action develop the reader's image of the character and her feelings?
5. How would other people in the story react to this character's feelings and actions?

C. Think about the following characters and situations.

—A student is unprepared for an important examination.
—A child is given a puppy as a surprise gift.
—A new teacher is confronted with a class of unruly students.
—A mother is given a surprise birthday party by her children.
—A new member of a soccer team scores the winning goal.
—A student finds out that she has been given a gift of $1,000.
—A hiker becomes separated from his companions in a wilderness area.
—A teenager loses the watch he has borrowed from his uncle.
—A teenager is waiting to be interviewed for her first job.

1. Describe what the character in each situation thinks and feels.
2. Choose one of the characters. Think about what you would include in a narrative paragraph about that character. What sentence would you use to make a direct statement about the character's feelings?
3. Name at least three specific actions that you would include in the paragraph.
4. What specific words would you use to present each action in as clear and detailed a way as possible?
5. How would each action develop the reader's image of the character and of the character's feelings?
6. What other people might be mentioned in the paragraph?
7. How would those other people react to the character's feelings and actions?

DRAFTING

■ Think of three different characters you might present in stories. The characters may be real people or people you make up. For each character, write a name and three words or groups of words that describe the character.

For example:

Monica—high school student
        athletic
        friendly and easy-going

■■ Imagine that something has happened to make each of your three characters angry. Decide what has happened and how each character responds. List three specific actions that each character would take.

For example:

Monica—clenches her fist but smiles to hide her anger
        waves good-bye to her friend and leaves the room without speaking
        hurries to the tennis court, where she practices violent serves for an hour

■■■ Read your list of actions for each character. Choose the list in which the actions best show the thoughts and feelings of the character. Think about how you might develop that list into a paragraph about the character. Write a sentence that makes a general statement about the feelings of the character. Your sentence may also include the reasons for the character's feelings.

For example:

When the drama teacher announced that someone else would have the role she had wanted, Monica felt hurt and angry.

■■■■ Read your sentence and the list of actions that goes with it. As you read, ask yourself the following questions:

—How does the character feel?
—What words, if any, in the sentence about the character's feelings are vague?
—What specific word might be used in place of each vague word?
—What specific actions are included in the list?
—How does each action show the character's thoughts and feelings?
—Which items on the list, of any, are not specific actions?
—How can you change those items to portray the character's specific actions?

—Which words might be changed to present each action in as clear and detailed a way as possible?

—What other actions might be added to show more of the character's thoughts and feelings?

After you have reviewed your sentence and your list of actions, make any changes or additions that seem necessary.

COMPOSING

Use your sentence and your list of actions to compose a narrative paragraph. Be sure your paragraph tells who the character is, where the character is, and what has made the character angry. Your paragraph should also present the specific actions that show what the character thinks and feels.

REVISING

Read your paragraph carefully. As you read, ask yourself the following questions:

—Which sentence in the paragraph introduces the character and makes a general statement about the character's feelings?

—Which words in that sentence, if any, are vague?

—What more precise word should be used in place of each vague word?

—Which actions show the character's thoughts and feelings?

—Which actions, if any, do not help show the character's thoughts and feelings?

—What other actions should be added to develop more fully the reader's image of the character?

—Which actions, if any, are not as specific as possible?

—Which words should be changed or added to make those actions more specific, clear, and detailed?

Make any changes that are necessary to improve your paragraph. After you have made your changes, you may have to recopy the paragraph.

PROOFREADING

Proofread your paragraph. Follow the steps presented in the PROOFREADING CHECKLIST on page 105. Correct any mistakes you have made in sentence structure, capitalization, punctuation, or spelling.

3 Using Dialogue to Develop Characters

Conversations between characters are an important part of many stories. Usually, conversations in stories are recorded in direct quotations and tell the exact words that each character says. They give specific information about each character. Such conversations are called **dialogue.**

Like a character's actions, dialogue can show who a character is. Dialogue can show what is happening to a character and how the character responds. Dialogue can let the characters express for themselves what they think and feel. Dialogue that is natural to the characters in a story contributes to the reader's full understanding of those characters.

WORKING
WITH
THE MODEL

Read the following paragraphs from a short story. Notice the details about the little girl that are presented in the first paragraph. Then notice how the dialogue develops that character.

The little girl said nothing. She unbuttoned her coat and folded it across her lap. Her dress underneath was prim and dark blue. A gold chain dangled about her neck, and her fingers, sensitive and musical-looking, toyed with it. Examining her more attentively, Mrs. Miller decided the truly distinctive feature was not her hair, but her eyes; they were hazel, steady, lacking any child-like quality whatsoever and, because of their size, seemed to consume her small face.

Mrs. Miller offered a peppermint. "What's your name, dear?"
"Miriam," she said, as though, in some curious way, it were information already familiar.
"Why, isn't that funny—my name's Miriam, too. And it's not a terribly common name, either. Now don't tell me your last name's Miller!"
"Just Miriam."
"But isn't that funny?"
"Moderately," said Miriam, and rolled the peppermint on her tongue.
Mrs. Miller flushed and shifted uncomfortably. "You have such a large vocabulary for such a little girl."
"Do I?"
"Well, yes," said Mrs. Miller, hastily changing the topic to: "Do you like the movies?"
"I really wouldn't know," said Miriam. "I've never been before."

Truman Capote
"Miriam"

A. Think about the little girl in the story.

1. The woman in the story, Mrs. Miller, has the impression that the little girl lacks "any child-like quality whatsoever." What details in the description support Mrs. Miller's impression of the little girl?

2. What specific words that the little girl uses develop that impression?

3. What do the little girl's words show about her thoughts and feelings?

4. How does the little girl make the woman feel?

5. What do the woman's words show about her thoughts and feelings?

B. Imagine that the woman in the story had started the conversation with a different little girl. Unlike the girl in the model, this little girl is a typical, talkative child.

1. How would this different little girl answer each of the woman's questions?

2. What specific words would she use?

3. How would this child make the woman feel?

4. What specific words might the woman say to reflect this different attitude?

C. Imagine you are preparing to write a story in which two important characters are an impatient shopper and a harried store clerk. The customer is late for an important appointment and wants to be helped with a complicated purchase. The clerk has a customer on the phone and three other customers waiting.

1. The clerk might begin a dialogue by saying, "Look, I can only do one thing at a time. Just wait your turn." Describe the thoughts and feelings the customer would probably have. What might the customer say to show those thoughts and feelings?

2. On the other hand, the clerk might say, "I'm sorry to keep you waiting. I'll be with you as soon as possible." Describe the thoughts and feelings the customer would probably have under those circumstances. What might the customer say to show those thoughts and feelings?

3. The customer might begin a dialogue by saying, "I don't have time to stand here waiting. If you can't take care of this for me, I'll have to go directly to the manager." Describe the thoughts and feelings the clerk would probably have. What might the clerk say to show those thoughts and feelings?

4. On the other hand, the customer might say, "I can see you're very busy. Would you mind just telling me how much these watches cost?" Describe the thoughts and feelings the clerk would probably have under those circumstances. What might the clerk say to show those thoughts and feelings?

DRAFTING

■ Look at the four people pictured below. Choose two of the people to use as story characters. Imagine that in part of the story those two characters collide accidentally on a crowded sidewalk.

Write two sentences about the characters you choose. In each sentence, name one of the characters and describe the thoughts and feelings of that character.

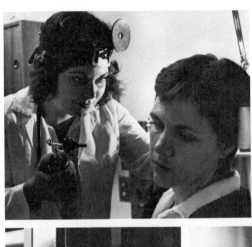

■■ Think about how your two characters will express their thoughts and feelings in a conversation. Write the words, phrases, or sentences the two characters will say at the beginning of their conversation.

■■■ Write at least three other specific words, phrases, or sentences that each character will say to express his or her thoughts and feelings.

■■■■ Read the words, phrases, and sentences you have planned for each character. As you read, ask yourself the following questions:

—What has happened to each character?

—How does each character feel?

—What does each word, phrase, or sentence show about the character who says it?

—What other words, phrases, or sentences might each character say?

Make any changes or additions that will improve the dialogue you are planning for the two story characters.

COMPOSING

Use your notes to write a story dialogue for your two characters. In your dialogue, have each character speak at least four different times. Have each character use words and expressions that help express who he or she is, as well as how he or she feels.

REVISING

Read your dialogue carefully. As you read, ask yourself the following questions:

—What specific words and expressions do the characters use?

—How do those words and expressions show who the characters are and how the characters feel?

—Which words should be changed to make the identity and the attitude of each character more vivid?

—Which expressions or sentences, if any, are not appropriate for a conversation between the two characters?

—How should those inappropriate expressions or sentences be made more natural?

Revise your dialogue so that it is as vivid and as natural as possible. After you have made the necessary changes, you may have to recopy your work.

PROOFREADING

Proofread your dialogue. Follow the steps presented in the PROOF-READING CHECKLIST on page 105. If necessary, also review the rules on pages 376 and 407 for using capital letters and punctuation marks in direct quotations. Correct any mistakes you have made in sentence structure, capitalization, punctuation, or spelling.

4 Developing a Story Plot

The series of events presented in a story is called the story **plot.** The events of a plot may be physical, packed with action—a pioneer faces hardship and adventure in a trip across the plains. The events of a plot may be psychological, related only to ideas and feelings—a young man changes his attitudes toward other people and so feels happier about himself. Most plots involve a combination of physical events and psychological events.

An interesting story has an interesting plot. The story makes the reader care about each event in the series. A story with a good plot, then, usually does not relate everything the main character thinks, feels, and does. It presents only those events that are important, that keep the story moving. Unimportant or irrelevant events detract from the story development. A good plot often depends as much on what events are left out as on what events are included.

WORKING
WITH
THE MODEL

Read the following narrative paragraphs. Notice the events that have been left out of the story, as well as those that have been included.

One day a man came to town on a donkey and began loafing around in the public library where I used to spend most of my time in those days. He was a tall young Indian of the Ojibway tribe. He told me his name was Locomotive 38. Everybody in town believed he had escaped from an asylum.

Six days after he arrived in town, his animal was struck by the Tulare Street trolley and seriously injured. The following day the animal passed away, most likely of internal injuries, on the corner of Mariposa and Fulton Streets. The animal sank to the pavement, fell on the Indian's leg, groaned and died. When the Indian got his leg free, he got up and limped into the drugstore on the corner and made a long-distance telephone call. He telephoned his brother in Oklahoma. The call cost him a lot of money, which he dropped into the slot as requested by the operator as if he were in the habit of making such calls every day.

William Saroyan
My Name Is Aram

A. Think about the events that are presented in the paragraphs.

1. How many days are covered in this part of the story?

2. What happened on the first day?

3. What happened on the sixth day?

4. What happened on the seventh day?

5. What event is presented at the end of the second paragraph? Why is that event presented in such detail? How does that action help develop the main character?

B. Think about the events that might have taken place but are not presented in the paragraphs.

1. Name at least three events that might have taken place on the first day but are not included in the story. Why are those events not included?

2. Name at least three events that might have taken place on the sixth day but are not included in the story. Why are those events not included?

C. In a later part of the same story, Locomotive 38 buys a car to replace his dead donkey. Imagine you are developing that part of the story plot. Read the following list of events.

—Locomotive 38 walked to the Packard dealership in town.
—On the way, he walked by three women, four men, and six children.
—He stopped and bought a hamburger on his way to the dealership.
—The cook put too many pickles on the hamburger.
—He saw a beautiful light green Packard at the dealership.
—The Packard had been made in Detroit.
—He paid cash for the Packard.
—Somebody else in town bought a Ford that day.
—He drove away in his new car.

1. If you were writing that part of the story, which events would you include in the plot? Which events would you leave out?

2. Which event would you present fully, in the most detail? Which events would you present briefly, without much detail?

3. Compare your ideas with the ideas of other students. Different people will probably have different ideas about how to develop the plot.

DRAFTING

■ Think of an experience in your own life about which you could write a story. Write one sentence that presents your main impression of the experience. If you want, you may choose a specific experience suggested by one of the following topics:

—making a new friend
—feeling embarrassed
—succeeding at a difficult task

■■ Think of all the events that might be part of your story. Do not worry yet about choosing the most important events. Write a list of all the possible story events.

■■■ Read your sentence and your list of events. Think about which events should be included in your story plot. Include only those events that help develop the main impression of the experience or that are necessary to an understanding of what happened. Underline the events that you want to include in your story.

■■■■ Reread the list of events that you will include in your story plot. Choose one important event that will be part of your story. List at least six details about that event. Your details may be about the appearance or attitude of characters, the actions of characters, and the dialogue of characters.

COMPOSING

Write one part of the story for which you developed a plot. Use your list of details to present one important event in the story. Use specific words to show clearly the character or characters in your story and to develop the action or the decision of that story event.

REVISING

Read the story section you have written. As you read, ask yourself the following questions:

—What main story event is presented in this section?
—What are the most important details about that event? Which sentences present those details?
—What specific words help make the details clear?
—Which words, if any, should be changed to make the details more clear?

Make any changes that are necessary to improve your story section. After you have made the changes, you may have to recopy your work.

PROOFREADING

Proofread your story section. Follow the steps presented in the PROOFREADING CHECKLIST on page 105. Correct any mistakes you have made in sentence structure, capitalization, punctuation, or spelling.

Using Chronological Order in Stories

The events of any story take place over a period of time. That period may be as short as a few minutes or as long as many years. No matter how long the period, however, the events of the story can be organized according to their occurrence in time. That is, they can be organized in **chronological order.**

The main events of a story can be presented in chronological order. The details of thought and action that develop each major event can also be presented in chronological order. Presenting the main events and the details of a story in chronological order usually makes the story interesting and easy to follow.

Certain words and groups of words, called **transitional words and phrases,** may be used in paragraphs and stories organized according to chronological order. These words and phrases sometimes help make the order of the events or details clear. Examples of transitional words include *eventually, next,* and *finally.* Examples of transitional phrases include *at first, in an hour,* and *at the same time.*

WORKING
WITH
THE MODEL

The following narrative paragraph presents one major event from a short story. Read the paragraph, and notice the organization of the actions.

The baker's shop, like everything else, was in ruins. No one was there. At first she saw nothing but the mass of crumpled earthen walls. But then she remembered that the oven was just inside the door, and the door frame still stood erect, supporting one end of the roof. She stood in this frame, and, running her hands in underneath the fallen roof inside, she felt the wooden cover of the iron caldron. Under this there might be steamed bread. She worked her arm delicately and carefully in. It took quite a long time, but, even so, clouds of lime and dust almost choked her. Nevertheless she was right. She squeezed her hand under the cover and felt the firm smooth skin of the big steamed bread rolls, and one by one she drew out four.

Pearl S. Buck
"The Old Demon"

A. Think about the actions presented in the paragraph.
   1. What did the woman do first?
   2. What did she do last?
   3. What other actions took place between the first action and the last action?
   4. In what order are the actions presented?

> 5. How does the organization of actions help make the event interesting and easy to understand?
>
> B. Think about the transitional words and phrases used in the paragraph.
>
> 1. Identify each transitional word or phrase.
> 2. How do the transitional words and phrases help make the organization of actions clear?
>
> C. Imagine you are preparing to write a story about your experiences on a typical school day.
>
> 1. What events would you include in your story?
> 2. Which event would you present first?
> 3. Which event would you present last?
> 4. How would you organize the other story events?
> 5. What transitional words and phrases would you use to make your organization clear?
>
> D. Choose one of the important events you would include in your story of a typical day.
>
> 1. What details of action and thought would you include in presenting that event?
> 2. Which detail would you present first?
> 3. Which detail would you present last?
> 4. How would you organize the other details of that event?
> 5. What transitional words and phrases would you use to make your organization clear?

DRAFTING

■ For the previous lesson, you wrote a list of important story events. Use that list, or write a new list of events for a new story. If you write a new list, remember to include only the important events that will help keep the story moving. Organize your list of major events in chronological order. Write a number next to each event to show the position it will have in the story.

■■ For at least three events in your list, write a transitional word or phrase that will help make the organization of events clear.

■■■ Choose one of the major events in your list. If you are using the same list of events that you used in the previous lesson, do not choose the same event you chose before. List at least six details of actions and thought that you would include in presenting that event.

■■■■ Organize your list of details in chronological order. Write a number next to each detail to show its position.

■■■■■ For at least two details in your list, write a transitional word or phrase that will help make the organization of details clear.

■■■■■■ Reread your organized list of details. As you read, ask yourself the following questions:

—Which details, if any, are not in chronological order?
—Which details, if any, are not important enough to be included in the list?
—What other details, if any, should be added to the list?

Make any changes that will improve your list of details.

COMPOSING

Use your list of details and your transitional words and phrases to write one part of your story. Present the details of the event in chronological order. Remember to use specific words that will make the details of thought and action clear and vivid for the reader.

REVISING

Read the story section you have written. As you read, ask yourself the following questions:

—In what order did the details of thought and action occur? In what order are they presented?
—Which details, if any, are not presented in chronological order? Where should those details be presented?
—What transitional words and phrases make the organization of the details clear? What other words and transitional phrases should be added to make the organization more clear?
—What specific words help make the details clear? Which words, if any, should be changed to make the details more clear?

If necessary, revise your story section so that it is as clear and as carefully organized as possible. After you have made the changes, you may have to recopy your work.

PROOFREADING

Proofread your story section. Follow the steps presented in the PROOFREADING CHECKLIST on page 105. Correct any mistakes you have made in sentence structure, capitalization, punctuation, or spelling.

6 Writing a Short Story

A short story should be carefully planned, clearly organized, and developed with specific details that will interest the reader.

DRAFTING

■ Think of a short story you would like to write. Write a sentence that states the main idea of your story.

■■ List in chronological order the most important events of your story.

■■■ For each event, list at least three details of thought and action.

■■■■ Write the name of the main story character. List at least four specific details about the appearance and attitude of the character.

■■■■■ If you plan to use dialogue, write the most important words, phrases, and sentences your main character will say.

COMPOSING

Use your lists and other notes to write a short story.

REVISING

Read your story carefully, and ask yourself the following questions:
—Which events and details, if any, are not presented in chronological order? Where should those events and details be presented?
—What transitional words and phrases, if any, should be added to make the chronological organization more clear?
—In the presentation of details, which words, if any, are vague? Which specific words should be used to make those details clear?

Make any changes that are necessary to improve your story. After you have made the changes, you may have to recopy the story.

PROOFREADING

Proofread your story. Follow the steps presented in the PROOFREADING CHECKLIST on page 105. Correct any mistakes you have made in sentence structure, capitalization, punctuation, or spelling.

CHAPTER 4

Expository Writing

The word **expository** comes from a Latin word that means **to explain.** The purpose of expository writing, then, is to explain. Expository writing, or exposition, usually uses facts to present ideas and information.

Examples of expository writing include directions, many magazine articles, most nonfiction books, factual essays, and reports.

In this chapter, you will learn more about developing paragraphs and essays as you practice expository writing. You will

- write paragraphs of directions
- use comparison in expository paragraphs
- use contrast in expository paragraphs
- use examples in expository paragraphs
- write expository essays

1   Writing a Paragraph of Directions

People read for many different reasons. One of the most important reasons is to find out how to do things. For example, before friends can play a new game, someone must read the directions for the game. Reading the directions is also an important first step in assembling a model, using a new machine, cooking an unfamiliar dish, or performing a scientific demonstration.

The essential qualities of a set of directions are clarity and thoroughness. Directions should be presented in direct and simple writing. They should present all of the steps necessary for completing the task. To be as clear as possible, the steps should be presented in chronological order. In addition, the directions may include a word or two of encouragement to help the reader along in the task.

WORKING
WITH
THE MODEL

Read the following paragraph of directions about pet safety. Notice how the paragraph leads the reader through the process of training a pet.

One of the best ways to combat accidents is never to let your pet get away with bad habits that could eventually become harmful. Don't wait for situations to occur; set them up. For instance, put an electric fan on the floor and let your pet see you fiddling with it. Curiosity will bring your pet over to it. Never call your pet, just tempt it. When it starts sniffing at the fan, give your pet a good whack and say, "No." This might seem a bit harsh, but just think of what the blades could do if your pet went to play with the fan any other time.

Jo and Paul Loeb
"Accident Prevention for Your Pet"

A. Think about the process presented in the paragraph.
1. What general statement about avoiding accidents is presented at the beginning of the paragraph?
2. What general direction about training a pet is presented in the paragraph?
3. What specific type of potential accident is discussed in detail in the paragraph?
4. What steps for preventing that type of potential accident are presented?
5. In what order are the steps presented?
6. Which statements in the paragraph provide explanation rather than actual directions? Why are those statements included in the paragraph?

B. Imagine you are giving directions about pet safety or about safety in sports. Your paragraph might begin with one of the following topic sentences:

Another potential danger for pets is traffic.
Proper warm-up exercises before strenuous activity provide protection against serious injury.

  1. Choose one of the topics and statements above. Think about the steps you would include in your paragraph of directions. Plan the order in which you would present each step. Then list the steps.

  2. Consider the steps in your list. Which necessary steps, if any, have you left out? Which unnecessary steps, if any, have you included?

C. Imagine you want to teach a friend to make a sweater similar to yours, or build a model like the one you built, or do something else that you have done successfully.

  1. With what general statement would you begin your directions?

  2. What are the steps, from first to last, in completing the task?

  3. What words of encouragement or guidance would you include in your directions?

DRAFTING

■ A friend in another state has written to you, asking for your advice. Your friend wants to know how to develop a certain skill you have or to do something you have done successfully. For example, you may be able to make macramé wall hangings or build model ships inside bottles. You may have run your own paper route, baby-sat for young children, written a column for the school newspaper, or gotten along with a troublesome younger brother or sister. Choose a skill or experience for which you can give directions. Write one sentence that makes a general statement about how to develop that skill or succeed with that experience.

■■ Think of all the steps involved in the task you have selected. List each step. Then think about the order of those steps. Next to each step, write a number to indicate its position in chronological order.

■■■ Write two comments that will help your friend understand the directions or that will encourage your friend to complete the task.

■■■■ Read your list and comments. As you read, ask yourself the following questions:

—Which necessary steps, if any, have not been included in the directions?

—Which unnecessary steps, if any, have been included in the directions?

—Which steps, if any, are not presented in chronological order?

—Which step, if any, is not presented clearly enough for my friend to understand it easily?

—How will each comment help my friend complete the task?

—Where among the steps should those comments be included?

COMPOSING

Use your list of steps and your comments to compose a paragraph of directions. You may want to begin the paragraph with a general statement of the task or with an encouraging comment for your friend. Present the steps clearly and in chronological order. Since you are now writing a paragraph and not a list, you may need transitional words and phrases, such as **first, next, after that,** and **when you have completed.**

REVISING

Read your paragraph carefully. Try to assume you are unfamiliar with the task for which your paragraph presents directions. Consider whether your directions are presented clearly and thoroughly. Ask yourself the following questions:

—Which steps, if any, should be added, taken out, or reorganized?

—Which steps, if any, should be presented more specifically or in more detail?

—What comments or words of encouragement, if any, should be added to help the reader complete the task?

—Which transitional words or phrases, if any, should be added to make the organization of the directions more clear?

Revise your paragraph to make your directions as clear and as thorough as possible. After you have made the changes, you may need to recopy the paragraph.

PROOFREADING

Proofread your paragraph. Follow the steps presented in the PROOFREADING CHECKLIST on page 105. Correct any mistakes you have made in sentence structure, capitalization, punctuation, or spelling.

Using Comparison in an Expository Paragraph

In many cases, a writer can help the reader understand a given subject by explaining how it is similar to another subject. In such cases, the writer uses a comparison. A comparison points out the similarities between two different objects, activities, ideas, or persons.

A comparison can be used to develop an expository paragraph. Usually, the comparison is directly stated in the topic sentence of the paragraph. Each specific similarity presented in the paragraph supports that comparison.

The details within a paragraph of comparison should be carefully organized. In many paragraphs of comparison, all the characteristics of one subject are presented without interruption. Then all the characteristics of the other subject are presented.

WORKING
WITH
THE MODEL

Read the following expository paragraph. Notice the comparison it develops.

The human nervous system is like an electronic communications network. On the fringes of the network are the information sources —our five senses. These are like an array of cameras, microphones, radar, and computer terminals. The brain is at the center of the network. It receives and issues orders, much as a computer does. Both systems are electrical. The nervous system resembles the computer's circuits. Both are power-hungry. The brain uses some 20 percent of the body's blood supply. Both are likely to break down when overloaded, overheated, or subjected to shock.

A. Think about the comparison developed in the paragraph.

1. What two things are compared?

2. What is the topic sentence of the paragraph?

3. The paragraph presents five characteristics of the human nervous system. What are they?

4. The paragraph presents five characteristics of an electronic communications network. What are they?

5. In what order are the characteristics of each system presented?

6. Which characteristic of the human nervous system is compared to each characteristic of the electronic communications network?

7. What details that are included in the paragraph make the characteristics of each system vivid?

B. Think about the following subjects:

—people who play chess
—tap-dancing
—the oldest child in a family
—cats as pets
—learning a foreign language
—your school building
—the mayor of your city or town

1. Imagine you are preparing to present each subject in a paragraph of comparison. To what would you compare each subject?

2. Choose one of your comparisons. What statement would you use as the topic sentence of a paragraph developing that comparison?

3. What specific similarities would you present in the paragraph?

4. How would you organize the details within the paragraph?

DRAFTING

■ List four topics you could develop in paragraphs of comparison. Each topic should be a pair of objects, ideas, activities, or persons.

For example:
Dahlia and Grandma
learning French and learning math
goldfish and parakeets
the president of the United States and the prime minister of Canada

■■ Read your four topics, and choose one to develop in a paragraph of comparison. Write a sentence that states the comparison you plan to develop. That sentence will serve as the topic sentence of your paragraph.

■■■ Think about the first object, idea, activity, or person named in your topic sentence. List at least four important details about that subject.

■■■■ Think about the second object, idea, activity, or person named in your topic sentence. List at least four details about that subject that are similar to the details listed about the first subject. Be sure that the details in your second list are in the same order as the details in your first list.

■■■■■ Read your topic sentence carefully, and think about the comparison it states. Ask yourself whether the sentence includes any vague words that should be replaced by specific words. Revise your sentence to make it as clear as possible.

■■■■■ Read your lists carefully. As you read, ask yourself the following questions:

—What other similarities, if any, should be added to each list?
—Which similarities, if any, do not directly support the comparison stated in the topic sentence?

Then revise your lists. Reword, add, take out, or reorganize the items to make your lists as clear and as complete as possible.

COMPOSING

Use your topic sentence and lists of similarities to write a paragraph of comparison. Begin the paragraph with the topic sentence. Next, present all the details about the first object, idea, activity, or person named in the topic sentence. Then present all the details about the second object, idea, activity, or person named in the topic sentence.

REVISING

Read your paragraph carefully. As you read, ask yourself the following questions:

—How does the topic sentence introduce the comparison?
—What changes in wording would make the topic sentence more clear?
—What specific similarities support the comparison stated in the topic sentence?
—Which similarities, if any, do not directly support the comparison?
—Which other similarities, if any, should be added to support the comparison?
—In what order are the details about the first object, idea, activity, or person presented?
—In what order are the details about the second object, idea, activity, or person presented?

Revise your paragraph to make the comparison as clear and as complete as possible. After you have made any necessary changes, you may need to recopy the paragraph.

PROOFREADING

Proofread your paragraph. Follow the steps presented in the PROOF-READING CHECKLIST on page 105. Correct any mistakes you have made in sentence structure, capitalization, punctuation, or spelling.

3 Using Contrast in an Expository Paragraph

Often, a writer can explain two somewhat similar subjects by presenting the differences between them. In such cases, the writer uses contrast. Contrast points out the differences between two objects, activities, ideas, or persons.

Like a comparison, a contrast can be used to develop an expository paragraph. Usually the contrast is directly stated in the topic sentence of the paragraph. Each specific difference presented in the paragraph supports that contrast.

The details within a paragraph of contrast should be carefully organized. In many paragraphs of contrast, the characteristics of the two subjects are presented alternately. This kind of organization highlights the direct contrast of each pair of details.

WORKING
WITH
THE MODEL

Read the following expository paragraph. Notice the contrast it develops.

Although crocodiles and alligators are closely related, there are important differences in the appearance of these two kinds of reptile. In most crocodiles, the snout comes to a point in front, where an alligator's snout is rounded. The American crocodile is only about two-thirds as heavy as an American alligator of the same length. Crocodiles can move quite quickly and often act rather vicious. Alligators, on the other hand, move more slowly and are less likely to attack. The unusually long fourth lower tooth of the crocodile fits into a groove in the side of the upper jaw. In the alligator, however, that extra-long tooth fits into a pit in the upper jaw.

adapted from *The World Book Encyclopedia.* © 1979
World Book-Childcraft International, Inc.

A. Think about the contrast developed in the paragraph.

1. What two things are contrasted?
2. What is the topic sentence of the paragraph?
3. The paragraph presents four characteristics of crocodiles. What are they?
4. The paragraph presents four characteristics of alligators. What are they?
5. How are the characteristics of crocodiles and alligators organized?
6. Which characteristic of alligators is contrasted with each characteristic of crocodiles?
7. What specific words in the paragraph help make the contrast between crocodiles and alligators clear?

B. Think about the following subjects:

—winter sports
—playing soccer
—compact cars
—riding a bicycle
—folk songs
—life in a big city

1. Imagine you are preparing to present each subject in a paragraph of contrast. With what would you contrast each subject?

2. Choose one of your contrasts. What statement would you use as the topic sentence of a paragraph developing that contrast?

3. What specific differences would you present in the paragraph?

4. How would you organize the details within the paragraph?

DRAFTING

■ List four topics you could develop in paragraphs of contrast. Each topic should be a pair of somewhat similar objects, ideas, activities, or persons.

For example:
my cousin and I
science fiction movies and science fiction books
parakeets and canaries
members of the Senate and members of the House of Representatives

■■ Read your four topics, and choose one to develop in a paragraph of contrast. Write a sentence that states the contrast you plan to develop. That sentence will serve as the topic sentence of your paragraph.

■■■ Think about the first object, idea, activity, or person named in your topic sentence. List at least four important details about that subject.

■■■■ Think about the second object, idea, activity, or person named in your topic sentence. List at least four details about that subject that contrast with the details listed about the first subject. Be sure that the details in your second list are in the same order as the details in your first list.

■■■■■ Read your topic sentence carefully, and think about the contrast it states. Ask yourself whether the sentence includes any vague words that should be replaced by specific words. Revise your sentence to make it as clear as possible.

■■■■■■ Read your lists carefully. As you read, ask yourself the follow-ing questions:

—What other specific differences, if any, should be added to each list?
—Which differences, if any, do not directly support the contrast stated in the topic sentence?

Then revise your lists. Reword, add, take out, or reorganize the items to make your lists as clear and as complete as possible.

COMPOSING

Use your topic sentence and lists of differences to write a paragraph of contrast. Begin the paragraph with the topic sentence. Then present one detail about the first object, idea, activity, or person named in the topic sentence, followed by the contrasting detail about the second ob-ject, idea, activity, or person. Use the same pattern in presenting all the details from your lists.

REVISING

Read your paragraph carefully. As you read, ask yourself the follow-ing questions:

—What contrast does the paragraph present?
—How does the topic sentence introduce that contrast?
—What changes in wording would make the topic sentence more clear?
—What specific differences support the contrast stated in the topic sentence?
—Which differences, if any, do not directly support the contrast?
—Which other differences, if any, should be added to support the contrast?
—Which specific words help make the contrast clear?
—What other specific words, if any, should be added to help make the contrast more clear?

Revise your paragraph to make the contrast as clear and as complete as possible. After you have made any necessary changes, you may need to recopy the paragraph.

PROOFREADING

Proofread your paragraph. Follow the steps presented in the PROOF-READING CHECKLIST on page 105. Correct any mistakes you have made in sentence structure, capitalization, punctuation, or spelling.

4 Using Examples in an Expository Paragraph

Many kinds of information can be communicated much more clearly through showing rather than through telling. But how does a writer show with words? Perhaps the best way is by using examples. Strong writing presents specific examples to support general statements.

An expository paragraph that is developed with examples usually presents a single general statement. That statement, the topic sentence of the paragraph, most often occurs at the beginning or at the end of the paragraph. The other sentences in the paragraph present examples to support that general statement. The examples must be clear and specific to fully support the general statement.

WORKING
WITH
THE MODEL

Read the following expository paragraph. Notice the statement and the examples that support it.

Even American kids are out of shape. In one Massachusetts school only eight fifth-graders out of a class of fifty-two were fit enough to earn presidential physical fitness awards. In a class in Connecticut, only two students out of forty qualified. Not long ago a study at Massachusetts General Hospital showed that 15 percent of 1,900 seventh-graders had high cholesterol levels and 8 percent had high blood pressure. (Both conditions are associated with an increased likelihood of heart attacks and strokes.)

James F. Fixx
The Complete Book of Running

A. Think about the information in the paragraph.
   1. What main idea does the paragraph present?
   2. What is the topic sentence of the paragraph? What general statement does it make?
   3. What examples does the paragraph present?
   4. How does each example support the general statement made in the topic sentence?
   5. What words and numbers make the examples clear and specific?

B. Read the following examples:
   —In one junior high school, more than half the students were overweight.
   —Many adults eat too much and exercise too little.
   —In some school districts, most sixth-grade students are reading on the second-grade level.

—In a recent test of 100 fourteen-year-olds, only 23 were able to run one mile without stopping.

—Some young athletes are in very good physical condition.

—At one summer camp, only a third of the teenage campers were able to complete a 24-mile hike.

1. Which examples might be included in the model paragraph? How do those examples support the general statement made in the topic sentence of the paragraph?

2. Which examples should not be included in the paragraph? Why do those examples not belong in the paragraph?

C. Imagine you are preparing to compose a paragraph similar to the model. However, instead of writing about American youth, you will write about the poor physical condition of American adults.

1. What general statement would you make in the topic sentence of your paragraph?

2. What specific examples would you use to support that general statement?

3. What words and numbers would you use to make the examples clear and specific?

DRAFTING

■ Think about the following topics. For each topic, write one general statement that you might support with examples. In addition, write a general statement about another topic of your own choice.

1. extracurricular activities at your school
2. the uses of books
3. ways to conserve energy
4. a personality trait of a specific friend
5. the importance of physical exercise
6. the appeal of cartoons

■■ Read your seven general statements, and choose one to use as the topic sentence of a paragraph. List at least four examples to support that general statement.

For example:

Last Friday's school dance was attended by only 17 students.

Only five students tried out for the baseball team this year.

Not even the cheerleaders attended every basketball game last season.

We have no drama club, although fifty students want to join one.

■■■ Read your general statement and your list of examples. Ask yourself the following questions:

—How does each example support the general statement?
—Which examples, if any, do not support the general statement?
—What other examples might be added to the list?

COMPOSING

Use your general statement and list of examples to write an expository paragraph. Begin the paragraph with your general statement. Use your examples to develop the paragraph and to support your general statement.

REVISING

Read your paragraph carefully. As you read, ask yourself the following questions:

—What main idea does the paragraph present?
—What general statement does the topic sentence make?
—Which words in the topic sentence are vague?
—What specific words should be used in place of each vague word in the topic sentence?
—What examples are presented to support the general statement made in the topic sentence?
—How does each example support that general statement?
—Which examples, if any, do not support the general statement and should not be included in the paragraph?
—What other examples, if any, should be added to support the general statement made in the topic sentence?
—What words and numbers make the examples in the paragraph clear and specific?
—What other words and numbers should be added to make the examples more clear and specific?

Make any changes that are necessary to improve your paragraph. After you have made your changes, you may need to recopy the paragraph.

PROOFREADING

Proofread your paragraph. Follow the steps presented in the PROOF-READING CHECKLIST on page 105. Correct any mistakes you have made in sentence structure, capitalization, punctuation, or spelling.

5 | Writing an Expository Essay

Many explanations require more than a single paragraph. In such examples of expository writing, the first paragraph usually makes a general statement about the subject and introduces the main ideas that will be developed in the essay. Each of the other paragraphs presents a main idea with details or examples to support it.

DRAFTING

■ Think about the question below, or make up your own question. Then write a general statement in answer to the question.

What effects do television commercials have on teenage audiences?

■■ Think about the three most important ideas you will present in your essay. State each main idea in a different topic sentence.

■■■ List at least four details or examples to support each topic sentence.

COMPOSING

Use your general statement, your topic sentences, and your lists of supporting details or examples to write a four-paragraph expository essay.

REVISING

Read your expository essay carefully. As you read, ask yourself the following questions:

—How is each main idea introduced in the first paragraph?
—What topic sentence states the main idea of each paragraph?
—What details or examples are presented in each paragraph?

Revise your essay to make your explanation as complete and as clear as possible.

PROOFREADING

Proofread your essay. Follow the steps presented in the PROOFREADING CHECKLIST on page 105. Correct any mistakes you have made in sentence structure, capitalization, punctuation, or spelling.

CHAPTER 5

Research Reports

For students, the research report is usually the most important form of expository writing. Students may be assigned research reports on a variety of subjects, from the theories of economics to the life of Jane Austen. The steps involved in preparing a research report on any subject, however, are the same.

In this chapter, you will follow the various steps involved in preparing a research report. You will

- plan research topics
- take notes
- prepare outlines
- write research reports

1 Planning a Research Report

When one of your teachers assigns a research report, your first concern may be, "How will I ever write that much?" But a research report involves a great deal more than sitting down and writing. Preparing a research report is a major project with a number of important steps. The actual writing of the report is one of the last steps. If you have carefully followed all the preliminary steps, you will find the last steps quite easy.

The first step in preparing a research report is deciding upon a topic. The topic may be assigned, or you may be allowed to select it yourself. If you choose the topic yourself, make your choice thoughtfully. Select a subject with which you are already somewhat familiar and which you would like to learn more about. Further, be sure your topic is narrow enough that you will be able to research it within a limited period of time and write about it within a limited number of pages.

Once you have a topic in mind, you need to find sources of information on that topic. This step in preparing the research report involves going to the library and finding the books, magazine articles, and encyclopedia articles which you will read for your report. Look through each possible source to see what kind of information it has. This is the time to be sure you can find enough information to write a full report. If you cannot find more than two good sources for your topic, you should probably change your plans and choose a new topic for your report.

At the library, you should record certain kinds of information about each of your sources. Make a record of each source on an individual card. These cards will be the bibliography cards for your report. Later, you will organize and use these cards to write a final bibliography, an organized list of all the sources used for your research report.

The third major step in preparing a research report is the development of a preliminary outline. Once you have decided on a topic and looked through the sources you will use, you should have some idea of the kinds of information you will be able to include in your report. Your plans will be recorded in your preliminary outline.

The outline should begin with a general question about your report topic. This question will help you when you read your sources. You can consider any information that will help answer that question important enough to include in your notes. The question should be followed by the main headings of an outline. These main headings will indicate the main ideas you expect to develop in your report. Of course, you will not yet know what information will be included under each heading. As you do your research, you may even decide to change your original headings. It is useful to develop them at this point, however, so that you can use them as guides in your research and note-taking.

WORKING WITH THE MODEL

Read the following examples from the first three steps in preparing a research report.

Possible Report Topics:

Social Problems—Problems of the Elderly in the United States
Europe—History of the European Economic Community
Painting—Characteristics of Impressionist Painting
Physics—Contributions of Marie Curie to Physics

Bibliography Cards:

Book:

Knopf, Olga, <u>Growing Old Gracefully</u>, New York, The Viking Press, 1975.

Magazine Article:

Richmond, Julius B., "Health Promotion and Disease Prevention in Old Age," <u>Aging</u>, May–June 1979, pp. 11–15.

Encyclopedia Articles:

Johnson, Marilyn, "Old Age," <u>The World Book Encyclopedia</u>, Vol. 14, Chicago, World Book–Childcraft International, Inc., 1979, pp. 558b–559.

"Gerontology and Geriatrics," <u>Encyclopedia Britannica</u>, Vol. 10, Chicago, William Benton, Publisher, 1972, pp. 363–365.

Preliminary Outline:

What special kinds of problems do elderly people in the United States face?

I. Definition of elderly
II. Physical problems
III. Financial problems
IV. Psychological problems

A. Think about the possible report topics.

1. Which topic in each pair is too general for a research report? What problems would students have in trying to prepare research reports on those topics?

2. Which topic in each pair is limited enough for a research report?

3. Suggest at least one other limited topic for each of the general topics.

B. Notice the information on each bibliography card.
 1. How is the author's name listed?
 2. What titles are included for each source?
 3. What information about the publishing company is recorded?
 4. On which cards are page numbers included?
C. Think about the preliminary outline.
 1. What question will be a guide for the student preparing this report?
 2. What are the main ideas about which the student expects to find information?

DRAFTING / COMPOSING

■ List at least five possible topics for research reports. Be sure each topic is limited enough to be presented in a single report. Then study your list of topics, and select one to use for your own research report. Underline that topic on your list.

■■ In a library, find at least four different sources for your research report. Look through each source to discover what general kind of information it offers. Prepare a bibliography card for each source.

■■■ Write a preliminary outline for your research report. Begin your outline with a question that will guide your research. Then list in outline form the main ideas you expect to develop in your report.

REVISING

Check the information on each of your bibliography cards. Ask yourself the following questions:

—Is each card complete?
—Is the handwriting on each card clear?
—Are all the names and titles spelled correctly?

If your answer to any of the questions is **no,** check your sources and revise your bibliography cards.

PROOFREADING

Your bibliography cards and your preliminary outline are for your own use, so they need not be perfectly understandable to others. Be sure, however, that they are clear and complete, or they will not help you as you continue working on your research report.

2 | Taking Notes for a Research Report

Taking notes is one of the most important steps in your research project, because it is the means by which you collect the information for your report. If you take good notes, you will be more than likely to write a good report.

All your information should be recorded on cards rather than on sheets of paper. The cards will help you organize the information when you outline and write your report.

You should follow the same format in preparing each note card. In the top right corner, write the last name of the author of the book or article. If the article is unsigned, write the title of the article instead of the author's name. After the author's name, write the number of the page on which you read the information. Then write a heading that identifies the general subject of the information recorded on the card. You can use the headings from your preliminary outline as headings for your note cards.

In the note below the heading, record only one item of information. Write the note in your own words, either in sentences or in phrases. In special cases, you may plan to use a quote from one of your sources. Then write the words exactly as they appear in the book or article, and use quotation marks around those words. On all other note cards, however, use your own words to record the information.

WORKING
WITH
THE MODEL

Read the following note cards.

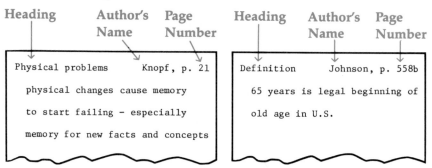

A. Notice the information on each note card.
  1. What information is recorded about the source of each note?
  2. What does the heading on each note card tell?
  3. How many notes are recorded on each card?
  4. In whose words are the notes written?

B. Imagine you are doing research on the problems faced by elderly people in the United States. You might read the following passage on page 12 of "Health Promotion and Disease Prevention in Old Age," an article by Julius B. Richmond. Think about how you would record the information in the passage on a note card.

Some changes are part of the aging process, but many others can be prevented. Moreover, like the aged themselves, normal age-related changes are subject to individual variability. In general, though, bones become more brittle with age and muscle loses some of its elasticity. Sensory "blurring" results in decreased sensitivity to light, noise, odor, and pain. Blood pressure increases and glucose tolerance declines.

1. What information would you record at the top of the note card?
2. What heading would you use for the note card?
3. What specific information would you record on the note card? What words would you use to record that information?

DRAFTING / COMPOSING

■ Read the books, magazine articles, and encyclopedia articles you have planned to use as sources for your research report. As you read, record the important information on note cards. Use the headings from your preliminary outline as the headings for your note cards. However, do not be too limited by your preliminary outline. If you find important information that does not fit under one of your original headings, create a new heading for that information.

REVISING

At the end of each note-taking session, check each new note card. As you read your cards, ask yourself the following questions:

—Is each note card clear and complete?
—Is the summary on each note card meaningful? Can the notes easily be expanded into sentences for the report?
—Are all proper nouns and all new words spelled correctly?

If the answer to any of the questions is **no,** check your sources and revise your note cards.

PROOFREADING

Like your bibliography cards and your preliminary outline, your note cards are for your use only. However, you should be sure that you can read and understand all the information on your cards.

3 | Outlining a Research Report

After you have completed most of your research, the next step in your project is preparing a detailed plan for the report. You must decide what information you will present, and you must decide how you will organize that information. The best way to make and record those decisions is by writing a final outline.

Your final outline should be based on your preliminary outline. The main headings of your final outline may be exactly those you used in the preliminary outline. If you added or changed any of those headings as you prepared your note cards, however, you should use the new headings in your final outline.

Prepare your final outline by organizing your cards into groups according to their headings. Then organize all the cards with the same heading into smaller groups. The cards in those smaller groups should all present related information. You can use each smaller group as a subheading in your outline. The note on each card will present a supporting detail to use within each section of your report.

As you review and organize your note cards, think about the main ideas you will present in your report. You should state those main ideas in a single sentence to be used in your outline. That sentence is called the thesis statement of your research report. The thesis statement should be a brief answer to the general question you composed when you started planning your research report.

WORKING
WITH
THE MODEL

Read the following outline for a research report. Notice the structure of the outline and the information it presents.

PROBLEMS OF THE ELDERLY—Outline

Thesis Statement:
Elderly people in the United States often face special physical, financial, and psychological problems.

  I. Definition of elderly

 II. Physical problems
 A. Illness
 B. Reduced ability and energy
 C. Decreased mobility

III. Financial problems
 A. Low wages
 B. Low retirement benefits
 C. Rising costs

IV. Psychological problems
    A. Impact of health problems and financial problems
    B. Low self-esteem
    C. Loneliness
    D. Fear

A. Think about the elements of the outline.

1. What is the title of the outline? What will be the title of the research report? What does the title tell about the contents of the report?

2. What is the thesis statement of the report? How does the thesis statement answer the question posed in the preliminary outline? What does the thesis statement tell about the contents of the report?

3. What is the first major heading of the outline? What main idea does it present?

4. What is the second major heading of the outline? What main idea does it present? What subheadings are listed under the main heading? What supporting ideas do they present?

5. What is the third major heading of the outline? What main idea does it present? What subheadings are listed under the major heading? What supporting ideas do they present?

6. What is the fourth major heading of the outline? What main idea does it present? What subheadings are listed under the main heading? What supporting ideas do they present?

B. Imagine that, instead of doing research on the special problems faced by the elderly in the United States, you had done research on the various groups that offer aid to the elderly. You might find that the headings on most of your note cards fell into the following four groups:

—reasons elderly need aid
—federal government agencies to aid elderly
—state and local government agencies to aid elderly
—private organizations to aid elderly

1. What main headings would you use in the outline for your report?

2. What thesis statement would you use?

3. What title would you give your report?

DRAFTING

■ Organize your note cards. Put them into groups to represent the main headings of your outline.

■■ Decide on the order in which you want to present the main ideas represented by the main headings of your outline. Organize your groups of cards in that order.

■■■ Read the cards within each group. Think about the subheadings you want to use under each main heading. Organize the cards of each heading to represent those subheadings.

■■■■ Think about the topic of your research report and about the major ideas that you will present in your report. Write a thesis statement summarizing the main ideas of your report.

■■■■■ Think of possible titles for your research report. Write at least three different words or phrases based on your thesis statement. Re-read your words and phrases, and underline the one that will make the best title.

COMPOSING

Use your organized note cards, your thesis statement, and your title to write an outline for your research report.

REVISING

Read your outline carefully. As you read, ask yourself the following questions:

—What changes, if any, are needed in the format of the outline?

—What are the main headings of the outline? How does each main heading relate to the thesis statement? How do the main headings relate to each other?

—What are the subheadings under each main heading? How does each subheading relate to its main heading? How do the subheadings in each group relate to each other?

—What headings and subheadings, if any, should be added? Which should be taken out? Which should be moved?

—Which parts of the outline, if any, seem weak or incomplete? What further research is needed before the outline is complete and the report can be written?

Revise your outline so that it is as clear and as complete as possible. If any more research is necessary, read and take notes. Then add the information from that research to your outline.

PROOFREADING

Proofread your outline. Follow the steps presented in the PROOF-READING CHECKLIST on page 105. Correct any mistakes you have made in outline format or spelling.

4 | Writing a Research Report

Once you have written an outline for your research report, you have completed most of the work involved in the project. You have chosen and narrowed a topic for your report. You have found books and articles on that topic. You have read those books and articles and taken notes on the information there. You have organized your notes. You have written an outline that gives a detailed plan for your report. All that remains is to actually write the report.

When you write your research report, you will be putting together the facts and ideas you have gathered from many different sources. It is important that you put those facts and ideas together in your own words, with your own organization; then your report will have a theme and a style uniquely yours. It is important that you develop each paragraph to support your thesis statement; then your report will have unity and will develop the reader's interest and understanding. And it is important that you use transitional words and phrases, so that each paragraph develops from the one before it; then you will have an essay of related paragraphs instead of a list of facts.

DRAFTING

■ Think about the main ideas for your research report, as presented in your thesis statement. Write an introductory paragraph based on that thesis statement. Remember, this is only the first draft of the first paragraph of your report. If you want, you can change it later. But finishing even a rough draft of your first paragraph will help you get going on the rest of your report.

■■ Read over your outline and your note cards. The note cards should be arranged to correspond to the organization of your outline. As you read, mark on your outline the number of paragraphs that you plan to devote to the information covered in each main heading. Also write a transitional word or phrase that you might use at the beginning of the first paragraph under each new heading.

■■■ Review the plans you have made for the paragraphs of your report. Write a topic sentence for each of the paragraphs you have planned. Be sure that each topic sentence states the main idea you will develop in that paragraph. You may want to include the transitional words and phrases you have written in your topic sentences.

■■■■ Write a short concluding paragraph for your report. It should present either a brief summary of the information in your report or a statement of the conclusions you have drawn from your research. Like your introductory paragraph, this paragraph can and probably will be changed later. However, it will give you a sense of direction as you develop your report.

■■■■■ Reread your introductory paragraph, your list of topic sentences, and your concluding paragraph. As you read, ask yourself the following questions:

—What main ideas are introduced in the introductory paragraph?
—Which ideas introduced in that paragraph, if any, are actually supporting ideas, not main ideas from the report?
—Which main ideas from the report, if any, are not introduced in that paragraph?
—What main paragraph idea is stated in each topic sentence?
—What facts and details will you include in each paragraph? How will those facts and details support the main idea in the topic sentence?
—What summary or conclusion is presented in the concluding paragraph? Which parts of the summary or conclusion, if any, are not based on ideas developed in the report?

Make any necessary changes in your paragraphs and topic sentences.

■■■■■■ Use your bibliography cards to prepare the bibliography for your report. Follow the format presented in the handbook lesson **Bibliography,** on page 108. You should have one bibliography entry for each source you used in your research.

COMPOSING

Use your introductory paragraph, your outline, your list of topic sentences, your note cards, and your concluding paragraph to write a research report. As you write, be conscious of how each sentence contributes to its paragraph, of how each paragraph relates to the next paragraph, and of how each paragraph relates to the main ideas of your report.

Even at this stage, you may find that some parts of your outline have to be rearranged or perhaps deleted. That is fine. Such changes show that you are thinking and that the outline is only a tool for your own use.

As you write, prepare the footnotes you will use. Follow the format presented in the handbook lesson **Footnotes,** on page 110.

78

REVISING

Try to finish writing your research report before it is due, and put the report away for a few days. Then when you go back over your report, you can be more objective about it. You will be able to do a better job of spotting problems and recognizing sections that need improvement.

When you read your report, ask yourself the following questions:

—What clues to the report does the title give? How might the title be revised to make the subject of the report more clear to the reader?

—Which part of the report states clearly what main ideas will be presented? How might this section be reworded to make the main ideas more clear to the reader?

—Which statements make the main points indicated by the main headings of the outline? What examples and information support each of those statements?

—Which statements, if any, are not supported directly enough? What examples or information could be added to support those statements?

—Which headings or subheadings from the outline, if any, have been left out? Where should information on those topics be included?

—How do the transitional words and phrases help make the relationships between paragraphs and between sections clear? What other transitional words and phrases, if any, should be added?

Make any changes that are necessary to improve your report. Even if you have planned and developed your report carefully, you may find you need to rewrite entire sections or even go to the library for more information. You may need to reorganize paragraphs, reword sentences, or add or take out information. Do not hesitate to make such changes in your report at this stage. You have already spent a good deal of time and energy on the research project, and your completed report should reflect your efforts.

When you have finished revising, recopy your report, typing it if necessary.

PROOFREADING

Proofread your report. Follow the steps presented in the PROOF-READING CHECKLIST on page 105, and review the lessons on footnotes and bibliography in your handbook. Correct any mistakes you have made in sentence structure, capitalization, punctuation, spelling, or the format of footnotes and bibliography.

CHAPTER 6

Persuasive Writing

Persuasive writing often bears a strong resemblance to the three other kinds of writing. It may include explanations, stories, or even descriptions. Persuasion is distinguished, however, by its purpose. It is intended to persuade readers, to convince them to think or act in a particular way.

In this chapter, you will develop your ability to organize and use words, sentences, and paragraphs of successful persuasion. You will

- write persuasive slogans
- write persuasive paragraphs
- write persuasive essays

1 Writing Persuasive Slogans

Almost every day, you read or hear someone else read persuasive writing. A billboard tries to persuade you to visit a particular resort. A radio announcer tries to persuade you to buy a certain record. A television actress tries to persuade you to use a special brand of toothpaste. A magazine ad tries to persuade you to select a new kind of cat food. Many of these attempts are made in the form of short, clever expressions called **persuasive slogans.**

A persuasive slogan may be a phrase, a clause, or a complete sentence. It should be short and memorable; every word in the slogan should count. The words of the persuasive slogan should be carefully chosen; they should work together to present a strong, direct appeal.

The specific words in any persuasive slogan are chosen for their meanings. Every word has at least one specific meaning, called a **denotation.** In addition, a word may also have a suggested meaning, called a **connotation.** The connotation of a word is its overtones, the ideas and feelings that the word suggests. In general, a word may have a positive connotation or a negative connotation.

Two words that have nearly the same denotation, or denotative meaning, may have different connotations, or connotative meanings. For example, *persistent* and *stubborn* have very similar denotative meanings. However, if someone calls you persistent, you are likely to feel complimented. *Persistent* suggests positive overtones and has a positive connotation. If someone calls you stubborn, on the other hand, you are likely to feel insulted. *Stubborn* suggests negative overtones and has a negative connotation.

In a persuasive slogan, the connotative meanings of words can be especially important.

WORKING
WITH
THE MODEL

Read the following persuasive slogans.

FRUIT PUNCH WITH AN EXTRAORDINARY TASTE

FRUIT PUNCH WITH A STRANGE TASTE

A FANTASTIC MOVIE ABOUT TWO ADVENTUROUS TRAVELERS

AN UNBELIEVABLE MOVIE ABOUT TWO RECKLESS TRAVELERS

WATCH THIS CLEVER PUBLIC SERVANT.

LOOK OUT FOR THIS SNEAKY POLITICIAN.

A. Think about the two slogans for fruit punch.

    1. Which slogan presents a positive image of the fruit punch? Which word in that slogan has a positive connotation?

    2. Which slogan presents a negative image of the fruit punch? Which word in that slogan has a negative connotation?

    3. What other words with positive connotations could be used in the first slogan?

    4. What other words with negative connotations could be used in the second slogan?

B. Think about the two slogans for the movie.

    1. Which slogan presents a positive image of the movie? Which words in that slogan have positive connotations?

    2. Which slogan presents a negative image of the movie? Which words in that slogan have negative connotations?

    3. What other words with positive connotations could be used in the first slogan?

    4. What other words with negative connotations could be used in the second slogan?

C. Think about the two slogans for the political candidate.

    1. Which slogan presents a positive image of the candidate? Which words in that slogan have positive connotations?

    2. Which slogan presents a negative image of the candidate? Which words in that slogan have negative connotations?

    3. What other words with positive connotations could be used in the first slogan?

    4. What other words with negative connotations could be used in the second slogan?

D. Think about the connotations of each of the following words.

—thrifty
—hasty
—sly
—wisdom
—self-confidence
—inexpensive
—outlandish
—nosy

    1. Which of the words have positive connotations? For each of those words, suggest another word with the same denotative meaning but a negative connotation.

    2. Which of the words have negative connotations? For each of those words, suggest another word with the same denotative meaning but a positive connotation.

E. Read the following slogans, and think about how they could be improved.

—A package of biscuits that taste pretty much like those biscuits that your grandmother or your grandfather made long ago

—Each and every person in the whole nation will probably like the taste of these gooey snacks.

1. Eliminate the unnecessary words from each slogan.

2. Revise the shortened slogans by using words with positive connotations wherever possible.

DRAFTING

■ Look at the mop pictured below, and think about how you might describe it in a persuasive slogan. List at least six words with positive connotations that you might use in a persuasive slogan about the mop.

■■ Look at the student pictured in the poster below. Think about the student's positive qualities that might be presented in a persuasive slogan. List at least six words with positive connotations that you could use in a slogan favoring that student.

■■■ Now consider the campaign against the student in the poster. List at least six words with negative connotations that might be used in a slogan against the student.

■■■■ Make up your own product or activity. Think about what makes the product or activity special. Then list at least six words you might use in a persuasive slogan about your product or activity. Each of your words should have a strong positive connotation.

COMPOSING

Write four persuasive slogans. Write one slogan to persuade shoppers to buy the mop. Write one slogan to persuade other students to vote for the student in the poster. Write one slogan to persuade other students to vote against that student. Finally, write a slogan to persuade people to buy your product or participate in your activity.

Use your lists of words as guides in writing each slogan, but do not try to include all the words from each list in each slogan. Select the words that will work well together and will present a strong, direct appeal.

REVISING

Read your four slogans carefully. As you read, ask yourself the following questions:

—What is the purpose of each slogan? How does the slogan achieve its purpose?
—How long is each slogan? What unnecessary words, if any, can be taken out of each slogan?
—Which slogan words have strong connotations? What is the effect of those connotations?
—What words, if any, might be replaced by other words with more positive (or negative) connotations?

PROOFREADING

Proofread each of your persuasive slogans. Follow the steps of the PROOFREADING CHECKLIST on page 105. Be sure that any slogan which is a complete sentence has the correct capital letters and end punctuation mark. Correct any mistakes you have made in spelling or punctuation.

2 | Writing a Persuasive Paragraph

Most people enjoy expressing their opinions and trying to persuade others to share those opinions. The simple statement of an opinion, however, is usually not very persuasive. In order to be persuasive, an opinion must be supported by reasons. The most convincing reasons are usually specific; they often include facts and statistics.

A persuasive paragraph usually presents a single opinion and several reasons to support that opinion. The opinion is stated in the topic sentence of the paragraph. In some persuasive paragraphs, the topic sentence comes first and serves as an introduction. In other persuasive paragraphs, the topic sentence comes last and serves as a conclusion.

WORKING
WITH
THE MODEL

Read the following persuasive paragraph. Think about the opinion and the reasons it presents.

If your warm-weather plans include water sports, there's one thing you should do to make this summer safe as well as enjoyable for your family members: drownproof them! Drowning is the second leading cause of accidental death for people between the ages of 4 and 44, according to the American National Red Cross. Twenty-eight percent of those drowned were children under 15 years old. Even more shocking is the fact that many of the seven thousand annual drowning victims knew how to swim. With drownproofing, however, a poor swimmer or even a nonswimmer can survive in the water twelve hours or more—even when fully clothed and in rough water.

Carla Stephens
"Drownproofing"

A. Think about the purpose of the paragraph.

1. What is the topic sentence of the paragraph? What opinion does the topic sentence state?

2. What reasons does the paragraph present to support the opinion stated in the topic sentence? What specific facts and statistics make those reasons convincing?

B. Think about the structure of the paragraph.

1. Where is the topic sentence?

2. How does each reason develop from the topic sentence?

3. If the topic sentence were moved to the end of the paragraph, how would that sentence have to be changed? Give an example of a topic sentence that might be used at the end of the model paragraph.

C. Read the following reasons:

— Young children can drown even in the shallow water of a wading pool.

— Young swimmers are setting records in international swim meets.

— Statistics show that the incidence of drowning in private swimming pools has increased in recent years.

— Swimming exercises every major muscle group in the body.

— Most children play around some body of water—a swimming pool, a pond, a river, a lake, or an ocean—at some time during the summer.

— Traffic accidents are another major cause of accidental death.

— Adults who can swim well but have not been drownproofed may not be able to survive a boating accident.

— Lake Tahoe is a popular recreation center for boaters.

1. Which reasons might be included in the model paragraph? How do those reasons support the opinion stated in the topic sentence of the paragraph?

2. Which reasons should not be included in the paragraph? Why do those reasons not belong in the paragraph?

D. Imagine you are preparing to compose a paragraph similar to the model. However, instead of persuading people to drownproof their families, your purpose will be to persuade people that they should learn to swim well.

1. What topic sentence would you use for your paragraph? Where would you place that topic sentence in your paragraph?

2. What reasons would you present to support your topic sentence?

DRAFTING

■ Choose one of the following topics, or think of another topic. Write one sentence that states your opinion on that topic.

— allowances
— energy conservation
— dogs in the city
— exercise
— homework
— computers
— marriage
— Western movies
— fast-food restaurants

For example:

Teenagers should not receive allowances.

■■ List at least four reasons that support your opinion.

For example:

Allowances encourage laziness and dependence.
Allowances don't provide enough money anyway.
Allowances can be replaced by fees for chores done at home.
Allowances too often cause arguments between parents and teenagers.

■■■ Read your opinion and list of reasons. As you read, ask yourself the following questions:

—Which reasons, if any, do not directly support the opinion?
—What other reasons might be added to the list?
—What facts or statistics would make each reason more convincing?

Then make any changes that will improve your list of reasons.

COMPOSING

Use your statement of opinion and your list of reasons to write a persuasive paragraph. Use the statement of your opinion as the topic sentence of your paragraph. Decide whether you want to use your topic sentence as the introduction or the conclusion of your paragraph. Then use your reasons to develop or to lead into your topic sentence.

REVISING

Read your persuasive paragraph carefully. As you read, ask yourself the following questions:

—What is the topic sentence of the paragraph?
—Where does the topic sentence come in the paragraph? Does it serve as an introduction or as a conclusion to the paragraph?
—What reasons support the opinion stated in the topic sentence?
—Which are the most convincing reasons in the paragraph?
—What might be added to make the other reasons in the paragraph more convincing?
—Which words in the paragraph have strong positive connotations?
—What other words with positive connotations might be used in the paragraph?

PROOFREADING

Proofread your paragraph. Follow the steps presented in the PROOF-READING CHECKLIST on page 105. Correct any mistakes you have made in sentence structure, capitalization, punctuation, or spelling.

Writing a Persuasive Essay

An opinion that is supported by a variety of reasons may be presented in a persuasive essay rather than a single persuasive paragraph. You might write an essay of three to five paragraphs, for example, persuading readers to agree with your opinion of a given book, to support a special cause, or to join a certain organization.

The first paragraph of a persuasive essay should clearly state the opinion of the writer. The other paragraphs should present reasons to support that opinion. Each paragraph should present a group of related reasons, or a category of reasons. Usually the categories are organized in order of their importance. The most important category is presented first, and the least important category is presented last.

DRAFTING

■ Choose a subject on which you have a strong opinion. Write a single sentence that states your opinion on that subject.

For example:
Every person needs time to be alone.

■■ Jot down all your specific reasons for holding that opinion. If you cannot list at least six specific reasons, start over with another subject. Do not try to organize your reasons yet; just list as many as possible.

For example:
Every person needs time to be alone to—

do homework	pursue hobbies like playing music
think about self	figure out the world
listen to records	read magazines or books
complete chores	plan projects

■■■ Read your list of specific reasons, and think about how the reasons can be grouped into categories. Select two, three, or four categories for your reasons. After each specific reason on your list, write a word that identifies its category.

For example:
Every person needs time to be alone to—

do homework—Work	pursue hobbies like playing music—Relax
think about self—Think	figure out the world—Think
listen to records—Relax	read magazines or books—Relax
complete chores—Work	plan projects—Work

■■■■ Review the categories you have chosen. Decide which category you consider most important and which you consider least important. List your categories from most important to least important.

For example:
1. Relax   2. Think   3. Work

COMPOSING

Use your statement of opinion, your list of reasons with categories, and your organization of categories to write a persuasive essay. In the first paragraph, state your opinion clearly and introduce the categories of reasons you will present in the essay. In the second paragraph, develop the category of reasons you have listed as most important. Use a statement of the category as the topic sentence of the paragraph. Support the topic sentence with specific reasons from your list. In the other paragraphs of your essay, develop your other categories of reasons.

REVISING

Read your essay carefully. As you read, ask yourself the following questions:

—What opinion does the essay present? Where is that opinion stated? What words might be changed to make the statement of opinion more clear?

—What categories of reasons does the essay present? How does each of those categories support the opinion? Which categories, if any, do not directly support the opinion and should be taken out of the essay? What other categories of reasons, if any, should be added?

—What is the topic sentence that presents the category of reasons in each paragraph? How does each specific reason in that paragraph support the topic sentence? Which reasons, if any, do not support the topic sentence and should be taken out of the paragraph? What other reasons, if any, should be added?

Make any changes that are necessary to improve your essay. After you have made your changes, you may need to recopy the essay.

PROOFREADING

Proofread your essay. Follow the steps presented in the PROOFREADING CHECKLIST on page 105. Correct any mistakes you have made in sentence structure, capitalization, punctuation, or spelling.

CHAPTER 7

Practical Writing

Certain kinds of writing follow special formats. These practical kinds of writing are used regularly by high school students and by adults. Knowing how to recognize and use these special forms of practical writing will help you understand, evaluate, and communicate information effectively.

In this chapter, you will practice using three different forms of practical writing, the business letter, the movie review, and the application form. You will

- plan and write business letters
- write movie reviews
- complete application forms

Writing a Business Letter

The use of the business letter is not limited to people in business. You may need to write a business letter to place an order, to register a complaint, to request information, to apply for a job, or to express an opinion.

A business letter follows a specific format. It has six elements: heading, inside address, greeting, body, closing, and signature. All six elements, properly placed and correctly punctuated, are expected in every business letter. A letter that does not follow the appropriate format might not be treated seriously.

In addition to following the correct format, a business letter should be very neat. A business letter from a student does not need to be typed, but it should be easy to read. The appearance of a business letter may make an important impression on the person who receives it. Look at the following samples from two different business letters, and think about the impression each letter might make.

```
                    232 Ridgeway Road

                    Muncie, Indiana 19803

                    April 15, 1981
```

```
    232 Ridgeway Road

      Muncie, Indiana 19803

    April 15, 1981
```

Read the following business letter. Notice its format and its message.

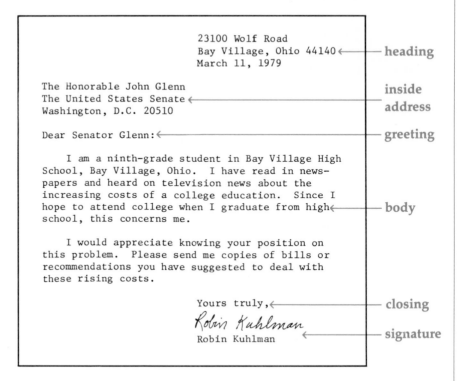

23100 Wolf Road
Bay Village, Ohio 44140 ←——— heading
March 11, 1979

The Honorable John Glenn   inside
The United States Senate ←———————— address
Washington, D.C. 20510

Dear Senator Glenn: ←———————————— greeting

    I am a ninth-grade student in Bay Village High
School, Bay Village, Ohio. I have read in newspapers and heard on television news about the
increasing costs of a college education. Since I
hope to attend college when I graduate from high ←——— body
school, this concerns me.

    I would appreciate knowing your position on
this problem. Please send me copies of bills or
recommendations you have suggested to deal with
these rising costs.

Yours truly, ←———— closing
Robin Kuhlman
Robin Kuhlman ←———————— signature

A. Think about the format of the letter.

1. What information does the heading include? What punctuation marks are part of the heading? Where is the heading written?

2. What information does the inside address include? What punctuation marks are part of the inside address? Where is the inside address written?

3. What words are used in the greeting? What punctuation mark is used? Where is the greeting written?

4. Which part of the letter contains the message of the letter? Where is that part written?

5. What words are used in the closing? What punctuation mark is used? Where is the closing written?

6. How is the signature given? Where is it written?

B. Think about the message of the letter.

1. What is the concern of the writer? What reasons for her concern does the writer give?

2. What does the writer want Senator Glenn to do? How does she request that action?

3. Does the writer use a formal style or an informal style?

DRAFTING

■ Prepare to write a letter to one of the United States senators from your state. Prepare the inside address of your letter. Use the title "The Honorable" before the name of your senator, and use the address used in the inside address of the model letter.

■■ Decide on the purpose of your letter. You may ask the senator for information on a specific issue or give the senator your opinion about an issue that affects the people in your state. Write one sentence stating the purpose of your letter. Then list the specific information you want to include and the specific requests you want to make.

COMPOSING

Write a business letter to one of your senators. Use the inside address and the list you have already prepared. Include all six elements of the business letter. In the body of the letter, state your business clearly and directly.

REVISING

Read your business letter carefully. As you read, ask yourself the following questions:

—Which six elements are included in this business letter? Which elements, if any, are misplaced? Which elements, if any, are missing? Which elements, if any, are not correctly punctuated?
—What concerns does the letter express? What requests does it make? What specific words make those concerns and requests clear? What essential information has been left out? What unimportant information has been included?

Make any changes that are necessary to improve your letter. Be sure that it follows the appropriate format and that its message is as clear and as direct as possible.

If you make any changes, rewrite or retype your letter.

PROOFREADING

Proofread your business letter. Follow the steps presented in the PROOFREADING CHECKLIST on page 105. Correct any mistakes you have made in sentence structure, capitalization, punctuation, or spelling.

2 | Writing a Movie Review

The film industry produces many more movies than the average person can ever hope to see. Rather than selecting movies according to titles or advertisements, many people read movie reviews to find out about current films. They use the reviews as a basis for deciding which movies are worth their time and money.

When you read a movie review, you can expect to find certain facts about the movie, as well as the reviewer's opinion of the movie. When you write a movie review, you have an obligation to share the same kinds of facts and an opportunity to give others your own opinion.

WORKING
WITH
THE MODEL

Read the following movie review. Notice the information and the opinions included in the review.

The Last Wave is a spellbinder, a tale of the supernatural that builds a fantastic sense of impending doom. Richard Chamberlain is riveting as an Australian lawyer whose familiar world crumbles after he turns from his area of corporate law to take on an odd criminal case. Several aborigines, the original Australians, are accused of murdering one of their own people. But Chamberlain has problems. There is confusion over the actual cause of death, and because of some terrifying secret area of knowledge relating to a concept of "Dreamtime"—the world of the spirit of their own culture—the aborigines refuse to answer his questions to aid in their defense. One of them even appears in his dreams. Somehow, Chamberlain is involved in other ways that he can't fathom. It's intimated that his own life is in peril, and his wife and children are drawn into the web.

Australian moviemaker Peter Weir, who directed *The Last Wave* from a screenplay based on his own original idea, gets top-notch performances from his players. With superb skill, he turns an everyday scene into one of terror. It's all the more frightening because the menace isn't simply based on sudden physical manifestations but on inexplicable events—a hailstorm, heavy rains, a swarm of frogs—that suggest natural forces are out of control. It's a movie you won't forget.

Edwin Miller
"Movie of the Month"

A. Think about the facts presented in the review.

1. What is the plot of the movie? What main story events does the review reveal? What story events does the review not reveal?

2. Who participated in making the movie? What was the role of each of those people?

3. What is the theme or main idea of the movie?

B. Think about the opinions presented in the review.

    1. What is the reviewer's opinion of the plot? Which words show that opinion?

    2. What is the reviewer's opinion of the main actor? Which words show that opinion?

    3. What is the reviewer's opinion of the director? Which words show that opinion?

    4. What is the reviewer's overall opinion of the movie? Where is that opinion most directly stated?

    5. What facts does the reviewer present to support each opinion?

C. Imagine you are writing a different review of *The Last Wave*. Unlike the writer of the model review, however, you think that the movie is slow, boring, and poorly acted.

    1. How would you change the first sentence of the review?

    2. How would you change the final sentence of the review?

    3. What other changes would you make in the review?

DRAFTING

■ Choose a movie that you have seen recently and that you would like to review. It may be a movie you saw in a theater or one you saw on television. Write the title of the movie you will review. Then write a sentence that summarizes your opinion of the movie.

■■ Make notes about the plot of the movie. List the most important story events, but do not reveal the whole story.

■■■ Make notes about the main story character or characters. After each character's name, write a phrase that describes the character's part in the story events.

■■■■ Make notes about the people who were involved in making the film and whom you want to mention in your review. You will probably want to include the names of the most important actors and actresses, as well as the name of the film's director.

■■■■■ Make notes about the style of the movie. This might include how the actors and actresses portrayed their characters, how the setting was developed, how the camera work set the mood of the film, how the music helped or hindered the film, how any special effects succeeded or failed. Your ideas on these subjects are your opinions; after each opinion you note, jot down at least one specific example from the movie to support your opinion.

■■■■■■ Write a sentence that summarizes the theme of the movie, the statement the movie tries to present. Then note your opinion of whether the theme is significant and of whether the theme is well developed in the movie.

■■■■■■■ Read your notes about the movie. Decide which aspect of the movie made the greatest impression on you, and underline your notes on that aspect. Those notes present information and opinions that will make a good beginning for your review.

COMPOSING

Use your notes to write a movie review. Begin with a statement about the aspect of the movie—plot, characters, style, or theme—that made the greatest impression on you. Remember to include both information and opinion in your review. Be sure that you present specific examples to support each of your opinions.

REVISING

Read your movie review carefully. As you read, ask yourself the following questions:

—What information about the movie's plot is presented in the review?
—Which details, if any, reveal too much about the plot?
—What other details should be added to make the plot more clear?
—What information about the characters is presented in the review?
—What details about those characters, if any, should be added?
—What information about the people involved in making the movie is presented in the review?
—What details about those people, if any, should be added?
—What opinions about the movie are presented in the review?
—What specific examples support those opinions?
—Which opinions, if any, are not supported by examples?
—What examples should be added to support those opinions?

Make any changes that are necessary to improve your movie review. After you have revised your review, you may need to recopy it.

PROOFREADING

Proofread your review. Follow the steps presented in the PROOF-READING CHECKLIST on page 105. Correct any mistakes you have made in sentence structure, capitalization, punctuation, or spelling.

3 | Completing an Application Form

Throughout their lives, most people need to complete a number of application forms for a variety of purposes. You may have to fill out an application form to change your class schedule, to be admitted to a college, to get a driver's license, to open a bank account, or to establish a charge account. One of the most important reasons you will have for filling out a form is to apply for a job.

Knowing how to fill out an application form completely and accurately will help you achieve your purpose—whether that purpose is to enroll in Consumer Mathematics II or to get a part-time job at an ice cream shop.

When you are given an application form to fill out, you should start by reading the entire form carefully. Think about the information that is called for in each item of the form. Think about how each of your responses should be presented. Does the form call for your last name first? Does the form require the street address on one line and the city and state names on another line? Be sure you know exactly what information should be presented on each line of the form before you start to write.

When you are ready to complete the application form, print each answer neatly and carefully. Printing is usually easier to read than cursive writing. Use a pen rather than a pencil. Writing in pencil may become smudged or faded. Information that is clear and easy to read will make a good impression on the person who reads your application form.

WORKING
WITH
THE MODEL

Read the application form on the following page. Notice the information that is requested in each item of the form. Also notice how each item has been completed.

A. Think about the application form.
   1. What information is called for in each item on the form?
   2. Which items have more than one part? In what order are those parts listed?
B. Think about how the application form has been completed.
   1. What information has been given for each item on the form?
   2. How has the form been filled out?
   3. What kind of impression will the completed form probably make?

B & B MANUFACTURING

APPLICATION FOR EMPLOYMENT

1. Date __JUNE 3, 1980__

2. Name __CHESNOVITCH   COURTNEY   ANN__
   Last   First   Middle

3. Address __3213   WEST SEVENTH ST.   #21__
   Number   Street   Apartment

   __WILMINGTON,   DELAWARE   19801__
   City   State   Zip Code

4. Telephone __555-6325__

5. Age __14__   6. Birthdate __MAY   21,   1966__
   Month   Day   Year

7. Education __9th GRADE   STANHOPE SCHOOL__
   Current Grade   School

8. Work Experience __MR. AND MRS. RICARDO MARTINEZ__
   Employer

   __3213   WEST SEVENTH ST.   #37__
   Number   Street

   __WILMINGTON ,   DELAWARE   19801__
   City   State   Zip Code

   __DAILY BABY-SITTING   JUNE-AUGUST 1979__
   Responsibilities   Dates

   __THE DAILY GAZETTE__
   Employer

   __4500 MAIN STREET__
   Number   Street

   __SANTA ANA , CALIFORNIA   94901__
   City   State   Zip Code

   __DAILY NEWSPAPER DELIVERY   JAN.-MAY 1979__
   Responsibilities   Dates

9. Reference __DR. JESSICA HELMHOLTZ__
   Name

   __538 WASHINGTON AVENUE__
   Number   Street   Apartment

   __WILMINGTON ,   DELAWARE   19804__
   City   State   Zip Code

C. Think about how you might complete the "Work Experience" item on the application form. It is usually important to give some information about the work you have done, even if that work has not been part of a paying job.

    1. What jobs have you held?

    2. If you have not yet had a paying job, what volunteer work have you done? What work have you done for clubs or service organizations? What household chores have you done regularly and responsibly over the past years?

D. Think about how you might complete the "Reference" item on the application form. Your reference should be an adult who knows you well, but who is not a relative. Your reference should be able to sincerely testify to your qualifications as a mature, responsible person who would make a good employee. Before you give a person's name as a reference, you should ask that person for his or her permission.

    1. Whom might you list as a reference on a job application form?

    2. Why would that person be a good reference?

DRAFTING

■ Read the application form on the following page carefully. Notice the exact information it calls for. Write your own name as you will write it for item [2] of the application form. Also write the name of the person you will use as a reference. Write that name as you will write it for item [9] of the application form.

■■ Think about what you will write for each line of the application form. If there is any information you are unsure of, check the facts now. Write out the information you will use in those parts of the application. Be sure that you can spell the names of people, streets, and cities correctly. Also be careful to describe your previous job duties accurately and in a way that emphasizes the responsibility involved. For example, "daily newspaper delivery" reminds your prospective employer that you were dependable enough to carry out your job every day.

COMPOSING

Write the information you would present on the application form. Write the number of each item from the form. After each number, write the information you would write on that part of the form. Print as clearly and as neatly as you would if you were actually filling out the application form.

REVISING

Read the information you have written for the application form. Be sure you have included the correct information for each part of the form. If you find any mistakes, rewrite the entire form. In general, it should not be necessary to revise the information on an application form. You should plan your responses carefully and write them correctly the first time you fill out the form.

PROOFREADING

Proofread the information for your application form. Be sure that you have spelled each name correctly and that you have used every necessary punctuation mark.

B & B MANUFACTURING

APPLICATION FOR EMPLOYMENT

1. Date _____

2. Name _____
   Last   First   Middle

3. Address _____
   Number   Street   Apartment

   City   State   Zip Code

4. Telephone _____

5. Age _____ 6. Birthdate _____
                    Month   Day   Year

7. Education _____
   Current Grade   School

8. Work Experience _____
   Employer

   Number   Street

   City   State   Zip Code

   Responsibilities   Dates

   Employer

   Number   Street

   City   State   Zip Code

   Responsibilities   Dates

9. Reference _____
   Name

   Number   Street   Apartment

   City   State   Zip Code

Composition Handbook

Sentences   102

Forms and Guidelines   105

Paragraphs   115

1 Sentence Variety

1a. Variety of Sentence Length

Vary the length of the sentences in a paragraph. Include both short and long sentences in order to hold the reader's interest. Too many short sentences can make writing seem choppy and juvenile. Too many long sentences can make the reader lose interest.

Living in a large family can be a problem. First, there is the problem of privacy. Sometimes a person wants to be alone, to sit and think, or listen to music, or make a very personal phone call. Try to do any of these in a house full of people! Then there is the problem of closet space. Sharing a two-by-four closet with a brother or sister is like asking a sardine to move over and make room. It's impossible. Finally, there is the problem of attention. One day I tried for an hour to speak with my mother about something important. Every five minutes, someone came barging in to interrupt us. I finally told her my problem in a note.

PRACTICING COMPOSITION SKILLS

■ Write answers to the following questions about the model paragraph.

1. How many sentences are in the model paragraph?
2. How many short sentences are there? How many long sentences?
3. Where are the short sentences placed?
4. What does the writer achieve with these short sentences?

■■ Rewrite the following paragraph, varying the length of the sentences.

The man stopped. He looked into the store window. The diamond sat in full view. The man looked up and down the block. The street was deserted. A single car drove by. The man drew the hammer from his sleeve. He raised the hammer slightly. The hammer slammed against the glass. Glass shattered. Bells jangled. The man reached a gloved hand through the glass. He picked up the diamond. He slid the diamond into his pocket. He slipped the hammer back into his sleeve. He walked calmly up the street. He did not even notice the police cars.

■■■ Write a paragraph of six or seven sentences on the advantages of living in a big family. Vary the length of your sentences. Place the short sentences carefully to make them most effective.

■■■■ Write a paragraph of six or seven sentences on one of the following topics, or choose a topic of your own. Vary the length of the sentences and place the short sentences carefully.

1. an accident
2. a busy store
3. a surprise exam
4. an audition
5. an unexpected victory
6. a disappointing game

1b. Variety of Sentence Beginnings

A sentence presents some or all of the following information: who or what, did what, when, where, why, and how. The kinds of information in many sentences can be arranged in several ways.

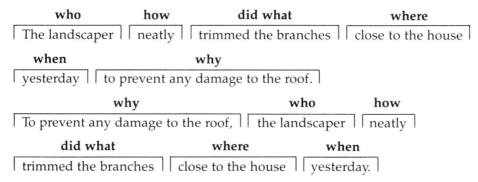

A paragraph of sentences that all begin in the same way or with the same kind of information can sound monotonous. Vary the beginnings of the sentences within a paragraph.

On graduation day, Karla woke up excited and nervous. She was thinking of the speech she was to make that evening. Having been selected from a large class, Karla felt proud, but her pride did not ease the tension. As she went in and out on errands, she kept reviewing the speech in her mind. Absentmindedly, instead of telling the grocer what was on her shopping list, Karla blurted out the part of her speech about the hungry and needy. That speech, no doubt, dominated Karla's day.

PRACTICING COMPOSITION SKILLS

■ Rewrite each of the following sentences in four ways. Begin each sentence by telling **when, where, why,** or **how.**

1. The clowns at the fair, hoping to raise money for charity, amused the audience all afternoon with their clever stunts.
2. The cashier at the restaurant carefully counts the money in the drawer each evening to determine the amount of the day's receipts.
3. The realtors in our town eagerly attend classes in their spare time to increase their sales.
4. The ghosts in the haunted house boldly frightened the new owners last week so that the house would remain in the possession of the ghosts.

■■ Rewrite the following paragraph. Vary the sentence beginnings.

I decided that morning to end our relationship cleanly. I had been their doormat long enough. I had been running their errands and doing their work for six months now. I had made myself their slave because I wanted to be their friend. I finally realized that they would never respect me if I did not respect myself. I gained a new respect for myself when I made my decision. I gained their respect when I carried it out.

1c. Combining Sentences

Combine related sentences to avoid the unnecessary repetition of words. Use a compound subject, compound predicate, appositive phrase, adverb clause, or adjective clause.

Compound Subject
Joe went on a bike hike. Jane went too.
Joe and Jane went on a bike hike.

Compound Predicate
The wind howled all night. The wind whistled also.
The wind howled and whistled all night.

Appositive Phrase
Arthur won a scholarship to college. Arthur is in my class.
Arthur, a boy in my class, won a scholarship to college.

Adverb Clause
I once visited the Grand Canyon. I was twelve years old then.
When I was twelve years old, I visited the Grand Canyon.

Adjective Clause
The bicycles were missing. We had left the bicycles on the sidewalk.
The bicycles that we had left on the sidewalk were missing.

PRACTICING COMPOSITION SKILLS

■ Combine the following sentence pairs to avoid the unnecessary repetition of words. Write the new sentences.

1. Delivering papers takes a long time. Collecting payments takes a long time, too.
2. I talk on the telephone at night. I also watch television.
3. The police officer brought the lost child home. The police officer is my neighbor.
4. We are building an addition to our house. We need more room.
5. That woman is a tennis pro. She is signing autographs.
6. I will do my homework. I will take a short nap first.
7. The lawnmowers hummed in the yards. The chain saws did the same.
8. Have you seen these pictures? I took these pictures at the party.
9. In college, Marci played varsity basketball. She also worked in the school library.
10. Dr. Reynosa is a respected surgeon. Dr. Reynosa also plays jazz.
11. I will go downtown. I will mail the letter at the main post office.
12. The telephone rang. At the same time, the doorbell rang.
13. Thea was disappointed when Martha said that. Thea was also hurt.
14. Sheri is fourteen years old. Sheri is my golden retriever.
15. The lifeguard leaped into the pool. She swam quickly to the floundering swimmer.

2 Proofreading

2a. Proofreading Checklist

Always proofread your work to eliminate errors. If you can, wait a day or more after finishing a major assignment such as a research report before proofreading it. First, proofread to be sure that it makes sense. Then proofread your work for specific problems in sentence structure, capitalization, punctuation, and spelling.

Proofreading Checklist

Sentence Structure

Proofread your work to avoid the following errors in sentence structure:

1. sentence fragments
2. run-on sentences
3. rambling sentences
4. wordy sentences
5. unnecessary changes in verb tense
6. double negatives
7. lack of agreement between subject and verb
8. incorrect placement of modifiers
9. unclear antecedents of pronouns
10. lack of parallel structure

Capital Letters

Proofread your work for capital letters where they are needed:

1. at the beginning of each sentence
2. at the beginning of a direct quotation
3. in proper nouns and proper adjectives
4. the personal pronoun **I**
5. in titles of people and relatives
6. in abbreviations
7. in titles of works of art

Punctuation Marks

Proofread your work for correct punctuation marks where they are needed:

1. at the end of each sentence: period, question mark, or exclamation mark
2. in a direct quotation: quotation marks, commas, period, question mark, or exclamation mark
3. periods in abbreviations
4. commas
5. quotation marks and underlines with titles
6. quotation marks within quotations
7. apostrophes in possessive nouns and in contractions
8. colons and semicolons
9. hyphens and parentheses

Spelling

Proofread your work for correct spelling of each word. Refer to a dictionary for the correct spelling of any word you are unsure of.

3 Note-Taking

3a. Summary Sentences

A summary sentence states in your own words the main idea of a passage you have read. When taking notes for research, use summary sentences to condense useful material.

Greek mythology is largely made up of stories about gods and goddesses, but it must not be read as an account of the Greek religion. According to the most modern idea, a real myth has nothing to do with religion. It is an explanation of something in nature; how, for instance, any and everything came into existence: people, animals, this or that tree or flower, the sun, the moon, the stars, storms, eruptions, earthquakes, all that is and all that happens. Thunder and lightning are caused when Zeus hurls his thunderbolt. A volcano erupts because a terrible creature is imprisoned in the mountain and every now and then struggles to get free. The Dipper, the constellation also called the Great Bear, does not set below the horizon because a goddess was once angry at it and decreed that it should never sink into the sea. Myths are early science, the result of people's first trying to explain what they saw around them.

Edith Hamilton
Mythology

Summary sentence:
Myths are early science, or explanations of nature, rather than religion.

PRACTICING COMPOSITION SKILLS

■ Read the following paragraphs. Then write a summary sentence for each paragraph.

1. Traveling by plane can be a difficult experience. Airports are usually out of the way and difficult to get to. Traffic builds up for miles as you approach the airport. At the airport, the maze of roads, the fleeting taxis, and the hundreds of signs require ten eyes and a carload of patience to get you where you have to go. Next you must wait in long lines to check your baggage and clear your ticket status. Then you take the long walk to the boarding gate. When you reach your destination, you go through the same difficulties in reverse.

2. Each generation of young people seems to find a new kind of music to make its own. In the roaring twenties, flappers danced to a wild music that shocked their parents. In the late thirties and forties, jazz came along to capture the fancy of the young. Rock 'n' roll caused a stir in the fifties, becoming a symbol for the youth of that decade. Songs of protest sparked the rebellion and demonstrations of the sixties and early seventies. And then came disco, bringing dancing and young people back together again.

3b. Bibliography Cards

Make a bibliography card for every source you read for a research report. Study the following types of bibliography cards:

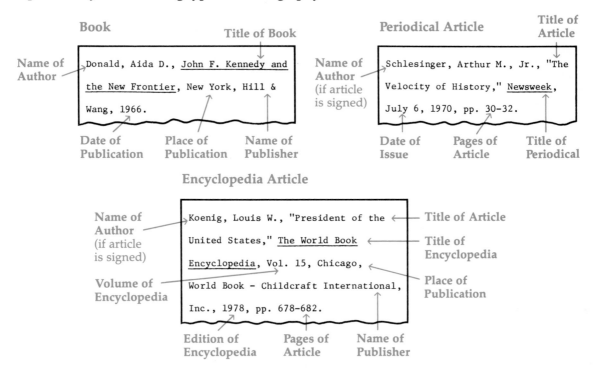

When an article in a periodical or encyclopedia is unsigned, begin the bibliography card with the title of the article. Everything else remains the same.

PRACTICING COMPOSITION SKILLS

■ Make a bibliography card for each of the following sources.

1. A book by Esther Forbes entitled <u>Paul Revere and the World He Lived In</u>, published in 1962 by Houghton Mifflin in Boston.

2. A magazine article by Daniel J. Boorstin entitled "A Case of Hypochondria" on pages 27–29 of the July 6, 1970, issue of <u>Newsweek.</u>

3. An article by Oscar Handlin entitled "United States History" on pages 86–126 of the 20th volume of the 1978 edition of The World Book Encyclopedia. The publisher is World Book–Childcraft International, Inc., in Chicago.

4. A magazine article by J. William Fulbright entitled "Reflections: In Thrall to Fear" on pages 41–62 of the January 8, 1972, issue of <u>The New Yorker</u>.

5. A book by Catherine Drinker Bowen entitled <u>John Adams and the American Revolution</u>, published in 1950 by Little, Brown in Boston.

3c. Bibliography

A bibliography is a list of the sources used in preparing a report. The sources are listed alphabetically by author (or by title, if an article is unsigned) on a separate sheet of paper. Compile the bibliography from the bibliography cards you prepared, including only those sources which are actually used in the final report. Include the bibliography at the end of your report. Study the following partial bibliography:

Bibliography

Apter, David E., "Government," International Encyclopedia of the Social Sciences, Vol. 6, New York, The Macmillan Company & The Free Press, 1968, pp. 214–229.

Donald, Aida D., John F. Kennedy and the New Frontier, New York, Hill & Wang, 1966.

"Federal Communications Commission," Collier's Encyclopedia, Vol. 9, New York, Crowell-Collier and Macmillan, Inc., 1967, p. 630.

Jensen, Amy LaFollette, The White House and Its Thirty-three Families, New York, McGraw-Hill, Inc., 1962.

Koenig, Louis W., "President of the United States," The World Book Encyclopedia, Vol. 15, Chicago, World Book–Childcraft International, Inc., 1978, pp. 678–682.

Schlesinger, Arthur M., Jr., "The Velocity of History," Newsweek, July 6, 1970, pp. 30–32.

Steele, Ronald, "The Kennedy Fantasy," The New York Review of Books, November 19, 1970, pp. 3–8.

PRACTICING COMPOSITION SKILLS

■ Compile a bibliography from the following sources.

Wicker, Tom, JFK and LBJ: The Influence of Personality upon Politics, New York, William Morrow, 1968.

Auchincloss, Kenneth, "The Kennedy Years," Newsweek, February 1, 1971, pp. 21–22.

"Arise, Ye Silent Class of '57!" Life, June 17, 1957, p. 94.

Ebenstein, William, "Democracy," Collier's Encyclopedia, Vol. 8, New York, Crowell-Collier Educational Corporation, 1969, pp. 75–83.

Lincoln, Evelyn, My Twelve Years with John F. Kennedy, New York, David McKay, 1965.

Hacker, Andrew, "We Will Meet As Enemies," Newsweek, July 6, 1970, pp. 24–25.

3d. Note Cards

Record research notes on individual cards. Follow these guidelines:

1. **In the top right-hand corner, write the author's last name and the page number on which you read the information. If an article is unsigned, write its title instead of the author's name.**

2. **In the top left-hand corner, write the general subject of the information recorded on the card. You can use the headings from your preliminary outline as headings for your note cards.**

3. **Record only one item of information on each card. Write the note in your own words. If you think you may use a direct quotation, copy the words exactly and use quotation marks around them.**

   Now that you are acquainted with some of the necessary substances in the food you eat, it is important for you to know a little about substances which are added to foods by food processors. A food additive is any substance which is added to a basic, natural food. An additive may change the taste, texture, appearance, nutritional value, or the "life span" of a food. Some additives are healthy or just harmless, and some are potentially dangerous for you.

Jill Pinkwater
The Natural Snack Cookbook

Heading   **Author's Name**

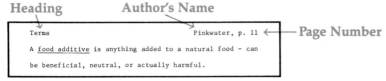

Terms   Pinkwater, p. 11   ——**Page Number**

A <u>food additive</u> is anything added to a natural food – can

be beneficial, neutral, or actually harmful.

PRACTICING COMPOSITION SKILLS

■ Make a note card for each of the following paragraphs. Use the heading "Abilities of the earthworm" for the first and "Kinds of reasoning " for the second.

1. Tested in laboratory experiments, fishbaits learn and remember maze problems. In the field they are good at turning and manipulating a small object, say a leaf or stick, so as to fit it into their tunnels. They react to and seem to interpret vibrations, and they scent trails made by others of their kind. They have a well-developed sense of taste, preferring, for example, carrot leaves to celery but choosing celery over cabbage.

   Bil Gilbert
   "They Crawl by Night," p. 55

2. I know that I like pizza more than I like apples, and that I like apples more than I like turnips. If I conclude from this series of preferences that I like pizza most of the three, or turnips least of the three, I have performed a *transitive inference*. The transitive inference is one form of reasoning sometimes measured on IQ tests.

   Robert J. Sternberg
   "Stalking the IQ Quark," p. 47

3e. Footnotes

Use footnotes in a report to identify the source of a quotation, statistic, or original idea. In the body of your paper, put a number (start with 1 for the first footnote) to the right and above the last word of the material to be footnoted. Put this same number to the left and above the actual footnote. Footnotes may be placed at the bottom of the page on which the information is used or on a separate sheet at the end of the report.

The first time a source is referred to in a report, the footnote must include all identifying information. For another footnote from the same source, use an abbreviated form of the initial footnote. Study the following types of footnotes.

Book

[1]Amy LaFollette Jensen, The White House and Its Thirty-three Families, p. 5.
[2]Jensen, p. 265.

Periodical Article

[3]Ronald Steele, "The Kennedy Fantasy," The New York Review of Books, November 19, 1970, p. 7.
[4]Steele, p. 8.

Encyclopedia Article

[5]David E. Apter, "Government," International Encyclopedia of the Social Sciences, 1968 Ed., Vol. 6, pp. 225–227.
[6]Apter, p. 216.

When an article in a periodical or encyclopedia is unsigned, begin the footnote with the title of the article. Everything else remains the same.

PRACTICING COMPOSITION SKILLS

- Write footnotes as indicated for each of the following sources.

1. A book by Fawn M. Brodie entitled Thomas Jefferson.
   First footnote: page 466
   Subsequent footnote: pages 466–467

2. An article by William S. Carleton entitled "Electoral College" in the 6th volume of the 1979 edition of The World Book Encyclopedia.
   First footnote: page 117
   Subsequent footnote: pages 115–117

3. A magazine article by Staughton Lynd entitled "Again—Don't Tread on Me" in the July 6, 1970, issue of Newsweek.
   First footnote: page 30
   Subsequent footnote: page 32

4. A magazine article by Kenneth Auchincloss entitled "Good-by to the '60s" in the December 29, 1969, issue of Newsweek.
   First footnote: pages 17–18
   Subsequent footnote: pages 12–14

4   Outlines

4a.   Writing Outlines

A clearly written outline will help you when you write your final report. Following your outline accurately will enable you to include in the proper sequence all the relevant information you have gathered. Study the following partial outline. Each Roman numeral indicates a main heading; each capital letter indicates a subheading; each Arabic numeral indicates a detail under a subheading. Always use two or more of the same kind of heading. Do not use only one Roman numeral or only one capital letter or only one Arabic numeral.

The Moon

I. General information
  A. Size
    1. Diameter
    2. Circumference
  B. Surface features
    1. Low, flat plains
    2. Rough, mountainous highlands
    3. Craters

II. The moon as seen from Earth
  A. Phases of the moon
  B. Orbit of the moon
  C. Lunar eclipses

PRACTICING COMPOSITION SKILLS

■ Imagine you are preparing an outline for a report on Marian Anderson, the famous American singer. Each heading is indicated for you by a Roman numeral. The remaining parts of the outline are out of order and are not labeled. They represent subheadings and details of subheadings. Give each part a capital letter or an Arabic numeral. Then arrange the entire outline in the proper sequence.

Marian Anderson

I. Early life
II. Musical career
III. Major accomplishments

Autobiography published in 1956
At New York Town Hall in 1935
Born in Philadelphia in 1902
Studied operatic voice in Europe
Awarded to promising singers in competition
Named U.S. delegate to U.N. in 1958

Famous performances
At Metropolitan opera in 1955
Spingarn Medal in 1939
Established Marian Anderson Award
Groups raised money for her studies
Awards received
Began singing in choir at age of eight
One thousand dollars awarded annually
Preparation

5 Letters

5a. Friendly Letters

People write friendly letters to exchange personal and social information with friends and relatives. A friendly letter often contains questions which will be answered in a letter of response.

The five elements of a friendly letter are: date, greeting, body, closing, and signature. Study the following model friendly letter.

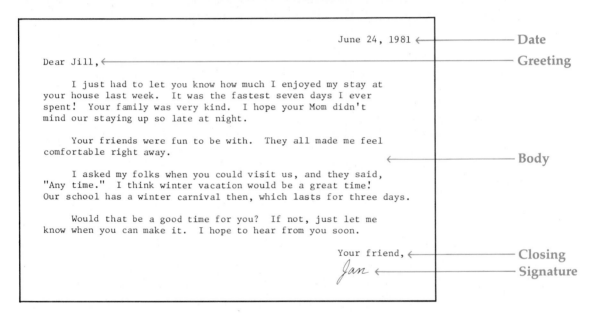

PRACTICING COMPOSITION SKILLS

■ Write answers to the following questions about the model letter.

1. What are the reasons Jan is writing to Jill?

2. Does Jan's letter ask any questions that she would like answered in a response letter from Jill? What are they?

■■ Write each of the following friendly letters. Use your own address and today's date.

1. Invite a cousin or friend (real or imaginary) to spend part of the summer vacation with you and your family.

2. Thank an aunt or uncle (real or imaginary) for the money she or he sent you as a birthday gift, and describe how you are going to use the money.

3. Introduce yourself to a new pen pal who is your age and lives in another country.

4. Ask a brother or sister (real or imaginary) who has been away at college for one month to describe his or her new life, and include news of your family and hometown.

5b. Business Letters

People write business letters for a number of reasons. They may want to obtain information, order goods or services, make a complaint, state an opinion, or apply for a job.

A business letter should be brief, clear, and simple. It should include all necessary information, such as specific names, dates, serial numbers, prices, or locations. It should also state exactly what the writer wants done. The letter should be typed or handwritten neatly.

The six elements of a business letter are: heading, inside address, greeting, body, closing, and signature.

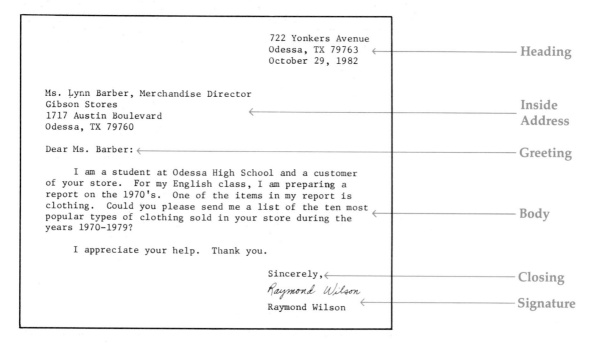

722 Yonkers Avenue
Odessa, TX 79763 ← ———————— Heading
October 29, 1982

Ms. Lynn Barber, Merchandise Director
Gibson Stores
1717 Austin Boulevard ← ———————— Inside Address
Odessa, TX 79760

Dear Ms. Barber: ← ———————— Greeting

    I am a student at Odessa High School and a customer of your store. For my English class, I am preparing a report on the 1970's. One of the items in my report is clothing. Could you please send me a list of the ten most popular types of clothing sold in your store during the ← ———————— Body years 1970-1979?

    I appreciate your help. Thank you.

        Sincerely, ← ———————— Closing
        Raymond Wilson
        Raymond Wilson ← ———————— Signature

PRACTICING COMPOSITION SKILLS

■ Write answers to the following questions about the model business letter.

1. What is the purpose of this business letter?

2. What necessary information to achieve that purpose does the writer include?

■■ Write each of the following business letters. Make up a different address in the heading of each letter.

1. Order information about activities, hotels, and prices for a summer vacation from the Cape Cod Chamber of Commerce, 16 Falmouth Avenue, Falmouth, Massachusetts 02543.

2. Request two replacement output transistors for your Rundfunk 1000 stereo receiver, which is still under warranty, from Laud Stereo, Inc., 617 Noyes Avenue, Tuttle, Oklahoma 73089.

5c. Envelopes

Prepare the envelope for a friendly letter and a business letter in the same manner. Write or type your name and address in the upper left-hand corner of the envelope. Write or type the name and address of the person to whom you are writing (the addressee) on the lower half of the envelope. Put a stamp in the upper right-hand corner.

When addressing an envelope for a business letter, be sure that the addressee's name and address on the envelope match the inside address of the letter. If you type a business letter, type the envelope also.

Use the ZIP code abbreviation for each state and the correct ZIP codes. Study the following model envelopes.

```
Raymond Wilson

722 Yonkers Avenue

Odessa, TX 79763

                    Ms. Lynn Barber, Merchandise Director

                    Gibson Stores

                    1717 Austin Boulevard

                    Odessa, TX 79760
```

PRACTICING COMPOSITION SKILLS

■ Prepare an envelope for each of the four friendly letters and each of the three business letters you wrote in the previous two lessons.

■■ Prepare the following envelopes.

1. Sender:
   Carol Gleason
   14757 Croydon Avenue
   Metairie, LA 70005

   Addressee:
   Mr. William Gleason
   Amherst College
   420 Seeley Hall
   Amherst, MA 01002

2. Sender:
   Ivan Green
   18 Century Place
   Los Angeles, CA 90067

   Addressee:
   Dr. Donald N. Adler
   433 Coldwater Canyon Avenue
   Sherman Oaks, CA 91403

3. Sender:
   Elizabeth Keyes
   3563 Ashbury Street
   Elmhurst, NY 11373

   Addressee:
   Mrs. Ronald Lewis
   9330 Clayton Street
   Maspeth, NY 11378

6 Paragraph Development

6a. Topic Sentences in Paragraphs

The topic sentence states the main idea of a paragraph. The topic sentence helps the writer concentrate on one main idea in a paragraph. It helps the reader understand the purpose of all of the supporting sentences. The topic sentence is often, but not always, the first sentence in the paragraph.

There is a great deal of variety in even the most ordinary aspects of life. For example, think of the hundreds of different kinds of flowers we see in gardens. Trying to name all of the different types of dogs or horses or birds would be a great challenge for anyone but an expert. Though we all can appreciate the beauty of the pine, the maple, the dogwood, and dozens of other trees, probably only a naturalist could list them all. And with all the human beings in the world, isn't it amazing that, with the possible exception of identical twins, no two of us look exactly alike?

PRACTICING COMPOSITION SKILLS

■ Read the following paragraph. Then write only the topic sentence of the paragraph.

To some people, success is measured in dollars. That is, the wealthier the individual, the more successful the person. To others, success depends on how much power and control over others an individual has. Still others think fame and popularity are the prime criteria of success. Happiness is the standard of success that some people use. Success, therefore, means different things to different people.

■■ Read the following incomplete paragraph. Then write a topic sentence for the paragraph.

When I was in first grade, I couldn't wait to join the Brownies. Soon after I had a complete uniform, I resigned. In second grade I cried for piano lessons. By third grade I had quit. In fourth grade I wanted desperately to learn ice skating. Six months after I started, my skates were gathering dust in the garage. In sixth grade I took up guitar. A short time later, I put it down.

■■■ Write a topic sentence for a paragraph on each of the following subjects.

1. parents
2. television
3. friends
4. dancing
5. sports
6. nature

■■■■ Choose one of the topic sentences you wrote in the previous activity. Use your topic sentence in a paragraph. Add four or five sentences that support the topic sentence.

6b. Using Details to Develop Paragraphs

Details are the specific elements that make a general statement clear. Details are especially important in descriptive paragraphs. In such paragraphs, observations of sight, sound, smell, touch, and taste make good details.

The kitchen showed no signs that humans were still living there. The odor of rotting fruit was overpowering. Packages of dry food, torn open by the cats, were strewn across the counter tops. A newspaper on the table bore a date already three weeks past. Webs of dust had begun to form on the lighting fixtures. A leaky faucet dripped into an overflowing sink, causing a slow but steady stream of water to cascade to the floor.

PRACTICING COMPOSITION SKILLS

■ List five more details that could be used to develop the topic sentence "The kitchen showed no signs that humans were still living there."

■■ Write each word or phrase that presents a detail in the following paragraph. After each word or phrase, write **sight, sound, smell, touch,** or **taste** to identify the sense to which the detail appeals.

Rotating the ball in his hand, the pitcher glares in at the batter. The batter returns the glare, clenching his sweaty hands around the handle of the bat. In the stands, the pleas and jeers of the fans echo around us. The warm summer sunshine, the smell of hot dogs, the refreshing taste of an ice-cold soda, and the excitement of a close ball game make a day at the ballpark one of our favorite activities.

■■■ List seven details which could be used to support this topic sentence: "We entered the cafeteria at the height of its activity." Try to use at least one detail from each of the five senses.

■■■■ Write a paragraph using your list of details and the topic sentence from the previous activity.

■■■■■ Write a paragraph about one of the following subjects. Use details to develop your paragraph.

1. an airport   3. a nursery   5. a person
2. a haunted house   4. your room   6. painting

■■■■■■ Write a paragraph about one of the following subjects. Develop your paragraph by using details of sound, smell, touch, and taste. Do not use any details of sight.

1. a crowded city street   4. an open field
2. the home of a large family   5. a gym
3. a party   6. the beach

6c. Using Incidents to Develop Paragraphs

An incident is a brief story. An incident can be written for one of two purposes: 1) to entertain readers, as any story would; and 2) to make a point clear.

Incident to Entertain

Once, on a long vacation with my parents, I was very bored because there was no one else my age staying at the hotel. Then one day a family checked in with a girl my age named Janet. My boredom quickly gave way to fun. That morning, we swam in the pool. In the afternoon, we explored the mountains around the hotel. After dinner, we took a rowboat out onto the lake and shared a long talk about school, parents, and the future. We made plans for the next day. But when I looked for Janet at breakfast, the manager said that there had been a death in Janet's family. She and her parents had had to leave for home immediately. I never saw or heard from Janet again.

Incident to Make a Point Clear

Sometimes an emergency will bring out unexpected abilities in a person. One Sunday morning, my parents had left me to watch my little sister, who was only a year old. All of a sudden, she began choking. I ran to her and saw only a part of a cellophane wrapper in her hand. The other part of it—a small piece—was lodged in her throat. Without really thinking, I put my hand into her little mouth. I reached my two fingers down into her throat to grasp the cellophane. My usually awkward hands worked like a surgeon's, and I drew the paper out. Only after it was all over did I realize how serious the situation had been. That's when I became frightened.

PRACTICING COMPOSITION SKILLS

■ Think of an incident that once happened to you or that you witnessed, which other people might enjoy reading about. It could be exciting, sad, or funny. Write a paragraph relating the incident as you remember it. Include enough details to help the reader visualize the scene. Describe the events that took place and the feelings you had at the time. Remember, you are not trying to prove a point. You are simply writing to entertain.

■■ Select one of the points listed below, or decide upon your own point. Write a paragraph using an incident to make the point clear.

1. Honesty is the best policy.
2. You always hurt the ones you love.
3. We appreciate things and people best after they are gone.
4. Laughter is the best medicine.
5. Beauty is in the eye of the beholder.
6. The best things in life are free.
7. If you don't succeed, always try again.

6d. Using Reasons to Develop Paragraphs

Reasons are usually used to develop paragraphs that explain, prove, persuade, or state an opinion.

Frances chose Felicity College after careful consideration of the things it had to offer. She wanted a small school where she could get more individual attention. The college had to have a good pre-med program to assist her in becoming a doctor. Because of her financial situation, Frances had to find a school which was close to home, had reasonable tuition rates, and offered an opportunity for part-time work. In addition, if the school had a varied array of extracurricular activities, so much the better. As Felicity met all of these requirements, Frances enrolled there.

PRACTICING COMPOSITION SKILLS

■ List three other reasons Frances might have considered in choosing her college.

■■ Complete the following paragraph of opinion. Add four sentences giving reasons to support the topic sentence.

Too much television viewing can be harmful to children. For one thing, television can make us believe that all problems are solved in thirty or sixty minutes. For another, it suggests that women are only housecleaners or assistants. . . .

■■■ Read the following topics. Write only the topics that you could develop with reasons.

1. a summary of the plot of a novel
2. the appearance of a character
3. your opinion of a book
4. an explanation of the causes of the Civil War
5. a description of an accident you witnessed
6. your defense against the accusation of a crime
7. your request for an increase in allowance or pay
8. an outline of the steps in a recipe
9. a request to the city council for a recreation center
10. the steps by which your little brother learned to read
11. your favorite movie of all time
12. your first day at a new school

■■■■ Write a paragraph on one of the following topics. Use reasons to develop your paragraph.

1. Convince the public to buy Shine-O toothpaste.
2. Prove that your client is innocent of the charge of being boring.
3. Defend your preference for a four-day school week.
4. Present the weaknesses in the way your school is run.

■■■■■ Write a paragraph that will be an argument against the paragraph you wrote in the previous activity. Use reasons to develop your new paragraph.

6e. Using Examples to Develop Paragraphs

Examples are illustrations or instances given to demonstrate, prove, or explain a point. Examples are often used to develop points in paragraphs.

Knowing how to "read" the signs of nature can help you forecast the weather. For example, dew on the grass at night or in the morning is a sign of fair weather. Birds perch more just before storms because low-pressure air is less dense, making it harder to fly. Smells are more distinct before a rainstorm. High clouds won't rain on you no matter how menacing they look. Lightning to the west or northwest of you is usually in a storm that will reach you. Aching corns and other pains can forecast bad weather, because as the air pressure falls, the tissues of the body swell.

PRACTICING COMPOSITION SKILLS

■ Which of the following would be effective examples to prove the statement "Wastefulness is part of American living"?

1. Early American farmers often worked a piece of land until it became barren, then moved on to another.
2. We use many throwaway products, such as bottles, cans, napkins, and cups.
3. During the Great Depression of the 1930's, Americans had to learn to stop wasting things.
4. Advertising encourages waste by enticing customers to buy something new, regardless of the condition of the old product they are replacing.
5. Consumers of the 1980's are buying compact automobiles with good gasoline mileage so eagerly that dealers cannot keep them in stock.

■■ List two examples to develop each of the following points or opinions.

1. At times, even the slightest noise can be a big distraction.
2. Engaging in team sports can help to develop character.
3. There are many advantages to being an only child.
4. Some forms of exercise can be fun as well as healthful.
5. Learning to play a musical instrument requires patience.

■■■ Select one of the topics from the previous activity. Add two or three more examples to those you have already listed. Then use your list to write a paragraph with examples.

■■■■ Write a paragraph on one of the following topics or on a topic of your own choice. Compose a topic sentence that makes a point about the topic. Then use examples to develop the paragraph.

1. nature's power
2. a sense of humor
3. dating
4. a successful person
5. friends
6. pressure on teenagers

6f. Using Comparison or Contrast to Develop Paragraphs

Comparison shows the likenesses between two or more things. Contrast shows the differences. Paragraphs can be developed by comparison or by contrast.

Comparison

Though they are the heroes of two novels set many years apart, Huckleberry Finn and Holden Caulfield are very much alike. Both are teenagers who care little for school. Each is pretty much on his own in the world, and each spends time moving in and out of various levels of society. Holden and Huck are both keen observers of people. They have no use for cheats, liars, and bullies, but they are very sympathetic to the downtrodden. They each go through adventures which are humorous as well as sad; and, in his own way, each boy seems to mature as a result.

Contrast

The two kinds of comedy, high comedy and low comedy, are quite different from one another. High comedy appeals to the mind and uses humor to make audiences recognize their own flaws and faults. Low comedy appeals to the emotions, and its purpose is simply to make people laugh. High comedy achieves laughter through wittiness and clever situations. Low comedy gets laughs through more physical means, such as a pie in the face or a slip on a banana peel.

PRACTICING COMPOSITION SKILLS

- ■ List the points of comparison in the first model paragraph.

- ■■ List the points of contrast in the second model paragraph.

- ■■■ Write a paragraph of comparison on one of the following topics or on a topic of your own choice.

1. Compare sports heroes to show-business idols.
2. Compare the society of a school to society at large.
3. Compare the way human parents raise their children to the way animal parents raise their offspring.
4. Compare soccer players to modern dancers.

- ■■■■ Write a paragraph of contrast on one of the following topics or on a topic of your own choice.

1. Contrast city life with country life.
2. Contrast life in a small family with life in a large family.
3. Contrast tennis with table tennis.
4. Contrast competition in team sports with competition in individual sports.
5. Contrast daytime television programs with evening television programs.
6. Contrast dogs as pets with cats as pets.
7. Contrast people who own dogs as pets with people who own cats as pets.
8. Contrast going to school with working.

7 Paragraph Organization

7a. Using Chronological Organization in Paragraphs

The steps or details in a paragraph may be arranged in the order of time, from first to last. This kind of organization is called chronological order. Chronological order is often used in narrative paragraphs and in expository paragraphs.

Narrative

When I arrived at my cousin's house, I noticed a blue van parked in front of the house. I rang the door bell, but there was no answer. I rang three or four more times; but again, no answer. Just as I was about to leave, I heard a clanking noise inside. I rang the bell and waited, but still I got no answer. I walked around to the back of the house and saw the rear door wide open. As I approached, a strange man and woman dashed out the door, carrying a bulging pillowcase and a portable television set. I froze in my tracks. The two strangers ran right by me and out to the blue van. I ran after them, only to see the van pulling away. I did, however, get the license plate number and call the police.

PRACTICING COMPOSITION SKILLS

■ The sentences in the following expository paragraph are not arranged in chronological order. Rewrite the paragraph, using chronological organization to arrange the steps.

Place the dirty clothes in the washing machine. While the clothes are being rinsed for the last time, add a capful of fabric softener. After the clothes are washed, take them out of the washing machine and put them in the dryer. Once the machine starts to wash the clothes, check to see that you have added enough detergent. Decide how much water will be necessary to cover the laundry in the machine, and press the appropriate button for a small, medium, or large load. When the clothes are dry, take them out of the dryer and fold them or put them on hangers. As the machine is filling with water, evenly sprinkle one cup of low-sudsing, biodegradable detergent into it. Put the clean, dry clothes away in dresser drawers and closets.

■■ Write a narrative paragraph on one of the following topics or on a topic of your own choice. Organize the details of your paragraph in chronological order.

1. a frightening experience   2. an accident   3. a tiring day   4. a typical morning

■■■ Write an expository paragraph on one of the following topics or on a topic of your own choice. Organize the details of your paragraph in chronological order.

1. directions to a movie theater
2. your team's progress this year
3. how to get to know a person
4. how to study for an exam

7b. Using Spatial Organization in Paragraphs

A paragraph that describes a setting should be organized to help the reader locate the objects and the people within the setting. This kind of organization is called spatial organization **. The description of a setting can be organized from left to right, top to bottom, far to near, or outside to inside. A description can also be organized in the reverse of any of those patterns. Shape, size, and relationship of one object to another can help the reader. Some words and phrases that show spatial relationship are listed in the box below.**

above	at the rear or front
below	at the top or bottom
beyond	to the left or right
across from	surrounding
next to	opposite

The yard was almost square, about fifty feet by fifty feet. A white picket fence lined each side, and wild forsythia bushes about seven feet high closed off the rear. Plants and flowers added color to the fence on the left, and a long, narrow vegetable garden livened the right side. Toward the rear of the yard, on the right, stood a children's gym set, complete with swings, a slide, and monkey bars. A thick green carpet of grass covered the entire yard. Standing majestically in its center was an apple tree.

PRACTICING COMPOSITION SKILLS

■ Draw a diagram of the yard described in the model paragraph.

■■ Rewrite the following paragraph. Choose a pattern of spatial organization, and organize the details according to that pattern. Add words and phrases that would locate details in the scene and give the reader some idea of the size and relationship of things.

The ninth-grade English classroom showed signs of much activity. Students' and teacher's desks had been rearranged. Projects, some half-finished and some completed, were all around. The presence of many plants added a homey feeling to the room. One group of students was reciting into a tape recorder. Another group was practicing a skit on the American Revolution. The teacher was talking with a third group. Only one student seemed to be uninvolved. She was leaning back in a chair, drawing cartoons in her notebook.

■■■ Use a pattern of spatial organization, aided by words that show relationships and size, to write a paragraph describing one of the following settings or a setting of your own choice.

1. a set in a play
2. a room in your house
3. an interesting building in your town
4. a schoolyard at lunchtime in warm weather

Speech

Narrative Speaking   124

Expository Speaking   130

Persuasive Speaking   140

Listening   146

CHAPTER 8

Narrative Speaking

Everyone enjoys hearing an interesting, well-told story. Certain people seem to have a talent for telling stories well. There is, however, no secret to their success. They choose their stories thoughtfully, they develop their stories carefully, and they tell their stories clearly.

In this chapter, you will develop your skills by telling stories in different kinds of situations. You will plan and tell your own stories, and you will listen as others tell their stories. You will

- tell stories in conversations
- make narrative speeches

1   Telling a Story

When you are talking with other people, you may sometimes want to tell a story that will inform or entertain them. Such stories can be an important part of conversation.

Your story will be interesting and enjoyable if you keep certain guidelines in mind. Select an appropriate story to tell. The story you choose should have a beginning, a middle, and an end. It should also be of some interest to your listeners. If your listeners are not interested in sports, for example, you should not choose a story that is filled with the details of a hockey game.

When you tell your story, relate each event in sequence, from beginning to end. Build up to the most exciting part of your story, but don't give away too much information too early. Remember to include enough details to help your listeners follow the story. Omit any details that are unimportant or irrelevant. Your listeners will enjoy the story more if you keep to the point and tell the story as directly as possible.

WORKING WITH THE MODEL

Read the following two conversations. The same story is told in two different ways. Notice in which conversation the story is presented more effectively.

ALICE: Welcome back, Don. How was your vacation?

DON: It was great. And something really funny happened on the way back. It was late at night, and while my mother was driving the family camper, my father and I were sleeping in the back, wearing our pajamas. Suddenly, my mother saw a red light and slammed on the brakes. Everything in the back of the camper fell down on our heads, and my father and I thought there'd been an accident. Naturally, we jumped out the back door. Just then, the light turned green, and my mother drove off down the road!

SUE: Hi, Don! Did you have fun on your vacation?

DON: Yes. And when my mother drove off and left us in the middle of the road, it was really funny. You see, I was sleeping in the back of the camper. It's a 1972 deluxe National Motors model, blue with a white top. We bought it used last year. Anyway, I was sleeping when all at once everything fell onto my head. And then my mother drove off down the road! But before that, I'd jumped out, of course. And my father was in the back with me, so he jumped out, too. And we were both wearing pajamas.

A. 1. What was the actual sequence of events in the story Don told to both Alice and Sue?

2. In which conversation did Don describe the events in the order in which they actually occurred?

3. In which conversation did Don describe the events in a confusing order?

4. Why do you think Don told the story to Sue in the way he did?

5. What relevant details did Don forget to tell until the end of the story he told Sue?

6. What irrelevant details did Don include in the story he told Sue?

7. If you had been Sue, at what points would you have wanted to interrupt Don to ask questions?

8. If you had been Sue, what questions would you have asked Don? Why would you have asked those questions?

9. Which story was more entertaining? Why?

B. It is often possible to tell the last part of a story first in order to heighten a listener's interest. Suppose Don had begun his story, "Would you like to hear how my father and I came to be stranded in the middle of County Road 5 in our pajamas with no money and no car?" After this introduction, how would he have told the rest of his story?

C. Suppose that the following events, listed out of sequence, occurred after Don's mother drove off down the road. How would you reorganize and retell them in entertaining story form?

1. At last, Don's mother stops for gas and sees the empty camper. She goes back for her husband and son.

2. Don's mother drives for 30 miles without stopping.

3. A police car drives up to Don and his father. The officers don't believe their story.

4. The first thing Don's father tries to do is flag down a station wagon.

5. The station wagon owner is shocked at the sight of Don's father in pajamas. She calls the police.

6. The whole family is reunited in the police station.

7. Don's mother drives back and sees her husband and son being taken away in a police car.

8. Don tries running after the camper, but he isn't wearing shoes.

9. Don and his father bear a strong resemblance to two escaped convicts. The police decide to take them to the station to check them out.

10. Don's mother has to show the police all the family pictures she carries in her wallet in order to convince them.

11. A reporter wants to put a picture of Don and his father on the front page of the local paper. Fortunately, she changes her mind.

PREPARING

Decide on several topics about which you might want to tell a story. Think of your own topic, or choose one of the following:

—your favorite joke
—your most embarrassing memory
—a time when you were really frightened
—something that happened on your vacation
—something silly you used to believe as a child
—what you think you would do if you saw an unidentified flying object

Think about your topic. Plan the beginning, the middle, and the end of your story. Decide how you will introduce your story and how you will conclude it.

Think about the important details you will need to include in order for your listener to understand your story. Then decide on the sequence in which you want to present the events you are describing. Tell your story to yourself, silently.

PRESENTING

With a partner, act out a conversation in which you tell the story you have just told yourself. You may want to have your partner ask you a question that will lead into your topic, such as, "What was the most embarrassing thing that ever happened to you?" After you have told your story, give your partner time to tell you his or her story.

EVALUATING

Ask your partner to evaluate the story you told in your acted-out conversation. Then evaluate your partner's story. Be sure to consider these questions:

—What was the point of the story?
—In what ways were you, the listener, entertained or informed?
—How appropriate was the length of the story? If it should have been longer, what material would you have added? If it should have been shorter, what material would you have taken out?
—Were the events of the story told in the right order?
—Were any details in the story irrelevant or distracting? How would leaving these details out have improved the story? Were there places in the story where you felt more details were needed? What kind of details do you think should have been included?

2 Making a Narrative Speech

You may sometimes be called upon to make a short speech that illustrates a particular point. In many cases, the best way to accomplish that purpose is to tell a story. If you choose your story carefully and present it in an interesting and entertaining way, you will succeed both in illustrating your point and in entertaining your audience.

When you are preparing a speech to illustrate a point, select your story carefully. Have one specific idea in mind, and then choose a story that develops that idea. Keep your idea simple and straightforward. Don't try to accomplish too much with a single story.

When you are telling the story, include only the details that are necessary to support your point. Don't give away the ending of the story by presenting too many details at the beginning. Hold your listeners' interest by building up to your point.

As you speak, make your story as clear and as entertaining as possible. Speak clearly, and be brief.

WORKING
WITH
THE MODEL

At the beginning of the school year, Morton High School held an assembly to welcome the new freshmen. Ann, the president of the student council, spoke first.

"I notice that many of you freshmen look nervous and confused," she said. "You've never been in a school this large before. You've never had to deal with class schedules or locker assignments. You're wondering if you'll ever feel at home here. I can't make predictions, but I would like to tell you a story.

"Three years ago a small, frightened freshman arrived on the first day of class. It was raining, and she had forgotten her umbrella. She had left her lunch on the bus. She was late for homeroom, tripped on the gym steps, and couldn't find the science lab at all. She went to the wrong room for French 1 and sat for an hour listening to an advanced Spanish class because she was too embarrassed to leave. At noon she sat on one of the old oak benches; she was hungry, miserable, and ready to cry.

"Then two seniors sat down next to her. They asked if they could help her, and she started to tell them about her morning. It was lunchtime, but the seniors spent 40 minutes explaining class schedules to her. They led her all the way to where the science lab was hidden. They showed her the secret of opening lockers. One of them loaned her an umbrella, and the other gave her a peanut butter sandwich from his lunch.

"You've probably guessed that I was that freshman. That sandwich is long since gone, and both those seniors are now in college—but I'll never forget my first days at Morton, and I believe you'll never forget yours."

A. 1. How did Ann make her story entertaining? What details did she include?

   2. What point was Ann trying to make about the students at Morton High School? Is the point clear? How did she build up to her point?

B. 1. Think of a story from your own experience that shows how strangers can help a person feel at home in a new setting.

   2. Think of a story, either true or fictitious, that shows how unhelpful people can be when a person is lost or confused.

PREPARING

Think of a point you would like to make by telling a story. Choose your own point, or use one of the following:

—why my neighborhood is or is not a pleasant place to live
—why watching television is or is not a waste of time
—why having a full-time job during summer vacation is or is not a good idea

Think of a brief story that illustrates the point you have chosen to make. List at least three details you will need to include.

Write a few notes to remind you of the sequence of events in your story.

PRESENTING

Write the point of your story on a piece of paper. Then tell your story to the class. After you have told the story, ask your audience to tell you what point you had in mind. See how close they can come to what you wrote on the paper.

EVALUATING

Ask yourself the following questions about the story you presented.

—How effectively did the story illustrate my point?
—How well did I present the story? Was it well organized? Did all the material in the story support the point I wanted to make? Was the story the right length?
—Did I speak clearly and effectively?
—How well did my audience respond to the story? Did they understand the point I wanted to make?
—Which details made my story entertaining? Which details could have been left out?

CHAPTER 9

Expository Speaking

Expository speaking is the oral presentation of information and ideas. Students are called upon to relate information and ideas to others several times a day.

Examples of expository speaking include directions, instructions, speeches, lectures, and reports.

In this chapter, you will develop your skills in expository speaking by presenting facts formally and informally. You will

- present information in a conversation
- give a summary speech
- use visual aids in a speech
- present a research report

Presenting Information in a Conversation

You may sometimes be asked to present information such as facts, directions, or instructions to another person. It is important to remember that your explanation or description may be your listener's introduction to the subject. Your information, therefore, should be presented accurately and precisely.

When you are asked to present certain information, take a moment to reflect on what you are going to say. Organize your thoughts in your mind. Then speak as clearly and as simply as possible. Give a complete description or explanation so that your listener has all the necessary information. Don't include unimportant details.

If you are giving instructions, try to demonstrate them. If you are giving directions, use landmarks and be specific. For example, if you say, "Go three blocks to the next traffic light," your listener will have a better picture in mind than if you say, "Go to the next traffic light."

When you have finished, make sure that your listener has understood the information you have presented. Clarify any missing or unclear points, if necessary.

WORKING
WITH
THE MODEL

Read the following two sets of directions. Notice in which set the directions are presented more effectively.

You want me to tell you how to get out to Boiling Springs Road? Well, I guess I ought to know. My cousin used to live out that way. She's lived in Indianapolis for the past five years. Or is it six? Anyway, what you need to do is pick up Pershing Road. Take that all the way out of town. First, go up here a few blocks to the stop sign. Well, maybe it's really the second stop sign you'll see. Then turn there and keep going till you come to Pershing. Though if you want to save time, you'll turn off before you get to Pershing. The name of the road you really want is either Clifford or Clinton. Anyway, stay on it, and it will take you right on out to Boiling Springs.

You want to get out to Boiling Springs Road? Now, let me see. When you leave here, turn right and go east for two blocks to Main Street. Turn left on Main and keep going north for about three miles until you get to Pershing Road. You'll know you're approaching Pershing Road when you see Dave's Donut Delight on your right. Turn left on Pershing and go west about four miles. Now your next turn will be Boiling Springs Road, but it's very hard to see. So, when you pass Carroll's Cabinet Shop on your right, slow down and go another hundred yards or so. You'll see a little dirt road just before the railroad tracks. Turn left onto it. That's Boiling Springs Road.

A. Think about the two sets of directions.

   1. Which directions were presented in the sequence in which they were to be followed?

   2. Which directions were given clearly and simply?

   3. Which directions included all the necessary information?

   4. Which directions included unimportant details?

   5. Which directions were more easily understood?

   6. Which directions were more likely to have been useful to the listener?

   7. If you were the listener, which directions would you prefer to have been given?

B. Think about the first set of directions.

   1. What important details did this speaker omit?

   2. What unnecessary details did this speaker include?

   3. If you had been listening to this speaker, what questions would you have needed to ask?

C. Think about the second set of directions.

   1. What landmarks did this speaker include?

   2. If you had forgotten some of this speaker's directions and had to use a map, would you still have a general idea of where you were going? Why?

D. Imagine that you have been asked to tell a new classmate how to locate and check out a particular book at your school library.

   1. What details would you include?

   2. How would you organize and present the information?

PREPARING

Think of a subject that you would like to give information about. Decide on your own subject, or choose one of the following:

—how to serve the ball in tennis
—how to prepare vegetable soup
—how to play backgammon
—how to use a movie camera
—how to build a model biplane
—how to get to the beach by bus
—the least congested route from your home to downtown
—the most scenic route in your town
—how to find the school's new cafeteria

—the shortest route from school to the public library
—what to look for when buying a new bicycle
—the kinds of music available on various local radio stations
—the exhibits presented at the museum this month
—how to choose a good radio
—how to organize your day to include school, chores, study, and play

Think about the subject you have chosen. Assume that your listener is hearing for the first time the information you will present.

Think about the details you will include and the sequence in which you will present them. Include all the details that are necessary for a complete and accurate explanation. Omit any details that are unimportant. Present your details in the order in which they will be most easily understood.

Rehearse what you will say to your listener. Then imagine that you were the listener. Revise your explanation, if necessary, for greater accuracy. Include additional necessary details that you forgot to include the first time. Change the order in which you present the details if your original presentation was not organized clearly.

PRESENTING

With a partner, act out a conversation in which you present your information. Before you begin, think about what you are going to say. Then speak clearly and simply. When you have finished, make sure that your listener has clearly understood you. If necessary, clear up any missing or confusing points. Then give your partner a chance to present information to you.

EVALUATING

Ask your partner to evaluate your presentation of information. Be sure that the following questions are considered:

—In what ways could the information have been presented more simply and more clearly?
—What essential details, if any, were omitted?
—What unnecessary details, if any, were included?
—What questions did the listener have to ask?
—How could the need for those questions have been avoided?
—If the same information were to be presented again to another person, how should it be reorganized?

2 Giving a Summary Speech

You may sometimes be asked to summarize orally an event or a piece of writing, such as the content of a lecture, meeting, book, or article. Include in your summary speech only the most important facts or ideas about your subject.

As you are listening or reading in preparation for your summary speech, jot down a few notes to help you remember important points. Use the notes to help you organize your thoughts for your summary speech. If you are summarizing an event, you may find chronological organization useful.

When you give a summary speech or any other kind of speech, follow certain general guidelines.

Project your voice and speak clearly so that you can be heard and understood by every one of your listeners. Maintain eye contact with your audience and do not read from prepared material. Know in advance how much time has been allotted to you and be sure your speech fits that length of time. Convey your interest in your subject by speaking in a lively manner.

WORKING WITH THE MODEL

Read the following portions of two summary speeches. In each instance, the speaker is the newly elected class representative to the student council and is reporting to the class what went on at the most recent council officers' meeting.

JENNY: Well, I went to my first meeting a couple of days ago, and a lot of things were brought up. Some votes were taken, too. I remember one vote was about changing the regular meeting day and we decided to meet on Tuesdays, I think, from now on. I think it's Tuesdays, anyway. Either Tuesdays or Thursdays. Well, I'll find out for sure from someone. I'll ask the tenth-grade representative, Mona. I want to borrow one of her record albums, anyway. Oh! Can any of you help out with the carnival?

JEFF: The student council officers met this past Monday afternoon from three to five, and I attended for the first time as your class representative. I'd like to summarize for you the major points that were brought up or discussed or voted upon.

First of all, when the meeting began, the council vice-president made a motion to change the day of the officers' meetings from Monday to any other school day. A vote was taken after discussion on both sides, and, beginning next week, the officers will meet on Thursdays from three to five.

The main purpose of this meeting was to discuss the fund-raising carnival that will be held in April. Each of us was asked to recruit volunteers from our class to serve on the various committees, such as food, games, and rides. I'd like to describe to you the functions of each committee, and after you've heard about them all, I hope that you'll each volunteer for the one you're most interested in.

First, I'll tell you about the food committee.

A. 1. In which summary speech had the speaker organized his or her thoughts before reporting to the class?

2. Which speaker probably did not take notes during the meeting?

3. What particular information that was omitted by Jenny in her speech was included by Jeff in his?

4. Which speaker—Jenny or Jeff—is more likely to enlist volunteers for the carnival committees? Why?

B. Imagine that you have been asked to summarize in a speech the content of a magazine article that you have recently read. How would you organize your information? What details would you include?

PREPARING

Decide on an event you would like to attend or a book or article you would like to read, and about which you will make a summary speech. Choose your own subject, or use one of the following:

—a sports event   —a class lecture   —a nonfiction book
—a news documentary   —a club meeting

While you are watching the event or reading the material, jot down brief notes about the important points you want to remember and relate.

Think about how to organize the material you have decided to include in your summary speech.

PRESENTING

Give your summary speech to the class.

EVALUATING

Ask your classmates to evaluate your summary speech. Be sure that they consider the following questions:

—What main points were made in the speech?
—How were the main points organized? How did that organization make the summary clear?
—What details, if any, should have been omitted? Why?

Using Visual Aids in a Speech

A visual aid is an instructional device that appeals chiefly to the sense of sight. Visual aids include charts, graphs, diagrams, maps, models, films, filmstrips, and slides. Such visual aids can often help a speaker clarify or emphasize an important point in a speech.

When you are considering using one or more visual aids in a speech, keep in mind the following guidelines.

Your visual aids should be simple, clear, accurate, and interesting. Everyone in the room should be able to see them easily. Charts, graphs, and pictures should be large and simple enough to immediately make their point. Maps should be current and should clearly show the area you want to discuss. If you are preparing your own aids, round off numbers and use abbreviations whenever possible. Don't make your visual aid material too detailed or too complicated. As you speak, you can add details that may not be shown by the aid.

Plan ahead. Decide whether you will use the aid throughout your speech, or merely to emphasize one or two points. Know how to operate any machinery you are using. Put slides and overhead projector transparencies in order and right side up. Place charts, graphs, pictures, and models in position at the front of the room before you begin your speech.

WORKING
WITH
THE MODEL

Read the following portion of a speech. Notice how effectively the speaker refers to a graph.

You can see on the graph behind me that in 1890 the population of Maine was greater than that of Oregon. As we move to the right, we can see that this was still true in 1910, although the gap is smaller. But notice what happened between 1930 and 1960! The population of Oregon took a gigantic leap, while that of Maine increased only slightly. Now, at the far end of the graph, observe the difference between the population of the two states in 1970.

A. Think about the speech.

1. What points did the speaker emphasize by using the graph?

2. Why was it effective to show these facts visually?

B. Look at the visual aids pictured on the next page. Identify each aid and describe how you might use it in a short speech.

C. Imagine that you have been asked to give a short speech on attendance patterns in your school. Think of an appropriate visual aid for this speech. What points might you emphasize with the aid?

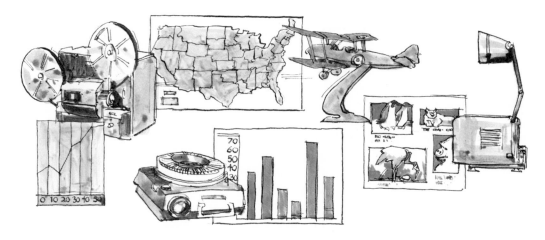

PREPARING

Think of a topic for a speech in which you could use a visual aid. Choose your own topic, or use one of the following:

—how a newcomer could best find his or her way around your school or town

—how to operate a simple piece of machinery, such as a small calculator

—how to make an effective play in a sport such as football or basketball

Think about the topic you have chosen. Decide on the visual aid you will use.

Plan a short speech about your topic. Decide whether you will use your visual aid throughout your speech or at one or two points in your speech. Your may make your own visual aid, or you may use a visual aid supplied by your school.

PRESENTING

Present your speech to the class. Make full use of your visual aid.

EVALUATING

Ask your classmates to evaluate your speech and your use of a visual aid. Be sure that the following questions are considered:

—What points, if any, did the visual aid help to emphasize or clarify?

—What other visual aid, if any, might have been used in the speech?

—How would this other aid have also served the speaker's purpose?

4 Presenting a Research Report

As a student, you may be required to give several oral reports each year. Preparing and presenting an oral research report gives you an opportunity to learn more about a subject that interests you and to share information on that subject with other students.

When you give an oral research report, you should present to your listeners an organized, logical sequence of ideas. You should include information that interested you and that will interest your audience, rather than giving a boring recitation of dry facts. (For information on how to do the research for your report, see Chapter 5, **Research Reports**.)

After you have completed the research for your report, make an outline. Then develop an introduction, a body, and a conclusion for your report.

The introduction should include a general statement of the main idea of your report. It should be interesting enough that your listeners will want to hear the report. It should lead into the body of the report. The body should consist of your main topics, subtopics, and supporting details. The conclusion should tie together in a general statement all the information in your report. It may be worded to reflect the statements you made in your introduction.

As you present your report, refer to the notes in your outline. Do not write out the report and memorize it. It is usually helpful, however, to practice giving your report a few times. You will find that your exact words will change each time you speak. The sense of what you are saying will remain the same as long as you are thoroughly familiar with your subject.

WORKING
WITH
THE MODEL

Read the following introduction to an oral research report. Notice how it leads into the body of the report.

The Aztec Indians are generally regarded as having had a powerful and uniquely advanced culture. In my research, however, I discovered that early in their history the Aztecs were a poor, nomadic people with no real culture of their own. In the thirteenth century, the Aztecs migrated from somewhere in the north to the Valley of Mexico. For the next hundred years or so, they absorbed the already advanced cultures of earlier inhabitants of the region and of neighboring states. Gradually, though, a unique Aztec culture began to develop and flourish; and through warfare and alliances, the Aztecs extended their power and influence from the Valley of Mexico to the north, the south, and the east. The history of the development of this famous Aztec culture involved three major stages.

A. Think about the introduction and the rest of the report that will follow.

 1. What is probably the topic of the report?

 2. What main ideas are mentioned in the introduction?

 3. What information do you expect to find out in the body of the report?

 4. How does the speaker lead into the body of the report from this introduction?

B. Imagine that you have been asked to give a report on the history of your school. What main topics would you cover? What supporting details would you include? How would you arrange your ideas?

PREPARING

Think of a topic on which you would like to present a short oral research report. Choose your own topic, or use one of the following topics:

—the history of basketball
—the accomplishments of a famous American
—the protection of an endangered species of wildlife
—the problems caused by air pollution

Do research on your topic. Take notes, using more than one source.

Organize your research material into outline form. Develop an introduction, a body, and a conclusion for an oral report that you can present in about five to eight minutes.

PRESENTING

Present your research report to the class. Refer to your outline notes, putting them in your own words. Maintain eye contact with your audience and project your voice in a lively, interesting manner.

EVALUATING

Ask your classmates to evaluate your oral research report. Be sure they consider these questions:

—How did the introduction make the listeners interested in hearing the body of the report?
—What were the main topics covered in the body of the report? What were the supporting details?
—How did the conclusion tie together all the information presented in the report?

CHAPTER 10

Persuasive Speaking

Nearly every day, occasions arise when it is desirable or even necessary to persuade others to adopt a particular viewpoint. Such occasions may involve persuading a friend to share a valued possession or persuading the city council to install a new traffic light.

In this chapter, you will develop your skills in speaking by attempting to persuade others to adopt a particular point of view, and you will listen critically as others attempt to persuade you. You will

- speak persuasively in an informal meeting
- give a formal persuasive speech

Speaking Persuasively in Informal Meetings

You may sometimes want to persuade another person or a group of people to agree with a particular opinion or take a certain course of action. You will be more likely to accomplish your goal if you follow certain guidelines.

State your position early, clearly, and confidently. Tell your listeners exactly what you think about the issue in question. Convince them by your manner that you are well informed about the issue and that you sincerely believe in your position.

Present reasons or evidence to support your position. Be sure the reasons you present are accurate, convincing, and logical. Do not present reasons that are merely personal preferences. For example, imagine that you are in a meeting discussing whether to cancel the school's Friday afternoon dances. If you say, "We should cancel the dances because very few people attended last year," your reason is much more convincing than if you say, "We should cancel the dances because I find them boring."

Be sure that everything you say applies to the issue being discussed. Do not bring up unrelated matters. Speak about the issue and not about other people. Don't restate what someone else has said unless you have something new to add.

Conclude your comments confidently and restate your position in your final remarks.

WORKING
WITH
THE MODEL

Mr. Monroe's English class was discussing the best method of raising money for a neighborhood project. Read the comments of the two speakers below. Notice which comments are presented more effectively.

MELANIE: I think the best way to raise money would be to have a car wash. Last year, the Ski Club had a car wash to raise money for a trip, and they made over $200. If we do a good job washing the cars, we will provide a service and improve the image of the school in the neighborhood. The owners of the Main Street gas station like student car washes because they attract business. Most important, whenever we've had a car was to raise money in the past, everyone has said how much fun it was!

OLIVER: If Melanie will let me get a word in edgewise, I have something to say. I guess she wants to have a car wash because her family just bought a new car, and she wants to show it off. Anyway, I think there are better ways to raise money. There's a company in town that will help us do this.

We can call them and tell them we want to raise money. Then they'll sell us cartons of canned nuts at a low price, and we can resell them door-to-door for more money. I think it's a good idea because my family really likes nuts. But if no one else agrees with me, it's all right.

A. Think about the comments Melanie makes.

1. At what point in her comments does Melanie state her position on a method for raising money?

2. How clearly does Melanie state her position?

3. Which words and expressions that Melanie uses show that she is confident about her idea?

4. What reasons does Melanie give in support of having a car wash?

5. How convincing are Melanie's reasons for having a car wash?

6. Which of her reasons, if any, are merely personal preferences?

7. What unrelated matters, if any, does Melanie bring up in her comments on raising money?

8. How does Melanie restate her position in her final remarks?

9. How well informed does Melanie seem to be?

B. Think about the comments Oliver makes.

1. At what point in his comments does Oliver state his position on a method for raising money?

2. How clearly does Oliver state his position?

3. Which words and expressions that Oliver uses show that he is not confident about his idea?

4. What reasons does Oliver give in support of selling canned nuts?

5. How convincing are Oliver's reasons for selling canned nuts?

6. Which of his reasons, if any, are merely personal preferences?

7. What unrelated matters, if any, does Oliver bring up in his comments on raising money?

8. How does Oliver conclude his comments?

9. How well informed does Oliver seem to be?

C. Imagine that you are in Mr. Monroe's English class and that you agree with Oliver's plan.

1. How would you begin your comments in support of selling canned nuts to raise money?

2. What words and expressions would you use to show that you were confident about your idea?

3. What reasons would you give in support of selling canned nuts?

4. How would you conclude your comments?

5. How would you show that you were well informed?

PREPARING

Imagine that your class is discussing an issue. Decide on your own issue, or choose one of the following:

—whether to rearrange the chairs and desks in a different pattern
—whether to allow students to sit next to their friends in class
—whether to have a student teach one class each week
—whether to start a project in which students create movies in their spare time
—whether to have monthly class meetings

Think about the issue you have chosen. Decide what position you will take on it. Decide how you will state your position at the beginning of your comments.

Think about the reasons with which you hope to persuade your classmates to adopt your point of view. Then decide on the sequence in which you will present your reasons.

PRESENTING

Working in a small group, act out a class meeting in which each of your chosen issues is discussed. Present your comments to try to persuade the group to adopt your point of view.

EVALUATING

Ask the other members of your group to evaluate the persuasive comments you made. Be sure to consider these questions:

—What was the speaker's position on the issue?
—How early was the position stated?
—How clearly was the position stated?
—What specific reasons were presented in support of the position?
—How convincing were the reasons?
—Which reason was the most convincing?
—Which reasons, if any, were merely personal preferences?
—Which words and expressions showed the speaker's confidence or lack of confidence?
—What unrelated matters, if any, were brought up?
—What final remarks concluded the comments?
—How well informed did the speaker seem to be?

You may sometimes be called upon to make a short persuasive speech. A formal persuasive speech follows many of the same guidelines as informal persuasive speaking. When you make a formal persuasive speech, also keep in mind the following guidelines.

Know your topic thoroughly. For example, if you are speaking in favor of purchasing new band uniforms, you should know how much each new uniform will cost, how many need to be ordered, where they are available, and so on.

Know the nature of your audience. If you are not a football player and you are speaking to the football team, don't make jokes at the expense of athletes. Try to establish an area of common ground with your audience. For example, you could say, "I am not a football player, but I'm a great football fan. I attended every home game last season."

Appeal to your audience's intelligence by presenting logical arguments and supporting details. Appeal to your audience's emotions by being positive and by using lively, energetic language. For example, instead of saying, "We should probably help out this cause," say, "We must stand behind this worthwhile cause."

WORKING
WITH
THE MODEL

Read the following formal persuasive speech. Notice the presentation of evidence and the language used by the speaker.

My fellow students, I am here to tell you why I believe that Sandy Wilson is your best possible choice for president of the student council. No other person in this school is more actively involved in student government. No one else has had as much experience chairing meetings. No one but Sandy has accomplished so many "nearly impossible" things.

Who can forget the bitter controversy that developed last year over the drabness of the lunchroom? Then Sandy Wilson thought of having the ninth-grade art classes paint a series of beautiful murals over the ugly gray walls. And it was also Sandy who convinced the school administration that the students could do it!

For too many years, the student council in this school has been unimportant and irresponsible. Well, I say it's time that we—the students—started speaking out and making some much-needed changes around here. And electing Sandy Wilson president of the student council is the best way to begin!

A. 1. What reasons does the speaker give for electing Sandy Wilson president of the student council? How does the speaker show a thorough knowledge of Sandy's capabilities?

2. How does the speaker fit the speech to the nature of the audience?

3. In what ways does the speaker appeal to the intelligence of the audience?

4. In what ways does the speaker appeal to the emotions of the audience? What persuasive language does the speaker use?

5. How does the speaker show confidence about Sandy's ability to serve effectively as class president? What lively, energetic language does the speaker use?

B. Imagine that you are speaking in support of one of your friends for president of the student council. What arguments would you use in your speech? How would you organize and phrase them?

PREPARING

Imagine that your class is electing a president. Make a list of the qualities you feel a good class president should have. Then choose someone in your class who has those qualities. Decide to support this person for class president. If you wish, you may choose yourself, or you may make up a person with those qualities.

Think about the candidate you have chosen. Decide how best to describe your candidate's qualifications for the office of class president.

Make a list of persuasive words and phrases that might convince your classmates to support your candidate.

Organize your material into a brief, persuasive campaign speech.

PRESENTING

Working in a small group, act out a pre-election assembly. Present your campaign speech in support of your chosen candidate.

EVALUATING

Ask the other members of your group to evaluate the persuasive speech you made. Be sure to consider these questions:

—How thoroughly were the candidate's qualifications presented to the audience?

—How effectively did the campaign speech fit the nature of the audience?

—In what ways did the speech appeal to the intelligence of the audience?

—In what ways did the speech appeal to the emotions of the audience? How effective was the persuasive language used?

—How persuasive was the campaign speech? How many members of the group decided to support the candidate?

CHAPTER 11

Listening

Aha!

Listening is an important part of the communication cycle. Although people spend a great deal of time listening to others, they frequently do not listen carefully. Careful listening to what is being said makes it more likely that communication will be accurate and complete.

In this chapter, you will develop your listening skills by listening and responding in formal and informal situations. You will

- listen in a conversation
- listen in a formal meeting
- ask questions in an interview
- listen and respond in an interview

1 Listening in a Conversation

You can participate actively in a conversation as a speaker and as a listener. Participating actively as a listener involves being alert, paying attention to the speaker, thinking about what you are hearing, and giving appropriate responses. An appropriate response is one that shows you are following what the speaker is saying. An appropriate response encourages the speaker to continue.

While you are listening in a conversation, look directly at the speaker to indicate that you are paying attention. Let the speaker finish each thought without interruption. If you wait impatiently for your own chance to talk, you will not be able to listen intelligently. You will also convey to the speaker the message that you are not really interested in what he or she is saying.

WORKING
WITH
THE MODEL

Read the two conversations below. Notice in which conversation the listener is a more active participant.

TED: Hi, Dora. Do you want to hear the latest story about my cousin Gary?

DORA: Of course! What's Gary done now?

TED: Well, he was walking down a street when two thugs came up to him and demanded all his money. Gary put up a terrific fight, but finally the thugs pinned him against a wall. When they took out his wallet, they discovered Gary had only one quarter. So one of the thugs asked, "Why did you fight like that over one quarter?" And do you know what Gary said?

DORA: What? I can hardly wait to hear!

TED: Gary said, "I wasn't fighting over the quarter. I was protecting the twenty dollar bill I have hidden in my shoe!"

DORA (laughing): What a great story! Did that really happen?

KATE: Hello, Ron. Did you hear what happened to my father in the hospital?

RON: No! But that reminds me. I have a great doctor joke to tell you when you finish your story.

KATE: Okay. My father was standing by the nurses' station in the hospital when a man shuffled up. Then the man—

RON: Say, Kate. Look at the time! It's almost 12:00. Let's eat lunch soon.

KATE: Okay. Then the man said to the nurse, "Can you tell me how Mr. Jones is doing?" Ron, what are you doing?

RON: Oh, sorry. I was looking in my pockets for my lunch money. Go on with your story. I'll bet I know how it ends. The man turns out to be Mr. Smith himself, right? Or was it Jones?

KATE: Never mind.

A. 1. In the first conversation, how did Dora actively participate as a listener? What were her appropriate responses? How were they appropriate?

   2. In the second conversation, what were Ron's inappropriate responses? How were they inappropriate?

B. Imagine that you are Ron in the second dialogue. What responses would you make in order to participate more actively as a listener?

C. Imagine that you are telling your favorite joke or story to a friend. What kind of responses would you like him or her to make?

PREPARING

Think of a subject for a conversation. Decide on your own subject, or choose one of the following:

—career goals
—hobbies
—music
—movies
—travel

Work with a partner with whom you will act out two conversations. You will be the speaker in a conversation about the subject you have chosen, and your partner will be the listener. Your partner will be the speaker in a conversation about the subject he or she has chosen, and you will be the listener. Decide which of you will portray a poor listener who gives inappropriate responses. Decide which of you will portray an active participant who listens intelligently and gives appropriate responses.

PRESENTING

In front of the class, act out your conversations with your partner.

EVALUATING

Ask your classmates to evaluate the conversations in which you participated. Be sure they consider the following questions:

—Who portrayed the poor listener? Who portrayed the actively participating listener?
—What inappropriate responses did the poor listener make?
—How did the actively participating listener indicate that he or she was listening intelligently?

148

When you attend a meeting or a lecture, listen courteously to the speaker. Sit quietly and give the speaker your full attention. Listen critically to the speaker. Concentrate on what is being said. Think about what you are hearing. Be on the alert for inaccuracies and for personal bias on the part of the speaker.

Taking notes during a formal meeting is a good aid for recalling the material later. When you take notes, do not attempt to write down everything the speaker says. Record only the main points and a few supporting details. To save time, you will probably want to use some abbreviations. Be sure, however, that your notes will be readable when you consult them again.

WORKING
WITH
THE MODEL

Study the sample notes below. They were taken in a science class during a lecture on snakes. Notice how the main topics and supporting details of the lecture are identified in the student's notes.

Snakes

Most snakes have similar gen. characteristics: no limbs, shed skin sev. times a yr., narrow body. Large number of vertebrae. Most have only one lung. No ears, but gd. vision.

Many harmless snakes in N. America: garter, water, green, black, racer, king, hognose, rat.

Few poisonous snakes in N.A.:   copperhead, water moccasin, rattlesnake, coral.

Snakes useful in many ways: pest controllers (kill mice, rats). In Orient, some eaten by people. Skin made into belts, shoes, etc. Some venom used in medicine.

First aid for snakebite involves slowing circ. of poison through blood: methods—ice pack, or constricting band. If recent bite, venom sometimes sucked out.

A. Think about the format of the student's notes.

1. How many main topics are recorded in the notes?

2. What are the main topics?

3. How are the main topics distinguished from the supporting details and examples in the notes?

4. What supporting details or examples are recorded in the notes for each main topic?

5. What abbreviations are used in the notes? For what word does each abbreviation stand?

B. Some prefer to use informal outlines when they take notes on meetings or lectures. Their notes usually follow the format of a formal outline but do not include the numerals and letters of an outline. For example, an informal outline of notes on the lecture about snakes might begin like this:

Most snakes have similar gen. characteristics
   no limbs

1. What other supporting details would be listed under that first main heading in an informal outline?
2. How would the other main headings be listed in an informal outline?
3. What supporting details or examples would be listed under each main heading in an informal outline?

PREPARING

Work with a partner. Decide upon a formal meeting during which you can both practice your listening and note-taking skills. If you wish, you may take notes on a television or radio documentary or special news report.

When you and your partner attend the meeting, listen courteously and critically. Take careful notes, being sure to identify the main topics and supporting details.

Later, look over your notes and try to recall as much as you can of the substance of the material you listened to.

PRESENTING

Prepare a neat copy of your notes. Exchange them with your partner. Compare the information in your notes with that recorded in your partner's notes.

EVALUATING

Ask yourself the following questions about your listening and note taking.

—What were the main topics discussed? How were they indicated in the notes?

—What supporting details were given? In the notes, how were they distinguished from the main topics?

—What points were missed that were recorded in your partner's set of notes?

3 | Asking Questions in an Interview

An interview is a meeting during which one person obtains information from another person by asking questions. The information sought may be about the life or work of the person being interviewed. It may be about a subject which interests or affects the person being interviewed. It may be a combination of both.

When you have decided to interview another person, prepare for the interview as thoroughly as possible. Decide exactly what information you—the interviewer—hope to discover. If the person you will interview—the interviewee—is a public figure, familiarize yourself through research with the publicly known facts about his or her life. Such research may suggest areas to investigate in the interview that you had not previously considered.

Prepare questions that will help your interviewee share with you the information you are seeking. In general, avoid asking questions which can be answered with a word or two, such as "yes," "never," or "last year." Such questions provide little information. Avoid asking questions which are too personal. It is important, however, that your questions and your manner show your interest in the interviewee.

You may write out on individual cards each question you plan to ask. Group together cards with related questions. As you ask each question during the interview, glance at the card, if necessary.

During the interview, you may briefly jot down the most important part of the interviewee's answer. Be sure, however, that you do not break the flow of the interview by constantly writing down long answers.

WORKING
WITH
THE MODEL

Study the two sets of interview questions that follow and the note cards that are shown on page 153. The interviewee is a trainer of wild animals. Notice which set of questions produces more useful information. Notice how the second interviewer condenses the answers on the note cards.

INTERVIEWER: When did you start training wild animals?
ANIMAL TRAINER: About twenty years ago.
INTERVIEWER: Do you enjoy working with them?
ANIMAL TRAINER: Yes, I do.
INTERVIEWER: Are they easy to train?
ANIMAL TRAINER: Some are.
INTERVIEWER: Have you ever been attacked by one of your animals?
ANIMAL TRAINER: Yes.

INTERVIEWER: Ms. Kelly, you've been a wild animal trainer for nearly twenty years. How did you first become interested in training wild animals?

ANIMAL TRAINER: Well, I always had lots of pets when I was growing up. For a while, I thought I might become a veterinarian. But when I was about fifteen, I went to the circus at Madison Square Garden. I was fascinated by the wild animal acts. So after I graduated from high school, I joined a traveling circus. My job was feeding the animals. I became friendly with the wild animal trainer and told him I was fascinated by the idea of working with the wild animals. He let me assist him, and then gradually he trained me.

INTERVIEWER: What do you enjoy most about working with wild animals?

ANIMAL TRAINER: It's a tremendous challenge to train an animal, and there's a great sense of satisfaction when you succeed. And the animals seem to enjoy it, too! As for wild animals, when you work with them, there's always the knowledge that if you make a mistake, you could really be in trouble! I guess the excitement appeals to me almost as much as the challenge of doing a job well.

INTERVIEWER: You've trained several different types of wild animals. How do your methods differ with each type?

ANIMAL TRAINER: Well, a trainer has to remember that no wild animal is ever completely tame, even if you've raised it from birth. So with all the wild animals, you have to remember, first of all, never to be careless. And it almost goes without saying that you should never be cruel to any animal. As for different methods, they don't differ between types of animals as much as between individual animals. Animals are individuals, just as humans are—and just as plants are, for that matter. Some of my animals respond better to firmness, for example, than others. Some of them even have their "bad days"! You have to be responsive to each animal. Training is a two-way process. It's a real communication between the animal and the trainer.

INTERVIEWER: Tell us about the time one of your tigers tried to attack you during a performance. How did you handle that situation?

ANIMAL TRAINER: You must be referring to that first show I did in Chicago. It was my second year as a full-fledged trainer. One of the tigers was apparently frightened by something that was going on in the audience. It was a rather unruly crowd. Anyway, I should have seen the signs of restlessness and thought of a way to get that one tiger out of the performing cage and still make it look like part of the act. What happened was that while

I was putting another tiger through a stunt, I carelessly turned my back to the restless one for a split second—something you should never do! That was all it needed. It sprang at me, but, luckily, I had sensed what was happening and managed to get out of the way. I let it know that I was in control of the situation. I didn't show fear. And, since it was used to obeying me, it gradually calmed down. Had it actually landed on my back, however, I would have needed outside help—a lot of it!

```
Q.  When did you start training wild animals?

A.  abt. 20 yrs ago
```

```
Q.  How did you first become interested in training wild
    animals?  (she started almost 20 years ago)

A.  many pets as child - vet?
    @ 15 - circus (M. Sq. G.) - wow!
    1st job: feeding animals - then assisted wild-animal
    trainer - trainer trained her
```

```
Q.  Do you enjoy working with them?

A.  yes
```

```
Q.  What do you enjoy most about working with wild animals?

A.  challenge to train      satisfaction w/success
    excitement (they're wild!)
```

```
Q.  Are they easy to train?

A.  some are
```

```
Q.  How do your methods of training differ with each type of
    wild animal?  (she's trained several different types)

A.  rule for all: they're never really tame -
    don't be careless (or cruel).
    animals differ in personality just like we do &
    respond to different methods.  trainer has to understand
    the individual animal.
    training: a 2-way process of communication
```

```
Q.  Have you ever been attacked by one of your animals?

A.  yes
```

```
Q.  How did you handle the situation when one of your tigers
    tried to attack you during a performance?

A.  tiger was excited & restless - trainer was careless
    (turned her back) - boom!  trainer was firm & showed no
    fear - showed tiger she was still in control (luckily no
    actual physical contact)
```

153

A. Compare the two interviews and the questions asked in each.

1. In which interview do the questions produce answers that are not informative? What is wrong with each of those questions?

2. In which interview do the questions encourage the animal trainer to give full, informative answers? Why do you think this is so?

3. Which interviewer probably did research before the interview? How can you tell?

B. Compare the second interview with the second set of note cards. What information was recorded in the answer section of each card?

C. Imagine that you are going to continue the second interview with the animal trainer. Think of four more questions you would like to ask her. Phrase each question so that the animal trainer is likely to fully share information with you.

PREPARING

Think of a person you would like to portray in an interview. You may choose to be a public personality (alive or dead) or a made-up person engaged in a particular profession or occupation. You may choose to be interviewed as yourself. If you choose to be a public personality, you may want to do some research about that person.

Work with a partner with whom you will act out the interview. If you have chosen to be a public personality, your partner should also do some research about that person. Your partner should prepare on individual cards four questions to ask in interviewing you.

Then find out which person your partner will portray in an interview. Prepare four questions to ask when you interview that person.

PRESENTING

In front of the class, act out your interview with your partner. When you portray the interviewer, write the main idea of each answer on the appropriate card.

EVALUATING

Ask your classmates to evaluate the interviews in which you participated. Be sure they consider the following questions:

—How did each interviewer indicate that he or she had researched the subject?

—How did the interviewer indicate interest in the interviewee?

Listening and Responding in an Interview

When you are conducting an interview, give your interviewee enough time to fully respond to each question. Do not interrupt a thought or break the flow of important information.

As you ask each question you have prepared, listen carefully to the answer. Respond with an appropriate follow-up question. This will elicit even more information from the interviewee.

For example, you may be interviewing a ski instructor who says, "I enjoy teaching at Sun Valley much more than at Aspen." Don't rush on to your next prepared question. Instead, ask a follow-up question, such as, "What are the major differences between those two areas?" or, "What experiences have you had at each of those resorts?"

During an interview, let the interviewee do most of the talking while you concentrate on listening. If your interviewee strays from the subject, ask another question to bring him or her back to it. If you fail to obtain a complete or satisfactory answer to a question, rephrase it and ask it again.

WORKING
WITH
THE MODEL

Read the following portion of an interview. The interviewee is an author. Notice the ways in which the interviewer responds to the interviewee's answers.

INTERVIEWER: Mr. Gorman, you've written over fifteen novels. Is there one in particular that you consider your favorite?

AUTHOR: Well, I'm not sure I have a real favorite. I like them all!

INTERVIEWER: Which one stands out in your mind as having been the most enjoyable to write?

AUTHOR: Well, I guess I'm partial to all my books that have to do with sports. I used to be a minor-league baseball pitcher, you know. I guess my favorite would be the first one I wrote, The Old Grapefruit. It's about a minor-league baseball pitcher!

INTERVIEWER: What's the meaning of that unusual title?

AUTHOR: Well, "grapefruit" is a slang term for a baseball. Actually, I can't stand to eat grapefruit. For breakfast, I usually eat an egg. Although this morning I didn't eat anything. I'll be starving by lunchtime!

INTERVIEWER: I know the feeling! Now, let me see. You were telling me about your first novel. Was it based on your own experiences?

AUTHOR: Oh, yes, indeed. Most of the characters were modeled on people I played ball with.

A. 1. What question had to be rephrased to elicit a more satisfactory response? How was it rephrased? What response was finally obtained?

2. What follow-up question did the interviewer ask?

3. At what point in the interview did the author stray from the subject? With what question did the interviewer bring him back to it?

B. Imagine you are continuing the interview with the author. What follow-up questions might you ask him in response to his last answer?

PREPARING

Think of a person you would like to interview. You may choose a public personality, a made-up person, or a classmate. If you have chosen a public personality, do any research necessary to familiarize yourself with him or her.

Work with a partner with whom you will act out the interview. If your partner will be acting the role of a public personality, he or she may also need to do some research.

Prepare your questions on individual cards.

Your partner will also have the opportunity to interview you as you play the part of the person he or she has chosen to interview.

PRESENTING

In front of the class, conduct your interview with your partner. Ask at least two follow-up questions during the interview.

On the backs of the appropriate cards, note your follow-up questions and their answers.

EVALUATING

Ask your classmates to evaluate the interview you conducted. Be sure that they consider the following questions:

—Which questions were follow-up questions? What additional information did they provide?

—Which question led to the most complete and interesting answer?

—Which questions, if any, did not provide complete and satisfactory answers? Were they rephrased? How were they rephrased? Did the rephrasing provide the desired information?

—At what points, if any, did the interviewee stray from the subject? Did the interviewer bring him or her back to it? How?

Speech Handbook

Communication   158

Forms and Guidelines   172

1 The Communication Cycle

1a. Analyzing Communication

Communication is a cycle. The speaker must decide what idea to communicate to the listener, how to present the facts, what words to use, and how to use his or her voice and body to make the clearest and strongest impression possible.

The listener, in turn, reacts to the speaker. The listener may react by showing interest, boredom, or amusement. The speaker observes the listener's response and alters his or her speech, word choice, voice, or body movements to achieve better communication with the listener. The listener reacts to these changes, and the communication cycle goes on.

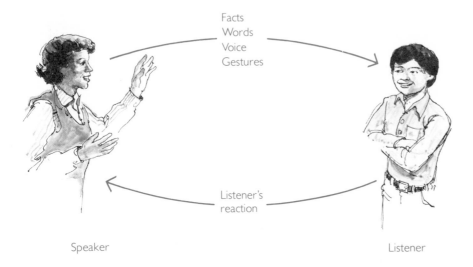

Facts
Words
Voice
Gestures

Listener's reaction

Speaker   Listener

The communication cycle is not always complete. The cycle can break down at one or more points. The following are some common causes of communication breakdown:

—inappropriate choice of subject
—illogical sequence of ideas
—badly chosen examples
—inappropriate language for the subject or the audience
—lack of information on the part of the listener or the speaker
—weak or unclear speaking voice
—inappropriate or distracting body movements
—misinterpretation of the listener's responses
—inattention by the listener
—inappropriate responses by the listener

PRACTICING SPEECH SKILLS

■ Each of the following paragraphs describes a communication cycle that has broken down. Read the paragraphs. Explain why each breakdown occurred.

1.   Mr. Emerson was telling Michael about his new stereo system. He said, "It has an integrated preamp-amplifier with class AB operation, a quartz-locked scanning digital-display tuner, a servo-controlled direct-drive turntable with a moving-coil cartridge, and three-way electrostatic speakers." Michael responded, "It doesn't sound so great to me."

2.   Luis told the class about his family's vacation. Later, they asked him questions and made comments about his speech. "Did you say you were gone three weeks, five weeks, or nine weeks?" asked Jan. "Did you go to Norwood, Norwalk, or Norfolk?" asked Chris. "Did you say you caught many fish or you bought many dishes?" asked Elaine. "I was sitting in the back row," said Mark, "and I didn't understand anything."

3.   Julie gave a speech about the life of Thomas Edison. She asked the class if they had enjoyed the speech. "Not me," said Carl. "I didn't have any breakfast this morning." "I don't know about your speech," said Marie, "but did you know that your socks don't match?" "It was pretty exciting," said George. "Two dogs were fighting outside the whole time you were speaking."

■■ Imagine that you have to present the following topics to each of the listeners indicated. Explain what approach you would take with each listener to make sure that you would be understood. Consider the facts you would use, the order in which you would present them, the language and examples you would use, and anything else that might help you communicate with each listener. Describe also the ways in which each of your listeners might react, and how you would respond to these reactions.

1. Explain the fun of roller-skating
   a. to a four-year-old who has never skated
   b. to a teacher who thinks it's dangerous
   c. to a classmate who has been skating for two years
   d. to a friend who loves skiing

2. Describe a folk music festival
   a. to your little brother, who hates music
   b. to a friend who plays guitar and sings
   c. to a student from a foreign country who has never heard American folk music
   d. to a friend who thinks everything but classical music is stupid and primitive

3. Describe the way a jet plane operates
   a. to the president of your school's science club
   b. to your friend, who isn't sure when the law of gravity was passed
   c. to your aunt, who has flown small planes for fifteen years
   d. to your little brother, who is about to take his first airplane flight

4. Tell about a very funny comedy act
   a. to a foreign student who speaks very little English
   b. to your school's drama coach
   c. to a five-year-old child
   d. to an adult who has no sense of humor

2   Using Your Voice

2a.   Speaking Strongly and Clearly

Your first duty as a speaker is to be heard clearly and comfortably. If your voice is too loud, it will sound harsh and unpleasant. If your voice is too soft, your audience will not be able to understand you and will soon give up trying. Suit your voice to the occasion. How loudly you speak will depend upon

—the size of the room
—the distance between you and your audience
—the amount of background noise coming from outside the room

In your speech, do not use unclear expressions, such as "um," "you know," "like," "anyway," "I mean," or "where was I?" If you must pause, pause silently.

2b.   Speaking Distinctly

Look at the cartoon. It shows a breakdown in communication. Notice why the listener cannot understand the speaker. Decide what the speaker is trying to say.

You must speak clearly in order to communicate effectively. Follow these rules:

—Do not drop the first syllables of words. (Say *did you,* not *joo.*)
—Do not drop final consonants. (Say *going,* not *goin'.*)
—Do not slur over consonant sounds. (Say *interesting,* not *inneresting.*)
—Do not drop syllables from the middle of words. (Say *probably,* not *probly.*)
—Do not substitute one consonant for another. (Say *water,* not *wadder.*)
—Do not mumble your vowels. (Say *independent,* not *induhpundunt.*)

If you pronounce words carelessly or incorrectly, your audience will pay attention to the sounds you are making, not to what you are saying. Before you make a speech, go over the words you are going to use. Be certain you know how to pronounce all of them. Check any pronunciations you are unsure of in a dictionary.

PRACTICING SPEECH SKILLS

■ Read the following sentences to a friend from indoor distances of 5 feet, 10 feet, 20 feet, and 30 feet. Have your friend raise his or her hand when your voice is not loud enough or clear enough.

1. Do you think it will rain?
2. I finished reading the book.
3. Meet me for lunch.
4. Lend me a pencil.
5. The library is closed.
6. There's a good program at 8 o'clock.

■■ Read the same sentences at the same distances as in the preceding exercise, but with background noise. Open the doors or windows. Turn on a radio, or have other people talk to each other. Have your friend raise his or her hand when your voice is not loud enough or clear enough.

■■■ Read aloud one or more of the following lists of words with your back turned to your listeners. Have your listeners write down each word as you pause between words. Were you understood?

thistle	fern	scheme	better	cross
system	firm	scream	petal	cough
missile	foam	screen	battle	cloth
distant	burn	green	meadow	clap
bristle	term	stream	medal	clan
whistle	turn	steam	metal	crop

■■■■ Read aloud the following tongue-twisters. You will have to pronounce each sound carefully and distinctly to avoid tripping over your tongue.

1. He sawed six long, slim, sleek, slender saplings.
2. Around the rough and rugged rock the ragged rascal ran.
3. Five wives wearily weave bright red rugs.
4. Theo Thistle thrust three thousand thistles through the thick of his thumb.

■■■■■ The following common words are frequently mispronounced. Say each word aloud. Next, refer to a dictionary to be sure you pronounced them correctly. Then say them again.

popular	probably	genuine	library	arctic	iron
inevitable	often	preferable	nuclear	February	irrelevant

2c. Using Vocal Variety

To become an effective speaker, you must learn how to vary the volume, rate, and pitch of your voice. You must also learn where to pause while speaking. Such variations help you to emphasize particular points. They also make your speech more interesting.

Volume is the loudness of your voice. When you raise the volume of your voice, you are letting your audience know that your words are exciting or important. When you lower your voice, you may indicate that your subject is sad or sensitive. Changing volume enables you to emphasize important words in a sentence.

Rate is the number of syllables you speak per minute. Your rate of speech will often go up when the subject is thrilling or funny. Your rate will slow down if your subject is solemn, or if you want to keep your audience in suspense.

Pitch is the highness or lowness of the sound of your voice. You naturally raise the pitch of your voice at the end of a sentence when you ask a question. You usually lower the pitch at the end of a sentence when you make a statement. Good speakers also learn to vary the pitch of their voices within a sentence in order to avoid monotony.

A *pause* is a slight delay in speaking. Pausing before or after a word, a phrase, or a sentence gives it emphasis.

PRACTICING SPEECH SKILLS

■ Read the following sentences. Think of three different meanings you could give to each by varying volume, rate, pitch, and pauses. Then read each sentence aloud three times, conveying the meaning you chose.

1. I don't know who she is.
2. You're going in the morning?
3. You must do that now.
4. He wouldn't understand.
5. Did we win the game?
6. She'll tell us what to do.

■■ Read the following sentences aloud, using the volume, rate, pitch, and pauses appropriate to their meaning.

1. Hurry up, Michael, or we'll miss the bus!
2. The only sound in the hushed room was the low, steady hum of the air conditioner.
3. With screeching tires and grinding gears, the racing car skidded around the turn, belching smoke and raising clouds of dust.
4. Holding his breath, Jimmy slowly and carefully pushed open the creaking door.
5. After the huge lunch, Olaf lay snoring on the sofa with a fat white cat asleep on his stomach.
6. With its rockets shut off, the spacecraft glided noiselessly down toward the eerie stillness of the Martian surface.

3 Listening

3a. Participating in a Conversation

Listening well, like speaking well, takes a certain amount of skill. Good speakers make themselves worth listening to by choosing interesting subjects, giving the right amount and kind of detail, choosing their words carefully, and appropriately varying their voices.

Good listeners must do their share to make a conversation enjoyable. Here are some rules for listeners:

1. Pay attention.
2. Show by your expression and comments that you are interested in what the speaker is saying.
3. Ask for clarification if the speaker's words or ideas are unclear.
4. Don't yawn, fidget, or wander away.
5. Don't interrupt the speaker in the middle of a sentence.
6. Don't use what the speaker is saying as an excuse to talk about your favorite subject.
7. Don't try to "top" the speaker by bragging about something you've said, done, or seen.

PRACTICING SPEECH SKILLS

■ Think about someone you enjoy talking to because he or she is a good listener. How does this person show interest in what you are saying? How does he or she encourage you to talk about interesting subjects? How does this person make you feel that he or she understands you? Write a short list of this person's best listening habits.

■■ Think about someone who is difficult to talk to because he or she is a poor listener. What does this person do that suggests he or she is uninterested in what you are saying? What does this person do that makes you feel that he or she does not understand you? Write a short list of this person's worst listening habits.

■■■ Are you a good listener or a bad listener? Perhaps you have some of the characteristics of both. Think of a conversation you have had during the past week. What poor listening habits did you show? What good listening habits did you practice? Write a short list of your good and poor listening habits. Then write a way to improve each of your poor listening habits.

■■■■ Take part in a conversation. (Don't tell the other people you are talking to that this is an exercise.) Try to practice only good listening habits. When you are alone, evaluate the conversation. What poor listening habits, if any, did you still show? Was the conversation a success? If not, what were the causes? Write a short list of ways in which the conversation could have been improved.

3b.   Listening to a Speech

When you are listening to a speech, you should practice all the good listening habits you learned for taking part in a conversation. In addition, you must learn how to follow a speech so that you can take notes. These rules will help you follow the important points in a speech:

1. Follow the speaker's signposts. A good speaker often tells the audience what part of the speech he or she has reached by using such phrases as "first of all," "a second fact is," "finally," and "in conclusion."

2. Notice what points the speaker is trying to emphasize. Pay attention to such phrases as "I want to point out" and "the important thing to remember is."

3. Follow the cues in the speaker's voice. Note changes in volume, pitch, and rate. Note the use of pauses. These are all signs of important points or of a change in topic.

4. Follow the speaker's physical cues. Notice the gestures or movements that he or she uses to emphasize important parts of the speech.

Taking good notes is an important skill. Notes help you later to recall important points. When you take notes, follow the speaker's signposts and cues listed above. They will help you recognize main topics and subtopics. Write in outline form, indenting the subtopics under the major topics:

> Major topic
> 1. first subtopic
>   example
> 2. second subtopic
>   example

Don't write too much. Write phrases and words rather than sentences. Use abbreviations. A good note-taker should have no trouble keeping up with a speaker.

PRACTICING SPEECH SKILLS

■ Read the following portion of a speech Jerry gave to her history class:

We have seen that Thomas Jefferson was an able statesman and a great president. We should remember that he was also an amateur scientist, inventor, and architect. As president of the American Philosophical Society, Jefferson shared scientific knowledge—for instance, the discovery of a fossil sloth—with other learned people. He was one of the first Americans to learn about vaccination, and he had his family inoculated against smallpox. As an inventor, Jefferson filled his home with ingenious devices, including a combination writing-desk and stepladder. Jefferson the architect designed Monticello, one of the finest American homes of its period, where he lived and worked. Near the end of his life, he designed the beautiful campus of the University of Virginia at Charlottesville. In all three fields, Jefferson showed the same intelligence and vision that gave us the Declaration of Independence.

Now read the notes that two students made on that portion of the speech.

A	B
Jefferson was also:	Thomas Jefferson was a statesman and president
1. amateur scientist	And he was an amateur scientist, etc.
Pres. of Amer. Philosophical Soc.	American Philosophical Society
shared scientific knowledge	Fossil sloth
encouraged vaccination	His family was inoculated against smallpox
2. inventor	Combination desk and stepladder
ingenious devices in his home	He lived in Monticello, which was one of the finest homes of its period
3. architect	University of Virginia is beautiful
Monticello (his home)	It is at Charlottesville
U. of Va.	Thomas Jefferson also wrote Declaration of Independence

Which set of notes gives a better idea of what the speaker was trying to say? What mistakes did the second note-taker make? Describe the bad listening habits of the second note-taker, and suggest ways this person could improve each of them.

■■ What information did the good note-taker leave out entirely? Why? How much of this omitted information would you have included if you had been taking notes on the speech? Rewrite the better set of notes so that they contain everything you think was important in this portion of the speech.

■■■ What kind of notes do you think Jerry used when she gave this portion of her speech? Would they be more detailed or less detailed than the notes taken by students A and B? Write out the notes you think the speaker would have used.

■■■■ When a member of your class gives a short speech based on notes, everybody in the class should take notes on the speech. Afterwards, compare your notes with the notes taken by other students. Did your classmates take better notes, or did you? Now compare the notes taken by the listeners with the notes used by the speaker. What are the differences? Work with other students in writing the very best notes that a listener could have taken on the speech.

4 Using Your Body

4a. Communicating Meaning and Emotions

Communication does not always require words. For example, the people in the picture below are using facial expressions and gestures to communicate different messages.

You can communicate emotions by the posture of your body, the expression on your face, and the gestures of your hands. You can also use body language to reinforce the meaning of what you are saying. Here are some basic rules for using your body while speaking:

1. Walk confidently to the place where you will be speaking. Keep your head up. If you are nervous (you probably are), don't show it.
2. Stand straight when you speak. Don't slouch, sway from side to side, or lean on the podium. Keep your hands out of your pockets.
3. Be sure your posture and expression suit the meaning of your words. Don't look dejected when you're telling your audience to feel proud. Don't grin like a clown when you describe sad events.
4. Use hand gestures to emphasize important points. But be careful not to distract your listeners; it is better to use too few gestures than too many.
5. Look directly and confidently at your audience. Try picking out a few listeners and looking each of them straight in the eye for a few seconds. (It's hard not to pay attention when you're being watched.)

4b. Understanding Audience Response

A good speaker is alert to the responses of his or her listeners. Every audience sends out signals that show how it feels about the speech it is listening to. These are some typical signals:

1. Facial expressions showing interest or lack of interest, approval or disapproval.
2. Shifts in body positions, showing whether the listeners are attentive or restless.
3. Obvious expressions of approval or disapproval: laughter, applause, boos, or hisses (of course, good listeners don't boo or hiss).

PRACTICING SPEECH SKILLS

■ Read the following sentences, using body posture, facial expression, and hand gestures to reinforce the meaning of the words and the emotion they convey.

1. This is absolutely vital. He must do it!
2. Drive east two blocks and turn right onto Oak Avenue.
3. Never in my life have I been so embarrassed!
4. Here are the facts. Look at them!
5. Hold the violin with your left hand and the bow with your right. Tuck the violin under your chin, then draw the bow across the strings.
6. This report will not do. Take it away!

■■ Read the following statements. Without using words (or making any other sounds), communicate each statement to one or more other students. Ask the students in your audience to write down their interpretations of your body language. Compare their interpretations with the messages you were trying to communicate.

1. I am tired and discouraged.
2. I am tired but pleased with my efforts.
3. I am frightened by an unusual sound.
4. I know everything and can do anything.
5. I am impatient.
6. I am very hungry.

■■■ Deliver a short speech giving directions. Use appropriate gestures, expressions, and movements to make your directions clear. Speak on one of the following topics, or choose one of your own.

1. how to get from your classroom to the school gym
2. how to shoot a free throw in basketball
3. how to knit a sweater
4. how to throw a Frisbee
5. how to put together and frost a wedding cake
6. how to stand before an audience

■■■■ Prepare and present a two-minute speech on a topic of your choice. Carefully observe your listeners' responses. Write a paragraph that describes the audience's reaction to your speech. Then talk to several classmates about their actual reactions to your speech. Find out if you judged their responses accurately from what you observed. Write a paragraph describing your audience's true response to your speech.

5 Word Choice

5a. Using Specific Words and Vivid Language

Specific words communicate your message clearly. Use specific words to get your listeners' attention and to create sharp images in their minds. For example, compare the following two sentences:

> They predicted that the weather would worsen soon.

> The weather forecaster predicted that six inches of snow would fall on Thursday.

The first sentence above gives only general information. The second sentence, which uses specific language, gives more information, and the information is clearer and more useful.

Vivid language appeals to the listener's senses of sight, sound, smell, touch, and taste. Use vivid language to encourage your listeners to pay close attention and to help them follow the points you are making. For example, compare the following two sentences:

> Jimmy's parents served us a good dinner.

> Jimmy's parents served us sizzling pork chops with apple sauce, mounds of steaming mashed potatoes, and crisp spinach salad with a tangy French dressing.

The first sentence above gives only a vague description of the dinner. The second sentence gives vivid details and appeals to all of the listener's senses.

5b. Using Appropriate Language

You probably use three different levels of language every day.
Formal English is used in most serious writing and speaking.

> I thought the film was well directed.

Informal (or colloquial) English is used in conversation and in light or humorous writing.

> I thought the movie was great.

Slang is used in conversations among close friends.

> I thought the flick was out of sight.

Formal English is the appropriate language for most speeches.

5c. Using Direct Language

Good speakers use direct and simple language in order to be easily understood. They keep their sentences fairly short—about ten to fifteen words. They use words they know their listeners will understand, and they use normal word order (subject before predicate). To make your language direct and simple, shorten clauses and phrases to single words whenever you can. Use active verbs rather than passive verbs or the verb **be.** For example, compare the following two sentences:

> The new coach is a man who has a sense of being impressed by his own achievements.

> The new coach is conceited.

The first sentence is a string of vague phrases and clauses that leaves the listener uncertain of the coach's real character. The second sentence is short and direct.

PRACTICING SPEECH SKILLS

■ Select the more specific expression from each pair.

1. bronchitis   a respiratory disease
2. He cheats at checkers.   He is dishonest.
3. building   cottage
4. a class of freshmen   audience
5. amphibian   frog
6. Irish setter   dog
7. faculty member   math teacher
8. Astronomy 10   a science course

■■ Reword the following sentences to make them more specific and vivid.

1. The dinner was undercooked.
2. The leaves were colorful.
3. There were many insects in the room.
4. Juan did well on several exams.
5. The bedroom was not neat.
6. His clothes were unusual.
7. The hall was crowded.
8. Her hair was an odd color.

■■■ In the following sentences, substitute a formal word or phrase for each word or phrase that is underlined.

1. The guy with the best record gets a medal.
2. The busted bike can be fixed.
3. It was a lousy way to start the vacation.
4. I bombed-out on the last test.
5. She thought the play was a turkey.
6. Mario went ape when he saw the new uniform.
7. When Eric was in the Army, he was nuts about the grub.

■■■■ List ten current slang expressions. Translate each of them into formal English.

■■■■■ Reword each of the following sentences to make it shorter, clearer, and more direct.

1. The young married man and woman were unable to make the adjustments in their life-style necessary to meet the demands of their budget.
2. I am sympathetic to the efforts being made on behalf of the movement to protect whales from being killed.
3. A written evaluation of a student's progress is issued to each student at the end of each marking period.
4. It is my painful duty to inform you that your performance on this paper is unfortunately such that you cannot hope to receive a passing grade in this course.

6 Attitudes

6a. Attitudes toward Yourself

Some actors experience "stage fright" before going on stage. You may feel "speech fright" when you speak to a group of people. You may have trembling hands, knocking knees, a quavering voice, a dry mouth, and a pounding heart. Here are some things you can do to feel more confident:

1. Prepare your speech carefully and thoroughly. Know everything you are going to say, the key points you will emphasize, and the gestures you will use.

2. Practice giving your speech several times. If possible, give it before your family or friends. Practice looking in the mirror while you speak to be sure you look confident and enthusiastic. Time yourself, to avoid the embarrassment of a speech that comes out too long or too short.

3. Become familiar with the place where you are to speak. If possible, speak a few sentences when the room is empty and have a friend in the back row tell you how well your voice carries.

4. Walk, stand, and speak confidently. Never apologize for your subject, manner, or speaking abilities. Remember: your audience wants to hear what you have to say.

6b. Attitudes toward Your Listeners

The way you speak, stand, and move projects an attitude to your listeners. Your listeners will react to your speech on the basis of this attitude as well as on the basis of what you have to say. Follow these rules in order to project attitudes of friendliness and confidence to your listeners:

1. Know your audience. When you prepare your speech, make sure that the subject matter and language are not too difficult for them. Take into account how much they already know (or don't know) about the subject.

2. Be prepared for your listeners' reactions. Know where they will laugh or where they may disagree. Be prepared to answer the questions they will ask after your speech. Keep your sense of humor.

3. Be confident; show that you are worth listening to. Show that you want your listeners to be interested and to understand you.

6c. Attitudes toward Your Subject

Your listeners will pay more attention if you project a positive attitude toward your subject. You must be interested in your subject. You must know your subject well. You must be able to communicate your knowledge and your interest. Here are some suggestions:

1. Know more about your subject than you plan to cover in your speech. This gives you a reserve of information with which to answer questions.

2. Be enthusiastic about your subject. Ask yourself: Why am I interested in this subject? Then try to arouse that same enthusiasm in your listeners.

3. Have facts, names, dates, and figures readily available. Write the facts and figures you think you might need on note cards. Practice using your cards without having to pause to shuffle through them.

4. Be aware of any attitudes or prejudices your listeners may have towards your subject. If there are two opposing points of view, be fair to both sides.

5. Show respect for your subject. Don't joke about, belittle, or apologize for the topic you have chosen.

PRACTICING SPEECH SKILLS

■ The following paragraphs describe what happened when three different people gave speeches. For each example, write a brief paragraph describing what the speaker did wrong. List the rules he or she should follow in order to speak better in the future.

1. "I'm going to be speaking about the emperor Constantine," said Marie. "He's very important because he was the first Christian emperor . . . well, actually, I didn't think he was very interesting, but Mrs. Phillips assigned Constantine to me, so what could I do? Anyway . . . this Constantine was born about 280 A.D. in Nay— . . . Naw— . . . oh, I can't pronounce it . . ."

2. "I'm supposed to talk about the Boston Tea Party today," said Lester. "I'm not very well prepared, because I didn't know the library was going to be closed last night, and I didn't do all the research I should have. So I apologize in advance. Am I speaking loud enough?

Can you hear me in the back? . . . Oh, that's good . . . for some reason I thought you couldn't hear me. I guess I didn't realize how big the room would look when I was standing up here. . ."

3. "My report is about nuclear submarines," announced George. "The first thing you have to understand is how nuclear reactors operate. You have learned that in your science classes, so I won't go into the subject now. The submarine's reactor powers a steam turbine; the principle is that of any electrical power plant, and I assume you understand it. The development of early submarines might interest you. There are several good books on the subject."

7 Kinds of Speaking

7a. Narrative Speaking

In a narrative speech you tell a story in order to inform your listeners, to entertain them, or to make a particular point. The story you tell may have happened to you or to someone you know, or it may be drawn from history. Here are some rules for good narrative speaking:

1. Pick an interesting story with a beginning, a middle, and an end. If you are telling the story in order to illustrate a point, be sure the point will be clear to your listeners.
2. Tell your story in the right order. This will usually be chronological—the order in which the events occurred. If you are telling your story for entertainment, be careful not to give away the ending.
3. Focus your story. Decide which details are important, which are relatively unimportant, and which could be omitted altogether.
4. Know your audience. Be sure your listeners have sufficient background to understand your speech.
5. Be clear. A reader can reread a page he or she has not understood, but your listeners cannot "replay" your speech if they fail to understand it the first time.
6. Be entertaining, speak to the point, and be brief.

PRACTICING SPEECH SKILLS

■ The following list contains the outlines of a narrative speech, but without detail and with the items in the wrong order. Rearrange the items in chronological order, and add important details that will help make the speech interesting. Deliver the speech. Write a paragraph about your listeners' reactions.

Merchandise was scattered all over the sidewalk.

A car went through the window of a major downtown store.

It is located at the intersection of two busy streets.

Fortunately, no one was hurt.

One vehicle swerved to avoid another.

The manager says the insurance company will cover the damage.

Customers were protected by furniture and structures inside the store.

■■ Prepare and deliver a three-minute narrative speech on one of the following topics, or on a topic of your choice.

1. my first day at a new school
2. my most embarrassing moment
3. my most frightening moment
4. the origin of a holiday tradition in our family
5. my first trip to a different city
6. how I made friends with a person from a foreign country
7. how I learned an important lesson from a member of my family

7b. Expository Speaking

In an expository speech you explain to your listeners how to do something, how something operates, how and why some event took place. An expository speech may simply relate directions for getting from one place to another. It may give complicated instructions for operating a piece of machinery. It may summarize a book or a film. It may take the form of a research report about history or science. There are a few rules that apply to all kinds of expository speeches:

1. Be clear. Present only the essential details, and relate them to each other with such expressions as "first," "next," "on the other hand," and "in conclusion."

2. Organize your information. Present all your details in a logical sequence. Make sure your listeners can easily hear the transition from one point to the next. Unless it is specifically against the rules, write the outline of your speech on note cards which you can glance at while you speak.

3. Have a clear goal in mind. Begin your speech with a general statement of what you are going to explain, show, or prove. At the end of the speech, remind your listeners of the points you have just made.

4. Suit your speech to your listeners. Be sure they have enough background to understand what you are saying. If you use visual aids—such as maps, charts, slides, or photographs—they should be easy to understand and clearly visible from the back of the room.

5. Be brief. Your listeners can absorb only so much information at one time.

PRACTICING SPEECH SKILLS

■ Prepare a brief expository speech on one of the following subjects or on a similar subject of your own choice. Practice your speech. Would your listeners easily understand everything you said? Change anything that was unclear.

1. the fastest way to get from your home to downtown
2. how to go from the science lab to the gym on a rainy day while staying dry
3. how to take your favorite hike
4. how to change a tire on a car or bicycle
5. how to swim the crawl (or other stroke)
6. the best vacation you ever had

■■ Deliver the speech you prepared. Compare your listeners' reactions to the speech with your evaluation of it. Write a brief report on any differences between what you thought of the speech and what they thought.

7c. Persuasive Speaking

In a persuasive speech you try to convince or influence a person or group. You may be trying to persuade your listeners to vote for a candidate, to support a cause, or to agree with your view of events. Here are some rules for effective persuasive speaking:

1. Know your topic well. Know which facts you are going to use in your speech. Keep additional facts in mind in case you need further proof. Be sure your facts are accurate.

2. Take a clear stand. Let your listeners know at the beginning of your speech what you will try to persuade them to do or think. At the end of your speech, briefly summarize your arguments and restate your position.

3. Be clear and concise in your argument. Be sure all the evidence you use supports the point you are trying to make. Present your facts and arguments in logical order.

4. Know your audience. Be sure they can understand all your arguments. Avoid saying anything that might offend any of your listeners.

5. Anticipate objections. Decide in advance at what points in your speech your listeners may disagree with you. Meet these possible objections as they occur: "Some people may disagree with what I have just said, but there are several facts that prove my case . . ."

6. Show confidence in your beliefs. Don't qualify your position with "maybe," "possibly," or "it seems to me" (your listeners already know they are hearing your opinion). Be as forceful as you can.

PRACTICING SPEECH SKILLS

■ Prepare a speech on one of the following topics or on a similar topic of your own choice. When you practice your speech, imagine that your audience is unsympathetic to your position. Anticipate their possible objections and think of facts to refute them. When you deliver the speech, have your classmates pretend to be this audience. After the speech, have them raise the objections such an audience would have raised. Answer their objections as forcefully as you can.

1. Persuade a group of fur-coat manufacturers that they should not hunt seals.

2. Persuade a gathering of Republicans (or Democrats) that they should support a Democrat (or Republican) for the presidency.

3. Persuade an organization opposed to nuclear energy that a nuclear power plant should be built in your county.

4. Persuade a convention of oil company executives that they should not drill in the center of your town.

7d. Interviewing

Good interviewing requires careful preparation. Here are some rules to follow in conducting an interview:

1. Write a polite letter requesting the interview. Suggest a date, a time, and a place that will be convenient for the interviewee. If you want to use a tape recorder, get the person's permission first. After the interview, write a letter thanking the person.

2. Be prepared. Do research into the person's life, education, and achievements before the interview. If the person is well known, check in reference books and in magazine and newspaper articles. If the person is not well known, talk to people who know the interviewee personally.

3. Plan your questions so that the interviewee will give you informative answers. Don't ask questions that can be answered with a simple "Yes" or "No." Don't ask questions that are too personal.

4. Write out your questions. You may want to put a check or a star next to the important questions on which you should spend the most time. Group related questions together. You can write your questions on cards, and later write the answers underneath them.

5. Record the answers accurately. If you want to use direct quotes, write these answers with quotation marks around them. Ask the interviewee to repeat anything you think you may have missed.

6. Ask follow-up questions. The interviewee will probably say several interesting things you had not expected. Don't waste the chance to ask him or her for more detail on the new subject.

7. Keep the interview in focus. If the interviewee starts talking about subjects that have nothing to do with his or her career, tactfully guide the conversation back to the area of interest. Let the interviewee do most of the talking.

PRACTICING SPEECH SKILLS

■ Prepare for an interview with a celebrity in the world of politics, business, or entertainment. Do research at the library into the person's background and achievements. Prepare at least fifteen questions you would ask the person. Select five of these as the most important questions. For each of these five questions, write at least two follow-up questions you might find it useful to ask.

■■ Interview a person in your town or community. Afterwards, write an article based on the interview. Include in your article information you have learned in your research. Use both direct and indirect quotes.

8 Special Speeches

8a. Introducing a Speaker

The purpose of a speech of introduction is to tell the audience about the speaker they will be listening to. You should tell only the speaker's name, achievements, and qualifications and the subject of the speech. Follow these rules for a speech of introduction:

1. Write or talk to the speaker in advance, requesting some facts you can use as background in your speech.

2. Gather information that shows why the speaker is qualified to talk about this subject and why the audience should be interested.

3. Organize your facts into a speech. Your speech should emphasize the speaker's abilities, but not overpraise the person.

4. Deliver your speech warmly and enthusiastically. You may be humorous, but don't show off or try to steal attention from the speaker.

5. Be brief. Remember, the audience didn't come to hear you.

6. End by saying the speaker's name again.

8b. Nominating a Candidate

A nominating speech explains why a candidate is qualified for a particular office, and makes the audience feel interested in him or her. Here are some basic rules for speeches of nomination:

1. Describe the requirements of the office, and tell how your candidate is especially qualified to fulfill them.

2. Praise your candidate's character, but avoid irrelevant personal details.

3. Be positive in your approach. Don't attack or ridicule another candidate.

4. Deliver your speech with conviction and enthusiasm. End the speech with the name of your candidate.

PRACTICING SPEECH SKILLS

■ Prepare and deliver a speech of introduction for one of the following people or for a person of your own choice.

—a student from another country   —a newspaper reporter
—a local politician   —a professional athlete

■■ Prepare and deliver a nominating speech on behalf of a potential candidate for one of the following offices or for an office of your choice.

—president of your class   —mayor of your town
—treasurer of the student council   —member of your city council

8c. Presenting an Award

The purpose of a presentation speech is to tell both the recipient of an award and the audience why the award is being made or recognition given. Here are rules to follow while presenting an award:

1. Explain why the award was established, what it represents, and why it is being presented.
2. Describe the qualifications and achievements of the recipient.
3. Praise the recipient warmly and sincerely, but try not to embarrass the person.
4. Express congratulations and best wishes.
5. Be brief. Don't tell jokes, and don't talk about yourself.

8d. Accepting an Award

When you accept an award, make a brief speech expressing your appreciation. Your words and manner should be modest and sincere. Here are some rules:

1. Thank the donors of the award.
2. Tell the audience of the importance the award holds for you.
3. Mention, as modestly as you can, events or achievements that led to your receiving the award, if you think they will interest the audience.
4. Acknowledge the people whose assistance or inspiration helped you win the award.
5. Be brief and sincere. Conclude by thanking the donors once again.

PRACTICING SPEECH SKILLS

- Prepare and deliver a presentation speech for one of the following awards, or for an award of your own choice.

—a trophy for your school's basketball champion

—a ribbon for the winner of an art contest

—a book for the winner of the short-story contest

—a certificate for a parent who did volunteer work for your school

—an "Oscar" for the best performer in a school play

—a medal for the junior farmer who exhibited the largest hog at the county fair

—a watch for your school secretary who is retiring after twenty years

—a plaque for a fire fighter who rescued six people from a burning building

—a savings bond for the author of the best article in the school paper

■■ Prepare and deliver a speech accepting one of the awards listed in the preceding exercise, or an award of your own choice.

8e. Oral Book Reports

The purpose of an oral book report is to tell your listeners what the book is about, what your opinion of it is, and why you believe they would find it informative or enjoyable.

An oral book report is very similar to a written book report, but you will probably make the oral report livelier in order to interest your listeners. Here is a list of rules to follow in preparing an oral book report:

1. Give the title of the book and the name of the author at the beginning of your speech. If you can learn anything about the author's life or other works, describe these briefly.

2. Describe the setting, characters, and plot. Concentrate on the two or three principal characters, and try to make them interesting to your listeners. Summarize enough of the plot to make the problems of the story clear, but be careful not to give away the ending or any surprises in the book.

3. Give your opinion of the book. Say whether you found the characters interesting and the setting vivid. If the plot kept you reading eagerly, explain why it did. Read brief excerpts if you want to give an impression of the way the book is written. Give your opinion of the illustrations, if they are important.

4. If you disliked the book, or aspects of it, give specific reasons for your dislike. Don't simply say, "I hate all books about dogs." Remember, your listeners are interested in whether they would like to read the book. If you talk only about your own opinions, they will learn nothing of the book's quality.

5. If the book is nonfiction, describe why you found it clear and informative—or unclear and uninformative. Mention whether the book told you all you wanted to know about the subject, whether the maps and illustrations were helpful, and whether you now want to learn more about the subject.

6. Tell your listeners whether or not you recommend the book to them. Summarize in a sentence the reasons for your recommendation.

PRACTICING SPEECH SKILLS

■ Prepare and deliver an oral report on a book, either fiction or nonfiction. If you enjoyed the book and recommend that your listeners read it, be sure to explain why this particular audience would enjoy it. If you did not enjoy the book and recommend that your listeners do not read it, be sure to explain why they in particular would not enjoy it.

9 Group Speaking

9a. Group Discussions

The purpose of a group discussion is to enable people to share their knowledge and ideas, and often to arrive at some solution for a problem. You probably take part in group discussions every day. You may have group discussions with friends during or after school or with members of your family. These are **informal** group discussions.

A **formal** group discussion should be conducted more carefully than an informal one. Everyone should have a chance to speak, and the group should try to reach some agreement on the question being discussed. Here are some rules for taking part in a formal group discussion:

1. Listen carefully to what the other people say.

2. Speak only about the subject being discussed.

3. Ask questions whenever something seems unclear. Intelligent questions can often shed new light on the subject under discussion.

4. Be polite and considerate when you disagree with others in the group.

Any formal group discussion with more than three or four people should have a leader, or chairperson. Here are the rules to follow when you are the chairperson of a formal group discussion:

1. Make sure that all members of the group have a chance to speak.

2. Allow only one person to speak at a time.

3. Keep the discussion on the topic. If the members of the group stray away from the subject, politely remind them of it.

4. Keep the discussion polite. If members start making personal remarks, point out that these have nothing to do with the subject.

5. Ask speakers to clarify their remarks if you or the other members of the group did not understand what they meant.

6. Near the end of the discussion, summarize what has been said on each side. Be fair and impartial in your summary.

7. Guide the group toward a decision. If there are still differences, suggest ways in which the members of the group could compromise.

PRACTICING SPEECH SKILLS

■ Take part in a formal group discussion on one of the following topics, or on a topic of your own choice. Write a brief report summarizing the discussion.

1. Is it good to have dress codes at school?
2. What could be done to improve the quality of life in your community?
3. What measures could your school take in order to stay within a limited budget?
4. Is student government necessary?

9b. Panel Discussions

Panel discussions resemble group discussions, but they are different in several important ways. A panel discussion is held before an audience. Usually, each person on the panel is an expert on the subject being discussed, or on one aspect of the subject. The purpose of the panel discussion is to inform the audience. Generally, the members of the panel do not try to reach a decision on the subject being discussed.

A panel discussion always has a chairperson, who is introduced to the audience by another person not on the panel. These are the rules to follow when serving as the chairperson of a panel discussion:

1. State and explain the subject under discussion.
2. Briefly introduce the panelists to the audience, emphasizing their qualifications to discuss the subject.
3. Begin the discussion by asking a panel member one of the questions you have prepared. When he or she has answered, continue the discussion by asking another member of the panel to respond.
4. Keep the discussion going by asking questions of panel members. Ask follow-up questions when you think they will produce interesting answers, but don't let the panel spend too much time on a single question.
5. Ask members of the panel to clarify their remarks if you find them unclear, or if you think the audience may find them unclear.
6. Follow the rules for the chairperson of a group discussion: keep the discussion orderly, polite, and on the subject.
7. Near the end of the discussion, ask the members of the panel for brief closing statements summarizing their views on the subject.
8. When the formal discussion is over, call for questions from the audience. Some listeners will have questions for specific members of the panel. Others will have general questions, and you will have to decide which panel member is best qualified to answer each question.
9. To conclude the discussion, briefly summarize the panel discussion and the audience's questions, and thank the members of the panel.

Here are rules to follow for taking part in a panel discussion.

1. Be prepared to discuss the subject. Know what position you will take and what questions you are likely to be asked. Bring notes with any useful facts or figures.
2. Listen carefully to the questions and answer them precisely and thoroughly. Stay on the subject.

3. When responding to a particular question, address the other members of the panel, but be sure that the audience can hear and understand you.

4. When you disagree with the other panelists, be polite. Limit your objections to questions of fact, and don't bring in personalities.

5. Keep your remarks brief. Each member of the panel should speak for about the same length of time.

6. Be prepared to answer questions asked by the audience or by the chairperson of the panel.

PRACTICING SPEECH SKILLS

■ Take part in a panel discussion on one of the following topics, or on a topic of your own choice.

1. Is there too much violence on television?
2. What is the most important issue facing your city or community?
3. What rules can students follow in order to do better in school?
4. In what ways will the world be different ten or twenty years from now?
5. What are the best careers for young people?
6. What new sources of energy will we use over the next few decades?
7. What measures can young people follow now in order to have longer, healthier lives?
8. What can ordinary citizens do about the rising crime rate?
9. How can schools help students become more intelligent consumers?

■■ Watch a panel discussion on television or listen to a panel discussion on the radio. The discussion should be at least half an hour long and should have at least three panelists besides the chairperson. Write a brief report on the panel discussion. Describe how the panel was conducted, whether the discussion was informative, and how questions were handled. Summarize your impressions of the panel discussion.

■■■ Decide with your classmates on a topic that is important to your school or community and that is appropriate for a panel discussion. The topic could be a major public issue facing your state, town, or community. Invite several experts to your school to participate in a panel discussion on the topic. They might be local politicians or other public officials, doctors, police officers, teachers, or scientists. A student should serve as chairperson, and the entire class should participate in preparing the chairperson's questions. After the discussion is over, write a report evaluating the panel discussion. Decide which panel members were best prepared and which ones gave the most informative answers. List the facts you learned from the panel. Then list the ways in which the panel discussion could have been improved.

9c. Parliamentary Procedure

Senates, assemblies, and other legislative bodies operate according to a set of rules called **parliamentary procedure.** Clubs and student councils also follow this system. The purpose of parliamentary procedure is to ensure that every member of the organization has a chance to be heard. Members speak one at a time about one proposal (called a **motion**) at a time. Every motion that is brought up is voted on, and the majority vote rules.

The complete system of parliamentary procedure is very complicated. Even experienced legislators have to refer to handbooks to know what to do in certain situations. However, you can use a simplified version of parliamentary procedure in club and class meetings.

Every meeting conducted according to parliamentary procedure has a **chairperson.** The chairperson is usually the president of the group that is meeting. The chairperson

—must be fair and give every member a chance to speak.
—must limit the discussion to the motion being considered.
—does not participate in the discussion.
—does not vote, except to break a tie, or if the voting is by secret ballot.

Each member of the group must

—speak only after being recognized by the chairperson.
—speak only about the motion under discussion.

The meeting begins when the chairperson raps on the table and says, "The meeting of _____ will come to order." Then comes the roll call, the reading of the minutes of the last meeting, and the reports of committees. When old business has been taken care of, the chairperson asks if there is any new business. The usual order for dealing with motions is the following:

1. A member raises his or her hand. The chairperson **recognizes** the member by saying that person's name. The member now **has the floor** and is allowed to speak.

2. The member who has the floor states the **motion.** The correct form to use is: "I move that . . ." or "I move to. . . ." For example, the member might say, "I move that we hold our meetings on Thursdays instead of Wednesdays."

3. Another member raises his or her hand, is recognized, and says, "I second the motion." Unless the motion has been **seconded,** it cannot be considered.

4. The chairperson repeats the motion in the exact words of the member who made it. For example, "It has been moved and seconded that we hold our meetings on Thursdays instead of Wednesdays." The chairperson then asks, "Is there any discussion?"

5. The members discuss the motion. Members raise their hands, and the chairperson recognizes those who want to speak for or against the motion.

6. When the discussion is finished, the chairperson asks for a vote by repeating the motion and saying, "All those in favor, say **aye.** All those opposed, say **nay.**" (Or the members can respond by saying "yes" or "no.")

7. The members vote. The chairperson counts the votes and announces the result: "The ayes have it. The motion is carried." ("The nays have it. The motion is defeated.")

After all the motions have been considered, the members agree on the business to be dealt with at the next meeting. Then a member moves that the meeting be **adjourned.** After the motion for adjournment has been seconded, and if there are no objections, the chairperson says, "The meeting stands adjourned."

PRACTICING SPEECH SKILLS

■ Read the following descriptions of what happens at a club meeting. Then answer each question by writing out what the person named would say if the meeting were being conducted according to parliamentary procedure.

1. The meeting of the Science Club is about to begin. What does the chairperson do and say?

2. Bill O'Hara raises his hand to speak. What does the chairperson say?

3. Bill thinks the club should take a field trip to the State Observatory. What does Bill say?

4. Erica Montano thinks Bill has a good idea. What does she do and say?

5. It is time for Bill's suggestion to be discussed. What does the chairperson do?

6. After the discussion, it is time to vote. What does the chairperson say?

7. A majority of the members vote for Bill's idea. What does the chairperson say?

■■ Conduct a class meeting according to parliamentary procedure. One person should act as temporary chairperson until the group elects a president. Then elect a vice-president, a secretary, and a treasurer. Propose, discuss, and vote on motions about meeting days, class projects, field trips, or other activities that the class is involved in. Try to follow the rules as closely as possible.

9d.   Debates

A debate is a competition between speakers. There are usually two teams of speakers. The teams argue on opposing sides of an issue, and each team tries to persuade the audience that its position is the right one. Debates have very specific rules and procedures. Every debate is based on a statement called a **proposition.** The proposition states something that people believe ought to be done. It does not state something that is clearly true or false. A proposition is always worded in a positive way; for example, "<u>Resolved</u>, That the United States should continue to build nuclear power plants." The proposition should be about an issue that has good arguments on both sides.

The **affirmative** team argues in favor of the proposition. The **negative** team argues against it. There are usually two speakers on each team. The debate begins when the chairperson announces the topic, briefly introduces the speakers, announces the order in which they will speak, and tells how many minutes each speaker will have.

The debate begins when the chairperson announces the topic, briefly introduces the speakers, announces the order in which they will speak, and tells how many minutes each speaker will have.

The debaters give their **main speeches** first. They speak in the following order: first affirmative speaker, first negative speaker, second affirmative speaker, second negative speaker. The chairperson times each speech carefully and tells the debater when he or she has only one minute left to speak. When a debater's time is up, he or she may finish a sentence but must then sit down.

Then the debaters give their **rebuttal** speeches, in which they try to **rebut,** or tear down, the arguments used by the other team. The debaters speak in the following order: first negative speaker, first affirmative speaker, second negative speaker, second affirmative speaker. The rebuttal speeches are also timed, and they are usually shorter than the main speeches.

If the debate is being judged, the judges now vote, and the chairperson announces which side has won the debate. If there is no judging, the chairperson thanks the speakers, and the debate is over.

PRACTICING SPEECH SKILLS

■ For each of the following sentences, write a correctly worded proposition that could be the subject of a debate. Remember that a proposition must be stated in positive language and must begin with the word **resolved.**

1. "If this country doesn't get a national health insurance program soon, we're going to be in trouble!"

2. "How are schoolteachers going to keep their kids in line if they can't swat or spank them?"

9e. Speaking in Debates

In most debates, you must be prepared to speak on either the affirmative or the negative side of the proposition. Whichever side you are assigned, you will have to make an effective argument in a limited period of time. Follow these rules for preparing and delivering a main speech.

1. If you are part of a team, decide in advance how you and your partner will divide the arguments. Each of you should speak about one aspect of the proposition. Do not let your arguments overlap.

2. Make your position clear at the beginning of your speech.

3. Remember that your time is limited. Use only the strongest facts to support your case. Make your arguments brief and direct.

4. Base your arguments on published facts and figures wherever possible. Always be specific when you cite facts; for example: "The Mayor's 1979 Crime Survey shows a 12 percent rise in violent crimes."

5. Summarize your arguments briefly at the end of your speech, and end by again strongly emphasizing your position.

Rebuttal speeches are shorter than the main speeches in debates. The purpose of the rebuttal is to tear down the arguments used by the debaters on the other team. Follow these rules for rebuttal speeches:

1. Work out in advance what arguments and facts your opponents will use. Decide what you would say if you were in their position.

2. Point out any unsound statements or untrue facts used by your opponents; for example: "The Police Commissioner has shown that the mayor's crime survey was biased, incomplete, and unscientific."

3. Point out any faulty logic used by your opponents; for example: "The fact that the elm trees died after the swimming pool was opened does not mean the trees died because the pool was opened."

4. Try to persuade your listeners that your opponents' arguments are less important than yours; for example: "It is true that our school's athletic budget has been cut—but our need for expanded athletic facilities is more important than mere dollars-and-cents."

5. Avoid personal attacks on the other debaters.

PRACTICING SPEECH SKILLS

■ Form teams, and prepare both affirmative and negative speeches on one of the propositions you wrote for the preceding lesson.

■■ Prepare rebuttal speeches to counter the speeches you think will be delivered by the other team.

■■■ Your teacher will assign the position each team will argue. Hold a debate on the proposition for which you have prepared the speeches.

10 Diagnostic Checklists

10a. Using Your Voice

Good speakers train their voices to be clear, natural sounding, pleasant, and easily understood. They pronounce all words correctly and distinctly, and they vary their delivery to keep their listeners' attention and to emphasize the meaning of their words.

Use the following checklist to evaluate your speaking voice. Answer each of the statements **yes** or **no.** You can also ask one of your listeners to answer the questions about your speaking voice.

The speaker

—can be heard by all listeners.
—can be easily understood.
—pronounces all words correctly.
—effectively varies the rate of speech.
—effectively varies the volume of speech.
—effectively varies the pitch of speech.
—makes effective use of pauses.
—avoids hesitating or saying "um," "you know,"
　　"like," and "I mean."

10b. Listening

Good listeners pay attention to a speaker's words and manner. When listening to speeches, they watch and listen carefully for the cues that tell them which points are important and which part of a speech they are listening to. When taking part in conversations, they do not interrupt other speakers or try to monopolize the conversation.

Use the following checklist to evaluate yourself as a listener. Answer each of the statements **yes** or **no.** You can also ask a speaker to evaluate his or her listeners by answering many of the statements in the checklist.

When taking part in a conversation, the listener

—avoids interrupting the speaker.
—listens politely to what is being said.
—avoids taking over the conversation.
—avoids trying to "top" the speaker.

When listening to a speech, the listener

—pays close attention.
—avoids yawning, fidgeting, or talking.
—follows the signposts in the speech.
—follows the speaker's emphases.
—follows the speaker's vocal cues.
—follows the speaker's physical cues.
—takes notes.
—asks intelligent questions after the speech.

10c. Using Your Body

A good speaker uses gestures, posture, and expression to reinforce the meaning of his or her speech. A good speaker moves and stands confidently, and avoids using distracting or inappropriate gestures.

Use the following checklist to evaluate your use of your body while speaking. Answer **yes** or **no** to each of the statements. You can also ask your listeners to use this checklist to evaluate the way you use your body while speaking.

The speaker

—walks confidently to the podium.
—stands straight while speaking.
—suits his or her posture and expression to what is being said.
—uses appropriate gestures to emphasize important points.
—avoids using distracting gestures or other movements.
—looks directly at the audience.

10d. Word Choice

Good speakers use accurate and vivid language that appeals to the listeners' senses. They use direct, precise language and short, straightforward sentences.
Use the following checklist to evaluate your choice of words in speaking. Answer **yes** or **no** to each of the statements. Your listeners can also use the checklist to evaluate your word choice.

The speaker

—uses specific language that creates sharp images in the listeners' minds.
—uses vivid language that appeals to the listeners' senses.
—uses language that is suited to the speech and audience.
—avoids slang while giving a speech.
—speaks in short sentences of ten to fifteen words.
—uses words the listeners will understand.
—uses normal word order in sentences.

10e. Attitudes

Good speakers are well prepared and confident, and they communicate their enthusiasm to their listeners. They pay attention to their listeners' responses and modify their words and delivery accordingly.

Use the following checklist to evaluate your attitudes as a speaker. Answer **yes** or **no** to each of the statements. Your listeners can also use many of the statements to evaluate your attitudes as a speaker.

The speaker

—prepares his or her speech carefully and thoroughly.
—practices giving the speech several times.
—makes sure that the speech will be the right length.
—is familiar with the place where he or she is to speak.
—responds to the listeners' reactions.
—conveys enthusiasm about the subject.
—has facts and figures available and uses them skillfully.
—is fair to opposing points of view.
—takes the subject seriously.
—is prepared to answer questions.

10f. Speaking in Groups

Speaking in groups, whether in a group discussion, a panel discussion, or a meeting conducted according to parliamentary procedure, must be governed by the rules the group has established. The chairperson makes sure that members of the group respect one another's rights.

Use the following checklists to evaluate your performance as a participant in, or chairperson of, a group discussion. Answer **yes** or **no** to each of the statements. Participants can also use these lists to evaluate one another's performance or that of the chairperson.

The member

—raises his or her hand in order to speak.
—speaks only when called upon.
—speaks only about the topic under discussion.
—keeps his or her remarks brief.
—is polite when disagreeing with the other members of the group.

The chairperson

—gives every member a chance to speak.
—asks members to clarify unclear statements.
—guides the discussion back to the topic when it has strayed.
—keeps members from personal arguments.
—helps the group come to a decision (if appropriate).

Grammar Handbook

Sentences   190

Parts of Speech   196

Sentence Patterns   248

Phrases and Clauses   286

Usage   320

Mechanics   376

Spelling and Vocabulary   416

1 Kinds of Sentences

1a. Declarative, Interrogative, and Imperative Sentences

The sun radiates heat and light.   Don't stare at the sun.
The sun is fascinating!   Be careful!
What causes a sunburn?

Read the sentences in the box.

- Which sentences make statements?
- Which sentence asks a question?
- Which sentences give commands?

A sentence that makes a statement is called a declarative sentence.
A sentence that asks a question is called an interrogative sentence.
A sentence that gives a command is called an imperative sentence.
A declarative or imperative sentence that expresses strong feeling and ends with an exclamation mark may sometimes be called an exclamatory sentence

PRACTICING LANGUAGE SKILLS

- Read each sentence below. Write **declarative sentence, interrogative sentence,** or **imperative sentence** to identify which kind of sentence it is.

1. Think about the sun.
2. Exactly what is it?
3. The sun is the most important star in our universe.
4. Compare the size of our sun with the size of other stars.
5. Why does the sun appear so large?
6. The sun seems larger than other stars because it is closer to us.
7. The sun is a yellow dwarf star.
8. Red giant stars may be 1,000 times as large as the sun.
9. Some stars are huge!
10. How do scientists get information about the sun?
11. Scientists study the sun with special telescopes.
12. Never look at the sun without protecting your eyes.
13. You can't be too careful!
14. What have scientists discovered about the sun?
15. The sun is made up of many gases.
16. Great storms occur on the sun's surface.
17. Consider the importance of the sun.
18. Solar energy is used in some homes.

APPLYING LANGUAGE SKILLS TO COMPOSITION

- Write three declarative sentences about our need for the sun.

■■ Write three interrogative sentences you would ask a scientist about the sun.

■■■ Write three imperative sentences that will help people protect themselves from too much exposure to the sun.

2 Subjects and Predicates

2a. Subjects and Predicates in Most Declarative Sentences

Oceans	contain many mysteries.
Modern equipment	brings new discoveries.
Research about the sea	will continue in the future.

Read the declarative sentences in the box. Each sentence is divided to show its two main parts.

- What is the first part of each sentence?
- What is the second part of each sentence?

Every sentence has two main parts, the **subject** and the **predicate.**

The subject of a sentence tells who or what the sentence is about. In most declarative sentences, the subject is the first part.

The predicate tells what the subject does or is. In most declarative sentences, the predicate is the second part.

PRACTICING LANGUAGE SKILLS

■ Write each of the following declarative sentences. Draw one line under the subject. Draw two lines under the predicate.

1. Oceans cover more than 70 percent of the surface of the earth.
2. They affect all forms of life.
3. Marine biologists study plant and animal life in the sea.
4. Marine geologists study rocks beneath the sea.
5. These scientists investigate the bottom of the sea, too.
6. Physical oceanographers study the currents and tides of the sea.
7. The chemicals in seawater interest chemical oceanographers.
8. Many oceanographers work on ships.

APPLYING LANGUAGE SKILLS TO COMPOSITION

■ Add a predicate to each of the following subjects. Write the declarative sentences you make.

1. sea life
2. the crashing waves
3. several large whales
4. colorful coral
5. seaweed
6. driftwood
7. deep-sea divers
8. dolphins
9. chemicals in the sea

■■ Add a subject to each of the following predicates. Write the declarative sentences you make.

1. may become a source of food
2. is a valuable resource
3. frightened early sailors
4. were lying in the sand
5. endangers many sea creatures
6. can be dangerous to divers
7. provides information to oceanographers
8. is helping to preserve our oceans

2b. Subjects and Predicates in Declarative Sentences with Inverted Order

The musicians	waited behind the curtain.
Behind the curtain waited	the musicians.

Read the declarative sentences in the box.

- In which sentence is the subject the first part?
- In which sentence is the predicate the first part?

In a few declarative sentences, the predicate is the first part and the subject is the second part. Such declarative sentences have **inverted order.** In most writing, declarative sentences with inverted order are used only occasionally for variety or for special emphasis.

2c. Subjects and Predicates in Imperative Sentences

Listen to the music.

Read the sentence in the box.

- What kind of sentence is it?
- Which main sentence part—the subject or the predicate—does not seem to be included in the sentence?

Every imperative sentence has the same subject: **you.** That subject is understood to be part of the sentence, even though it is not said or written.

PRACTICING LANGUAGE SKILLS

■ Write each of the following sentences. If the sentence subject is understood to be **you,** write **(you)** before the predicate of the sentence. Then draw a vertical line between the two main parts of the sentence. Write **subject** above the subject. Write **predicate** above the predicate.

1. Out of ragtime and blues developed a new musical form.
2. People around the world became jazz fans.
3. Play another jazz record.
4. Turn the volume up.
5. Listen carefully to the trumpet.
6. From Louis Armstrong's trumpet came unforgettable sounds.
7. He developed the scat style of singing.
8. Try to imitate Armstrong's style.
9. You may find it difficult.
10. Among the greatest jazz singers is Ella Fitzgerald.
11. Her voice has impressed listeners of several generations.
12. In concert halls across the country sat spellbound audiences.
13. Remember the feeling in Fitzgerald's voice.
14. Tell us about the concert.
15. Not all jazz musicians are Americans.

2d. Subjects and Predicates in Interrogative Sentences

Are most people **eating well?** Most people **are eating well.**	**What should** we **eat?** We **should eat what.**
What vitamins do you **need?** You **do need what vitamins.**	Which foods **have those vitamins?** Which foods **have those vitamins.**

Read the interrogative sentence in each box. Then read the declarative sentence below it.

- How have the words in the interrogative sentence been used to form the declarative sentence?
- What are the subject and predicate of the declarative sentence?
- What are the subject and predicate of the interrogative sentence?

The words of an interrogative sentence can be used to form a declarative sentence. That declarative sentence may not always sound natural, but it will help you find the subject and predicate of the interrogative sentence. The subject and predicate of the interrogative sentence are the same as the subject and predicate of the declarative sentence.

PRACTICING LANGUAGE SKILLS

■ Write each of the following interrogative sentences. Draw one line under each word in the subject. Draw two lines under each word in the predicate.

1. Are you taking good care of your body?
2. What did you eat for breakfast this morning?
3. Did your breakfast give you enough energy?
4. Which breakfast foods provide the best nutrition?
5. Should all people regulate their calories?
6. How long do you sleep each night?
7. How many hours of sleep does a healthy person need?
8. Do adults need less sleep than teenagers?
9. Are you getting enough exercise?
10. How often should the average person exercise?
11. Which forms of exercise are most healthful?
12. Is jogging good for everyone?
13. How far did you run this morning?
14. Do you need to improve your posture?
15. Why is fresh air important?
16. Are you breathing properly?
17. Do you know how to relax?
18. How can relaxation improve your health?
19. Do you exercise by yourself?
20. Is there a tennis team at your school?
21. Have you tried out for the swimming team?
22. Are you serious about exercising?
23. Why are warm-up exercises important?
24. Will you use the school's new gym equipment?
25. When did you begin your exercise program?

Reviewing **1** Kinds of Sentences and **2** Subjects and Predicates

1a. Declarative, Interrogative, and
Imperative Sentences

Read each sentence below. Write
declarative sentence, interrogative sentence,
or **imperative sentence** to identify which
kind of sentence it is.

1. Where did you go last night after the party?
2. Meet us at Gerry's house at 7:30 or 8:00.
3. The storm ended abruptly.
4. It's wonderful to see you!
5. Has anyone seen Margo since class let out?
6. Mercury is the closest planet to the sun.
7. Imagine the heat on Mercury!
8. Life on earth would not be possible without the sun.
9. How much do you expect to earn this summer?
10. How much energy does the sun give off?
11. Don't you think sunsets are the most beautiful thing in nature?
12. My sister has photographed many sunsets.
13. Once no one understood the cause of eclipses.
14. Are you afraid of eclipses?
15. There is nothing to be afraid of!
16. An eclipse of the moon may last more than an hour.
17. Clouds hid the last eclipse from our view.
18. Have you ever seen an eclipse of the sun?
19. Tell us about it.
20. When did it take place?
21. How long did it last?
22. You should never look directly at the sun.
23. Use a pinhole projector.
24. Sunglasses do not provide enough protection during an eclipse.

Write each of the following sentences. If
the sentence subject is understood to be **you,**
write **(you)** before the predicate of the
sentence. Then draw one line under each
word in the subject. Draw two lines under
each word in the predicate.

2a. Subjects and Predicates in Most
Declarative Sentences

25. Ramses II ruled Egypt for nearly seventy years.
26. Ramses' long reign lasted from 1292 to 1225 B.C.
27. The war against the Hittites occupied the early part of his reign.
28. He supervised a vast building program in Egypt after the war.
29. Ramses' mummy is in the Egyptian Museum in Cairo.
30. Oceanographers may help us find food supplies in the future.
31. The color and variety beneath the sea make scuba diving a fascinating hobby.
32. Atomic research will certainly have important effects on life in the future.
33. Nuclear fusion may someday be a safe, efficient source of energy.
34. Mr. Burdett told us to study carefully for our science test.
35. Our school gym is one of the oldest buildings in town.
36. The project took me more than a week.
37. Water company records do not go back beyond the year 1923.
38. I finally found the date in an old newspaper.
39. Everyone in my class is in favor of saving the old gym.
40. The building may be torn down anyway.
41. We are organizing a committee.
42. The committee already has more than one hundred members.

2b. Subjects and Predicates in Declarative Sentences with Inverted Order

43. Down the stairs walked the students.
44. From the kitchen came the aroma of freshly baked bread.
45. Around the corner ran the thief.
46. Out the door scampered the puppy.
47. Into the woods ran the fox.
48. Among the great blues singers stands Billie Holiday.
49. Among her most famous songs is "Strange Fruit."
50. From coast to coast spread the rumor of his retirement.
51. Beyond those mountains lies a fertile valley.
52. Around that story have grown a thousand legends.
53. Behind this door is a secret passage.
54. Under the old couch was an antique silver watch.
55. Into the pitch dark tunnel roared the train.
56. Next to the guest speaker sat the class president.
57. Out of the house ran three small dogs.

2c. Subjects and Predicates in Imperative Sentences

58. Tell me about your trip.
59. Have a good time!
60. Stay calm.
61. Take a deep breath.
62. Please open the window.
63. Listen to your mother.
64. Please give me just a few more minutes.
65. Leave my mail alone!
66. Tell me about your trip.
67. Let me know about the job offer.
68. Drop me a line.
69. Please come to our new apartment on Kremer Street.
70. Let me know.
71. Please bring me a glass of water.

2d. Subjects and Predicates in Interrogative Sentences

72. Have you heard this song before?
73. Will you teach me the rules of chess?
74. Did anyone see a spaceship on the football field?
75. Is Marguerite meeting us later?
76. Where is the science lab?
77. Do you pay attention to your diet?
78. Can a human being survive on liquids?
79. What is your favorite form of exercise?
80. Do you prefer tennis or handball?
81. When do you like to exercise?
82. Would you like to join my gymnastics class?
83. Do you see anything tempting on the menu?
84. Is the school track good for running?
85. Will you show me the best method for this project?
86. What made Harry so happy yesterday afternoon?
87. Which one of those baseball players broke that window?
88. Where is my overcoat with the fur collar?
89. Have you been listening to the principal's speech?
90. Did you hear me calling you?
91. Has Marjorie already finished her dinner?
92. How many times has he told us that story?
93. Why hasn't Anne put the lawn mower away?
94. Do you believe the stories about the old house on Calhoun Street?
95. What time did you put the pie in the oven?
96. Will Patricia be taking part in the holiday show at school?
97. Who made that decision?
98. Why did you disagree with me?
99. Are the other paints still in the cabinet?
100. When will the next plane for New York City take off?

3 Verbs

3a. Recognizing and Using Verbs

Many skiers **enjoy** the mountain air.	A skier **enjoys** the mountain air.
Many skiers **try** a difficult maneuver.	A skier **tries** a difficult maneuver.
Many skiers **glide** down the slopes.	A skier **glides** down the slopes.

Read the sentences in the boxes. The words in dark type, and others like them, are called **verbs.**

- What is the verb in each sentence?
- Does each verb tell about something that is happening now or something that happened in the past?

The predicate of every sentence includes a verb.

A verb tells what happens or what is. Every verb has several different forms to express differences in time.

The verbs in the sentences in the boxes are called **present tense verb forms. Present tense verb forms may be used to tell about present action or existence. They may also be used to tell about repeated action or existence.**

Most verbs have two present tense forms to go with different kinds of sentence subjects. One present tense verb form is called the **plural form.** It goes with plural subjects and with the subjects **I** and **you.** The other present tense verb form is called the **singular form.** It goes with singular subjects.

Subjects	Present Tense Verb Forms	
many skiers	glide	plural form
I, you, we, they	glide	plural form
one skier	glides	singular form
he, she, it	glides	singular form

PRACTICING LANGUAGE SKILLS

- Read the following sentences. Write the present tense verb form from each sentence. After each verb, write **plural form** or **singular form** to identify its form.

1. In autumn, the weather turns crisp.
2. Colorful leaves drift from the trees.
3. Animals sense the approach of winter.
4. Ice crystals form on paths and rooftops.
5. A light snow flurry signals the onset of winter.
6. Soon the sky darkens overhead.
7. Winds whistle through the barren trees.
8. The harsh winter begins.
9. Silent snowfalls shroud the earth in white.
10. Housebound people restlessly await the warmth of spring.
11. Milder weather quickens the pace of life.

3b. Past Tense Verb Forms

> A great fire **raged** through Chicago.
> The fire **destroyed** the entire downtown area.
> Citizens **rebuilt** Chicago from its ruins.

Read the sentences in the box.

- What is the verb in each sentence?
- Does each verb tell about something that is happening now or something that happened in the past?

The verbs in the sentences in the box are called **past tense verb forms.** **Past tense verb forms are usually used to tell about action or existence in the past.**

Many past tense verb forms are made by adding **-ed** or **-d** to the present tense plural form. Some verbs, called irregular verbs, change in different ways to show the past tense.

- Which sentence in the box has an irregular verb?

PRACTICING LANGUAGE SKILLS

■ Read the following sentences. Write the past tense verb form from each sentence.

1. Spanish settlers founded San Francisco in 1776.
2. Spanish soldiers built a military fort, or presidio, there.
3. Spanish priests established a mission near the fort.
4. Prospectors discovered gold near present-day Sacramento in 1848.
5. Gold seekers came to California from all parts of the world.
6. San Francisco became the supply center for these fortune hunters.
7. The city grew tremendously during the gold rush.
8. A severe earthquake shook San Francisco on April 18, 1906.
9. Fires swept through the city for three days.
10. The United Nations chose San Francisco for its first meeting.
11. Representatives from all over the world met there.
12. The meeting lasted for several weeks.
13. International leaders believed in the importance of this meeting.

APPLYING LANGUAGE SKILLS TO COMPOSITION

■ Use each of the following past tense verb forms in a sentence. Write the sentences.

1. visited
2. climbed
3. drove
4. saw
5. returned
6. enjoyed
7. spent
8. took
9. selected

3c. Forms of Be

> Cuzco, Peru, **was** the center of the ancient Inca empire.
> Cuzco **is** thousands of feet above sea level.
> The Andes mountains **are** all around Cuzco.

Read the sentences in the box.

- What is the verb in each sentence?

The verb in each sentence is a form of **be. Be** is an unusual verb. It has three present tense forms and two past tense forms.

Subjects	Present Tense Forms	Past Tense Forms
I	am	was
he, she, it, one city	is	was
you, we, they, many cities	are	were

PRACTICING LANGUAGE SKILLS

■ The verb in each of the following sentences is a form of **be.** Write only the verb from each sentence. After each verb, write **present** or **past** to identify its tense.

1. Stonehenge is an ancient monument in England.
2. It is now in ruins.
3. These ruins are the most famous prehistoric artifacts in England.
4. Stonehenge is a collection of huge stones.
5. Probably the stones were originally in a circle.
6. An earthen wall was around the largest circle of stones.
7. Other stone formations were inside the circle.
8. Some stones are from a part of Wales nearly 300 miles, or 480 kilometers, away.
9. Some stones were nearly six tons in weight.
10. The transportation of these stones was a remarkable achievement.
11. Stonehenge was an accomplishment of the New Stone Age.
12. Archaeologists are unsure about the purpose of Stonehenge.
13. Perhaps it was a place of worship.
14. Possibly it was an astronomical calendar.
15. I am curious about Stonehenge.
16. Stonehenge is near Salisbury, a city in southern England.
17. Another famous ancient monument is not far from Stonehenge.
18. That monument is Woodhenge.

APPLYING LANGUAGE SKILLS TO COMPOSITION

■ Write three sentences, each with a different present tense form of the verb **be.**

■■ Write two sentences, each with a different past tense form of the verb **be.**

3d. Be as an Auxiliary

> Many people **are choosing** simple life-styles.
> Everyone **is limiting** the use of resources.
> Some people **were encouraging** this kind of change years ago.

Read the sentences in the box. The two words in dark type in each sentence are the **verb phrase** of the sentence.

- What is the verb phrase in each sentence?

In some sentences, two or more words make up the verb. Those words are called the **verb phrase** of the sentence.

The first word in a verb phrase may be a form of **be.** When a form of **be** is the first word in a verb phrase, it is called an **auxiliary.**

An auxiliary in a verb phrase is always followed by a main verb form. The auxiliary **be** is followed by the **present participle** form of a verb. A present participle form ends with **-ing.**

PRACTICING LANGUAGE SKILLS

■ Write only the verb phrase from each of the following sentences.
Underline the auxiliary in each verb phrase.

1. The scientific community is studying the effects of pollution.
2. Perhaps we are depending too heavily upon technology.
3. Several years ago, relatively few people were investigating environmental pollution.
4. Rachel Carson was warning the public about pesticides nearly twenty years ago.
5. Pesticides are damaging delicate ecological balances.
6. Carelessness is destroying some species completely.
7. All over the world, other species are facing extinction.
8. Animals are dying needlessly every day.
9. Today we are learning more about the ecology of our planet.
10. The government is restricting the use of pesticides.
11. Many people are recycling materials.

■■ Add two different verb phrases to complete each of the following sentences in two different ways. First, use a present tense form of the auxiliary **be** and the present participle form of the verb in parentheses. Second, use a past tense form of **be** and the present participle form of the verb. Write the sentences.

1. Scientists (learn) about the control of weather.
2. Harsh weather conditions (create) problems.
3. Hurricanes (kill) many people.
4. Drought (cause) severe famines in parts of the world.
5. Tornadoes (destroy) property.
6. Unusually cold weather (damage) crops.

3e. Have as an Auxiliary

> Many people **have chosen** simple life-styles.
> Everyone **has limited** the use of resources.
> Some people **had encouraged** this kind of change years ago.

Read the sentences in the box. The verb phrase of each sentence is in dark type.

- What is the verb phrase in each sentence?

Like **be, have** can be used as an auxiliary in a verb phrase. The auxiliary **have** is followed by the **past participle** form of a verb. Most past participle forms end with **-n** or **-d.** A few past participle forms do not change or change in special ways.

PRACTICING LANGUAGE SKILLS

- Write only the verb phrase from each of the following sentences. Underline the auxiliary in each verb phrase.

1. Political cartoonists have criticized industrial pollution for over fifty years.
2. Some cities have improved the quality of the air.
3. In the past, such efforts had been rather unsuccessful.
4. In the 1970's, people had demanded cleaner air.
5. In the 1980's, scientists have solved some of the problems of urban pollution.
6. Private citizens, too, have contributed to the effort.
7. Even young children have studied these problems in school.
8. Older students have devised solutions in class projects.
9. In the past, only a few people had campaigned for clean air.
10. Now parents and students have organized for a better environment.
11. These efforts have given many people renewed hope.
12. In many communities, birds have returned to the trees.

■■ Add two different verb phrases to finish each of the following sentences in two different ways. First, use a present tense form of the auxiliary **have** and the past participle form of the verb in parentheses. Second, use the past tense form of the auxiliary **have** and the past participle form of the verb. Write the sentences.

1. The visit to the museum (give) me a vivid picture of our city's past.
2. I (learn) that it was founded over 200 years ago.
3. Trappers (build) the first settlement on the banks of the river.
4. Several Indian tribes (live) in the same area.
5. The settlement (grow) rapidly from its humble beginnings.
6. Many different people (contribute) to its growth.
7. Trade (cause) an increase in traffic on the river.
8. Merchants (arrive) from all parts of the country.

3f. Modals

> Reptiles **can live** only in warm climates.
> They **must have** heat for survival.
> They **will hibernate** during a cold winter.

Read the sentences in the box.

- What is the verb phrase in each sentence?
- What is the first word in each verb phrase?
- What verb form follows each of those words?

The first word in each of the verb phrases in the sentences in the box is called a **modal.** The words in the box below are all modals.

can	might	should
could	must	will
may	shall	would

A modal can be part of the verb phrase of a sentence. When it is, it is always followed by a main verb form. The main verb form that follows a modal in a verb phrase is the present tense plural form. The modal **shall** is not used as often as the other modals. **Shall** is usually used only with the subjects **I** and **we.**

PRACTICING LANGUAGE SKILLS

- Write only the verb phrase from each of the following sentences. Underline the modal in each verb phrase.

1. Certain snakes may look dangerous.
2. Some harmless snakes might resemble dangerous snakes.
3. The python and the anaconda may grow to a length of 30 feet, or 9 meters.
4. We should be very careful around snakes.
5. Some snakes would make good pets.
6. A new owner must handle a snake gently.
7. Snakes can move very rapidly.
8. Snakes will follow the scent of their prey.
9. Rattlesnakes will warn their enemies.
10. A rattling sound could indicate danger.
11. Fights between male snakes could occur during the breeding season.
12. A snake can strike accurately in the dark.
13. A snake's stomach can expand greatly.
14. A snake will swallow an animal larger than its own head.
15. Snakes can survive a long time without food.
16. Snakes may remain inactive for long periods of time.
17. Snakes in captivity might live fifteen to thirty years.
18. No snakes can hear ordinary sounds.
19. They must sense vibrations of the ground.
20. A snake will investigate its environment with its tongue.
21. A cobra's bite could kill you in a few seconds.
22. Several kinds of snakes might be useful around the house.

3g. Separated Verb Phrase Words in Declarative Sentences

> Scientists **had** rather cautiously **predicted** the appearance of a comet.
> The public **was** mistakenly **expecting** a brilliant show.
> Most observers **could** not **see** Comet Kohoutek without instruments.

Read the declarative sentences in the box.

- What is the verb phrase in each sentence?
- What word or words come between the two words of the verb phrase in each sentence?

In some declarative sentences, the words of the verb phrase are separated by one or more other words. **Not** is the word which most frequently separates the words of the verb phrase in a declarative sentence. (See **Recognizing and Using Adverbs,** page 236.)

3h. Separated Verb Phrase Words in Interrogative Sentences

> **Had** scientists **predicted** the appearance of a comet?
> **Was** the public **expecting** a brilliant show?
> **Could** most observers **see** Comet Kohoutek without instruments?

Read the interrogative sentences in the box.

- What is the verb phrase in each sentence?
- What word or words come between the two words of the verb phrase in each sentence?

In many interrogative sentences, the two words of the verb phrase are separated by one or more other words.

PRACTICING LANGUAGE SKILLS

■ Write only the two words of the verb phrase from each of the following sentences.

1. Comets have always fascinated people.
2. Have you ever seen a comet?
3. Scientists can usually predict a comet's appearance.
4. Halley's Comet has now become a regular visitor to earth.
5. People had first observed this comet before 86 B.C.
6. It will not appear again until the late 1980's.
7. Some people may superstitiously consider a comet a sign of disaster.
8. A collision between a comet and earth could indeed be destructive.
9. This would surely be an unusual occurrence, however.
10. Can comets emit light?
11. When will Comet Kohoutek appear again?

202

12. Have you ever read a science fiction story about a comet?
13. I have recently read the "The Star," by H. G. Wells.
14. You might not enjoy science fiction.
15. It has lately become a very popular form for short stories, novels, and movies.
16. A science fiction writer may sometimes predict real events.
17. At the beginning of this century, people were not yet using the term "science fiction."
18. Most people can probably guess the origin of that term.
19. Science fiction stories may often involve the exploration of space.
20. Have you ever thought about the possibilities of space travel?
21. Would you volunteer for a years-long voyage?
22. Only a few unusual people would voluntarily agree to such a trip.
23. Some very famous science fiction stories have also dealt with changes in time.
24. Can you imagine a real time machine?
25. Would you use it?
26. To what century would you travel in the time machine?

■■ Rewrite each of the following declarative sentences in two ways. The first time, add the word **not** between the two words of the verb phrase. The second time, change the order of the words in the original declarative sentence to form an interrogative sentence.

1. Most people have seen many meteors.
2. Meteors should make you nervous.
3. Most meteors will collide with the earth.
4. Those students are looking for meteors.
5. They have watched the sky every night.
6. They have recorded every sighting.
7. That meteor is leaving a long trail.
8. We can photograph it.
9. That planetarium is displaying meteorites now.
10. Chemists have analyzed those meteorites.
11. You would enjoy a trip to the planetarium.
12. The planetarium has added several other new exhibits recently.
13. The city is planning a new museum.
14. They will build it near the planetarium.
15. Many people will ride the bus to the planetarium.
16. You can walk to the new museum from there.
17. The museum will display crafts and artifacts from ancient civilizations.

APPLYING LANGUAGE SKILLS TO COMPOSITION

■ Use each of the following verb phrases in a declarative sentence. Add the word **not** between the two words of the verb phrase. Write the sentences.

1. were observing
2. may reach
3. will make
4. had found
5. might explain
6. could discover
7. must follow
8. have exploded
9. am watching

■■ Use each of the following verb phrases in an interrogative sentence. Write the sentences.

1. is explaining
2. can explore
3. have wondered
4. will reappear
5. are searching
6. has traveled
7. were using
8. have investigated
9. had seen

3i.   Do as an Auxiliary

> **Do** comic strips **portray** our society?
> Some people **did** not **recognize** comics as American folk art.
> A comic book collection **does become** valuable.

Read the sentences in the box.

- What is the verb phrase in each sentence?
- What is the first word in each verb phrase?
- What other word or words come between the two words of the verb phrases in the first two sentences?

Like **be** and **have, do** can be an auxiliary in the verb phrase of a sentence. The main verb form that follows the auxiliary **do** is the present tense plural form.

The auxiliary **do** is used only in certain situations. Usually it is used in declarative sentences with the word **not** and in some interrogative sentences. It is occasionally used for emphasis.

PRACTICING LANGUAGE SKILLS

■ Write only the two words of the verb phrase from each of the following sentences. Underline the auxiliary in each verb phrase.

1. Do you read many comic books?
2. I do not know the name of the first comic strip.
3. Does anyone remember "Mutt and Jeff"?
4. Did "Mutt and Jeff" become very popular?
5. Chester Gould did not write "Mutt and Jeff."
6. Chester Gould did create "Dick Tracy."
7. Do you read "Little Orphan Annie"?
8. Does Annie represent the children of this country?
9. Do many people worry about the influence of comic books?
10. Does any comic teach history?
11. Did some college students collect comic books?
12. Many comics did not become classics.
13. Some comics do not deal in fantasy.
14. A few comics do relate biographical stories.
15. Criticism of comic books does not lessen their popularity.
16. Readers do find comics enjoyable.

APPLYING LANGUAGE SKILLS TO COMPOSITION

■ Write an interrogative sentence you would ask about each of the following comic strip characters. Use a form of the auxiliary **do** in the verb phrase of each sentence.

1. Clark Kent
2. Dagwood
3. Lucy
4. Dennis the Menace
5. Olive Oyl
6. Snoopy
7. Popeye
8. Blondie
9. Momma

3j. Modals with the Auxiliary Be

> You **might be visiting** Alaska.
> You **would be enjoying** its spectacular scenery.

Read the sentences in the box.

- What is the verb phrase in each sentence?
- What modal is the first word in each verb phrase?
- What auxiliary follows the modal in each verb phrase?
- What main verb form follows the auxiliary in each verb phrase?

In a verb phrase, a modal may be followed by the auxiliary **be** and the present participle form of a main verb.

3k. Modals with the Auxiliary Have

> You **might have visited** Alaska.
> You **would have enjoyed** its spectacular scenery.

Read the sentences in the box.

- What is the verb phrase in each sentence?
- What modal is the first word in each verb phrase?
- What auxiliary follows the modal in each verb phrase?
- What main verb form follows the auxiliary in each verb phrase?

In a verb phrase, a modal may be followed by the auxiliary **have** and the past participle form of a main verb.

PRACTICING LANGUAGE SKILLS

- Write only the verb phrase from each of the following sentences.

1. At one time, glaciers might have covered most of North America.
2. Glaciers may be changing the earth's surface even now.
3. They might be decreasing in size each summer.
4. They may be increasing in size each winter.
5. Glaciers could be depositing debris on the land.
6. They might be creating new land formations.
7. Glaciers must have begun their retreat centuries ago.
8. People might have heard the thunderous sound of the ice.
9. Tons of glacial ice may have fallen into the bay.
10. The glaciers must have expanded during the last Ice Age.
11. The Ice Age may have caused large-scale migrations.
12. American Indians must have migrated from Asia during the Ice Age.
13. They could have crossed the Bering Straits on the solid ice.
14. Some scientists may be expecting a radical change in the climate.

3l. The Auxiliary Have **with the Auxiliary** Be

> Those detectives **have been investigating** the case.
> One detective **has been questioning** the witnesses.
> She **had been looking** for you.

Read the sentences in the box.

- What is the verb phrase in each sentence?
- What form of the auxiliary **have** is part of each verb phrase?
- What form of the auxiliary **be** follows **have** in each verb phrase?
- What main verb form is part of each verb phrase?

In a verb phrase, the auxiliary **have** may be followed by **been,** the past participle form of the auxiliary **be. Been** is followed by the present participle form of a main verb.

3m. Modals **with the Auxiliary** Have **and the Auxiliary** Be

> Those detectives **may have been investigating** the case.
> One detective **should have been questioning** the witnesses.
> She **might have been looking** for you.

Read the sentences in the box.

- What is the verb phrase in each sentence?
- What modal is the first word in each verb phrase?
- What form of the auxiliary **have** follows the modal in each verb phrase?
- What form of the auxiliary **be** follows **have** in each verb phrase?
- What main verb form is part of each verb phrase?

In a verb phrase, a modal may be followed by the auxiliary **have. Have** is followed by **been,** the past participle form of the auxiliary **be. Been** is followed by the present participle form of a main verb.

PRACTICING LANGUAGE SKILLS

■ Write only the verb phrase from each of the following sentences.

1. The secret agent had been feeling nervous for several days.
2. She had been hearing footsteps behind her.
3. Someone might have been following her.
4. An enemy could have been watching all her activities.
5. Perhaps another agent had been talking too much.
6. The agent had been hearing strange noises on her telephone, too.
7. Somebody might have been listening to her conversations.
8. She has been worrying all day about these sounds.

9. She should have been concentrating on her work.
10. She may have been imagining everything.
11. Perhaps she has been reading too many novels about secret agents.
12. The characters in those novels may have been stimulating her imagination.

■■ Finish each of the following sentences by adding a verb phrase. Use a form of the auxiliary **have, been,** and the present participle form of the verb in parentheses.

1. Arlo (work) on this puzzle for eighteen months.
2. He (consider) all the possible solutions.
3. He (ask) his friends for advice.
4. His friends (study) the puzzle with him.
5. They (make) suggestions.
6. Arlo's parents (worry) about him.
7. They (try) to interest Arlo in other activities.
8. Arlo (ignore) their suggestions.
9. He (spend) all his time on the puzzle.
10. He (lose) sleep.
11. He (concentrate) on nothing else.
12. Arlo's teachers (wonder) about the importance of the puzzle.
13. They (encourage) him to pay more attention to his classes.
14. Fortunately, Arlo (make) good progress with the puzzle recently.
15. His work (near) an end.

■■■ Finish each of the following sentences by adding a verb phrase. Use a modal, **have, been,** and the present participle form of the verb in parentheses.

1. The stranger (wear) a wrinkled trenchcoat.
2. He (lurk) around that corner.
3. He (watch) us.
4. His accomplice (listen) to our conversation.
5. They (record) our words.
6. The stranger (send) messages to somebody else.
7. They (gather) information about our project.
8. We (guard) the laboratory more carefully.
9. Other people (watch) our laboratory.
10. They (observe) our work for a long time.
11. We (act) more cautiously.
12. We (post) guards at every door.
13. The enemies of the project (use) the information against us.
14. Those people (attempt) to stop the work on our secret project.
15. The people in charge of the project (listen) to our enemies.
16. They (prepare) to withdraw their support of the project.

APPLYING LANGUAGE SKILLS TO COMPOSITION

■ Use each of the following verb phrases in a sentence. Write the sentences.

1. has been looking
2. have been reading
3. had been considering
4. may have been thinking
5. might have been going
6. must have been talking
7. could have been watching
8. should have been listening
9. have been asking
10. would have been smiling
11. might have been waiting
12. should have been attending
13. had been hoping
14. has been rushing

3n. Verb Tenses

Tense	Examples	Verb Forms
present	know, knows	present tense plural form, present tense singular form
past	knew	past tense form
future	will know, shall know	modal **will** or **shall** + present tense plural form
present perfect	have known, has known	present tense form of auxiliary **have** + past participle verb form
past perfect	had known	past tense form of auxiliary **have** + past participle verb form
future perfect	will have known, shall have known	modal **will** or **shall** + auxiliary **have** + past participle verb form

Read the chart above. It shows the six verb tenses. Verb tenses are used to express differences in time.

- What are the names of the six tenses?
- What are the six tenses of the verb **know**?

Follow the examples in the chart to form the tenses of other verbs.

- What are the six tenses of the verb **like**?
- What are the six tenses of the verb **think**?

Verbs in the present tense are used to express action or existence that occurs in the present or that is repeated habitually.

Only three people **know** the secret.
Sulla always **knows** what to do.

Verbs in the past tense are used to express action or existence that occurred in the past and is not occurring in the present.

I **knew** the address yesterday, but now I can't remember it.

Verbs in the future tense are used to express action or existence that will occur in the future.

We **shall know** the answer tomorrow.

Verbs in the present perfect tense are used to express action or existence that occurred in the past or that occurred in the past and continues into the present.

> I **have known** several honest people in my life.
> Harry **has known** that joke for more than five years.

Verbs in the past perfect tense are used to express action or existence that occurred in the past before some other event.

> No one **had known** about the party until you mentioned it.

Verbs in the future perfect tense are used to express action or existence that will be completed in the future before some other event.

> By the time they graduate from high school, they **will have known** each other for fifteen years.

PRACTICING LANGUAGE SKILLS

■ Write each verb or verb phrase from the following sentences. (Some sentences have more than one verb or verb phrase.) Then write the name that identifies the tense of the verb.

1. Monica understood every word in the poem.
2. They speak both Spanish and English.
3. Randall will help the beginners.
4. Before the cake exploded, nothing unusual had happened.
5. Crystal has worked in the library since September.
6. Angel will arrive in Dallas tomorrow night.
7. I shall drive him to the airport.
8. You have already postponed the meeting three times.
9. By the time summer ends, we will have run a total of two hundred miles.
10. Carmine had already left when we arrived.
11. Terrance did his best work.
12. Emily raises hamsters and gerbils.
13. Until the telegram arrived, nobody had suspected anything.
14. This bus stops at every corner between the beach and downtown.
15. Danielle waited patiently.
16. The class has studied fractions and decimals.
17. I had changed my plans before I heard from you.
18. Joe will meet you at the theater.
19. By the time Miss Castenega arrives, we will have completed the project.
20. We always keep the scissors in that drawer.
21. By the end of December, I will have earned more than three hundred dollars.
22. Will you really earn that much?
23. I have calculated everything down to the last cent.
24. I had a similar job last winter.
25. Before I began this job, I had been a baby-sitter for two years.
26. Next summer I will work on the clean-up crew at the beach.
27. You certainly work hard!
28. For several years, we have planned a trip to Alaska.
29. My mother had thought about the trip for months before she told me about it.

30. Progressive Verb Tenses

Tense	Examples	Verb Forms
present progressive	am talking, is talking, are talking	present tense form of auxiliary **be** + present participle verb form
past progressive	was talking were talking	past tense form of auxiliary **be** + present participle verb form
future progressive	will be talking, shall be talking	modal **will** or **shall** + auxiliary **be** + present participle verb form
present perfect progressive	have been talking, has been talking	present tense form of auxiliary **have** + **been** + present participle verb form
past perfect progressive	had been talking	past tense form of auxiliary **have** + **been** + present participle verb form
future perfect progressive	will have been talking, shall have been talking	modal **will** or **shall** + **have** + **been** + present participle verb form

Read the chart above. It shows the progressive forms of the six verb tenses. The progressive form of each tense is used to show continuing action or existence.

- What are the six progressive tenses of the verb **talk**?
- What are the six progressive tenses of the verb **like**?
- What are the six progressive tenses of the verb **think**?

Progressive verb tenses **are usually used to express continuing action or existence in the past, present, or future.**

PRACTICING LANGUAGE SKILLS

■ Write each verb or verb phrase from the following sentences. (Some sentences have more than one verb or verb phrase.) Then write the name that identifies the tense of the verb.

1. Corliss has been wondering about your question.
2. Joshua is waiting for your answer.
3. Nobody had been listening.
4. On November 14th, I shall have been living in this apartment for eight years.
5. Artis is looking for it.
6. Mr. Feingold had been working there for twenty years before he retired.
7. I shall be looking for you.
8. They have been talking on the phone for more than an hour.

9. Jamie has been asking about you.
10. Anya was studying.
11. I am baking two loaves of bread for the dinner party.
12. Dara, Penny, and Stu were swimming in the Pacific Ocean.
13. Marty will be driving four of us to camp every day.
14. In December, you will have been living at college for four months.
15. The members of the drama club are preparing for the school play.
16. Moira is studying at the library.
17. Charley is waiting for a bus.
18. The Jeffersons had been planning their Hawaiian vacation for three months.
19. The soccer team has been practicing every afternoon.
20. He will be buying his plane ticket at the airport.
21. I shall be meeting him in Chicago.
22. You are drinking your milk too noisily.
23. Lightning was flashing, and thunder was crashing.
24. The baby has been crying for several minutes.
25. They will be leaving for the movie at six o'clock.
26. I have been looking for you all afternoon.
27. I am shopping for a present for my sister.
28. The boys have been asking for a puppy.
29. We will be learning a new language this year.
30. I have been dieting for three weeks.
31. I have been losing weight steadily.
32. People have been remarking on my weight loss.

■■ Complete each of the following sentences by adding a progressive tense form of the verb in parentheses. Write the sentences.

1. Sally (play) softball for the past three months.
2. The birds (fly) south very soon.
3. She (rest) now.
4. They (play) tennis before the storm.
5. They (ride) their bicycles to school from now on.
6. I (perform) in tomorrow's concert.
7. The musicians (rehearse) until lunch time.
8. The contestants (compete) for valuable prizes.
9. The train (arrive) in less than an hour.
10. She (study) Spanish since ninth grade.
11. You (disturb) my concentration with all that noise.
12. We (wait) for your call.
13. John (explore) that cave with his brother.
14. She (save) her allowance for a catcher's mitt.
15. Kelly (call) you tomorrow or the next day.
16. They (watch) television last night.
17. It (rain) for two and a half days.
18. The water (boil).
19. They (ask) many questions.
20. I (visit) New York next month.
21. The store (close) in ten minutes.
22. They (watch) his progress with interest.
23. The movie company (film) on our street all next week.
24. The candidate (issue) a statement on that subject tomorrow.
25. She (jog) each morning.
26. The wind (howl) all night.
27. Our branch store (open) next month.
28. We (look) for a larger apartment.
29. The play (end) soon.
30. That dog (bark) for the past fifteen minutes.

211

3p. Sentences with Passive Verb Phrases

> The director **chooses** the cast.
> The cast **is chosen** by the director.

> The writer **has revised** the script.
> The script **has been revised** by the writer.

Read the sentences in the first box.

- What is the subject of the first sentence?
- What is the verb in the first sentence?
- What is the subject of the second sentence?
- What is the verb phrase in the second sentence?
- What is the auxiliary in the verb phrase?
- What main verb form is part of the verb phrase?

Read the sentences in the second box.

- What is the subject of the first sentence?
- What is the verb phrase in the first sentence?
- What is the auxiliary in the verb phrase?
- What is the subject of the second sentence?
- What is the verb phrase in the second sentence?
- What are the two auxiliaries in the verb phrase?
- What main verb form is part of the verb phrase in both sentences?

The first verb or verb phrase in each box is in the **active voice.** An active verb tells what the subject does or did.

The verb phrase in the second sentence in each box is in the **passive voice. A passive verb phrase tells what is done or was done to the subject.** Every passive verb phrase contains a form of the auxiliary **be** and the past participle form of a main verb. When the passive verb phrase refers to an action in the past, the verb phrase contains a form of the auxiliary **have.** In a passive verb phrase, a form of **have** is followed by the past participle form of **be** and by the past participle form of the main verb.

When the auxiliary **be** occurs in active verb phrases, it is followed by the present participle form of the main verb.

> She **is playing** the game.

Only when the auxiliary **be** is followed by the past participle form of the main verb is the verb phrase passive.

> The game **is played** with a net.

The passive voice is wordier and less forceful than the active voice. You should use the passive voice only occasionally, when you want to emphasize to whom or to what something was done.

PRACTICING LANGUAGE SKILLS

■ Read the following sentences. Write only the sentences that have passive verb phrases. Underline the passive verb phrase in each sentence you write.

1. That movie was seen by millions of people.
2. Audiences around the world are enjoying it.
3. Elaborate sets were built for the film.
4. The sets were designed by Thom Wronka.
5. An unusual location was selected for the outdoor scenes.
6. The entire crew traveled to the location.
7. The outdoor scenes were filmed by a special camera crew.
8. Sketches were submitted by the costume designer.
9. Suggestions were made for changes in the costumes.
10. The final sketches were approved.
11. The cast had rehearsed that scene many times.
12. No mistakes were made.
13. Several technicians were processing the film.
14. Two reels were lost by accident.
15. Retakes were ordered by the director.
16. Perhaps the actors had given better performances the first time.
17. The producer was becoming nervous at the tight schedule.

■■ Finish each of the following sentences by adding a passive verb phrase. Use a form of the auxiliary **be** and the past participle form of a main verb.

1. The script |||||||||||||| by a talented author.
2. Suggestions |||||||||||||| by several of her friends.
3. Most of the suggestions |||||||||||||| by the writer.
4. The script |||||||||||||| by the writer's agent.
5. Then it |||||||||||||| to the film studios.
6. The script |||||||||||||| by a major studio.
7. The story |||||||||||||| by people at the studio.
8. The writer |||||||||||||| with her script.
9. Preparations |||||||||||||| for the film.
10. A young man |||||||||||||| to direct.
11. Although young, he |||||||||||||| much responsibility.
12. The cast |||||||||||||| by the writer, the director, and the producer.

APPLYING LANGUAGE SKILLS TO COMPOSITION

■ Use each of the following passive verb phrases in a sentence. Write the sentences.

1. am pleased
2. is offered
3. are arranged
4. was delivered
5. were suggested
6. has been made
7. have been tried
8. had been written
9. was shown

213

3q. Subjunctive Form of Be

> You **are** not our representative.
> If you **were** our representative, for whom would you vote?

> I **am** not voting.
> If I **were** voting, I would vote for Dana.

Read the pair of sentences in each box.

- What form of **be** is used in the first sentence in each box?
- What form of **be** is used in the second sentence in each box?
- With what word does the second sentence in each box begin?

The second sentence in each box includes a special form of the verb **be.** This form is called the **subjunctive form.**

The most common subjunctive form of **be** is **were.** This form is used with all subjects. It is used as a main verb or as an auxiliary in a verb phrase.

The subjunctive form of **be** is used only in special circumstances to show conditions contrary to fact. For that reason, the subjunctive form of **be** is used most often in groups of words following **if.** (See **Adverb Clauses,** page 304.)

Read the two sentences in the box below.

- In which sentence is the subjunctive form of **be** used?

> If Lee **is** going to the show, we can go with him.
> If Lee **were** going to the show, we could go with him.

The subjunctive form of **be** is not always used in groups of words after **if.** The form of **be** in the first sentence shows that Lee may or may not go to the show. The subjunctive form of **be** in the second sentence shows that Lee has already decided not to go to the show. It shows a condition contrary to fact.

PRACTICING LANGUAGE SKILLS

■ Read the following sentences. Write only the sentences that have the subjunctive form of **be.** Underline the subjunctive form of **be** in each sentence you write.

1. If Shelly were sixteen, she would be allowed to drive.
2. Because it is raining, we will have to eat inside.
3. If this movie were funny, I would be laughing.
4. If it were sunny, we could eat outdoors.
5. If the store were open now, we could buy the other ingredients right away.
6. If the snow were not so deep, the bus could travel safely on this road.

7. Unless the snowplows clear this road, nobody will be able to use it.
8. If Dr. Tseng were here, she would help us.
9. If Marla is ready, we can leave.
10. If the instructions for this model were clear, it would not be so difficult to assemble the parts.
11. Although Derek is reading the instructions carefully, he does not understand them.
12. If the salary were higher, Ms. Cajigas would accept the job.
13. If the radio were on, I would be unable to concentrate on my homework.
14. Although the television was on, no one was watching it.
15. If the trains were not running, many people would be unable to get to work.
16. If I were wrong, I would admit it.
17. If Eduardo were in your place, he would do the same thing.
18. When Hank is in charge, he can make that decision.
19. If you were really concerned, you would offer to help.
20. If Jorge were directing the play, the cast would be better prepared.
21. If it were not so late, we could start the next project right away.

APPLYING LANGUAGE SKILLS TO COMPOSITION

■ Add a group of words to finish each of the following sentences. Use the subjunctive form of **be** in each sentence. Write the sentences.

1. If |||||||||||||||| , everyone would be happier.
2. If |||||||||||||||| , we could be swimming in the lake now.
3. If |||||||||||||||| , the project would be simpler.
4. If |||||||||||||||| , he would advise us.
5. If |||||||||||||||| , she could answer that question.
6. If |||||||||||||||| , you would understand them.
7. If |||||||||||||||| , I would follow the instructions.
8. If |||||||||||||||| , it would be over now.
9. If |||||||||||||||| , I would give it back to him.
10. If |||||||||||||||| , we would have no difficulty with it at all.
11. If only |||||||||||||||| , she would be extremely happy.
12. If |||||||||||||||| , I would enjoy my summer job more.
13. If |||||||||||||||| , I would go with you.
14. If |||||||||||||||| , she would probably tell you to wipe your feet.
15. If |||||||||||||||| , he would not feel so tired.
16. If only |||||||||||||||| , we could relax for a change!
17. If |||||||||||||||| , I would be happy to deliver it.
18. If |||||||||||||||| , we could begin work soon.
19. If |||||||||||||||| , anything could happen.
20. If |||||||||||||||| , I would take it to the veterinarian.
21. If |||||||||||||||| , I would sweep the kitchen floor.
22. If |||||||||||||||| , she would probably buy a new one.
23. If |||||||||||||||| , you could have it.
24. If |||||||||||||||| , I would be very pleased to accept it.
25. If |||||||||||||||| , everyone would say that it was a mistake.
26. If |||||||||||||||| , everyone would be listening to it.
27. If |||||||||||||||| , she would show us how to use those machines.
28. If |||||||||||||||| , the plane would already be in the air.
29. If |||||||||||||||| , I would not try to answer all those questions.

Reviewing   3   Verbs

3a. Recognizing and Using Verbs

Finish each of the following sentences by adding a present tense form of the verb in parentheses. Write the sentences.

1. Marisa (study) engineering.
2. She (design) satellites in class.
3. Her parents (encourage) her ambitions.

3b. Past Tense Verb Forms

Finish each of the following sentences by adding a past tense form of the verb in parentheses. Write the sentences.

4. We all (go) to the beach on the Fourth of July.
5. We (grill) hamburgers and corn on the cob.
6. Beautiful fireworks (explode) in the evening sky.

3c. Forms of Be

Finish each of the following sentences by adding a present or past tense form of the verb **be.** Write the sentences.

7. Mary Cassatt, born in 1845, |||||||||||||||| a famous American artist.
8. Her birthplace |||||||||||||||| Pittsburgh.
9. The subjects of many of her paintings |||||||||||||||| mothers and children.

3d. Be as an Auxiliary

Add a verb phrase to finish each of the following sentences. Use either a present or past tense form of the auxiliary **be** and the present participle form of the verb in parentheses. Write the sentences.

10. Technology (advance) rapidly.
11. It (solve) many problems.
12. Some technological advances (create) new problems.

3e. Have as an Auxiliary

Add a verb phrase to finish each of the following sentences. Use either a present or past tense form of the auxiliary **have** and the past participle form of the verb in parentheses. Write the sentences.

13. We (call) you all week.
14. Joe (ask) everyone about you.
15. No one (see) you.
16. It (be) in the shop.
17. Nothing (arrive) yet.

3f. Modals

Add a modal to complete the verb phrase of each of the following sentences. Write the sentences.

18. We |||||||||||||||| give a party.
19. I |||||||||||||||| invite the guests.
20. You |||||||||||||||| decorate the room.
21. Everyone |||||||||||||||| have a good time.

Write the following sentences. Draw a line under the two words of each verb phrase.

3g. Separated Verb Phrase Words in Declarative Sentences

22. We had never seen anything like it.
23. I should not leave until three o'clock.
24. They are definitely arriving tomorrow.
25. You will never guess the answer.
26. We are not leaving yet.

3h. Separated Verb Phrase Words in Interrogative Sentences

27. Will the Service Club sponsor a fair?
28. Has Cynthia finished her report?
29. Is Kevin watching a news program?
30. Are the buses running on schedule?
31. Would you like another sandwich?

3i. Do as an Auxiliary

Change each of the following declarative sentences to an interrogative sentence. Use a form of the auxiliary **do** in each new verb phrase. Write the sentences.

32. Henry writes a music column for the school paper.
33. The reporters give their articles to the editor.
34. The editor needed two more items.

Write the following sentences. Draw a line under the three words of each verb phrase.

3j. Modals with the Auxiliary Be

35. We could be relaxing in the warm sun.
36. They might be swimming in the lake.
37. The tourists will be enjoying a mild climate.

3k. Modals with the Auxiliary Have

38. The package should have arrived by now.
39. Kurt must have forgotten the address.
40. He might have sent it to our old house.

3l. The Auxiliary Have with the Auxiliary Be

41. I have been watching the news on television each evening.
42. One reporter has been covering local government.
43. The ratings had been rising steadily.

3m. Modals with the Auxiliary Have and the Auxiliary Be

Finish each of the following sentences by adding a verb phrase. Use a modal, **have, been,** and the present participle form of the verb in parentheses. Write the sentences.

44. Paul (work) late last night.

45. The dogs (bark) while we were gone.
46. They (wait) for over two hours.

Write each verb or verb phrase from the following sentences. (Some sentences have more than one verb or verb phrase.) Then write the name that identifies the tense of the verb.

3n. Verb Tenses

47. They will return this evening.
48. Hana had visited us once before.
49. I exercise every other morning.

3o. Progressive Verb Tenses

50. Nikki had been studying for three hours before she took a break.
51. We were looking all over for you!
52. My parents will have been living in Alaska for sixteen years when September comes.

3p. Sentences with Passive Verb Phrases

Finish each of the following sentences by adding a passive verb phrase. Use a form of the auxiliary **be** and the past participle form of a main verb.

53. The diamonds |||||||||||||||| in Africa.
54. The largest diamond |||||||||||||||| to the bidder.
55. The diamond mine |||||||||||||||| by a small company.

3q. Subjunctive Form of Be

Add a group of words to finish each of the following sentences. Use the subjunctive form of **be** in each sentence. Write the sentences.

56. If |||||||||||||||| , we could start the rehearsal.
57. If |||||||||||||||| , I would build a snow castle.
58. If |||||||||||||||| , he would certainly answer the phone.

4 Nouns

4a. Recognizing and Using Nouns

> Three famous **entomologists** attended the **meeting**.
> Unusual **insects** are being displayed in the **mall**.
> The **beauty** of this **insect** amazes many **people**.

Read the sentences in the box.

- What words are in dark type?
- What does each of those words name?
- Which word in dark type is used in two different forms?

The words in dark type, and others like them, are called **nouns**

Nouns are naming words. A noun may name a person, a place, a thing, an event, or an idea.

Most nouns have two forms. The **singular form** of a noun means "one." The **plural form** of a noun means "more than one."

PRACTICING LANGUAGE SKILLS

■ Write only the nouns from each of the following sentences. After each noun, write **singular** or **plural** to identify its form.

1. Insects are found throughout the world.
2. All insects have six legs.
3. Some common insects are the bee, the ant, the butterfly, and the ladybug.
4. Spiders are not insects.
5. Every spider has eight legs.
6. Butterflies display brilliant colors.
7. A fly has a tongue like a sponge.
8. Bees and ants often live in groups.
9. In these colonies, each member has a special job.
10. Natural defenses take the place of strength.

■■ Finish the following sentences by adding a noun in each blank space. Write the sentences.

1. The |||||||||||| devoured the |||||||||||| .
2. The |||||||||||| flew around the |||||||||||| .
3. A |||||||||||| was eating some |||||||||||| .
4. The |||||||||||| buzzed around the |||||||||||| .
5. Some |||||||||||| and some |||||||||||| were blooming in the |||||||||||| .
6. Certain |||||||||||| may be harmful to other |||||||||||| .
7. A |||||||||||| has landed on your |||||||||||| .
8. The |||||||||||| of those |||||||||||| are very colorful.
9. The |||||||||||| noticed two large |||||||||||| on its |||||||||||| .

APPLYING LANGUAGE SKILLS TO COMPOSITION

■ Use each of the following nouns in a sentence. Write the sentences.

1. butterflies 3. ladybug 5. bee 7. fleas
2. ants 4. firefly 6. moths 8. cricket

4b. Proper Nouns and Common Nouns

> There are **museums** in many **cities.**
> The **Brooklyn Museum** is in **New York City.**

Read the sentences in the box.

- What nouns are in each sentence?
- In which sentence do the nouns name particular places?

A noun that names a particular person, place, thing, event, or idea is called a proper noun. Each important word in a proper noun begins with a capital letter.

Nouns that do not name particular people, places, things, events, or ideas are called common nouns

PRACTICING LANGUAGE SKILLS

■ Write only the nouns from each of the following sentences. After each noun, write **proper** or **common** to identify which kind of noun it is.

1. New York City has many museums.
2. The works of painters and sculptors are exhibited in the Museum of Modern Art.
3. Pablo Picasso was the most famous painter of this century.
4. Picasso was born in Spain and lived in France.
5. His works can be seen in museums throughout the world.
6. The American Museum of Natural History has exhibits of dinosaurs and other extinct animals.
7. Baskets and pottery made by the Indians of North America and South America are also displayed.
8. One special part of the museum is the Hayden Planetarium.
9. Emma goes to the planetarium often.

■■ Finish the following sentences by adding a proper noun in each blank space. Write the sentences.

1. |||||||||||||| visited |||||||||||||||| in |||||||||||||||| .
2. They saw |||||||||||||||| and |||||||||||||||| .
3. |||||||||||||| came all the way from |||||||||||||| to see them.
4. Those students are reading novels by |||||||||||||||| and |||||||||||||| .
5. They have also studied the plays of |||||||||||||||| and |||||||||||||| .
6. |||||||||||||| and |||||||||||||||| are among their favorite books.
7. The members of that class are studying the art of |||||||||||||||| .

APPLYING LANGUAGE SKILLS TO COMPOSITION

■ Think of a proper noun to use in place of each of the following common nouns. Use each of your proper nouns in a sentence. Write the sentences.

1. museum
2. artist
3. holiday
4. country
5. state
6. city
7. friend
8. teacher

4c.   Gerunds

Ramon **is swimming.**
Swimming is good exercise.
Ramon enjoys **swimming.**

Read the sentences in the box.

- What present participle is part of the verb phrase in the first sentence?
- What noun is the subject of the second sentence?
- What noun in the third sentence names the activity Ramon enjoys?

The present participle verb form **swimming** is part of all three sentences in the box. In the first sentence, it is the main verb form in the verb phrase. In the second and third sentences, however, **swimming** is used as a noun. **A present participle verb form that is used as a noun is called a** gerund

PRACTICING LANGUAGE SKILLS

■ Write only the gerund from each of the following sentences.

1. Competing is important for athletes.
2. Many track stars excel in running.
3. Sprinting requires strong muscles and good concentration.
4. Correct breathing is an essential part of any exercise.
5. Jogging has become very popular.
6. Marathon runners must learn pacing.
7. Relaxing helps the runner conserve needed energy.
8. Hurdling is a specialized track event.
9. Competitors in this event must practice jumping.
10. The shouting of the fans encourages the racers.

■■ Finish each of the following sentences by adding a gerund. Write the sentences.

1. Those athletes enjoy ||||||||||||||| .
2. ||||||||||||||| does not tire them.
3. The coach helps each competitor with her ||||||||||||||| .
4. ||||||||||||||| is good for almost everyone.
5. That athlete is proud of her ||||||||||||||| .
6. He excels in ||||||||||||||| .
7. The fans like ||||||||||||||| .
8. ||||||||||||||| before a game is beneficial for an athlete.

APPLYING LANGUAGE SKILLS TO COMPOSITION

■ Write five sentences about a sport you enjoy. Use a different gerund in each sentence. You may choose your gerunds from the box below.

skating	exercising	spinning
diving	turning	running
skiing	concentrating	jumping

4d. Infinitives as Nouns

> This ballet company **will succeed.**
> **To succeed** is the hope of all ballet companies.
> This ballet company has begun **to succeed.**

Read the sentences in the box.

- What verb form is part of the verb phrase in the first sentence?
- What pair of words is the subject of the second sentence?
- What pair of words in the third sentence names the activity that the ballet company has begun?

The verb form **succeed** is part of all three sentences in the box. In the first sentence, it is the main verb form in the verb phrase. In the second and third sentences, **succeed** follows the word **to. The pair of words, to and a verb form, is called an** infinitive. Infinitives may be used as nouns in sentences. In both the second and third sentences in the box, the infinitive **to succeed** is used as a noun.

PRACTICING LANGUAGE SKILLS

■ From each of the following sentences, write only the infinitive that is used as a noun.

1. Every serious dancer wants to perform.
2. To train requires energy and determination.
3. To improve is the goal of each dancer.
4. To practice may sometimes seem impossible.
5. To perform means even more physical and mental pressure.

■■ Finish each of the following sentences by adding an infinitive used as a noun. Write the sentences.

1. Every performer wants ⅠⅠⅠⅠⅠⅠⅠⅠⅠⅠⅠⅠⅠ .
2. ⅠⅠⅠⅠⅠⅠⅠⅠⅠⅠⅠⅠⅠ is a necessary part of the daily routine.
3. ⅠⅠⅠⅠⅠⅠⅠⅠⅠⅠⅠⅠⅠ can sometimes be extremely difficult.
4. Throughout their professional lives, they must continue ⅠⅠⅠⅠⅠⅠⅠⅠⅠⅠⅠⅠⅠ .
5. ⅠⅠⅠⅠⅠⅠⅠⅠⅠⅠⅠⅠⅠ is a fear of all performers.
6. ⅠⅠⅠⅠⅠⅠⅠⅠⅠⅠⅠⅠⅠ can lessen some of the disappointments.

APPLYING LANGUAGE SKILLS TO COMPOSITION

■ Write five sentences about one kind of dancing. Use a different infinitive as the subject of each sentence. You may choose your infinitives from the box below.

to train	to perform	to watch	to obey	to move
to learn	to applaud	to study	to turn	to relax
to practice	to listen	to teach	to leap	to bow

5 Pronouns

5a. Recognizing and Using Personal Pronouns

> **Diana** was the Roman goddess of the moon.
> **She** also ruled over forests and animals.
> Beautiful temples were built for **her.**

Read the sentences in the box.

- What word in the second sentence replaces **Diana**?
- What word in the third sentence replaces **Diana**?

Words such as **she** and **her** are called **personal pronouns.**

Personal pronouns are words that can take the place of nouns or of groups of words that include nouns.

Personal pronouns have more than one form. The form of a pronoun depends upon how the pronoun is used in a sentence. In the sentences in the box above, **she** and **her** are two different forms of the same personal pronoun. Two forms of personal pronouns are listed in the boxes below.

Subject Form Pronouns:	I	you	he	she	it	we	they
Object Form Pronouns:	me	you	him	her	it	us	them

A personal pronoun usually refers to the noun it replaces. That noun is called the **antecedent** of the pronoun. In the sentences in the box above, for example, the proper noun **Diana** is the antecedent of the personal pronoun form **she** and of the personal pronoun form **her.**

PRACTICING LANGUAGE SKILLS

■ Read the following pairs of sentences. For each pair, write the personal pronoun form or forms from the second sentence. Then find each pronoun's antecedent in the first sentence. After each personal pronoun, write the noun that is its antecedent.

1. The mythical city of Asgard stood high on a mountain in the sky. It was the home of the Norse gods and goddesses.
2. Odin was the father of the gods. He ruled over lesser gods and humans.
3. Frigg was married to Odin. She ruled the goddesses.
4. From the mountain top, Odin observed the people on the earth below. He wished them well.
5. Odin could also see the Jotuns. They were giants who wanted to destroy the people of earth.
6. Loki was an evil god. He was the son of a giant.
7. Odin had two ravens. They flew to earth and brought him back great knowledge.
8. Most people have heard of Thor, Odin's oldest son. According to myth, he was the god of thunder and lightning.

9. Balder was Thor's younger brother. He was the god of goodness and harmony.
10. Thor had great strength, even for a god. He was also extremely bad-tempered.
11. Thor carried a magic hammer. It always returned to Thor's hand.
12. One day, Thrym, the giant king, stole the hammer. "Before the hammer is returned, Freyja must marry me," Thrym declared.
13. Thor visited Freyja. He was unable to convince her to marry Thrym.
14. Then Thor had an idea. "I will dress as Freyja and fool Thrym," Thor decided.
15. In bridal clothes, Thor returned to Thrym's palace. He quickly recovered the stolen hammer.
16. Thrym was fooled. Thor killed him before the trick was discovered.

■■ Write the second sentence from each of the following pairs. Finish the sentence by adding a subject form pronoun. Choose the pronoun that will agree with the antecedent in dark type.

1. Greek mythology tells of **King Midas,** who was a powerful ruler. |||||||||||||| was also a very foolish person.
2. King Midas gave an elaborate **feast.** |||||||||||||| lasted several days.
3. The god **Dionysus** was pleased by the feast. |||||||||||||| granted Midas one wish.
4. Midas was sure of his **wish.** |||||||||||||| was for the power to turn all he touched into gold.
5. Midas touched some nearby **leaves.** |||||||||||||| changed into gold.
6. Midas ran excitedly around his garden, touching all the **flowers.** |||||||||||||| immediately turned into gold.
7. At first, **King Midas** was delighted with the results of his wish. Soon |||||||||||||| would be the wealthiest man in the world.
8. He quickly learned to regret his **wish,** however. |||||||||||||| began to cause him terrible difficulties.
9. The king sat down to dinner and touched his **food.** |||||||||||||| became inedible gold.
10. His beautiful **daughter,** whom Midas loved dearly, ran to kiss him. When they touched, |||||||||||||| became a golden statue.
11. **Midas** was inconsolable. |||||||||||||| prayed that he could lead a normal life again.
12. **Dionysus** heard the king's prayer. |||||||||||||| decided to end Midas' sorrow.
13. "Wash your hands in the **river,"** Dionysus instructed Midas. "|||||||||||||| will take the power of your wish from you."
14. **Midas** did as Dionysus had told him. Immediately, everything |||||||||||||| had touched just a short time before became alive again.
15. Once the god **Apollo** was angry with Midas. |||||||||||||| gave the king a pair of donkey's ears.
16. Midas hid his **ears** from everybody. |||||||||||||| could not be concealed from his barber, however.
17. The **barber** dug a hole in the ground. Into it |||||||||||||| whispered the secret.

APPLYING LANGUAGE SKILLS TO COMPOSITION

■ Write five sentences about a wish you might make. Use a different personal pronoun form in each sentence.

5b. Possessive Pronoun Forms

> We are looking for **our** dog.   Is this dog **yours**?
> Have you lost **your** dog?   That dog is **ours**.

Read the sentences in the box.

- What word in each sentence shows possession?
- Which possessive words are followed by a noun?
- Which possessive words are not followed by a noun?

Personal pronoun forms such as **our, ours, your,** and **yours** are called
possessive pronouns. Possessive pronoun forms can be used before
nouns in sentences, or they can be used alone in sentences. The
possessive pronoun forms in the first box below are used before nouns.
The possessive pronoun forms in the second box do not come before nouns.

my	your	his	her	its	our	their
mine	yours	his	hers	its	ours	theirs

PRACTICING LANGUAGE SKILLS

■ Write only the possessive pronoun forms from the following sentences.

1. Many people choose their pets for emotional reasons.
2. This dog has been my friend for years.
3. That sheep dog is hers.
4. Which of these puppies is yours?
5. Animals often warn their owners of danger.
6. One woman claimed that a pet bird saved her life.
7. Most pets are sensitive to their environment and its changes.
8. Does your pet act strangely before a storm?
9. Ours can sleep through anything.
10. Some people enter their dogs in shows.
11. Our dog likes cats.
12. My friend has a parrot that talks.
13. Its favorite word is "hello."
14. Yesterday, Lucy found two frogs in her garden.
15. The frogs hopped out of her yard and into mine.

■■ Finish each of the following sentences by adding a possessive
pronoun. Write the sentences.

1. We are teaching ||||||||||||||| pets to obey.
2. You should bring ||||||||||||||| dog to the next training session.
3. Allana is very pleased with the progress of ||||||||||||||| pet.
4. The best-trained dogs in the class are ||||||||||||||| and ||||||||||||||| .
5. That puppy under the chair is ||||||||||||||| .
6. It does not always obey ||||||||||||||| commands.
7. That huge dog is wagging ||||||||||||||| tail.
8. Three dogs are following ||||||||||||||| owners across the room.
9. ||||||||||||||| dog doesn't seem to be responding very well to training.
10. Whenever the trainer approaches, one dog rolls over on ||||||||||||||| back.

5c. Indefinite Pronouns

> Jay found the key. **He** had left it in the lock.
> Jay found the key. **Somebody** had left it in the lock.

Read the sentence pairs in the box. The words in dark type are two different kinds of pronouns.

- Which pronoun refers to a specific person?
- Which pronoun does not refer to a specific person?

Pronouns such as **somebody** that do not refer to specific persons or things are called **indefinite pronouns.** The words in the box below can all be indefinite pronouns. (Some of the words in the box can also be used as adjectives. See **Adjectives, Indefinite Pronouns, and Demonstrative Pronouns,** page 232.)

all	each	most	others
another	either	neither	several
any	everybody	nobody	some
anybody	everyone	none	somebody
anyone	everything	no one	someone
anything	few	nothing	something
both	many	one	such

PRACTICING LANGUAGE SKILLS

- Write only the indefinite pronouns from the following sentences.

1. The mimes waved to everybody in the theater audience.
2. One took an imaginary ball from an imaginary closet.
3. She tossed the ball to somebody else on the stage.
4. As hard as they tried, no one could catch the ball.
5. Someone even tripped over the imaginary ball.
6. Another tripped over her own feet.
7. Everything seemed to be going wrong for the performers.
8. Everyone in the audience watched them closely.
9. Most were amused by the mimes.

■■ Finish each of the following sentences by adding an indefinite pronoun. Write the sentences.

1. |||||||||||||| had completed the research in plenty of time.
2. |||||||||||||| had used only magazine articles as sources.
3. |||||||||||||| had read one or more complete books.
4. The teacher should probably have recommended |||||||||||||| .
5. |||||||||||||| had spent long hours in the public library.
6. |||||||||||||| had taken notes.
7. |||||||||||||| used many note cards.
8. Alfie had used |||||||||||||| .
9. |||||||||||||| worked in pairs.
10. |||||||||||||| worked in groups of three.
11. Finally, |||||||||||||| had finished.

225

5d. Reflexive Pronouns

> A cat will clean **itself.**   I **myself** do not like most cats.

Read the sentences in the box.

- What word in the first sentence refers to **cat**?
- What word in the second sentence emphasizes **I**?

Pronoun forms such as **itself** and **myself** are called reflexive pronouns. A reflexive pronoun is usually used to refer to a noun or pronoun in the same sentence. Reflexive pronouns are occasionally used for special emphasis. The words in the box below are reflexive pronouns.

myself	yourselves	herself	ourselves
yourself	himself	itself	themselves

5e. Interrogative Pronouns

> **Whom** have you invited?   **Who** is coming?

Read the interrogative sentences in the box.

- With what word does each sentence begin?

Words such as **who** and **whom** are called interrogative pronouns. They are used in interrogative sentences. The words in the box below can all be interrogative pronouns.

what	which	who	whom	whose

PRACTICING LANGUAGE SKILLS

- Write only the reflexive pronouns and the interrogative pronouns from the following sentences. After each pronoun, write **reflexive** or **interrogative** to identify which kind of pronoun it is.

1. Cats often like to be by themselves.
2. Who is in the yard?
3. Shana chose a black kitten for herself.
4. Which did Joey choose?
5. He picked a calico kitten for himself.
6. You should select a kitten yourself.
7. What does your cat like to eat?
8. We made a scratching post for our cat all by ourselves.
9. You yourselves can build one, too.
10. Rex is training his cat by himself.
11. Who wants another cat?
12. A cat can entertain itself.
13. My cat has won itself an important place in my life.
14. Which is the smallest kitten in the litter?
15. I myself have three cats.
16. What is the name of your cat?
17. Whose cat caught the fish?
18. Whom does your cat like most?
19. My cat likes itself most of all.
20. Whose is the big gray cat?

5f. Demonstrative Pronouns

> **This** is the best apple.
> **Those** are too ripe.

Read the sentences in the box.

• What is the word in dark type in each sentence?

Words such as **this** and **those** are called demonstrative pronouns. They are used to point out things or people. The words in the box below can all be demonstrative pronouns. (See **Adjectives, Indefinite Pronouns, and Demonstrative Pronouns,** page 232.)

that	these	this	those

5g. Relative Pronouns

> Ms. Goldring is the teacher **whom** you should see.
> She will give you the information **that** you need.

Read the sentences in the box.

• What is the word in dark type in each sentence?

Words such as **whom** and **that** are called relative pronouns. They are used to introduce adjective clauses. (See **Adjective Clauses,** pages 306–309.) The words in the box below can all be relative pronouns.

that	which	who	whom	whose

PRACTICING LANGUAGE SKILLS

■ Write only the demonstrative pronouns and the relative pronouns from the following sentences.

1. No one knows for sure about the people who first explored unknown regions.
2. This has never been fully determined.
3. It is a question that has fascinated many people.
4. There must have been someone who decided to expand the limits of the known world.
5. We can guess about the people who volunteered for such expeditions.
6. They were undoubtedly people who enjoyed adventure.
7. They left behind families and friends who waited anxiously for their return.
8. The expeditions were surely made in boats that would look unfamiliar to us.
9. These were pioneers whose courage we must admire.
10. Among them were explorers whom we have studied in school.
11. Crossing the ocean was an achievement that took courage.
12. This was a feat which we can only wonder at.

227

Reviewing ▌4▐ Nouns and ▌5▐ Pronouns

4a. Recognizing and Using Nouns

Write only the nouns from each of the following sentences. After each noun, write **singular** or **plural** to identify its form.

1. The beach was extremely crowded.
2. Children were wading in the ocean.
3. Some people were listening to radios.
4. Several teenagers were playing volleyball.
5. A girl and her dog were splashing in the surf.
6. The lifeguards watched the swimmers carefully.

4b. Proper Nouns and Common Nouns

Write only the nouns from each of the following sentences. After each noun, write **proper** or **common** to identify which kind of noun it is.

7. Our club is going to Jones Beach tomorrow.
8. Let's have a picnic in Forest Park.
9. Juneau is in Alaska.
10. The Smithsonian Institution is not only an important center for research but also a fine museum.
11. I have seen plays by Shakespeare in Central Park.
12. The Bronx Zoo and the San Diego Zoo both have special sections for children.

4c. Gerunds

Write only the gerund from each of the following sentences.

13. Exercising can be fun.
14. One good form of exercise is walking.
15. Running is quite popular now.
16. Surfing is very popular on the west coast.

17. Swimming is the way many people keep fit.
18. Have you enjoyed dancing?
19. My favorite activity is skating.

4d. Infinitives as Nouns

Write only the infinitive that is used as a noun from each of the following sentences.

20. I need to study.
21. To pass is my immediate goal.
22. I don't want to fail.
23. To succeed would make me very happy.
24. I have always tried to excel.
25. My family has told me to relax.

5a. Recognizing and Using Personal Pronouns

Write the second sentence from each of the following pairs. Finish the sentence by adding a pronoun that will agree with the antecedent in dark type.

26. **Maria** was angry. |||||||||||||| had been waiting for Tommy for over two hours.
27. Finally **Tommy** arrived. "Where have |||||||||||||| been?" Maria demanded.
28. "I was delayed by the **subway,**" he explained. "|||||||||||||| was stuck in the tunnel."
29. "Oh, no!" exclaimed **Maria.** "|||||||||||||| am so sorry for being angry at you."
30. "That's all right," **Tommy** assured Maria. "You had no way of knowing what had happened to |||||||||||||| ."
31. "Nevertheless," said **Maria,** "I apologize. |||||||||||||| should have asked you for an explanation before exploding at you."
32. The two **friends** made up after their quarrel. Later |||||||||||||| went out to dinner.

Finish each of the following sentences by adding a possessive pronoun, an indefinite pronoun, or a reflexive pronoun. Write the sentences.

5b. Possessive Pronoun Forms

33. Mozart is |||||||||||||| favorite composer.
34. I've learned to play all |||||||||||||| piano pieces.
35. One piece is particularly delightful to play because of |||||||||||||| liveliness.
36. |||||||||||||| performance at yesterday's recital was excellent.
37. Working harder at |||||||||||||| own practicing would be a good idea.
38. |||||||||||||| playing has improved a great deal.

5c. Indefinite Pronouns

39. |||||||||||||| had a different idea for the fair.
40. |||||||||||||| suggested a Western theme.
41. |||||||||||||| proposed a space motif.
42. |||||||||||||| insisted on having an auction.
43. |||||||||||||| remarked that the booth with homemade items had always raised the most money.
44. |||||||||||||| agreed that more volunteers would be needed to insure the success of the fair.

5d. Reflexive Pronouns

45. I |||||||||||||| have a different idea.
46. Can you do it by |||||||||||||| ?
47. He gave me some candy, but saved most of it for |||||||||||||| .
48. Maria keeps to |||||||||||||| most of the time.
49. Carol and Bill cleaned the house today all by |||||||||||||| .
50. We bought |||||||||||||| a new stereo.
51. Mike built |||||||||||||| a bookcase.
52. Joanne |||||||||||||| is very good at building furniture.

Write only the interrogative pronouns, the demonstrative pronouns, and the relative pronouns from the following sentences.

5e. Interrogative Pronouns

53. Who will perform tonight?
54. What is the name of the play?
55. To whom were the flowers delivered?
56. Which are our seats?
57. Whose are the coats on our seats?
58. Who wrote the play?
59. Which is the leading lady?
60. Who is the character with the beard?

5f. Demonstrative Pronouns

61. These are our seats.
62. This is my desk.
63. Those were difficult questions.
64. That was a silly movie.
65. Those are beautiful flowers.
66. This is a lovely day.
67. That was a clever remark.
68. These are the books you will read.

5g. Relative Pronouns

69. He is the man whose name I never can remember.
70. The song has a rhythm which is quite unusual.
71. The story is about a dog that saved a child's life.
72. I am the person who called earlier.
73. They know the woman whom you interviewed.
74. She has an idea that might prove very helpful.
75. This is a story which may sound incredible.
76. That man is the painter whose work you admired.
77. He is married to a woman who is even more famous.
78. She is the writer whom you praised so highly.

6 Adjectives

6a. Recognizing and Using Adjectives

> **Graceful** seagulls soared above us.
> **Several large** seagulls landed nearby.

Read the sentences in the box.

- What is the noun in each sentence?
- What word or words come before the noun in each sentence?

Words such as **graceful, several,** and **large** are called **adjectives.**

An adjective is a word that modifies a noun. In other words, an adjective limits or restricts the meaning of a noun. Very often, one or more adjectives may be used before the noun that is modified.

The word **several** is one of a special group of adjectives called **determiners.**

Determiners are adjectives that can only be used before the noun they modify. The words in the box below, and all cardinal numbers, can be determiners.

a	each	most	that
an	either	neither	the
another	every	one	these
any	few	several	this
both	many	some	those

The three determiners **a, an,** and **the** are sometimes called **articles.**

PRACTICING LANGUAGE SKILLS

■ Write each adjective from the following sentences. (Some of the adjectives are determiners.) After each adjective, write the noun it modifies.

1. Turquoise waves break gently on the brilliant sand.
2. Slender palms are swaying in the humid breeze.
3. A constant hum of small insects fills the air.
4. A few sleek yachts are lying at shallow anchor.
5. On the quiet beach, happy vacationers sunbathe on colorful towels.
6. Eager snorkelers are surveying the tranquil water.
7. A calm lagoon beckons those adventuresome divers.
8. Curious eyes peer at the strange underwater world.
9. A sea anemone is moving with silent grace before them.
10. Are any tiny fish hiding in the rough coral?

11. Several transparent jellyfish hover near nervous onlookers.
12. Those swimmers are moving slowly toward the hot shore.
13. The salty water can irritate bloodshot eyes.
14. Painful sunburns may be soothed by oily lotion.
15. The warm sun quickly dries damp swimsuits.
16. Curious children dig deep tunnels in the damp sand.
17. Several swimmers dry off in the bright sunlight.
18. Hungry picnickers open their delicious lunches.
19. They have hot chicken and cold milk.
20. Weary bathers pack up sandy towels.
21. Adults and children head for home after a delightful day.

■■ Finish the following sentences by adding an adjective in each blank space. Write the sentences.

1. ||||||||||||||| group of ||||||||||||||||| divers is exploring ||||||||||||||||| ||||||||||||||||| waters.
2. ||||||||||||||| ||||||||||||||||| fish are darting through ||||||||||||||||| ||||||||||||||||| coral.
3. ||||||||||||||| shells lie along ||||||||||||||||| ||||||||||||||||| shore.
4. ||||||||||||||| strands of seaweed ripple through ||||||||||||||||| water.
5. ||||||||||||||| ||||||||||||||||| diver spots ||||||||||||||||| wreckage of ||||||||||||||||| ||||||||||||||||| ship.
6. ||||||||||||||| ||||||||||||||||| divers swim toward ||||||||||||||||| wreck.
7. ||||||||||||||| ||||||||||||||||| anchor lies near ||||||||||||||||| ship.
8. All ||||||||||||||||| divers are excited by ||||||||||||||||| ||||||||||||||||| discovery.
9. ||||||||||||||| divers decide to board ||||||||||||||||| ||||||||||||||||| ship.
10. They spot ||||||||||||||||| ||||||||||||||||| chest below ||||||||||||||||| deck.
11. Together, ||||||||||||||||| ||||||||||||||||| divers bring ||||||||||||||||| ||||||||||||||||| chest to ||||||||||||||||| surface.
12. ||||||||||||||| group of divers looks in awe at ||||||||||||||||| ||||||||||||||||| chest.
13. ||||||||||||||| diver breaks ||||||||||||||||| ||||||||||||||||| lock.
14. Carefully, ||||||||||||||||| diver opens ||||||||||||||||| top of ||||||||||||||||| ||||||||||||||||| chest.
15. Inside ||||||||||||||||| chest are ||||||||||||||||| ||||||||||||||||| jewels.
16. "Look at all ||||||||||||||||| ||||||||||||||||| gems," says ||||||||||||||||| diver.
17. "This must have been ||||||||||||||||| ||||||||||||||||| chest," says ||||||||||||||||| diver.
18. "We'd better give ||||||||||||||||| chest and all ||||||||||||||||| ||||||||||||||||| jewels to the authorities," says ||||||||||||||||| leader of ||||||||||||||||| group of divers.
19. ||||||||||||||| divers take off ||||||||||||||||| ||||||||||||||||| equipment.
20. They divide ||||||||||||||||| treasure into ||||||||||||||||| piles.
21. ||||||||||||||| divers wash off ||||||||||||||||| jewels in ||||||||||||||||| surf.
22. They wrap ||||||||||||||||| jewels in ||||||||||||||||| ||||||||||||||||| piece of cloth.
23. "||||||||||||||||| treasure must be worth ||||||||||||||||| money," says ||||||||||||||||| diver.
24. "||||||||||||||||| authorities may give us ||||||||||||||||| reward."

APPLYING LANGUAGE SKILLS TO COMPOSITION

■ Use the noun **people** in the subject of five different sentences. In each sentence, use a different adjective to modify the noun. Write your sentences.

6b. Adjectives, Indefinite Pronouns, and Demonstrative Pronouns

> **Both** girls are working on the jigsaw puzzle.
> **Both** are making progress.

> **This** piece does not fit into the puzzle.
> **This** is the piece you need.

Read the sentences in the first box.

- In which sentence is **both** an adjective that modifies the noun **girls**?
- In which sentence is **both** an indefinite pronoun?

Read the sentences in the second box.

- In which sentence is **this** an adjective that modifies the noun **piece**?
- In which sentence is **this** a demonstrative pronoun?

Words such as **both** can be used either as adjectives or as indefinite pronouns. When the word modifies a noun, it is an adjective. When the word does not modify a noun, it is an indefinite pronoun.

The words **that, these, this,** and **those** can be used either as adjectives or as demonstrative pronouns. When one of these words modifies a noun, it is an adjective. When it does not modify a noun, it is a demonstrative pronoun.

PRACTICING LANGUAGE SKILLS

■ Write the following sentences. Write **a** above each adjective, **i.p.** above each indefinite pronoun, and **d.p.** above each demonstrative pronoun to identify the three kinds of words.

1. I wonder if another piece might fit into that area.
2. These are the two possibilities for this section.
3. Either might be correct.
4. This is the piece to try first.
5. Now try that piece.
6. Unfortunately, neither piece fits in here exactly.
7. Several pieces seem to be missing from this puzzle.
8. These were on the floor.
9. I see some pieces under that chair.
10. Each will help us complete the puzzle.
11. Those pieces do not fit into any part of this puzzle.
12. Some must belong to a different puzzle.
13. It takes days to finish some puzzles.
14. This must be one of those puzzles.
15. Some friends may offer to help us.
16. Most will only offer silly suggestions.
17. Others may have some useful ideas.
18. Those will stay to work with us.
19. Some may know where these pieces go.
20. I have done many puzzles.
21. None has been as difficult as this puzzle.
22. This is a challenge.
23. I prefer this puzzle, however, to a simpler one.
24. Any puzzle without certain pieces can surely be considered a challenge.

6c. Proper Adjectives

> Many people enjoy **French** food.   The **French** enjoy good food.

Read the sentences in the box.

- In which sentence is the word **French** used as an adjective that modifies the noun **food**?
- In which sentence is the word **French** used as a proper noun?

In the first sentence in the box, **French** is an adjective that refers to a particular place. **Adjectives which refer to particular people, places, things, events or ideas are called** proper adjectives. Each important word of a proper adjective begins with a capital letter.

Often, the same word can be used as a proper adjective or as a proper noun. If it is used as a proper adjective, it must modify a noun.

PRACTICING LANGUAGE SKILLS

■ From each of the following sentences, write the proper adjective and the noun it modifies. Underline the proper adjective.

1. More than 5,000 years ago, Egyptian cooks baked bread and prepared cakes.
2. Greek fish, cooked with oil and herbs, was praised by early poets.
3. Wealthy Greeks considered Athenian cheesecake a great delicacy.
4. In ancient times, a simple gruel was the most common Italian food.
5. However, Roman aristocrats enjoyed elaborate dishes with fine sauces.
6. Many of these sauces were made with Oriental spices.
7. Little is known of ancient British cookery.
8. Perhaps the Saxon people were not especially interested in food.
9. The Norman invaders apparently changed that attitude.
10. By the fourteenth century, English cookbooks were being written.

■■ Finish each of the following sentences by adding a proper adjective. Write the sentences.

1. The tourists will travel through several |||||||||||||||| countries.
2. They will be thrilled by impressive views of the |||||||||||||||| pyramids.
3. Several tourists hope to hike in the |||||||||||||||| mountains.
4. The travelers stayed at a |||||||||||||||| inn.
5. They enjoyed a |||||||||||||||| breakfast the next morning.
6. One of the guides taught them several |||||||||||||||| songs.
7. Someone demonstrated a |||||||||||||||| dance.
8. Next year, we will take a |||||||||||||||| tour.

APPLYING LANGUAGE SKILLS TO COMPOSITION

■ Write five sentences about different kinds of food. Use a proper adjective in each sentence.

6d. Adjectives after the Nouns and Pronouns They Modify

> The **happy** pilot landed successfully.
> The pilot was **happy.**
> She was **happy.**

Read the sentences in the box.

- What adjectives modify the noun **pilot** in the first sentence?
- What adjective comes before the noun **pilot** in the second sentence?
- What other adjective is part of the second sentence?
- What adjective is part of the third sentence?

In the first two sentences in the box, the adjective **happy** modifies the noun **pilot.** In the second sentence, the adjective **happy** comes after the noun **pilot.** An adjective may come after the noun it modifies.

In the third sentence in the box, the adjective **happy** modifies the personal pronoun **she.** Adjectives may modify personal pronouns, indefinite pronouns, and demonstrative pronouns, in addition to nouns. An adjective that modifies a pronoun usually comes after that pronoun.

PRACTICING LANGUAGE SKILLS

■ From each of the following sentences, write the adjective that comes after the noun or pronoun it modifies. Then write the noun or pronoun that the adjective modifies.

1. The Wright brothers were curious about gliders.
2. Their flights proved successful.
3. A large glider may appear clumsy.
4. It is graceful.
5. A glider flight can be fun.
6. The view may be spectacular.
7. The passengers remain secure.
8. A pilot should feel knowledgeable about air currents.
9. They may become unpredictable.
10. The currents near thunderclouds are especially hazardous.
11. A glider may stay airborne for hours.
12. The development of gliders has been rapid.
13. Their improvement is extraordinary.
14. Gliding may become popular.
15. Good weather will always be necessary.

■■ Finish each of the following sentences by adding an adjective. Write the sentences.

1. The plane on the runway was ||||||||||||| .
2. Many passengers on the flight felt ||||||||||||| .
3. Several passengers looked ||||||||||||| .
4. The engines' roar became ||||||||||||| .
5. The view from the windows was ||||||||||||| .
6. The countryside looked ||||||||||||| .
7. The landing was ||||||||||||| .
8. When the passengers emerged, they were ||||||||||||| .
9. They said the pilot had been ||||||||||||| .
10. The plane's wheels were ||||||||||||| .
11. They felt the flight had been ||||||||||||| .

6e. Participles as Adjectives

> The cold wind **was freezing** the explorers.
> The **freezing** wind hindered their progress.

> The explorers **had determined** to reach their goal.
> The **determined** explorers continued toward their goal.

Read the sentences in the first box.

- In which sentence is the present participle **freezing** the main verb form in the verb phrase?
- In which sentence is the present participle **freezing** an adjective modifying the noun **wind**?

Read the sentences in the second box.

- In which sentence is the past participle **determined** the main verb form in the verb phrase?
- In which sentence is the past participle **determined** an adjective modifying the noun **explorers**?

Participles may be used as adjectives in sentences. In the second sentence in the first box, the present participle **freezing** is used as an adjective. In the second sentence in the second box, the past participle **determined** is used as an adjective.

PRACTICING LANGUAGE SKILLS

■ From each of the following sentences, write the participle that is used as an adjective and the noun that each participle modifies. Then underline the participle.

1. The Arctic Ocean is a forbidding area.
2. Near the North Pole, the Arctic is a frozen sea.
3. In the summer, water from the melting ice runs into the ocean.
4. Huge pieces of floating ice crash together.
5. The packed ice is in constant motion.
6. Moving ice may make a loud noise.
7. Sometimes it sounds like rolling thunder.
8. A century ago, Jules Verne imagined a fascinating submarine named the Nautilus.

■■ Finish each of the following sentences by adding a participle used as an adjective. Write the sentences.

1. |||||||||||||||| explorers have been intrigued by new territories.
2. They are attracted by |||||||||||||||| missions.
3. |||||||||||||||| conditions do not discourage the explorers.
4. A |||||||||||||||| success can inspire an explorer.
5. Some explorers trek through |||||||||||||||| jungles.
6. Other explorers climb |||||||||||||||| mountain peaks.
7. Still other explorers sail through |||||||||||||||| oceans.

7 Adverbs

7a. Recognizing and Using Adverbs

> Anne Sullivan taught Helen Keller **daily.**
> Sullivan worked **tirelessly** with the young girl.
> Sullivan taught many lessons **outdoors.**

Read the sentences in the box.

- Which word in the first sentence tells when Sullivan taught?
- Which word in the second sentence tells how she worked?
- Which word in the third sentence tells where she taught?

In the sentences in the box, the words **daily, tirelessly,** and **outdoors** are used as **adverbs.**

An adverb modifies the verb or verb phrase of a sentence. Adverbs tell when, where, or how in a sentence.

The word **not** is usually used as an adverb. This special adverb can change the entire meaning of a sentence.

PRACTICING LANGUAGE SKILLS

- Write only the adverb from each of the following sentences.

1. Helen Keller's illness completely destroyed her sight and hearing.
2. The Kellers desperately hoped for improvement.
3. Their early attempts at education did not succeed.
4. Finally, they asked Anne Sullivan for help.
5. She accepted the project enthusiastically.
6. She helped Helen constantly.
7. Helen quickly learned the Braille reading system.
8. She eagerly mastered a special typewriter.
9. She was speaking soon.
10. Later, Helen Keller entered Radcliffe College.
11. Her work there was outstanding.
12. Helen Keller spoke courageously on behalf of disabled people.

■■ Finish each of the following sentences by adding an adverb. Write the sentences.

1. Many students learn ||||||||||||||| .
2. Those students are working ||||||||||||||| .
3. ||||||||||||||| , the teacher explains the problem.
4. ||||||||||||||| , one student suggests a possible solution.
5. The other students ask questions ||||||||||||||| .
6. Everyone thinks about the problem ||||||||||||||| .
7. The students ||||||||||||||| begin to work out a complete solution.
8. ||||||||||||||| the students have completed the project.
9. The teacher looks ||||||||||||||| at what they have accomplished.

7b. Adverbs That Modify Adjectives

> That **rather** romantic poem is by Edna St. Vincent Millay.
> Your essay about Millay is **too** long.

Read the sentences in the box.

- What is the adjective in each sentence?
- What word comes before each adjective?

In the sentences in the box, the words **rather** and **too** are used as **adverbs.** These adverbs modify the adjectives **romantic** and **long.** Adverbs that modify adjectives are sometimes called qualifying adverbs or qualifiers.

PRACTICING LANGUAGE SKILLS

▪ From each of the following sentences, write the qualifying adverb. After each qualifying adverb, write the adjective that the qualifying adverb modifies.

1. Emily Dickinson lived an unusually quiet life.
2. She had a very strict upbringing.
3. Dickinson went on very infrequent outings from her home in Amherst, Massachusetts.
4. Dickinson withdrew from society at a fairly young age.
5. In the privacy of her room, she began to write quite profound poems.
6. Many of her poems were rather short.
7. Dickinson created nearly two thousand highly original poems.
8. This unusually large collection of poems was discovered after Dickinson's death.
9. Her family was extremely surprised by the discovery of Dickinson's poems.
10. Dickinson's poems were published in a rather gradual manner over the next decades.
11. Finally, Dickinson gained the very special fame she deserved.

▪▪ Finish each of the following sentences by adding a qualifying adverb. Write the sentences.

1. Robert Frost became a |||||||||||||| popular poet.
2. Frost developed an interest in poetry when he was |||||||||||||| young.
3. He took a series of odd jobs to support himself, although he was |||||||||||||| reluctant to do so.
4. Throughout his life, he was a |||||||||||||| conscientious writer.
5. Frost achieved fame at a |||||||||||||| young age.
6. Readers have always been |||||||||||||| enthusiastic about Frost's poems.
7. Many people like the |||||||||||||| direct language of the poems.
8. Other readers praise Frost's |||||||||||||| graceful style.
9. Robert Frost had a |||||||||||||| long career as a poet.
10. After he became famous, he lived on his |||||||||||||| small New Hampshire farm.
11. It was a |||||||||||||| great honor to read a poem at President Kennedy's inauguration.

7c. Adverbs That Modify Other Adverbs

> Grandma Moses became a painter **quite** late in her life.
> Critics praised her paintings **very** enthusiastically.

Read the sentences in the box.

- What adverb in the first sentence tells when Grandma Moses became a painter?
- What adverb in the second sentence tells how critics praised her paintings?
- What word comes before each adverb?

In the sentences in the box, the words **quite** and **very** are used as adverbs. These adverbs modify the adverbs **late** and **enthusiastically.** Adverbs that modify other adverbs are sometimes called qualifying adverbs or qualifiers.

PRACTICING LANGUAGE SKILLS

■ From each of the following sentences, write the qualifying adverb. After each qualifying adverb, write the adverb that the qualifying adverb modifies.

1. Grandma Moses was born Anna Mary Robertson quite early in September, 1860, in northern New York state.
2. She and her husband, Thomas Salmon Moses, moved to Virginia fairly soon after their marriage in 1887.
3. In 1905, they returned rather eagerly to New York and bought a farm.
4. In her late seventies, Anna began very earnestly to paint pictures.
5. Critics almost immediately recognized her simple pictures as a genuine expression of American folk art.
6. Grandma Moses' paintings depict quite vividly her memories of life in Virginia and New York.
7. Quite soon, her work became famous.
8. Reproductions of many of her paintings have been rather widely distributed on calendars and greeting cards.

■■ Finish each of the following sentences by adding a qualifying adverb. Write the sentences.

1. Andrew Wyeth |||||||||||||| often has been called the most popular American painter of our time.
2. Andrew was taught |||||||||||||| carefully by his father, N. C. Wyeth.
3. The elder Wyeth |||||||||||||| vividly illustrated children's books, such as Treasure Island.
4. Andrew learned |||||||||||||| quickly.
5. He was only in his twenties when his first pictures were |||||||||||||| enthusiastically acclaimed.
6. Andrew Wyeth paints |||||||||||||| realistically.
7. He |||||||||||||| always portrays his friends and neighbors in his paintings.
8. Christina's World |||||||||||||| movingly depicts one of Wyeth's friends.

7d. Infinitives as Adverbs

Each player practices **regularly**. Each player practices **to win**.

Each player is **rather** anxious. Each player is anxious **to win**.

Read the sentences in the first box.

- What adverb in the first sentence modifies the verb **practices**?
- What pair of words in the second sentence modifies the verb **practices**?

Read the sentences in the second box.

- What adverb in the first sentence modifies the adjective **anxious**?
- What pair of words in the second sentence modifies the adjective **anxious**?

The second sentence in each box includes the pair of words **to win.**
The pair of words, to and a verb form, is called an infinitive.

Infinitives may be used as adverbs in sentences. An infinitive can
modify the verb or verb phrase of a sentence. When it does, the
infinitive usually follows the verb or verb phrase. An infinitive can also
modify an adjective in a sentence. When it does, the infinitive usually
follows the adjective.

PRACTICING LANGUAGE SKILLS

■ From each of the following sentences, write only the infinitive that is
used as an adverb. After each infinitive, write the verb or verb phrase
or the adjective that the infinitive modifies.

1. Tournaments can be fun to observe.
2. Many people will come to participate.
3. Other people might attend to relax.
4. Tennis tournaments are enjoyable to watch.
5. Each player battles to win.
6. Victory may be difficult to achieve.
7. The players are ready to begin.
8. The people in the audience stretch to see.
9. That last play was impossible to judge.
10. The decision of the referee is difficult to understand.
11. Most members of the audience must strain to hear.
12. The onlookers are standing to applaud.
13. The judges are there to listen.
14. The reporters are anxious to hear.
15. The candidate is happy to accept.
16. He is unwilling to try.
17. The game is easy to learn.

■■ Finish each of the following sentences by adding an infinitive used
as an adverb. Write the sentences.

1. Monopoly can be fun IIIIIIIIIIIIIIIII .
2. Once begun, the game is hard IIIIIIIIIIIIIIIII .
3. Each player throws dice IIIIIIIIIIIIIIIII .
4. The players buy property IIIIIIIIIIIIIIIII .
5. A Chance card might be risky IIIIIIIIIIIIIIIII .
6. A player may be too poor IIIIIIIIIIIIIIIII .
7. Players must be lucky IIIIIIIIIIIIIIIII .
8. People of all ages play this game IIIIIIIIIIIIIIIII .
9. Some players devise systems IIIIIIIIIIIIIIIII .

8 Prepositions

8a. Recognizing and Using Prepositions and Prepositional Phrases

> The magazine article was written **by** Margaret Mead.
> The magazine article was written **about** Margaret Mead.
> The student did research **with** her.
> The student did research **for** her.

Read the sentences in the box. Notice the words in dark type.

- In the first two sentences, what kind of word follows the word in dark type?
- In the second two sentences, what kind of word follows the word in dark type?

The words in dark type, and others like them, are called **prepositions.**

A preposition is a word that shows how a noun or a pronoun relates to another word or group of words in the sentence.

- In the first two sentences, what relationship is shown by the prepositions **by** and **about**?
- In the second two sentences, what relationship is shown by the prepositions **with** and **for**?

The words in the box below can be prepositions.

about	below	for	through
above	beneath	from	throughout
across	beside	in	to
after	besides	into	toward
against	between	like	under
along	beyond	near	underneath
amid	but (to mean "except")	of	until
among	by	off	unto
around	concerning	on	up
at	down	over	upon
before	during	past	with
behind	except	since	without

A preposition is always followed by a noun or pronoun. **The noun or pronoun that follows a preposition is called the** object of the preposition.

The preposition and the object of the preposition are called a prepositional phrase. Other words may come between the preposition and the object of the preposition. These words are also part of the prepositional phrase.

PRACTICING LANGUAGE SKILLS

■ Write only the prepositional phrases from the following sentences. In each prepositional phrase you write, circle the preposition and underline the object of the preposition.

1. Anthropology is the scientific study of human culture.
2. Anthropologists look for patterns in the behavior of different people.
3. They study the similarities among all people and the differences between groups.
4. Anthropology is divided into several branches.
5. Archaeology is one branch of anthropology.
6. Archaeologists learn from objects left by earlier peoples.
7. Tools and other artifacts provide clues about life in ancient times.
8. Archaelogists often work with other scientists.
9. Linguistic anthropologists study languages from different societies around the world.
10. Social anthropologists look at relationships within groups of people.
11. Margaret Mead became one of the most famous anthropologists in the world.
12. During her life, Mead traveled throughout the world.
13. Field studies were very important to her.
14. Mead wrote several books about her research.
15. Studies by Margaret Mead have improved our understanding of other peoples.

■■ Finish the following sentences by adding a prepositional phrase in each blank space. Write the sentences.

1. Most people live ||||||||||||||||| .
2. Many scientists have studied changes ||||||||||||||||| .
3. Living ||||||||||||||||| may provide individuals ||||||||||||||||| .
4. Teenagers and their parents often disagree ||||||||||||||||| .
5. Children ||||||||||||||||| may need help ||||||||||||||||| .
6. Children can help their parents ||||||||||||||||| ||||||||||||||||| .
7. Parents can help their children ||||||||||||||||| ||||||||||||||||| .
8. Many families ||||||||||||||||| enjoy playing ||||||||||||||||| .
9. Some families have experimented ||||||||||||||||| ||||||||||||||||| .
10. All societies should provide their members ||||||||||||||||| ||||||||||||||||| .
11. Small children enjoy playing ||||||||||||||||| .
12. Babies are happiest ||||||||||||||||| .
13. As children grow, they make friends ||||||||||||||||| .
14. When they go to school, children learn to get along ||||||||||||||||| .
15. Shy children sometimes have trouble ||||||||||||||||| .
16. Friendly, outgoing children may succeed ||||||||||||||||| .
17. A student who does not read well may also have difficulty ||||||||||||||||| .
18. Good teachers are experienced ||||||||||||||||| .

APPLYING LANGUAGE SKILLS TO COMPOSITION

■ Write five sentences about a real or imaginary family. Use at least one prepositional phrase in each sentence.

8b. Prepositional Phrases as Adjectives and as Adverbs

> The singer **in the leading role** performed well.
> She sang **with great feeling.**
> She was happy **with her performance.**
> She made a mistake early **in her performance.**

Read the sentences in the box.

- What is the prepositional phrase in each sentence?
- Which prepositional phrase modifies the noun **singer**?
- Which prepositional phrase modifies the verb **sang**?
- Which prepositional phrase modifies the adjective **happy**?
- Which prepositional phrase modifies the adverb **early**?

Prepositional phrases can be used in two different ways.

A prepositional phrase can be used as an adjective in a sentence. The prepositional phrase may modify a noun or a pronoun. A prepositional phrase used as an adjective usually follows the noun or pronoun it modifies.

A prepositional phrase can also be used as an adverb in a sentence. The prepositional phrase may modify a verb or verb phrase, an adjective, or an adverb.

PRACTICING LANGUAGE SKILLS

■ Write the prepositional phrases from the following sentences. After each prepositional phrase, write **adjective** or **adverb** to identify how the phrase is used.

1. The first operas were composed in Italy.
2. The art form spread across Europe.
3. Performers in an opera sing their lines.
4. Opera dates from the sixteenth century.
5. Groups of singers performed the first operas.
6. Solos developed during the seventeenth century.
7. The first public opera house opened in Venice during the seventeenth century.
8. The characters in many operas seem unbelievable to us.
9. The development of the plot may also seem unlikely.
10. The music of the opera appeals to most audiences.

APPLYING LANGUAGE SKILLS TO COMPOSITION

■ Use each of the following prepositional phrases in a sentence about a real or imaginary performance. Use prepositional phrases 1–4 as adjectives. Use prepositional phrases 5–9 as adverbs. Write your sentences.

1. in the audience
2. with them
3. by the door
4. near the front
5. with enthusiasm
6. throughout the auditorium
7. across the stage
8. into the microphones
9. in several other cities

9 Conjunctions

9a. Recognizing and Using Coordinating Conjunctions

> Mountain climbing is an exciting **and** challenging sport.

Read the sentence in the box.

- Which two words are joined by **and**?

Words such as **and** are called **coordinating conjunctions.**

Coordinating conjunctions join words or groups of words in sentences. The following words are coordinating conjunctions: **and, but, or, nor, for, yet.**

9b. Correlative Conjunctions

> Mountaineers carry **not only** compasses **but also** maps.

Read the sentence in the box.

- Which two words are joined by **not only . . . but also**?

Words such as **not only . . . but also** are called **correlative conjunctions.**

Correlative conjunctions join words or groups of words in sentences. Correlative conjunctions are always used in pairs.

The words in the box below are all correlative conjunctions.

> either . . . or   neither . . . nor   both . . . and
> whether . . . or   not only . . . but (also)

PRACTICING LANGUAGE SKILLS

- Write only the conjunction or conjunctions from each of the following sentences.

1. In 1920, British climbers vowed to conquer Mount Everest or die trying.
2. George Leigh-Mallory led the expedition, for he was a famous climber.
3. Both storms and avalanches doomed the climbing expedition in 1922.
4. Not only injuries but also deaths forced the climbers to retreat.
5. Neither Mallory nor the rest of his team felt another assault could be made.
6. Their routes had been altered either by blizzards or by avalanches.
7. Two teams planned to attack the summit, but one of the teams turned back.
8. Both Mallory and his friend Andrew Irvine pushed on.
9. The people below never saw Mallory or Irvine again.
10. Either the weather or the altitude defeated many expeditions.

9c. Subordinating Conjunctions

> Mountaineers feel a special thrill **whenever** they reach the summit of a mountain.
>
> Some mountains remain unconquered **while** higher ones have already been scaled.

Read the sentences in the box.

- Which two groups of words are joined by **whenever**?
- Which two groups of words are joined by **while**?

The words in dark type, and others like them, are called **subordinating conjunctions.**

Subordinating conjunctions **join word groups called clauses within sentences.** (See **Adverb Clauses,** page 304.)

The words in the box below are all **subordinating conjunctions** or **subordinators.**

after	if	when
although	since	whenever
as	though	where
because	unless	wherever
before	until	while

PRACTICING LANGUAGE SKILLS

- Write only the conjunction or conjunctions from the following sentences.

1. Most mountaineers consider either the Alps or the Himalayas the best range for climbing.
2. Mount Everest is one of the world's most famous mountains, yet it is one of the most mysterious.
3. It is remotely situated, and its peak is constantly shrouded in mist.
4. Annapurna was the highest mountain ever climbed until Hillary and Norgay conquered Everest in 1953.
5. Some people look upon a mountain as an obstacle while others regard it as a challenge.
6. In 1865, seven climbers reached the summit of the Matterhorn in the Alps after they had struggled and failed for years.
7. Tragically, four of the climbers fell to their deaths when their rope broke on the descent.
8. Climbers must be prepared to cope with storms, cold, wind, and the effects of less oxygen if they climb very high mountains.
9. Mountaineering became less difficult when items such as portable oxygen tanks and nylon rope were introduced.
10. Some climbing techniques are meant to overcome obstacles while others are meant to minimize dangers.
11. There has been controversy over the motives of mountain climbers since people first began to climb.
12. Most people climb mountains because they enjoy the climbing itself.

10 Interjections

10a. Recognizing and Using Interjections

> **Wow!** Is this really a photograph of the Loch Ness monster?
> **Well,** I'm not sure what it is.

Read the sentences in the box.

- Which two words express emotion?

Words such as **wow** and **well** in the sentences in the box are called **interjections.**

An interjection is a word that expresses emotion and that has no grammatical relationship to the other words of the sentence.

An interjection that expresses very strong emotion is often punctuated with an exclamation mark. Most interjections are separated from the other words of a sentence by a comma.

Interjections are very rarely used in formal writing.

PRACTICING LANGUAGE SKILLS

- Write only the interjections from the following sentences. If a sentence does not have an interjection, write **none.**

1. Say, what do you think of these stories about Big Foot?
2. Well, some of the stories sound pretty unlikely.
3. Oh, I've seen some pictures of Big Foot's prints.
4. Wow! Look at this one!
5. Oh, that looks as though it could be a fake.
6. Many people believe that this is a photograph of the real Big Foot.
7. Hey! Have you heard about the movies of Big Foot?
8. Say! That sounds interesting!
9. Gosh, are you sure that's accurate?
10. How could a creature that large avoid being captured?
11. Well, for one thing, it lives deep in the woods.
12. Wow! Do you think that big animal survives on plants and roots?
13. My! It must eat a lot of leaves!
14. Well, one man claimed he was carried off by Big Foot.
15. Wow! Was the man hurt?
16. He was returned unharmed after seven days.
17. Golly! That man must have had quite a story to tell!
18. Oh, he didn't tell anyone about that adventure for many years.
19. My! It's intriguing to think that this creature might be real.

APPLYING LANGUAGE SKILLS TO COMPOSITION

- Write a dialogue in which two friends talk about flying saucers. One friend claims to have seen a flying saucer. The other friend believes that no such thing exists. Use at least four interjections in the dialogue.

Reviewing 6 Adjectives 7 Adverbs 8 Prepositions 9 Conjunctions and 10 Interjections

6a. Recognizing and Using Adjectives

Write each adjective from the following sentences. (Some of the adjectives are determiners.) After each adjective, write the noun it modifies.

1. Most people like sunny days.
2. The old desk had a secret drawer.
3. A funny program was on television recently.
4. Seven new cars were parked in the lot.
5. An unusual event occurred.

6b. Adjectives, Indefinite Pronouns, and Demonstrative Pronouns

Write the following sentences. Write **a** above each adjective, **i.p.** above each indefinite pronoun, and **d.p.** above each demonstrative pronoun to identify the three kinds of words.

6. Several students were learning to use the new computer.
7. This is not an easy task.
8. Some learned more quickly than others.
9. Those students helped their classmates.

6c. Proper Adjectives

From each of the following sentences, write the proper adjective and the noun it modifies. Then underline the proper adjective.

10. Among Panamanian exports are bananas and petroleum products.
11. The Norwegian sovereign is King Olav V.
12. The Himalayan mountain range is dominated by Mount Everest.
13. German cooking is a favorite in those villages.

6d. Adjectives after the Nouns and Pronouns They Modify

From each of the following sentences, write the adjective that comes after the noun or pronoun it modifies. Then write the noun or pronoun that the adjective modifies.

14. Our hike in the mountains was wonderful.
15. The views of the valley were spectacular.
16. The entire day proved marvelous.
17. The lake looks peaceful.

6e. Participles as Adjectives

From the following sentences, write each participle that is used as an adjective and the noun that the participle modifies. Then underline the participle.

18. The scorching sun beat down on the burning sand.
19. Sweltering vacationers ran toward the refreshing water.
20. Exhausted bathers relaxed after an invigorating swim.
21. Concerned parents watched their children carefully.

7a. Recognizing and Using Adverbs

Write only the adverb from each of the following sentences.

22. We rehearsed daily for three weeks.
23. Opening night finally arrived.
24. The audience responded to the performance enthusiastically.
25. My parents visited me backstage.
26. They were smiling proudly.

From each of the following sentences, write the qualifying adverb. After each qualifying adverb, write the adjective or the other adverb that the qualifying adverb modifies.

7b. Adverbs That Modify Adjectives

27. An extremely loud noise woke me.
28. I had been having a very pleasant dream.
29. I felt quite irritable all morning.

7c. Adverbs That Modify Other Adverbs

30. Tracy and Kevin left rather early.
31. They rode unusually quickly to the baseball field.
32. The other players arrived fairly soon.

7d. Infinitives as Adverbs

From each of the following sentences, write only the infinitive that is used as an adverb. After each infinitive, write the verb or verb phrase or the adjective that the infinitive modifies.

33. A good play is fun to attend.
34. Some people come to learn.
35. The performers are hoping to entertain.

8a. Recognizing and Using Prepositions and Prepositional Phrases

Write only the prepositional phrases from the following sentences. In each prepositional phrase you write, circle the preposition and underline the object of the preposition.

36. Linguistics is the scientific study of language.
37. Linguists look for similarities among languages.
38. They study a language by talking to native speakers.

8b. Prepositional Phrases as Adjectives and as Adverbs

Write the prepositional phrases from the following sentences. After each prepositional phrase, write **adjective** or **adverb** to identify how the phrase is used.

39. The Nile River flows into the Mediterranean Sea.
40. America's only active diamond mine is in Arkansas.
41. The last piece of the puzzle is missing.

Write only the conjunction or conjunctions from each of the following sentences.

9a. Recognizing and Using Coordinating Conjunctions

42. I enjoy short stories and poetry.
43. He is friendly but shy.
44. She prefers volleyball or basketball.

9b. Correlative Conjunctions

45. Juan cooked not only dinner but also breakfast.
46. We can either fish or swim.
47. Neither Ned nor Nora knows Nancy.

9c. Subordinating Conjunctions

48. I enjoy sitting by a roaring fire whenever the weather is cold.
49. We drove carefully because the mountain road was treacherous.
50. I haven't seen him since he moved away.

10a. Recognizing and Using Interjections

Write only the interjections from the following sentences.

51. Say, did you see that UFO last night?
52. Wow! Sam said he saw it land!

11 Sentences with Intransitive Verbs

11a. Subject Nouns and Pronouns with Verbs and Verb Phrases

Snow falls.	Walruses are swimming.
Bears will be hibernating.	They fish.

Read the sentences in the box.

- What noun or pronoun is the subject of each sentence?
- What verb or verb phrase is the predicate of each sentence?

There are several different sentence patterns. Each sentence pattern has certain kinds of words in a certain order.

The sentences in the box follow the simplest sentence pattern. This pattern has only two basic sentence parts:

Subject Noun or Pronoun	+	Verb or Verb Phrase

The main verb in a sentence that follows this pattern is called an **intransitive verb.**

PRACTICING LANGUAGE SKILLS

■ Write only the subject noun or pronoun from each of the following sentences.

1. Winds have been blowing.
2. Drifts are forming.
3. Ponds freeze.
4. Water is dripping.
5. Icicles may form.
6. Clouds have been gathering.
7. Storms move.
8. Skies may darken.
9. Snowstorms will begin.

■■ Write only the verb or verb phrase from each of the following sentences.

1. Jungles swelter.
2. Thunder cracks.
3. Rain has fallen.
4. Plants are steaming.
5. Leaves are falling.
6. They have decayed.
7. Flowers will grow.
8. Monkeys are screeching.
9. Lizards might be climbing.

APPLYING LANGUAGE SKILLS TO COMPOSITION

■ Add a verb or verb phrase to each subject noun or pronoun. Write the sentences you make.

1. temperatures
2. we
3. grass
4. I
5. elephants
6. they
7. zebras
8. vultures

■■ Add a subject noun or pronoun to each verb or verb phrase. Write the sentences you make.

1. roam
2. are hunting
3. could be coming
4. can swim
5. should migrate
6. has disappeared
7. might have returned
8. will be sleeping

11b. Modifiers in Sentences with Intransitive Verbs

> Many animals live in the harsh tundra.
> Plants with bright flowers grow rapidly in the spring.
> Tall, graceful reindeer may graze on the shrubs.

Read the sentences in the box.

- What is the subject noun of each sentence?
- What is the verb or verb phrase of each sentence?
- What other words and word groups are part of each sentence?

Adjectives, adverbs, and prepositional phrases may be included in sentences that follow this sentence pattern:

| Subject Noun or Pronoun | + | Verb or Verb Phrase |

The modifiers add more information, but they do not change the pattern of the sentence.

PRACTICING LANGUAGE SKILLS

■ Write only the subject noun or pronoun and the verb or verb phrase from each of the following sentences.

1. The hot, humid climate of the jungle varies little.
2. A thundershower occurs almost every day.
3. Dense plant life thrives throughout tropical forests.
4. The cycle of growth and decay continues unceasingly.
5. The floor of a tropical rain forest lies in deep shade.
6. Tall trees rise from the forest floor.
7. Tiny rays of sunlight dance on the dark ground.
8. People can walk easily through most parts of the forest.
9. Insects buzz loudly within the shady forest.
10. Noisy animals run swiftly along the tangled branches.
11. Apes may swing from tree to tree.

APPLYING LANGUAGE SKILLS TO COMPOSITION

■ Add at least two modifiers to each of the following sentences. Use adjectives, adverbs, and prepositional phrases. Write the sentences you make.

1. Blizzards develop.
2. Winds may be howling.
3. Temperatures have dropped.
4. Glaciers might be breaking.
5. Icebergs could have floated.
6. Penguins are strutting.
7. Whales may float.
8. Seals might have been playing.
9. Bears have hunted.
10. Otters will swim.
11. They play.
12. You may wait.

11c. Sentences with Compound Subjects

> A snake lives in that cage.
> A lizard lives in that cage.
> Either a snake or a lizard lives in that cage.

Read the first two sentences in the box.

- What is the subject of each sentence?
- What is the predicate of each sentence?

Read the third sentence in the box.

- How have the first two sentences been combined to form the third sentence?

Two sentences with the same predicate can be joined to form a new sentence with a **compound subject**.

A sentence with a compound subject is a sentence that has two or more subject nouns or pronouns. In a sentence with a compound subject, the subject nouns or pronouns are usually joined by a coordinating conjunction or a correlative conjunction. (See **Recognizing and Using Coordinating Conjunctions,** page 243, and **Correlative Conjunctions,** page 243.)

11d. Sentences with Compound Predicates

> Horace stopped.
> Horace stared at the snake.
> Horace stopped and stared at the snake.

Read the first two sentences in the box.

- What is the subject of each sentence?
- What is the predicate of each sentence?

Read the third sentence in the box.

- How have the first two sentences been combined to form the third sentence?

Two sentences with the same subject can be joined to form a new sentence with a **compound predicate**.

A sentence with a compound predicate is a sentence that has two or more verbs or verb phrases with the same subject. In a sentence with a compound predicate, the verbs or verb phrases are usually joined by a coordinating conjunction or a correlative conjunction. (See **Recognizing and Using Coordinating Conjunctions,** and **Correlative Conjunctions,** page 243.)

PRACTICING LANGUAGE SKILLS

■ Combine the two sentences in each of the following pairs to form a sentence with a compound subject or a sentence with a compound predicate.

1. The science teachers were reading about the snake.
   Their students were reading about the snake.
2. Hallie went to the library.
   Hallie read about snakes.
3. She went home.
   She thought about the articles.
4. Hallie wondered about the snake.
   Everyone else in the class wondered about the snake.
5. The long orange snake hid under a rock in its cage.
   The long orange snake slept.

6. It moved slowly.
   It ate very infrequently.
7. A group of curious students stayed late.
   A group of curious students watched for changes in the snake's behavior.
8. You should have stayed with them.
   I should have stayed with them.
9. The snake slithered between the bars of the cage.
   The snake disappeared.
10. The students looked everywhere for the snake.
    Their friends looked everywhere for the snake.

APPLYING LANGUAGE SKILLS TO COMPOSITION

■ Finish each of the following sentences by adding two subject nouns or pronouns. If you wish, you may also add adjectives and prepositional phrases to modify the subject nouns and pronouns. Write the sentences you make.

1. |||||||||||||| and |||||||||||||| had been listening carefully.
2. |||||||||||||| and |||||||||||||| will be ready for the next project.
3. Both |||||||||||||| and |||||||||||||| should have been studying for the exam.
4. Either |||||||||||||| or |||||||||||||| must have been standing by the gate.
5. Neither |||||||||||||| nor |||||||||||||| could sleep on the night before the performance.
6. |||||||||||||| and |||||||||||||| have succeeded.
7. Either |||||||||||||| or |||||||||||||| will go to the movies with us.
8. Both |||||||||||||| and |||||||||||||| have been lying in that corner for weeks.

■■ Finish each of the following sentences by adding two verbs or verb phrases. If you wish, you may also add adverbs and prepositional phrases to modify the verbs and verb phrases. Write the sentences you make.

1. The frightened animals |||||||||||||| and |||||||||||||| .
2. Alfie |||||||||||||| but |||||||||||||| .
3. Everyone in that group |||||||||||||| or |||||||||||||| .
4. The antique train |||||||||||||| and |||||||||||||| .
5. The scientists |||||||||||||| but |||||||||||||| .
6. The news reporter for that station |||||||||||||| and |||||||||||||| .
7. Shocked by the news, he |||||||||||||| and |||||||||||||| .
8. The rest of the crowd |||||||||||||| or |||||||||||||| .

11e. Diagraming Sentences with Intransitive Verbs

A diagram shows the structure of a sentence. It shows the different parts of a sentence and the way those sentence parts fit together.

A sentence composed only of a subject noun or pronoun and a verb or verb phrase is the simplest kind of sentence to diagram. Each of the following two sentences, for example, has only a subject noun or pronoun and a verb or verb phrase.

> Entertainers arrived.
> They will be performing.

To diagram any sentence, begin by drawing a straight horizontal line. Then draw a short vertical line through the horizontal line.

Write the subject noun or pronoun on the horizontal line to the left of the vertical line. Write the verb or verb phrase on the horizontal line to the right of the vertical line.

| Entertainers | arrived | | They | will be performing |

In a sentence diagram, use the capital letters used in the sentence. Do not use the punctuation marks of the sentence.

PRACTICING LANGUAGE SKILLS

- Diagram each of the following sentences.

1. Vendors are beckoning.
2. Crowds have gathered.
3. They have been laughing.
4. Horns blast.
5. Bells will ring.
6. Buzzers may be sounding.
7. Stands have opened.
8. Baseballs are flying.
9. Dolls will topple.
10. We have won.
11. Rides have begun.
12. Riders have been waiting.
13. Calliopes are jangling.
14. Teacups spin.
15. Carts have stopped.
16. It has broken.
17. Everyone is shouting.
18. Jerome has been waving.
19. We will wait.
20. They will be laughing.
21. Cameras are clicking.
22. Carousels spin.
23. Puppets will entertain.
24. Clowns are winking.
25. Guides help.
26. Lines have been forming.
27. Spectators will be watching.
28. Elephants have paraded.
29. Lions will roar.
30. Tigers will jump.
31. We will applaud.
32. Everyone will eat.
33. Gilda waved.
34. Horses ran.
35. Parents will be waiting.
36. People have been smiling.
37. We will be leaving.
38. Carmen was crying.

11f.   Diagraming Sentences with Adjectives and Adverbs

Sentences with intransitive verbs may include adjectives and adverbs.
These modifiers can be diagramed to show their relationship to other
sentence parts.

The following sentence, for example, includes two adjectives that
modify the subject noun. It also includes an adverb that modifies the
verb phrase.

> The tiny dog was posing proudly.

To diagram such a sentence, begin by writing the subject noun and the
verb phrase on the horizontal line.

$$\text{dog} \mid \text{was posing}$$

Diagram each adjective on a slanted line below the noun it modifies.
Proper adjectives and possessive pronouns that come before nouns are
diagramed in the same way.

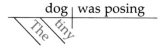

Diagram the adverb on a slanted line below the verb phrase it modifies.

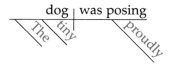

PRACTICING LANGUAGE SKILLS

- Diagram each of the following sentences.

1. All the dogs were waiting.
2. Their nervous trainers stood nearby.
3. Serious judges were observing closely.
4. Your hound is performing now.
5. That spaniel moves awkwardly.
6. The spectators applaud politely.
7. Obedient dogs have been standing motionlessly.
8. Competent handlers speak authoritatively.
9. Their dogs will respond eagerly.
10. Most breeds learn readily.
11. One outstanding dog poses arrogantly.
12. Their smooth coats are shining.
13. The judges have been conferring quietly.
14. Anxious owners are listening attentively.
15. A large poodle is trotting forward.
16. Its owner smiles proudly.
17. Several dogs are barking now.
18. The show ends suddenly.
19. The audience is clapping enthusiastically.
20. A large dog growled fiercely.
21. Two tiny dogs yap excitedly.
22. The owners are leaving.
23. The heavy doors slam noisily.
24. Another show will begin soon.

11g. Diagraming Sentences with Qualifying Adverbs

Sentences with intransitive verbs may include adverbs that modify adjectives and adverbs. These adverbs can be diagramed to show their relationship to other sentence parts.

The following sentence, for example, includes two qualifying adverbs. The adverb **fairly** modifies the adjective **good.** The adverb **extremely** modifies the adverb **rapidly.**

That fairly good student is reading extremely rapidly.

To diagram such a sentence, begin by writing the subject noun and the verb phrase on the horizontal line. Diagram each adjective on a slanted line below the noun it modifies. Diagram the adverb **rapidly** on a slanted line below the verb phrase it modifies.

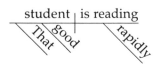

Then diagram each qualifying adverb on a slanted line below the adjective or adverb it modifies.

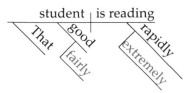

PRACTICING LANGUAGE SKILLS

- Diagram each of the following sentences.

1. The extremely tired students were studying.
2. A rather difficult test was coming.
3. Joelle read quite carefully.
4. Everyone wrote very quickly.
5. Their somewhat dull pencils scratched noisily.
6. One especially nervous student complained angrily.
7. Her friends argued quite forcefully.
8. Morning arrived too soon.
9. Everyone arose unusually early.
10. Each student reviewed fairly quickly.
11. Everyone had prepared quite carefully.
12. They wrote quite calmly.
13. The students answered extremely competently.
14. Their teacher spoke quite proudly.
15. Everybody passed very easily.
16. The relieved students celebrated rather noisily.
17. The extremely sensitive neighbor complained.
18. A rather excited student danced.
19. The cake arrived too late.
20. The ice cream melted quite rapidly.
21. Everyone ate very eagerly.
22. Carolyn stayed fairly late.

11h. Diagraming Sentences with Prepositional Phrases

Sentences with intransitive verbs may include prepositional phrases. The prepositional phrases may be used as adjectives to modify the subject noun or pronoun, or they may be used as adverbs to modify the verb or verb phrase. Prepositional phrases can be diagramed to show their relationship to other sentence parts.

The following sentence, for example, includes two prepositional phrases. The first prepositional phrase modifies the subject noun of the sentence. The second prepositional phrase modifies the verb.

A large group of tourists rushed through the famous palace.

To diagram such a sentence, begin by writing the subject noun and the verb on the horizontal line. Diagram each adjective on a slanted line below the subject noun. Then diagram the first prepositional phrase, which is used as an adjective, below the subject noun. Write the preposition on a slanted line below the subject noun. Write the object of the preposition on a horizontal line connected to the slanted line.

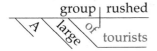

Diagram the second prepositional phrase, which is used as an adverb, in the same way. Write the preposition on a slanted line below the verb.

Write the object of the preposition on a horizontal line connected to the slanted line. Then diagram each adjective that modifies the object of the preposition on a slanted line below that noun.

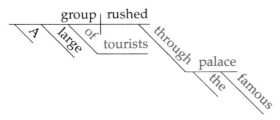

PRACTICING LANGUAGE SKILLS

- Diagram each of the following sentences.

1. The circus is in town.
2. Performers from the circus parade through the streets.
3. Several acrobats in bright costumes are performing.
4. One acrobat climbs up a sturdy rope.
5. She hangs from the rope.
6. Someone in the crowd gasps.
7. The people sit on wooden bleachers.
8. A clown from the show waves to us.

11i. Diagraming Sentences with Compound Subjects

Sentences with compound subjects can be diagramed to show their structure. The sentence below, for example, has a compound subject. Each subject noun is modified by two adjectives.

The talented drummer and the popular guitarist are playing well.

To diagram such a sentence, begin by writing the two subject nouns on horizontal lines, one above the other. Join the two lines to the horizontal line for the verb phrase. Add a dotted line between the two lines for the subject nouns, and write the conjunction on the dotted line.

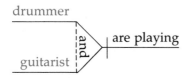

Then diagram the adjectives and the adverb below the nouns and the verb phrase they modify.

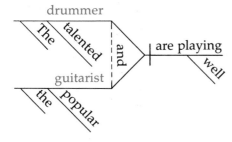

PRACTICING LANGUAGE SKILLS

- Diagram each of the following sentences.

1. Soloists and groups will perform.
2. Noise and laughter subside.
3. The singers and the musicians enter.
4. Reviewers and critics listen carefully.
5. Sonja and her friends applaud enthusiastically.
6. The pianist and a drummer perform together.
7. Sasha and Lucia are leaving already.
8. The manager of the concert and her assistants are waiting.
9. The singers and the members of the band are bowing.
10. One guitarist and two singers return to the stage.
11. Ricardo and Laura are waiting for the next concert.
12. A famous folksinger and her band will perform then.
13. Blythe and her parents have been talking about a party.
14. Jory and Nate will be going to the party.
15. Dr. Robles and the new teacher from Spain will be speaking at the next meeting.

11j. Diagraming Sentences with Compound Predicates

Sentences with compound predicates can be diagramed to show their structure. The sentence below, for example, has a compound predicate. The first verb is modified by an adverb, and the second verb is modified by a prepositional phrase.

The people applauded loudly and shouted with enthusiasm.

To diagram such a sentence, begin by writing the two verbs on horizontal lines, one above the other. Join the two lines to the horizontal line for the subject noun. Add a dotted line between the two lines for the verbs, and write the conjunction on the dotted line.

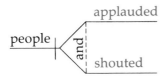

Then diagram the adjective, the adverb, and the prepositional phrase below the noun and the verbs they modify.

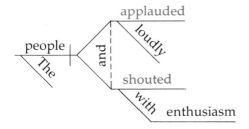

PRACTICING LANGUAGE SKILLS

■ Diagram each of the following sentences.

1. Everyone watches and listens.
2. Lights blink and flash.
3. The performers wave and bow.
4. The people in the audience clap and cheer.
5. Several performers leap gracefully and dance across the stage.
6. The fans laugh and shout.
7. The performers return and sing again.
8. The musicians bow and leave.
9. They wave to the fans and hurry off the stage.
10. The members of the audience stand and rush toward the exits.
11. They walk to the main gate and wait for their friends.
12. The bus arrives at the stop and waits for the passengers.
13. The photographer stood quietly and waited for the right moment.
14. Jessica turned and waved to her friends.
15. Dwayne jumped into the boat and rowed away.
16. They walked to the library and looked at the new magazines.
17. The tourists stayed at the hotel and rested.
18. Si ran ahead and waited for us.

257

Reviewing **11** Sentences with Intransitive Verbs

11a. Subject Nouns and Pronouns with Verbs and Verb Phrases

Write each sentence. Underline the subject noun or pronoun and circle the verb or verb phrase.

1. Clouds are approaching.
2. Rain will be falling.
3. Night comes.
4. They are sleeping.
5. It has happened.
6. Nobody has been listening.
7. Shelly might have been calling.
8. Everybody hurried.
9. Flowers are blooming.
10. He has graduated.
11. Melissa will perform.
12. Someone might succeed.

11b. Modifiers in Sentences with Intransitive Verbs

Write only the subject noun or pronoun and the verb or verb phrase from each sentence.

13. A hot, dry wind blows across the desert.
14. Certain plants grow well in the desert.
15. Some animals thrive there.
16. Lizards live under rocks.
17. Those coyotes sleep during the day.
18. Small gray insects scurry through the sand.
19. The young gymnast moved especially well on the uneven parallel bars.
20. Everyone in the room had been watching closely.
21. Joanna had walked for an hour in the rain.
22. The other people in the group were waiting there.
23. Her diamonds gleamed brilliantly.
24. Nobody in the building knew about the power failure.

11c. Sentences with Compound Subjects

Write the two subject nouns or pronouns from each sentence.

25. Armand and his brother have been arguing.
26. You and I should have been waiting.
27. The doe and her fawn were grazing in the meadow.
28. Photographers and reporters gathered at the scene.
29. The candidates and their supporters filed onto the stage.
30. An elephant and two monkeys performed for the judges.
31. The violinist and the pianist have been practicing.
32. Octavio and the other members of the club will be arriving soon.
33. George and Jessica presented their dance specialty.
34. Books and magazines were scattered about the room.

11d. Sentences with Compound Predicates

Write the two verbs or verb phrases from each sentence.

35. Everyone stopped and listened.
36. The tides ebb and flow.
37. The water drips from the leaky faucet and runs onto the floor.
38. Mario stood on the corner and waved to the passing motorists.
39. Dorian tried hard but failed.
40. The engine sputtered and finally stopped completely.
41. The little boy smiled and waved shyly.
42. The strange animal emerged slowly from the forest and lumbered toward us.
43. Bart mounted his horse and rode into town.
44. Brenda looked at the pictures and laughed loudly.

Diagram each of the following sentences.

11e. Diagraming Sentences with Intransitive Verbs

45. Everybody should be singing.
46. Alberto was juggling.
47. Paola has left.
48. We might win.
49. They will be watching.
50. Adam has finished.
51. Carla should complain.
52. Megan will be waiting.

11f. Diagraming Sentences with Adjectives and Adverbs

53. The runners are waiting nervously.
54. The final race began quickly.
55. A long line has formed outside.
56. The price has risen sharply.
57. A lonely stranger was standing there.
58. The funny show ended abruptly.
59. They had been watching carefully.
60. The new members will meet tomorrow.

11g. Diagraming Sentences with Qualifying Adverbs

61. The bus arrived quite early.
62. The rather lazy student has succeeded.
63. A very long story developed.
64. You are speaking too softly.
65. An especially funny actress will be performing.
66. That train must have stopped quite frequently.
67. They were moving rather quietly.
68. A very large freighter is sailing.

11h. Diagraming Sentences with Prepositional Phrases

69. The people in the auditorium were waiting.
70. A group of ushers stood in the aisle.
71. The musicians practiced for an extra hour.
72. A trio of dancers moved across the stage.
73. A small scrap of paper was lying on the floor.
74. Every student in that class will be waiting for your answer.
75. The contestants from the other schools will arrive soon.
76. Nobody in Toledo has heard about it.

11i. Diagraming Sentences with Compound Subjects

77. Corliss and Martina will be competing.
78. Giovanni and Tara hiked around the lake.
79. Ten students and four teachers have been talking about the problem.
80. Luz and her friends have been practicing together.
81. Two old textbooks and several magazines were lying on the table.
82. Derrick and his friends are waiting for us.
83. A famous old movie and a funny new movie are playing at the same theater.
84. Maurice and Antonio will be going to that theater.

11j. Diagraming Sentences with Compound Predicates

85. Leon called and talked to Horace.
86. Every student jogged or ran.
87. The plants withered and died.
88. They hiked up the mountain and fished in the lake.
89. Barbara reads rather slowly but writes quite quickly.
90. The students sat quietly and listened to the lecture.
91. Brad stumbled and fell.
92. The kite dropped unexpectedly and crashed into the tree.

12 Sentences with Direct Objects

12a. Direct Object Nouns and Pronouns

Camels can endure **heat.**
Fur protects **them.**
They waste **nothing.**

Read the sentences in the box.

- What is the subject noun or pronoun of each sentence?
- What is the verb or verb phrase of each sentence?
- What word in each sentence tells **who** or **what** after the verb or verb phrase?

Each sentence in the box has a **direct object.** The direct object of a sentence is a noun or pronoun that follows the verb or verb phrase. **The direct object noun or pronoun tells who or what after the verb or verb phrase.** Each sentence in the box follows this sentence pattern:

Subject Noun or Pronoun	+	Verb or Verb Phrase	+	Direct Object Noun or Pronoun

The main verb in a sentence with a direct object noun or pronoun is called a **transitive verb.**

PRACTICING LANGUAGE SKILLS

- Write only the direct object noun or pronoun from each of the following sentences.

1. Deserts can support life.
2. Sunlight raises temperatures.
3. It has caused evaporation.
4. Clouds have been losing moisture.
5. Wind has blown dunes.
6. It has shifted them.
7. Erosion has shaped rocks.
8. Plants have been storing water.
9. Wolves may visit deserts.
10. Camels can store fat.
11. Tortoises eat cacti.
12. Animals are avoiding heat.
13. Some may dig burrows.
14. Crevices may hide insects.
15. Burrows may be concealing lizards.
16. Animals need shelter.
17. Animals may eat meat.
18. Rainwater will fill lakes.
19. It nourishes plants.
20. Plants need it.
21. They also need sunlight.
22. Camels have humps.
23. Travelers should carry identification.
24. They will need it.
25. Somebody should bring food.
26. Bees spread pollen.
27. Flowers attract them.
28. Winds blow seeds.
29. Roots absorb water.
30. Plants produce oxygen.
31. Cacti may have blossoms.
32. Cacti contain water.

12b. Modifiers in Sentences with Direct Objects

> A forest usually has various layers of plants.
> The tops of the tallest trees form the canopy of the forest.
> Dead leaves cover the forest floor.

Read the sentences in the box.

- What is the subject noun of each sentence?
- What is the verb of each sentence?
- What is the direct object noun of each sentence?
- What other words and word groups are part of each sentence?

Adjectives, adverbs, and prepositional phrases may be included in sentences that follow this pattern:

Subject Noun or Pronoun	+	Verb or Verb Phrase	+	Direct Object Noun or Pronoun

The modifiers add more information, but they do not change the pattern of the sentence.

PRACTICING LANGUAGE SKILLS

■ From each of the following sentences, write only the subject noun or pronoun, the verb or verb phrase, and the direct object noun or pronoun.

1. The forest may provide a home for many different animals.
2. Many animals of the forest have small bodies.
3. Such animals include the lively chipmunk.
4. Chipmunks build their nests underground.
5. They store the food for the winter in their nests.
6. Most chipmunks gather seeds from trees.
7. A chipmunk must have sharp teeth.
8. Its teeth can break the tough cover on seeds.
9. A chipmunk usually has black and white stripes on its back and tail.
10. The deer ate the leaves.
11. Many deer grow antlers on their heads.
12. The antlers of a deer may indicate its age.
13. Young white-tailed deer have spots on their backs.
14. A deer loses its spots within a year.
15. All deer have long, powerful legs.
16. Most deer have a very keen sense of smell.
17. The trees in the forest provide lumber for industry.
18. They also provide shelter for birds and small animals.
19. Birds build their nests in the branches of trees.
20. Squirrels hide nuts for the long, cold winter.
21. Fires can threaten all life in the forest.
22. Some animals hunt other animals.

12c. Intransitive Verbs and Transitive Verbs

> The students have been studying.
> The students have been studying that poem.

Read the sentences in the box.

- What is the verb phrase of each sentence?
- What is the direct object noun of the second sentence?
- In which sentence is the main verb intransitive?
- In which sentence is the main verb transitive?

Many main verbs may be used either as intransitive verbs or as transitive verbs. These verbs are intransitive in sentences that do not have direct object nouns or pronouns. They are transitive in sentences that have direct object nouns or pronouns.

PRACTICING LANGUAGE SKILLS

■ Write the verb or verb phrase from each of the following sentences. Then write **intransitive** or **transitive** to tell how the main verb is used in that sentence.

1. The members of the orchestra have been practicing for the next concert.
2. They have been practicing the same piece for almost two hours.
3. Ethan acted the part with unusual conviction.
4. The rest of the family has eaten already.
5. The powerful horse stopped unexpectedly.
6. Marvin baked several red apples with honey and walnuts.
7. Lucinda usually speaks Japanese with her grandparents.
8. The gardener opened the rusty gate carefully.
9. Somebody may have eaten the rest of the watermelon.
10. Seth answered each question slowly and thoughtfully.
11. Even a child can stop this machine without assistance.
12. The lecturer had been speaking too softly.
13. The hikers rested their sore feet in the stream.
14. The detective searched every room for a clue.
15. They have been searching for the lost hikers all weekend.
16. Suddenly, the heavy door opened.

APPLYING LANGUAGE SKILLS TO COMPOSITION

■ Use each of the following main verbs in two different sentences. In the first sentence, use it as an intransitive verb. In the second sentence, use it as a transitive verb.

1. sing
2. read
3. paint
4. perform
5. play
6. shake
7. draw
8. write
9. watch

12d. Sentences with Compound Direct Objects

> Carmine will choose a pair of goldfish.
> Carmine will choose that noisy canary.
> Carmine will choose either a pair of goldfish or that noisy canary.

Read the first two sentences in the box.

- What is the subject of each sentence?
- What is the verb phrase of each sentence?
- What is the direct object noun of each sentence?

Read the third sentence in the box.

- How have the first two sentences been combined to form the third sentence?

Two sentences with the same subject and the same verb or verb phrase can be joined to form a new sentence with a compound direct object.

A sentence with a compound direct object is a sentence that has two or more direct object nouns or pronouns. In a sentence with a compound direct object, the direct object nouns or pronouns are usually joined by a coordinating conjunction or a correlative conjunction.

PRACTICING LANGUAGE SKILLS

- The following sentences have compound direct objects. Write only the two direct object nouns or pronouns from each sentence.

1. Each winner will receive both a certificate and a special prize.
2. The prizes include small pets and a few stuffed animals.
3. Some participants might prefer a book or a subscription to a magazine.
4. This kind of contest provided encouragement and fun for everyone.
5. All the contestants must have both knowledge and good luck.
6. Everyone should have been watching the other contestants and you.
7. The photographers are recording both the successes and the disappointments.
8. Nobody has noticed the duck on that chair or the rabbits in the corner.
9. At the carnival, Bob won a stuffed panda and an elegant necklace for Carol.
10. We all ate hamburgers and french fries for lunch.
11. Carol enjoys both the rides and the games.
12. She invited Justine and Christy to come with us.
13. One vendor was selling both peanuts and popcorn.
14. Justine bought a balloon and a baton.
15. Christy wanted a magic wand or a frightening mask.
16. After lunch, Justine could find neither Carol nor Christy.
17. She asked Bob and me for our help.
18. We found Carol and Christy on the ferris wheel.
19. I hurled baseballs at milk bottles and footballs at a stuffed clown's nose.
20. We enjoyed our day at the carnival and the prizes we won.

12e. Passive Verb Phrases from Sentences with Direct Objects

> Miranda has made that suggestion.
> That suggestion has been made by Miranda.
> That suggestion has been made.

Read the first sentence in the box.

- What is the subject noun of the sentence?
- What is the direct object noun?
- What is the verb phrase?

Read the second and third sentences in the box, and compare them with the first sentence.

- What is the subject noun of each sentence?
- What is the verb phrase? What kind of verb phrase is it?
- What noun follows the preposition **by** in the second sentence?
- What prepositional phrase is part of the second sentence but not part of the third sentence?

A sentence with a direct object can be made into a sentence with a passive verb phrase. The direct object noun or pronoun becomes the subject noun or pronoun of the sentence with the passive verb phrase. A sentence with a passive verb phrase usually emphasizes an action or the recipient of an action. (See **Passive Verb Phrases,** page 212.)

Most often, the subject noun or pronoun of the sentence with the direct object follows the preposition **by** in the sentence with the passive verb phrase. Sometimes, however, the person or thing that performs the action is not considered as important as the action itself. Then the prepositional phrase beginning with **by** may be left out of the sentence.

PRACTICING LANGUAGE SKILLS

- Each of the following sentences has a direct object noun or pronoun. Use each sentence to make a new sentence with a passive verb phrase. Write the sentences.

1. Sid reviewed the suggestions.
2. Miss Kim made several comments.
3. Someone took notes.
4. Arthur read the notes aloud.
5. Alberta asked several questions.
6. Carla answered most of the questions.
7. Somebody referred the other questions to Aurora.
8. Aurora has made a study of the situation.
9. Someone has consulted three experts.
10. Each expert gave a different opinion.
11. Ingrid ended the discussion.
12. Somebody has requested a vote on the suggestions.
13. The members wrote the votes on slips of paper.
14. Chuck collected the slips of paper.
15. The leader of the committee has counted the votes.
16. Somebody has announced the winner.
17. The panel approved the suggestions.

12f. Diagraming Sentences with Direct Objects

Sentences with direct objects can be diagramed to show their structure. The following sentence, for example, has a direct object noun. That noun is modified by an adjective and by a prepositional phrase.

   Eastman developed workable cameras for amateur photographers.

To diagram such a sentence, begin by writing the subject noun, the verb, and the direct object noun on the main horizontal line. The direct object noun or pronoun of a sentence follows the verb or verb phrase on the horizontal line. A short vertical line which goes to, but not through, the horizontal line separates the verb or verb phrase from the direct object noun or pronoun.

Then diagram the adjective and the prepositional phrase below the direct object noun.

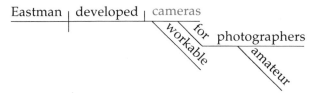

PRACTICING LANGUAGE SKILLS

- Diagram each of the following sentences.

1. Necessity may encourage inventors.
2. Judson developed zippers.
3. People could use zippers.
4. They had been using buttons.
5. Perkins designed refrigerators.
6. Goldmark created long-playing records.
7. Yale produced locks for banks.
8. Inventions can affect our entire lives.
9. Inventors have made many useful discoveries.
10. Lippershey built the first telescope.
11. McCormick revolutionized American farming techniques.
12. Mauchly paved the way for the electronic computer.
13. Computers may make important changes in your life.
14. Some inventions may have certain harmful effects.
15. People must evaluate the total effect of each invention.
16. Inventions may cause new kinds of problems.
17. Automobiles revolutionized transportation in this country.
18. The exhaust from those automobiles has polluted the air.
19. Pollution has affected the health of many people.
20. Sensitive people have left polluted cities.
21. Computers store useful information.
22. Computers may threaten our privacy.
23. Inventions improve life in many areas.

13 Sentences with Indirect Objects

13a. Indirect Object Nouns and Pronouns

> Janis Ian gave us "Society's Child."
> "Society's Child" brought Ian fame.

Read the sentences in the box.

- What is the subject noun of each sentence?
- What is the verb of each sentence?
- What is the direct object noun of each sentence?
- What pronoun in the first sentence tells to whom Ian gave "Society's Child"?
- What noun in the second sentence tells to whom "Society's Child" brought fame?

Each sentence in the box has an **indirect object. The indirect object of a sentence is a noun or pronoun that tells** to whom **or** for whom .
A sentence with an indirect object follows this sentence pattern.

Subject Noun or Pronoun	+	Verb or Verb Phrase	+	Indirect Object Noun or Pronoun	+	Direct Object Noun or Pronoun

PRACTICING LANGUAGE SKILLS

- Write only the indirect object noun or pronoun from each of the following sentences.

1. Elvis Presley gave audiences entertainment.
2. People wished him success.
3. Agents were offering Presley contracts.
4. They paid him money.
5. He was giving us concerts.
6. Fans would throw him flowers.
7. He might show them smiles.
8. Elvis brought everyone enjoyment.
9. Admirers were offering him gifts.
10. He had written them letters.
11. Secretaries mailed fans photographs.

APPLYING LANGUAGE SKILLS TO COMPOSITION

- Finish each of the following sentences by adding an indirect object noun or pronoun. Write the sentences.

1. Music has given |||||||||||||| enjoyment.
2. Musicians may bring |||||||||||||| jazz.
3. It offers |||||||||||||| relaxation.
4. Songs may tell |||||||||||||| stories.
5. Leaders have handed |||||||||||||| guitars.
6. She is showing |||||||||||||| chords.
7. Performers promise |||||||||||||| amusement.
8. Agents may promise |||||||||||||| success.
9. Audiences will give |||||||||||||| encouragement.
10. Reviewers may give |||||||||||||| criticism.

13b. Modifiers in Sentences with Indirect Objects

> Modern inventions have given many people freedom from
> time-consuming chores.
> Many stores now offer consumers a wide variety of time-saving
> gadgets.

Read the sentences in the box.

- What is the subject noun of each sentence?
- What is the verb or verb phrase of each sentence?
- What is the indirect object noun of each sentence?
- What is the direct object noun of each sentence?
- What other words and word groups are part of each sentence?

Adjectives, adverbs, and prepositional phrases may be included in
sentences that follow this pattern:

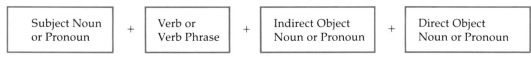

| Subject Noun or Pronoun | + | Verb or Verb Phrase | + | Indirect Object Noun or Pronoun | + | Direct Object Noun or Pronoun |

The modifiers add more information, but they do not change the
pattern of the sentence.

PRACTICING LANGUAGE SKILLS

■ From each of the following sentences, write only the subject noun or
pronoun, the verb or verb phrase, the indirect object noun or pronoun,
and the direct object noun or pronoun.

1. Early artifacts show us the inventiveness of human beings.
2. Prehistoric humans brought the world crude tools.
3. They gave people simple speech.
4. The cultivation of plants offered our ancestors a new means of survival.
5. They taught us the uses of fire.
6. Written language has brought everyone a means of communication.
7. Printed books have given us information about past discoveries.
8. They offer inventors a basis for further discoveries.

APPLYING LANGUAGE SKILLS TO COMPOSITION

■ Add at least two modifiers to each of the following sentences. Use
adjectives, adverbs, and prepositional phrases. Write the sentences you
make.

1. Inventions offer people convenience.
2. Automobiles gave us transportation.
3. Electricity brings homes light.
4. Television teaches children facts.
5. Supermarkets sell families food.
6. Telegraphs send friends messages.
7. Furnaces give rooms warmth.
8. Machines make people clothes.

13c. Sentences with Compound Indirect Objects

> The naturalist showed the campers slides of the area.
> The naturalist showed the other visitors slides of the area.
> The naturalist showed the campers and the other visitors slides of the area.

Read the first two sentences in the box.

- What is the subject of each sentence?
- What is the verb phrase of each sentence?
- What is the direct object noun of each sentence?
- What is the indirect object noun of each sentence?

Read the third sentence in the box.

- How have the first two sentences been combined to form the third sentence?

Two sentences with the same subject, the same verb or verb phrase, and the same direct object noun or pronoun can be joined to form a new sentence with a **compound indirect object**.

A sentence with a compound indirect **object is a sentence that has two or more indirect object nouns or pronouns.** The indirect object nouns or pronouns are usually joined by a coordinating conjunction or a correlative conjunction.

PRACTICING LANGUAGE SKILLS

■ The following sentences have compound indirect objects. Write only the two indirect object nouns or pronouns from each sentence.

1. She has given Conrad and me a map of the trails here.
2. Show Ramon and Mary your story.
3. The rangers gave my companions and me advice about the trails.
4. Many campers are buying their neighbors or their friends souvenirs of the park.
5. That clerk must have sold you and Carlotta a dozen postcards.
6. Give Addie and me your report.

APPLYING LANGUAGE SKILLS TO COMPOSITION

■ Finish each sentence by adding two indirect object nouns or pronouns. You may add adjectives and prepositional phrases to modify the indirect object nouns and pronouns. Write the sentences.

1. Ms. Enkojo has been buying ||||||||||||||| and ||||||||||||||| presents.
2. Hennie will show both ||||||||||||||| and ||||||||||||||| the best technique.
3. Arlo can give either ||||||||||||||| or ||||||||||||||| an extra copy of the book.
4. Somebody must have made ||||||||||||||| and ||||||||||||||| a special snack.
5. Marcelle can sell ||||||||||||||| and ||||||||||||||| tickets to the musical.
6. The messenger will hand either ||||||||||||||| or ||||||||||||||| the envelope.

13d. Passive Verb Phrases from Sentences with Indirect Objects

> The theater has sold thousands of fans tickets.
> Thousands of fans have been sold tickets by the theater.
> Thousands of fans have been sold tickets.

Read the first sentence in the box.

- What is the subject noun of the sentence?
- What is the indirect object noun?
- What is the verb phrase?

Read the second and third sentences in the box, and compare them with the first sentence.

- What is the subject noun of each sentence?
- What is the verb phrase? What kind of verb phrase is it?
- What noun follows the preposition **by** in the second sentence?
- What prepositional phrase is part of the second sentence but not part of the third sentence?

A sentence with an indirect object can be made into a sentence with a passive verb phrase. The indirect object noun or pronoun becomes the subject noun or pronoun of the sentence with the passive verb phrase. A sentence with a passive verb phrase is used to emphasize an action or the recipient of an action. (See **Sentences with Passive Verb Phrases,** page 212.)

Often, the subject noun or pronoun of the sentence with the indirect object follows the preposition **by** in the sentence with the passive verb phrase. Sometimes the prepositional phrase beginning with **by** may be left out of the sentence.

PRACTICING LANGUAGE SKILLS

■ Each of the following sentences has an indirect object noun or pronoun. Use each sentence to make a new sentence with a passive verb phrase. Use the indirect object noun or pronoun as the subject of each new sentence. Write the sentences.

1. Silent films promised audiences much pleasure.
2. Hollywood film companies paid the stars of the silent screen high salaries.
3. Most studios offered performers long contracts.
4. The star system offered Rudolph Valentino instant fame.
5. Charlie Chaplin's films give everyone enjoyment.
6. The advent of sound had given silent films unbeatable competition.
7. The large movie studios promised the public more talkies.
8. Color gave films more realism.
9. Early color films gave some people headaches.
10. Technicolor promised studios an exciting new color system.
11. Theaters sold movie fans more tickets.

13e.   Diagraming Sentences with Indirect Objects

Sentences with indirect objects can be diagramed to show their structure.

The following sentence, for example, has an indirect object noun. That noun is modified by an adjective and by a prepositional phrase.

> Mr. Kwok gave each student in the class advice.

To diagram such a sentence, begin by writing the subject noun, the verb, and the direct object noun on the main horizontal line. Then diagram the indirect object noun on a separate line. The indirect object noun or pronoun of a sentence is diagramed on a short horizontal line that is connected to the verb or verb phrase by an empty slanted line.

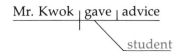

Then diagram the adjective and the prepositional phrase below the indirect object noun.

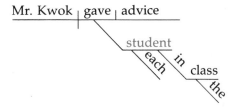

PRACTICING LANGUAGE SKILLS

■ Diagram each of the following sentences.

1. Bazaars may offer shoppers excitement.
2. Merchants are showing browsers merchandise.
3. They have promised us bargains.
4. Variety gives buyers choices.
5. Shopkeepers will offer customers advice.
6. Customers are handing merchants money.
7. Owners have sold them handicrafts.
8. One customer has been asking every clerk questions.
9. He is buying his young son a gift.
10. Each clerk has given the customer different advice.
11. Somebody finally sold the confused customer several toys.
12. The man will hand his son a huge box of toys.
13. Some customers pay the clerks in the store cash.
14. The store sends many customers monthly bills.
15. Those customers mail the store their checks.
16. The store may offer everyone in this area an account.

14 Sentences with Object Complements

14a. Object Complement Nouns and Adjectives

> We have elected them **leaders.**   Success has made Nora **proud.**

Read the sentences in the box.

- What is the direct object noun or pronoun of each sentence?
- In the first sentence, what noun follows and refers to the direct object pronoun?
- In the second sentence, what adjective follows and refers to the direct object noun?

Each sentence in the box has an object complement. **The object complement of a sentence is a noun or an adjective that follows the direct object and refers back to it.** An object complement noun renames a direct object noun or pronoun. An object complement adjective modifies a direct object noun or pronoun. A sentence with an object complement follows this sentence pattern:

Subject Noun or Pronoun	+	Verb or Verb Phrase	+	Direct Object Noun or Pronoun	+	Object Complement Noun or Adjective

Only verbs that have meanings similar to the meaning of either **make** or **consider** can be used in sentences with object complements.

PRACTICING LANGUAGE SKILLS

- Write only the object complement noun or adjective from each sentence.

1. Everyone had considered Antarctica wasteland.
2. Many believed it worthless.
3. Ice had made interiors inaccessible.
4. Snowstorms make winters dangerous.
5. Richard Byrd showed himself unafraid.
6. Explorers made Byrd leader.
7. Byrd found Antarctica fascinating.
8. Byrd considered himself fortunate.
9. He considered expeditions exciting.
10. Antarctica made Byrd famous.
11. Explorations made maps understandable.
12. They proved equipment functional.
13. Voters will elect them representatives.
14. Governments have appointed them advisors.
15. Discoveries may make you famous.
16. It made has them happy.
17. Somebody has appointed her secretary.
18. People may consider you lucky.
19. Explorers have proved themselves courageous.
20. We have proved ourselves capable.
21. We found the air polluted.
22. The accused man was proved innocent.
23. I consider the entire story unbelievable.
24. Ernesto was appointed treasurer of the club.

271

14b. Modifiers in Sentences with Object Complements

> The crew had jokingly named the project Mission Impossible.
> Technicians on the project made the spacecraft livable for the astronauts.

Read the sentences in the box.

- What is the verb or verb phrase of each sentence?
- What is the direct object noun of each sentence?
- What is the object complement noun or adjective of each sentence?
- What other words and word groups are part of each sentence?

Adjectives, adverbs, and prepositional phrases may be included in sentences that follow this pattern:

Subject Noun or Pronoun	+	Verb or Verb Phrase	+	Direct Object Noun or Pronoun	+	Object Complement Noun or Adjective

The modifiers add more information, but they do not change the pattern of the sentence.

PRACTICING LANGUAGE SKILLS

■ From each of the following sentences, write only the subject noun or pronoun, the verb or verb phrase, the direct object noun or pronoun, and the object complement noun or adjective.

1. The scientists had finally declared all plans complete.
2. They readily appointed Antonelli captain of the mission.
3. Antonelli had consistently proved herself skillful.
4. The captain found the members of her crew ready for the mission.
5. She considered their extensive training finished.
6. The work of many technicians had made the complex equipment functional.
7. The crew found the long countdown nerve-racking.
8. The scientists in the tower declared all systems perfect.
9. The long, dangerous mission had finally proved itself completely worthwhile.
10. Captain Antonelli showed herself most capable of command.

APPLYING LANGUAGE SKILLS TO COMPOSITION

■ Add at least two modifers to each sentence. Use adjectives, adverbs, and prepositional phrases. Write the sentences you make.

1. Leaders have named them trainees.
2. They considered themselves lucky.
3. Instruction made them competent.
4. Exercise kept bodies healthy.
5. Work made days endless.
6. Scientists declared experiments ready.
7. They will appoint Davis researcher.
8. He considered himself fortunate.
9. They found research enjoyable.
10. Officials declared trainees astronauts.

14c. Diagraming Sentences with Object Complements

Sentences with object complements can be diagramed to show their structure.

The following sentence, for example, has an object complement noun. That noun is modified by two adjectives and a prepositional phrase.

Everyone considers her a capable leader for this group.

To diagram such a sentence, begin by writing the subject pronoun, the verb, the direct object pronoun, and the object complement noun on the main horizontal line. The object complement noun or adjective of a sentence follows the direct object noun or pronoun on the horizontal line. A short slanted line that goes to, but not through, the horizontal line separates the direct object noun or pronoun from the object complement noun or adjective.

Everyone | considers | her \ leader

Then diagram the adjectives and the prepositional phrase below the object complement noun.

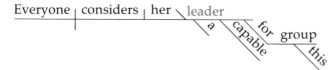

PRACTICING LANGUAGE SKILLS

- Diagram each of the following sentences.

1. Aviation has made some people famous.
2. Aviators may consider flights exciting.
3. Aviators must prove themselves courageous.
4. His flight to Paris made Charles Lindbergh famous throughout the world.
5. People believed Lindbergh fearless.
6. Lindbergh considered himself lucky.
7. He proved himself adventurous.
8. Exceptional flights may make some pilots very popular.
9. Amelia Earhart found planes fascinating.
10. She considered oceans especially challenging.
11. Her flights made Earhart a heroine to many people.
12. Many people considered her a brave pilot.
13. Some people thought her foolish.
14. Earhart considered each difficult flight an adventure.
15. Thick clouds might make navigation dangerously difficult.
16. The monotony of a flight may make a pilot less aware of possible dangers.
17. Modern instruments have made flight much safer.
18. The speed of jets has made the time in the air much shorter.

Reviewing 12 Sentences with Direct Objects
13 Sentences with Indirect Objects and
14 Sentences with Object Complements

Write only the direct object noun or pronoun from each sentence.

12a. Direct Object Nouns and Pronouns

1. Gerard raises hamsters.
2. It has been following us.
3. They have received awards.
4. Vanessa will explain it.
5. You can reserve seats.
6. We may see snow.

12b. Modifiers in Sentences with Direct Objects

7. Luis will probably invite his cousins to the next party.
8. The prospector discovered an unusual rock on the floor of the mine.
9. Roxanne will probably share her notes with you.
10. The participants have been planning the next meeting for three weeks.
11. Everybody in the group must approve the plan.
12. Carl will certainly read at least six books this month.

12c. Intransitive Verbs and Transitive Verbs

Write the verb or verb phrase from each sentence. Then write **intransitive** or **transitive** to tell how the main verb is used in that sentence.

13. Simone has been writing letters.
14. We should practice again soon.
15. Everybody was watching the parade.
16. Ilise performed a solo.
17. Elmer sang in a clear, deep voice.
18. Edie and Al danced a number from the musical comedy.

12d. Sentences with Compound Direct Objects

Write the two direct object nouns or pronouns from each sentence.

19. Jon has two cats and a parrot.
20. The cats will eat either fish or meat.
21. That cat is following you and me.
22. The parrot has a strong beak and claws.
23. This cartoon will amuse Sam and her.

12e. Passive Verb Phrases from Sentences with Direct Objects

Rewrite each sentence as a new sentence with a passive verb phrase.

24. The Beatles wrote that song.
25. Marta choreographed the next dance.
26. Amy Lewis won first prize.
27. Mr. Rojas took the message.
28. The girls rowed the first boat.

12f. Diagraming Sentences with Direct Objects

Diagram each sentence.

29. They should ride the bus.
30. Darlene will repair the bicycle.
31. Nobody will accept the responsibility.
32. They are rehearsing their speeches.

Write only the indirect object noun or pronoun from each sentence.

13a. Indirect Object Nouns and Pronouns

33. They have been telling us stories.
34. We wished Theo luck.
35. Everyone brought Erika presents.
36. Nobody can promise you success.
37. Ms. Knox gave him advice.

13b. Modifiers in Sentences with Indirect Objects

38. Yesterday Rod showed me his plans for the Service Club.
39. The administration has promised the students a wider variety of choices.
40. Several students offered the young children some assistance.
41. The author will send the company a letter of explanation.
42. Sulin has written Gloria another memo on that subject.
43. Lorene read us the story from the school paper.

13c. Sentences with Compound Indirect Objects

Write the two indirect object nouns or pronouns from each sentence.

44. Marcella has made Julio and Nancy a surprise.
45. The teacher asked Drew and Lexie the same question.
46. Lorie showed Gary and me the package.
47. Somebody may have told Lynn and Ollie the secret.
48. Cammie must be giving either you or me a present.
49. Raul sent both his aunt and his grandmother flowers for their birthdays.

13d. Passive Verb Phrases from Sentences with Indirect Objects

Use each sentence to make a new sentence with a passive verb phrase. Use the indirect object noun or pronoun as the subject of each new sentence. Write the sentences.

50. Her relatives gave Lena many gifts.
51. The judges have promised the winner a trip to Hollywood.
52. Seth has sold everybody a ticket.
53. First Bank offered Miss McFee a loan.
54. His brother sent Stanley a box of rocks.

13e. Diagraming Sentences with Indirect Objects

Diagram each sentence.
55. The students asked her many questions.
56. Kelvin brought them several books.
57. Kurt has baked his friends some cookies.
58. Nobody told me the answer.

Write only the object complement noun or adjective from each sentence.

14a. Object Complement Nouns and Adjectives

59. I considered it impossible.
60. They named her Julia.
61. We will elect Rita president.
62. Inez proved herself capable.
63. He has made history interesting.

14b. Modifiers in Sentences with Object Complements

64. Many students consider Ulrika the friendliest person in the school.
65. The voters will elect Benjamin their next representative to the council.
66. The members of the decorating committee made the gym unrecognizable.
67. Everyone found the new exhibit at the museum quite interesting.
68. The artist has proved herself an extraordinary painter.

14c. Diagraming Sentences with Object Complements

Diagram each sentence.
69. The students elected Lisa president.
70. He will find the work quite difficult.
71. They should have named the puppy Quisas.
72. Your reaction has made me confident.

15 Sentences with Linking Verbs

15a. Sentences with Predicate Adjectives

> They have been **unhappy.**
> Sonja seemed **friendly.**

Read the sentences in the box.

- What is the subject noun or pronoun of each sentence?
- What is the verb or verb phrase of each sentence?
- What adjective in each sentence modifies the subject noun or pronoun?

Each sentence in the box has a **predicate adjective.**

A predicate adjective **is an adjective that follows the verb or verb phrase in certain sentences and modifies the subject noun or pronoun.** A predicate adjective may sometimes be called a **completer adjective.**

A predicate adjective can only follow certain main verbs. Those verbs are called **linking verbs.** The most common linking verb is **be.** Some common linking verbs are listed in the box below.

act	appear	be	become	feel	grow	look	prove
remain	seem	smell	sound	stay	taste	turn	

A sentence with a predicate adjective follows this sentence pattern:

Subject Noun or Pronoun	+	Linking Verb or Verb Phrase	+	Predicate Adjective

15b. Sentences with Predicate Nominatives

> They were **strangers.**
> Strangers may become **friends.**

Read the sentences in the box.

- What is the subject noun or pronoun of each sentence?
- What is the verb or verb phrase of each sentence?
- What noun in each sentence renames the subject noun or pronoun?

Each sentence in the box has a **predicate nominative.**

A predicate nominative is a noun or pronoun that follows a linking verb and renames the subject noun or pronoun. A predicate nominative is sometimes called a **completer noun** or **completer pronoun.**

The linking verbs that are most commonly followed by predicate nominatives are listed in the box below.

be	become	remain	stay

A sentence with a predicate nominative follows this sentence pattern:

Subject Noun or Pronoun	+	Linking Verb or Verb Phrase	+	Predicate Nominative

PRACTICING LANGUAGE SKILLS

■ Write only the predicate adjective or the predicate nominative from each of the following sentences. Then write **predicate adjective** or **predicate nominative** to identify which kind of word it is.

1. Voters may seem enthusiastic.
2. Candidates will become representatives.
3. Representatives may become senators.
4. Winners feel elated.
5. It might be you.
6. You will look successful.
7. Everyone will feel proud.
8. It may appear simple.
9. It is complicated.
10. Campaigning may prove difficult.
11. Friends will remain supporters.
12. They may sound sympathetic.
13. Supporters will remain helpful.
14. Officials will become reformers.
15. Reforms may be successes.
16. Policies will remain unchanged.

■■ Finish each of the following sentences by adding a predicate adjective or a predicate nominative. Then write **predicate adjective** or **predicate nominative** to identify the kind of word you added.

1. Problems may remain |||||||||||||||| .
2. They are acting |||||||||||||||| .
3. It might have seemed |||||||||||||||| .
4. Orlando will be |||||||||||||||| .
5. Flowers smell |||||||||||||||| .
6. You look |||||||||||||||| .
7. Hamburgers should smell |||||||||||||||| .
8. We may have appeared |||||||||||||||| .
9. Oaks are |||||||||||||||| .
10. We should be |||||||||||||||| .
11. Members are |||||||||||||||| .
12. Enemies have become |||||||||||||||| .
13. It might have been |||||||||||||||| .
14. Laura has become |||||||||||||||| .
15. We will remain |||||||||||||||| .
16. They were |||||||||||||||| .

APPLYING LANGUAGE SKILLS TO COMPOSITION

■ Write four sentences about yourself. Use a linking verb and a predicate adjective in each sentence.

■■ Write two sentences about a friend. Use a linking verb and a predicate nominative in each sentence.

15c. Modifiers in Sentences with Predicate Adjectives and Sentences with Predicate Nominatives

> The first performance of the play was quite successful.
> Several students in the Drama Club may someday become stars on Broadway.

Read the sentences in the box.

- What is the subject noun of each sentence?
- What is the verb or verb phrase of each sentence?
- What is the predicate adjective of the first sentence?
- What is the predicate nominative of the second sentence?
- What other words and word groups are part of each sentence?

Adjectives, adverbs, and prepositional phrases may be included in sentences that follow this sentence pattern:

Subject Noun or Pronoun	+	Linking Verb or Verb Phrase	+	Predicate Adjective or Predicate Nominative

The modifiers add more information, but they do not change the pattern of the sentence.

PRACTICING LANGUAGE SKILLS

■ From each of the following sentences, write only the subject noun or pronoun, the linking verb or verb phrase, and the predicate adjective or predicate nominative.

1. The long rehearsals often seemed quite tedious for the students.
2. The director of the play is Ms. Mallen.
3. She was once a student at a rather famous drama school.
4. She has become an excellent teacher.
5. They felt quite confident during rehearsal.
6. Several players must have grown quite nervous before the first performance.
7. All the people in the audience proved extraordinarily enthusiastic.
8. The applause at the end of the first act sounded nearly thunderous.
9. The students on the stage felt very proud of their work.
10. The next project for the Drama Club will probably be a musical.

APPLYING LANGUAGE SKILLS TO COMPOSITION

■ Add at least two modifiers to each of the following sentences. Use adjectives, adverbs, and prepositional phrases. Write the sentences you make.

1. Actors may have felt nervous.
2. Actresses appeared confident.
3. Members may become successful.
4. They will remain members.
5. Performances might prove difficult.
6. Audiences might appear indifferent.

278

15d. Sentences with Compound Predicate Adjectives

> The campground was quite **crowded** last summer.
> The campground was very **noisy** last summer.
> The campground was quite **crowded** and very **noisy** last summer.

Read the first two sentences in the box.

- What is the subject of each sentence?
- What is the verb of each sentence?
- What is the predicate adjective of each sentence?

Read the third sentence in the box.

- How have the first two sentences been combined to form the third sentence?

Two sentences with the same subject and the same linking verb or verb phrase can be combined to form a new sentence with a **compound predicate adjective**.

A sentence with a compound predicate adjective **is a sentence that has two or more predicate adjectives.** In a sentence with a compound predicate adjective, the predicate adjectives are usually joined by a coordinating conjunction or a correlative conjunction.

PRACTICING LANGUAGE SKILLS

- Combine the two sentences in each of the following pairs to form a sentence with a compound predicate adjective.

1. A camping trip may be enjoyable.
   A camping trip may be difficult.
2. The campsite will appear comfortable after a long day of hiking.
   The campsite will appear inviting after a long day of hiking.
3. The other campers were helpful.
   The other campers were friendly.
4. Their advice might prove valuable.
   Their advice might prove worthless.
5. The inside of a camper's tent should remain warm at all times.
   The inside of a camper's tent should remain dry at all times.
6. The best vacations are long.
   The best vacations are restful.
7. The trip will prove exciting.
   The trip will prove dull.
8. For some people, a worthwhile hike should be slow.
   For some people, a worthwhile hike should be leisurely.
9. For other people, a worthwhile hike is long.
   For other people, a worthwhile hike is arduous.
10. The air should feel crisp.
    The air should feel invigorating.
11. It should smell clean.
    It should smell fresh.
12. The weather should remain clear.
    The weather should remain warm.
13. An entire summer at camp could prove boring.
    An entire summer at camp could prove rewarding.

15e. Sentences with Compound Predicate Nominatives

> The project will be a complete **success.**
> The project will be a complete **failure.**
> The project will be either a complete **success** or a complete **failure.**

Read the first two sentences in the box.

- What is the subject of each sentence?
- What is the verb of each sentence?
- What is the predicate nominative of each sentence?

Read the third sentence in the box.

- How have the first two sentences been combined to form the third sentence?

Two sentences with the same subject and the same linking verb or verb phrase can be combined to form a new sentence with a **compound predicate nominative**.

A sentence with a compound predicate nominative **is a sentence that has two or more predicate nominatives.** In a sentence with a compound predicate nominative, the predicate nominatives are usually joined by a coordinating conjunction or a correlative conjunction.

PRACTICING LANGUAGE SKILLS

■ Combine the two sentences in each of the following pairs to form a sentence with a compound predicate nominative.

1. The members of the committee were students.
   The members of the committee were teachers.
2. The leader of the group should have been Toria Svensen.
   The leader of the group should have been Mr. Giallorenzi.
3. The topic of the discussion will be pollution.
   The topic of the discussion will be conservation.
4. Each group member will become a leader.
   Each group member will become a follower.
5. The listeners may become enthusiastic organizers.
   The listeners may become supporters of the cause.
6. The speaker has been a teacher.
   The speaker has been a camp counselor.
7. Michael has long been an avid reader.
   Michael has long been an amateur sculptor.
8. Greta is an experienced surfer.
   Greta is an experienced ice skater.
9. The person who broke that vase must have been Ilse.
   The person who broke that vase must have been Bob.
10. Whoever takes that job will have to be a good teacher.
    Whoever takes that job will have to be a brilliant scientist.
11. That building is a fire hazard.
    That building is an eyesore.
12. Ms. Horowitz is a journalist.
    Ms. Horowitz is a short-story writer.

15f. Sentences with Adverbs after Linking Verbs

> Our helpers should be **here.**

Read the sentence in the box.

- What is the verb phrase of the sentence?
- What adverb follows the verb phrase?

In some sentences, a linking verb or verb phrase is followed by an adverb.

15g. Sentences with Prepositional Phrases after Linking Verbs

> The tools were **on the table.**

Read the sentence in the box.

- What is the verb of the sentence?
- What prepositional phrase follows the verb?

In some sentences, a linking verb or verb phrase is followed by a prepositional phrase.

PRACTICING LANGUAGE SKILLS

■ From each of the following sentences, write only the adverb or the prepositional phrase that follows the linking verb or verb phrase.

1. The instructions should be under the lid.
2. They must be somewhere.
3. The paintbrushes are in those cans.
4. The rollers should remain there.
5. Most of the tools are on this shelf.
6. It is near the box.
7. The hammer should be with the nails.
8. It might be on the floor.
9. The samples are in that heavy brown bag.
10. The bag is here.
11. The saw is under those pliers.
12. The screwdriver is with the wrench.
13. They may be outside.
14. The plans for this project were in the newspaper.
15. A diagram is on the workbench.
16. Your friends should be here.

APPLYING LANGUAGE SKILLS TO COMPOSITION

■ Finish each of the following sentences by adding an adverb or a prepositional phrase after the linking verb or verb phrase. Write the sentences.

1. The next meeting will be ||||||||||||||| .
2. Every member must be ||||||||||||||| .
3. Only the president was ||||||||||||||| .
4. That dog was ||||||||||||||| all the time.
5. Nobody else should be ||||||||||||||| .
6. You should have stayed ||||||||||||||| .
7. The bikes stayed ||||||||||||||| all night.
8. My bike should be ||||||||||||||| .
9. The tourists stayed ||||||||||||||| .
10. A message may be ||||||||||||||| .

15h. Diagraming Sentences with Linking Verbs

Sentences with predicate adjectives and sentences with predicate nominatives can be diagramed to show their structure. The first sentence below, for example, has a predicate adjective. The second sentence has a predicate nominative. The two sentences are diagramed in the same way.

Tracey has become quite skillful.   This is an example of her work.

To diagram such sentences, begin by writing the subject noun or pronoun, the verb or verb phrase, and the predicate adjective or predicate nominative on the main horizontal line. A short slanted line that goes to, but not through, the horizontal line separates the verb or verb phrase from the predicate adjective or predicate nominative.

Tracey | has become \ skillful   This | is \ example

Then diagram the adverb below the predicate adjective, and diagram the adjective and the prepositional phrase below the predicate nominative.

PRACTICING LANGUAGE SKILLS

- Diagram each of the following sentences.

1. Hobbies may be enjoyable.
2. The work looks easy.
3. We will become experts.
4. The materials have become rather expensive.
5. Our collection has grown quite large.
6. Some pieces are rather old.
7. They may prove valuable.
8. This model is an antique.
9. It looks very delicate.
10. Dana will be the leader of the next tour.
11. He seems somewhat nervous about the job.
12. The people on the tour are curious about the collection.
13. Their questions may be difficult.
14. The tour will be a success.
15. Dana might feel uncertain of his answers.
16. Dana will soon feel more confident.
17. His friends may become leaders on the tour.
18. The job looks quite interesting.
19. Susan seems very competent.
20. Her experience may prove useful.
21. The new teacher appears unusually confident.
22. Her office will soon feel comfortable.
23. Linda is very happy about her scholarship.
24. Our team may be victorious in the fall.
25. You should become an applicant.
26. The form for applicants is long.
27. Your handwriting should be neat.

15i. Simple Subjects and Simple Predicates

> The anxious **goalie is standing** near the net.
> **She has been guarding** the goal carefully.
> The **players** on both teams **are** nervous.

Read the sentences in the box.

- What is the subject of each sentence?
- What is the subject noun or pronoun of each sentence?
- What is the predicate of each sentence?
- What is the verb or verb phrase of each sentence?

The subject noun or pronoun of a sentence is called the simple subject.
The verb or verb phrase of a sentence is called the simple predicate.

The simple predicate of a sentence may be an intransitive verb or verb phrase, a transitive verb or verb phrase, or a linking verb or verb phrase.

PRACTICING LANGUAGE SKILLS

■ Write only the simple subject and the simple predicate from each of the following sentences.

1. Athletic events have captured the interest of many people.
2. Jogging has become a popular activity in every part of the country.
3. Some people play tennis every weekend.
4. Golf remains an especially popular pastime.
5. Many young people are now studying gymnastics.
6. During the summer, families may play volleyball.
7. Baseball is one of the most popular sports in the United States.
8. Another favorite game of many Americans is football.
9. Popular winter sports include skiing, tobogganing, ice-skating, and bobsledding.
10. Water sports provide good exercise.
11. Many students enjoy rowing or sailing.
12. Physical fitness has become an important concern of many people.
13. Some people ride their bikes to school or to work.
14. Other people roller-skate.
15. Wilderness areas attract a small group of sporting enthusiasts.

APPLYING LANGUAGE SKILLS TO COMPOSITION

■ Each group of words below includes a simple subject and a simple predicate. Use each simple subject and simple predicate in a sentence. Write your sentences.

1. you would have enjoyed
2. games entertain
3. athletes may enter
4. they might have been playing
5. competition is
6. coaches have given
7. I am learning
8. teams will compete

Reviewing 15 Sentences with Linking Verbs

15a. Sentences with Predicate Adjectives

Write the predicate adjective from each sentence.

1. Carlos felt hungry.
2. Everyone was enthusiastic.
3. Marcia remained confident.
4. They might have grown impatient.
5. It should taste spicy.
6. Mr. Walters may have felt nervous.
7. It seemed incomplete.
8. Stu remained convinced.
9. Animals may appear tame.
10. She sounded angry.

15b. Sentences with Predicate Nominatives

Write the predicate nominative from each sentence.

11. They have remained friends.
12. It could have been you.
13. Cissy will become president.
14. They are guests.
15. Students may become teachers.
16. Pictures can be symbols.
17. Oklahoma had been a territory.
18. It is a state.
19. Turnips are vegetables.
20. They might have been cousins.

15c. Modifiers in Sentences with Predicate Adjectives and Sentences with Predicate Nominatives

Write only the predicate adjective or the predicate nominative from each sentence.

21. The people in the lobby looked rather nervous.
22. The woman in that large office is the president of the company.
23. Barbara felt quite confident during the interview.

24. He might have become my best friend.
25. The yogurt tasted somewhat sour.
26. The cool water felt refreshing.
27. The solution to the problem was surprisingly simple.
28. The music sounded too loud to most of the dancers.
29. Lucille may become a photographer.
30. Vance may have been the secretary of the club.

15d. Sentences with Compound Predicate Adjectives

Write the two predicate adjectives from each sentence.

31. The mixture should be smooth and creamy.
32. The winter seemed too long and too cold.
33. Corliss seemed both shy and nervous.
34. Most examinations are either too easy or too difficult.
35. I felt neither strong nor brave.
36. Their firewood must have been either green or damp.
37. The final product was thick and rather gooey.
38. Only a few people will actually become rich and famous.
39. The results were complicated and confusing.
40. The winner of the speech contest had been confident and direct.

15e. Sentences with Compound Predicate Nominatives

Write the two predicate nominatives from each sentence.

41. Bryjid will become either an architect or a commercial artist.

42. His two best friends are still Leroy and Alfie.
43. The only necessary tools are a hammer and a small wrench.
44. The next contestant will be either Artis or you.
45. Gloria's assistants will be Setsuko and Orlando.
46. The dog's awards were a large cup and two blue ribbons.
47. He should have become either an actor or a singer.
48. We have become both friends and accomplices.
49. Our next dog will be either a poodle or a mutt.
50. Ms. Grabowski has been both a counselor and a principal.

15f. Sentences with Adverbs after Linking Verbs

From each sentence, write the adverb that follows the linking verb or verb phrase.

51. You should have been there.
52. The best performance will be tonight.
53. Silvia has been here for nearly an hour.
54. They must have been upstairs.
55. The tourists had been everywhere.
56. The diary must be somewhere in his desk.
57. The last meeting was yesterday.
58. The younger children were outside.

15g. Sentences with Prepositional Phrases after Linking Verbs

From each sentence, write the prepositional phrase that follows the linking verb or verb phrase.

59. The broom must be behind the door.
60. Nobody has been in this room.
61. The scissors should have been in the top drawer.
62. This package is for you.
63. Our parents will be in the audience.

64. Ada has been with her cousins.
65. The members of both teams were on the field.
66. Something must be under the rug.

15h. Diagraming Sentences with Linking Verbs

Diagram each sentence.

67. Their new neighbor is Verna.
68. I have been feeling hopeful.
69. The test was rather difficult.
70. The colt was acting skittish.
71. Your suggestion proved worthless.
72. Daphne has become an exceptional pianist.
73. These are samples of the material.
74. The red roses smell very sweet.
75. Several people in the crowded room felt uncomfortable.
76. The sky has become rather cloudy.

15i. Simple Subjects and Simple Predicates

Write only the simple subject and the simple predicate from each sentence.

77. A young boy in a red slicker was standing on the top step.
78. You should have acted more cautiously.
79. The driver of the old truck gave us a helpful suggestion.
80. The raft floated slowly down the river.
81. That particular symphony has always been my favorite.
82. Juliette plays the oboe rather well.
83. This old bike just needs a new chain and some fresh paint.
84. Our stroll through the countryside proved exhausting.
85. The butcher will probably cut you another chop.
86. The first two performers were Burgess and Belinda.
87. Every student in the class had a different opinion.

16 Phrases

16a. Identifying and Using Prepositional Phrases

> Naturalists have found examples **of animal cooperation.**
> Animals will cooperate **under certain conditions.**

Read the sentences in the box.

- What is the prepositional phrase in each sentence?
- In which sentence does the prepositional phrase modify the noun **examples**?
- In which sentence does the prepositional phrase modify the verb phrase **will cooperate**?

A phrase is a group of words that is used as a noun, as an adjective, or as an adverb. A phrase never contains both a subject and a predicate.

One kind of phrase is the prepositional phrase. A prepositional phrase is a phrase that begins with a preposition. A prepositional phrase ends with a noun or pronoun, which is called the object of the preposition. A prepositional phrase may be used as an adjective or as an adverb in a sentence.

PRACTICING LANGUAGE SKILLS

■ Write only the prepositional phrase from each of the following sentences. Then write **adjective** or **adverb** to show how the prepositional phrase is used.

1. Animals have a need for companionship.
2. We have made studies of rat behavior.
3. Rats sicken in isolation.
4. Rats in groups mature more rapidly.
5. Chimps will work with each other.
6. They may pass food between cages.
7. Small animals might hunt in teams.
8. Cooperative fishing is practiced by white pelicans.
9. They thrash the water with their wings.
10. Frightened fish move into smaller areas.
11. The birds then eat the haul of fish.

APPLYING LANGUAGE SKILLS TO COMPOSITION

■ Add a prepositional phrase to complete each of the following sentences. Write the sentences.

1. Many people own pets ||||||||||||||| .
2. These pets cooperate ||||||||||||||| .
3. A dog may protect a cat ||||||||||||||| .
4. You may see a cat sleeping ||||||||||||||| .
5. A bird can often eat safely ||||||||||||||| .
6. Some animals need companionship when they are ||||||||||||||| .
7. Often an animal will give food ||||||||||||||| .
8. A single tadpole ||||||||||||||| will often become sick.
9. Rabbits kept ||||||||||||||| may become irritable.
10. Animals, like humans, have a need ||||||||||||||| .

16b. Gerund Phrases

> **Communicating with animals** interests some scientists.
> They enjoy **studying animal speech.**
> They have developed methods for **talking to chimpanzees.**
> Their greatest achievement has been **communicating with a chimp.**

Read the sentences in the box. In each sentence, the phrase in dark type is used as a noun.

- With what verb form does each phrase begin?
- With what part of speech does each phrase end?

A **gerund phrase** **is a phrase that begins with a gerund. A gerund is a present participle verb form used as a noun. A gerund phrase includes one or more other words that add to the meaning of the gerund. It may contain nouns used as direct objects or as objects of prepositions.** A gerund phrase is used as a noun in a sentence.

PRACTICING LANGUAGE SKILLS

■ Write only the gerund phrase from each of the following sentences. Underline the gerund in each gerund phrase.

1. Washoe, a chimpanzee, succeeded in mastering a simple sign language.
2. By combining unrelated words, she even developed new concepts.
3. We now know chimps are capable of learning hundreds of words.
4. Putting words into meaningful sentences is also possible.
5. However, speaking through sign language can cause confusion.
6. Using computers can make communication more exact.

APPLYING LANGUAGE SKILLS TO COMPOSITION

■ Complete each of the following sentences by adding one or more words after the gerund to make a gerund phrase. Write the sentences.

1. Communicating |||||||||||||||| is common in many animals.
2. The rabbit warns of danger by thumping |||||||||||||||| .
3. Dancing |||||||||||||||| tells bees the location of food.
4. Birds can assemble flocks by calling |||||||||||||||| .
5. Rubbing |||||||||||||||| allows crickets to communicate.
6. Studying |||||||||||||||| is fascinating.

■■ Finish each of the following sentences by adding a gerund phrase.

1. Animals use signs for |||||||||||||||| .
2. Cats will communicate with their owners by |||||||||||||||| .
3. |||||||||||||||| brings a dog rapid attention.
4. |||||||||||||||| indicates a horse is angry.
5. |||||||||||||||| is a sign of canary contentment.
6. All animal owners have the duty of |||||||||||||||| .

16c. Diagraming Gerund Phrases Used as Subjects

Sentences with gerund phrases can be diagramed to show their structure. For example, the following sentence has a gerund phrase as a subject.

Studying law is difficult.

To diagram this sentence, begin by writing the verb and the predicate adjective of the sentence on a horizontal line.

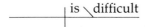

Now draw two horizontal lines connected by a vertical line above the subject of the main diagram line. Write the gerund in a curve at the angle of the top horizontal line and the vertical line. Write the direct object of the gerund phrase on the second horizontal line.

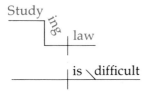

To show that the gerund phrase is used as a subject, connect the gerund phrase to the subject position on the main diagram line with this line (⋏).

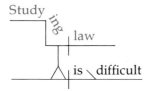

PRACTICING LANGUAGE SKILLS

- The following sentences have gerund phrases used as subjects. Diagram each sentence.

1. Studying medicine is a challenge.
2. Training doctors is a great responsibility.
3. Mastering new techniques becomes complicated.
4. Saving lives gives great satisfaction.
5. Teaching school is a worthwhile career.
6. Preparing lessons becomes a daily task.
7. Correcting papers is a nightly chore.
8. Supervising sports provides excitement.
9. Meeting new people gives real pleasure.
10. Writing reports may be time-consuming.
11. Stealing cars is a crime.
12. Checking the level of the oil is your job.
13. Washing the car is a bore.
14. Putting air in the tires will be necessary.
15. Leaving the house early is a habit.
16. Remodeling old houses can be fun.
17. Repairing the lawn mower was easy.
18. Meeting your train will be impossible.
19. Writing reports prepared me for college.
20. Shaking hands was the candidate's greatest talent.

16d. Diagraming Gerund Phrases Used as Direct Objects

Sentences with gerund phrases as direct objects can be diagramed to show their structure. For example, the following sentence has a gerund phrase as a direct object.

Students enjoy performing experiments in the lab.

To diagram this sentence, begin by writing the subject and the verb on a horizontal line.

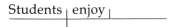

Now draw two horizontal lines connected by a vertical line above the direct object space of the main diagram line. Write the gerund in a curve at the angle of the top horizontal line and the vertical line. Write the direct object of the gerund phrase on the second horizontal line. Add the prepositional phrase that modifies the gerund.

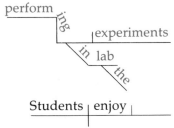

In order to show that the gerund phrase is used as a direct object, connect the gerund phrase to the direct object space of the main diagram line with this line (⋀).

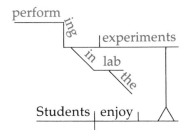

PRACTICING LANGUAGE SKILLS

■ The following sentences have gerund phrases used as direct objects. Diagram each sentence.

1. I do not enjoy washing the car.
2. Jerry likes sailing her boat.
3. Marie loves skating on the ice.
4. Michael teaches surfing during the summer.
5. Connie tried fishing for trout.
6. She preferred hiking in the mountains.
7. Ed studied dancing for two years.
8. Lola practiced repairing her car.
9. She also teaches dancing to children.

16e. Nonrestrictive Participial Phrases

> **Recognized as a period of learning,** the Renaissance was also a time of artistic achievement.
>
> The Renaissance, **recognized as a period of learning,** was also a time of artistic achievement.

Read the sentences in the box. In each sentence, the group of words in dark type is used as an adjective.

- In the first sentence, what phrase gives further information about **the Renaissance**?
- In the second sentence, what phrase gives further information about **the Renaissance**?
- With what part of speech does each phrase begin?
- Do the two sentences have the same meaning?

A participial phrase is a phrase that begins with a present participle or a past participle. A participial phrase includes one or more words that add to the meaning of the participle. It may include nouns used as the direct object of the participle or as the object of a preposition. A participial phrase is used as an adjective in a sentence.

If a participial phrase merely gives further information about the noun it modifies, it is called a nonrestrictive participial phrase. A nonrestrictive participial phrase is separated by commas from the rest of the sentence. Sometimes a nonrestrictive participial phrase precedes the noun it modifies.

Using new techniques, Leonardo painted the <u>Mona Lisa</u>.

Sometimes a nonrestrictive participial phrase follows the noun it modifies.

Leonardo, using new techniques, painted the <u>Mona Lisa</u>.

Whether it precedes or follows the noun it modifies, the nonrestrictive participial phrase has the same meaning.

PRACTICING LANGUAGE SKILLS

■ Write only the nonrestrictive participial phrase from each of the following sentences. Underline the participle in each participial phrase.

1. Destined to be a great Renaissance master, Leonardo da Vinci was born in 1452.
2. Having little education, Leonardo was apprenticed at an early age.
3. He became a pupil of Verrocchio, celebrated for his religious paintings.
4. His fame, colored by rumors of supernatural talents, spread rapidly.
5. Seeking both artist and engineer, the Duke of Milan commissioned him in 1482.
6. The Last Supper, painted in Milan, is one of his most famous works.

7. Capturing the profound emotions of the apostles, it is a masterpiece.
8. Painted with inferior materials, the mural has deteriorated.
9. Experimenting in his free time, Leonardo invented the first flying machine.
10. Engineering countless other devices, he discovered much about natural laws.
11. Many of his discoveries, based on scientific observation, remain valid.
12. His notebooks, unpublished for centuries, could have revolutionized science.
13. Often called his most famous portrait, the <u>Mona Lisa</u> was never finished.
14. Exemplifying the use of light and dark colors, it now hangs in the Louvre.
15. Studying anatomy, Leonardo made many drawings of the skeleton and muscles.
16. These drawings, filled with accurate detail, were centuries ahead of their time.
17. Working for the Duke of Milan, Leonardo designed fortifications and war machines.
18. Anticipating modern warfare, he invented tanks and machine guns.
19. An underwater breathing apparatus, sketched in Milan, resembles today's diving equipment.
20. Working in isolation, Leonardo seems to have had few friends.
21. His handwriting, written from right to left, can be read only in a mirror.
22. His discoveries, recorded in his notebooks, could not be read by the wrong people.
23. Leonardo's designs, worked out brilliantly, could not have been built in the sixteenth century.
24. Existing only on paper, they remained dreams until the twentieth century.
25. Leonardo's genius, unmatched in history, will always fascinate us.

APPLYING LANGUAGE SKILLS TO COMPOSITION

■ Complete each of the following sentences by adding a nonrestrictive participial phrase. Write the sentences.

1. ||||||||||||||| , we finally had enough money to go camping.
2. We decided to camp by Lake Pine Cone, ||||||||||||||| .
3. Our sleeping bags, ||||||||||||||| , were very warm.
4. We slept in a small tent, ||||||||||||||| .
5. Our meals, ||||||||||||||| , tasted delicious.
6. For breakfast we had oatmeal and dried fruit, ||||||||||||||| .
7. After breakfast my brother, ||||||||||||||| , went fishing.
8. My sister and I, ||||||||||||||| , went hiking.
9. The sunsets, ||||||||||||||| , were beautiful.
10. A few accidents, ||||||||||||||| , caused us some trouble.
11. My brother, ||||||||||||||| , fell in the lake.
12. My sister, ||||||||||||||| , wandered around the mountain all night.
13. ||||||||||||||| , I developed a rash on both legs.
14. My camera, ||||||||||||||| , was nearly flattened.
15. Raccoons, ||||||||||||||| , ate nearly all of our food.
16. A thunderstorm, ||||||||||||||| , left us soaking wet.
17. ||||||||||||||| , we were still sad to return home.
18. ||||||||||||||| , we plan to return next year.
19. ||||||||||||||| , we agreed that we had had a good time.
20. ||||||||||||||| , I have saved almost enough money for next year.

16f. Restrictive Participial Phrases

Painters **using new techniques** created unusual effects.
Churches **built of stone** have lasted for centuries.

Read the sentences in the box. In each sentence, the group of words in dark type is used as an adjective.

- In the first sentence, what phrase gives essential information about **painters**?
- In the second sentence, what phrase gives essential information about **churches**?
- With what part of speech does each phrase begin?
- Could these phrases be dropped from their sentences without changing the meaning of the sentences?

If a participial phrase gives essential information about the noun it modifies, it is called a restrictive participial phrase. A restrictive participial phrase cannot be removed from a sentence without changing the meaning of the sentence. Notice how removing the restrictive participial phrase changes the meaning of the following sentence.

All people **joining our club** must pay dues. (true)
All people must pay dues. (untrue)

A restrictive participial phrase always follows the noun it modifies. A restrictive participial phrase is not separated by commas from the rest of the sentence.

PRACTICING LANGUAGE SKILLS

■ Write only the restrictive participial phrase from each of the following sentences. Underline the participle in each participial phrase.

1. We had a banquet of food originating in many different cultures.
2. Dipak brought an Indian curry containing a number of vegetables.
3. Kimon made a salad topped with Greek olives and feta.
4. Feta is a strong cheese made from goat's milk.
5. Chili peppers stuffed with cheese were Agustina's favorite.
6. French bread spread with garlic butter accompanied the meal.
7. Mario prepared an Italian dessert made with beaten eggs.
8. Custard made with cinnamon tastes better than plain custard.
9. Lamb cooked with garlic is a tradition in Sheila's family.
10. Rye bread spread with sweet butter goes well with Swiss cheese.
11. Hot chocolate drunk at bedtime helps Stephanie fall asleep at night.
12. I prefer mild enchiladas, but Jay prefers them sizzling with hot sauce.
13. Peanut stew is a Nigerian dish found seldom in this country.
14. Pastries filled with jelly always have a surprise when you bite into them.

16g. Diagraming Participial Phrases

Sentences with participial phrases can be diagramed to show their structure. For example, both these sentences contain participial phrases.

Shoppers comparing prices have saved money.
Careful shoppers comparing sale prices have saved much money.

To diagram the first sentence, begin by writing the subject, the verb phrase, and the direct object of the sentence on a horizontal line.

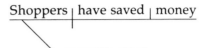

Now draw a second horizontal line under the first. Draw a slanting line connecting it with the noun modified by the participial phrase.

Write the participle in a curve along the slanted line and the lower horizontal line. Write the direct object of the participial phrase on the lower horizontal line.

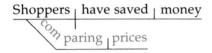

To diagram the second sentence, place the adjectives on slanted lines under the words they modifying.

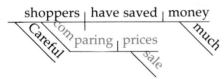

PRACTICING LANGUAGE SKILLS

■ The following sentences have participial phrases. Diagram each sentence.

1. Consumers making purchases must be careful.
2. They should evaluate advertisements promoting products.
3. Commercials promising bargains may be deceptive.
4. Congress has passed legislation requiring labels.
5. Buyers should study labels listing contents.
6. Brands stressing quality may be tested.
7. Shoppers considering nutrition are wise.
8. Groups protecting consumers have multiplied.
9. They provide information concerning products.
10. Consumer groups make tests determining product safety.
11. Accidents involving defective goods have decreased greatly.

293

16h. Infinitive Phrases Used as Nouns

> **To predict natural disasters** has been a goal of science.
> Scientists are trying **to save thousands of lives.**

Read the sentences in the box. In each sentence, the group of words in dark type is used as a noun.

- In which sentence is the phrase in dark type used as a subject noun?
- In which sentence is the phrase in dark type used as a direct object noun?

An infinitive phrase **is a phrase that begins with an infinitive. An** infinitive **consists of the word** to **and a verb form such as** predict **or** save. **An infinitive phrase includes one or more other words that add to the meaning of the infinitive.** An infinitive phrase may be used as a noun in a sentence. The word **to** may sometimes be omitted from the infinitive phrase.

PRACTICING LANGUAGE SKILLS

■ From each of the following sentences, write only the infinitive phrase that is used as a noun. Then write **subject** or **direct object** to show how the infinitive phrase is used.

1. To predict earthquakes is still impossible.
2. To worry about earthquakes is useless.
3. Geologists do not dare to explore active volcanoes.
4. To attempt this would be foolish.
5. Geologic changes in the earth begin to build stress.
6. The earth starts to relieve this pressure.
7. Its crust begins to show cracks.
8. Sudden splitting of the earth's surface starts to cause earthquakes.
9. To experience an earthquake can be frightening.
10. To remain calm is very important.
11. Scientists are trying to establish earthquake warning signals.
12. To gather data requires thousands of seismic stations.
13. To measure earthquakes takes sensitive instruments.
14. Each year seismologists attempt to study many earthquakes.

APPLYING LANGUAGE SKILLS TO COMPOSITION

■ Complete each of the following sentences by adding an infinitive phrase. Write each sentence.

1. |||||||||||||| is a great scientific achievement.
2. |||||||||||||| was considered impossible a century ago.
3. Now we have learned |||||||||||||| .
4. All of us expect |||||||||||||| .
5. |||||||||||||| would save lives and property.
6. |||||||||||||| could be a benefit to us all.
7. |||||||||||||| is still not possible.
8. Scientists are planning |||||||||||||| .
9. In the future, people hope |||||||||||||| .
10. One day we may begin |||||||||||||| .

16i. Infinitive Phrases Used as Adjectives

American women have not always had the right **to vote in elections.**

Read the sentence in the box. The group of words in dark type is used as an adjective.

- With what word does the group of words in dark type begin?
- What word does the group of words in dark type modify?

An infinitive phrase **is a phrase that begins with an infinitive. An infinitive phrase includes one or more other words that add to the meaning of the infinitive.** An infinitive phrase may be used as an adjective in a sentence.

PRACTICING LANGUAGE SKILLS

■ From each of the following sentences, write only the infinitive phrase that is used as an adjective. Then write the noun that the infinitive phrase modifies.

1. A conference to declare women's rights was held at Seneca Falls, New York, in 1848.
2. The convention to proclaim women's equality had many delegates.
3. The women demanded the right to vote in elections.
4. This move to gain the franchise was very radical.
5. Attempts to discredit the convention spread.
6. Newspapers called it a plot to destroy the American family.
7. For some, the convention became a bad dream to forget hurriedly.
8. For others, Seneca Falls provided the inspiration to act courageously.
9. A society to work for women's equality became active.
10. Plans to continue the work of the convention grew.
11. The struggle to gain the vote for women began.
12. Not until 1920 did American women have the chance to vote in national elections.

APPLYING LANGUAGE SKILLS TO COMPOSITION

■ Complete each of the following sentences by adding an infinitive phrase used as an adjective. Write the sentences.

1. Equality is a goal ||||||||||||||| .
2. The way ||||||||||||||| is through constant work.
3. The effort ||||||||||||||| may take strength.
4. Inability ||||||||||||||| might not affect you personally.
5. An agreement ||||||||||||||| might not be wise.
6. Trying ||||||||||||||| could take a long time.
7. Laws ||||||||||||||| should be enforced.
8. Legislators have the power ||||||||||||||| .
9. Do we need laws ||||||||||||||| ?
10. The right ||||||||||||||| should be guaranteed to all.
11. Every citizen should have the opportunity ||||||||||||||| .

16j. Infinitive Phrases Used as Adverbs

Reporters rushed **to file their stories.**
They were anxious **to inform the public.**

Read the sentences in the box. In each sentence, the group of words in dark type is used as an adverb.

- With what word does each group of words in dark type begin?
- In which sentence does the group of words in dark type modify a verb?
- In which sentence does the group of words in dark type modify an adjective?

An infinitive phrase **is a phrase that begins with an infinitive. An infinitive phrase includes one or more other words that add to the meaning of the infinitive.** An infinitive phrase may be used as an adverb in a sentence.

PRACTICING LANGUAGE SKILLS

■ From each of the following sentences, write only the infinitive phrase that is used as an adverb.

1. All newspapers are eager to gain subscribers.
2. Hundreds of publications compete to attract readers.
3. Newspapers print bold headlines to catch readers' eyes.
4. Journalists at the turn of the century were anxious to correct social conditions.
5. Reporters still frequently work to support causes.
6. Many write to promote social change.
7. Sometimes forces combine to prevent honest news reporting.
8. Dictatorships are careful to control the press.
9. The world was thrilled to watch astronauts land on the moon.
10. Radio and television are quick to report local news.
11. Television stations compete to get stories first.
12. People will read newspapers to get more extensive coverage.

APPLYING LANGUAGE SKILLS TO COMPOSITION

■ Complete each of the following sentences by adding an infinitive phrase used as an adverb. Write the sentences.

1. Reporters on our school newspaper are eager |||||||||||||| .
2. Throughout the school they gather |||||||||||||| .
3. Proofreaders are anxious |||||||||||||| .
4. The entire newspaper staff is careful |||||||||||||| .
5. Advertising agents must be sure |||||||||||||| .
6. As deadlines near, everyone rushes |||||||||||||| .
7. The journalists are relieved |||||||||||||| .
8. When the paper is distributed, students hurry |||||||||||||| .

16k. Diagraming Infinitive Phrases Used as Nouns

Sentences with infinitive phrases used as nouns can be diagramed to show their structure. For example, the following sentences have infinitive phrases used as nouns. The infinitive phrase in the first sentence is used as a subject noun. The infinitive phrase in the second sentence is used as a direct object.

> To have supporters is important.
> They are trying to get votes.

In both sentences, the infinitive phrase and the rest of the sentence are diagramed in the same way. Only the position of the line connecting the infinitive phrase to the rest of the sentence is changed. This connecting line is drawn to show the use of the infinitive phrase in the sentence.

To diagram the first sentence, begin by writing the verb and the predicate adjective on a horizontal line.

Now draw a second horizontal line above the subject position. Place the verb form and the direct object of the infinitive phrase on the second horizontal line. Place the word **to** on a slanted line in front of the second horizontal line. To show that the infinitive phrase is used as a subject, connect the infinitive phrase to the subject position on the main diagram line with this line ($\wedge$).

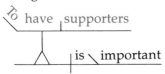

Diagram the second sentence in much the same way. Begin by writing the subject pronoun and the verb phrase on a horizontal line. Study the example below.

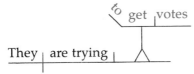

PRACTICING LANGUAGE SKILLS

■ The following sentences have infinitive phrases used as subjects or as direct objects. Diagram each sentence.

1. To gain confidence is important.
2. Students must try to inform themselves.
3. To investigate issues is essential.
4. To win votes is necessary.
5. They will try to read many papers.
6. We need to hear speeches.
7. To find candidates is difficult.
8. To uncover problems is vital.
9. They should work to find solutions.
10. To back leaders is your responsibility.

161. Diagraming Infinitive Phrases Used as Adjectives and as Adverbs

Sentences with infinitive phrases used as adjectives or as adverbs can
be diagramed to show their structure. For example, the first of the
following sentences has an infinitive phrase used as an adjective. The
second sentence has an infinitive phrase used as an adverb.

These are the plans to organize the parade.
Spectators hurried to see the band.

To diagram the first sentence, begin by writing the subject, the verb,
and the predicate nominative on a horizontal line.

These | are \ plans

Diagram the infinitive phrase under the noun it modifies, as you would
diagram a prepositional phrase. Place the word **to** on the slanted line.
Place the verb form and the direct object of the phrase on the
horizontal line.

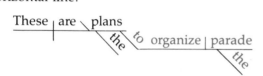

To diagram the second sentence, write the subject and the verb on a
horizontal line.

Spectators | hurried

Diagram the infinitive phrase under the verb it modifies, as you would
diagram a prepositional phrase. Place the word **to** on the slanted line.
Place the verb form and the direct object of the phrase on the
horizontal line.

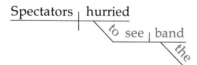

PRACTICING LANGUAGE SKILLS

■ The following sentences have infinitive phrases used as adverbs or as
adjectives. Diagram each sentence.

1. They are sure to enjoy the parade.
2. I paused to pet a horse.
3. We stood to watch the clowns.
4. We found volunteers to decorate floats.
5. We organized a group to lead everyone.
6. Onlookers strained to hear the music.
7. Food stands are places to buy snacks.
8. Ramon became the person to sell flags.
9. Everyone stretched to see the animals.
10. Noisy children waited to get balloons.

298

16m. Appositive Phrases

> Romulus was one of the founders of Rome.
> Romulus, **a son of Mars,** was one of the founders of Rome.

Read the sentences in the box.

- What is the subject of each sentence?
- In the second sentence, what group of words identifies or renames the subject?

An appositive phrase follows a noun or pronoun in a sentence. An appositive phrase is a phrase that identifies or renames the noun or pronoun it follows. An appositive phrase always contains an appositive noun. In the second sentence in the box, **son** is the appositive noun that identifies or renames Romulus. An appositive phrase is separated by commas from the rest of the sentence.

PRACTICING LANGUAGE SKILLS

■ Write the appositive phrase from each of the following sentences. Underline the appositive noun in each appositive phrase.

1. Julius Caesar, an ancient statesman, was born in Rome.
2. In 60 B.C., Caesar formed the First Triumvirate, a coalition of three powerful leaders.
3. During Caesar's absence, Crassus, a member of the Triumvirate, died.
4. This left Pompey, the third member, extremely powerful.
5. Pompey became jealous of Caesar, his young rival.
6. Caesar overcame Pompey's troops in Pharsalus, a town in Greece.
7. Julius Caesar wrote the Commentaries, a work about his campaigns.
8. Caesar, now dictator, had many enemies.
9. Caesar was assassinated on March 15, 44 B.C., a famous date in history.

APPLYING LANGUAGE SKILLS TO COMPOSITION

■ Combine each of the following pairs of sentences to make a new sentence. Use part of the second sentence as an appositive phrase in your new sentence. Write the new sentences.

1. Augustus ruled from 27 B.C. to A.D. 14.
   Augustus was the first Roman emperor.
2. He had changed his name from Octavian to Augustus.
   Augustus is a name meaning "sacred" or "exalted."
3. Octavian first became powerful after the death of Julius Caesar.
   Julius Caesar was his great-uncle.
4. Octavian shared power with Mark Antony.
   Antony was a powerful Roman tribune.
5. Octavian and Antony defeated Brutus.
   Brutus had been a conspirator in Caesar's assassination.
6. When Antony joined Cleopatra, Octavian declared war on both of them.
   Cleopatra was the queen of Egypt.

Reviewing [16] Phrases

16a. Identifying and Using Prepositional Phrases

Write only the prepositional phrase from each of the following sentences. Then write **adjective** or **adverb** to show how the prepositional phrase is used.

1. Amelia parked her car in the garage.
2. The boy in the corner seems very shy.
3. The book on the table looks easy.
4. The teacher with the beard is Mr. Richardson.
5. We roller-skated around the lake.
6. He put the old shoes in the attic.

16b. Gerund Phrases

Write only the gerund phrase from each of the following sentences. Underline the gerund in each gerund phrase.

7. My father learned to swim by falling in the river.
8. Racing cars is a hard profession.
9. Clara's duty is editing the paper.
10. Richard's science project will be designing an electronic adding machine.
11. Jamey lets us know how he feels by crying at the top of his lungs.
12. Aunt Eloise worked her way through college by selling encyclopedias.

16c. Diagraming Gerund Phrases Used as Subjects

The following sentences have gerund phrases used as subjects. Diagram each sentence.

13. Marking the prices is your job.
14. Washing the dishes is Eric's task.
15. Multiplying in his head is Bob's talent.
16. Shooting baskets is Sandra's skill.
17. Rescuing that cat was difficult.
18. Seeing that movie made her very happy.

16d. Diagraming Gerund Phrases Used as Direct Objects

The following sentences have gerund phrases used as direct objects. Diagram each sentence.

19. I enjoy napping in the hammock.
20. I avoid mowing the lawn.
21. We should try fishing for sea bass.
22. Consuela practiced throwing the discus.
23. Rudy hated delivering his speech.
24. He dreaded standing on the stage.

16e. Nonrestrictive Participial Phrases

Write only the nonrestrictive participial phrase from each of the following sentences. Underline the participle in each participial phrase.

25. Standing in line, Craig soon felt tired.
26. Asked to dance, Marie was embarrassed.
27. Elected class president, Jon thanked everyone who had voted for him.
28. Luis, having won the Junior Songwriter competition, was elated.
29. Walking in a daze, Norman fell into the irrigation ditch.

16f. Restrictive Participial Phrases

Write only the restrictive participial phrase from each of the following sentences. Underline the participle in each participial phrase.

30. Houses built of seasoned wood can resist dry rot.
31. My father gave me a necktie decorated with seahorses.
32. Divers using scuba equipment explored the wreck.
33. A man wearing a cape walked onstage.
34. Musicians playing Viennese waltzes entertained the guests.

16g. Diagraming Participial Phrases

The following sentences have participial phrases. Diagram each sentence.

35. My brother found a pamphlet promising wealth.
36. Shaking his head, he gave it to me.
37. Reading it, I was shocked.
38. People making false promises should be jailed!
39. Highly embarrassed, he said nothing.

16h. Infinitive Phrases Used as Nouns

From each of the following sentences, write only the infinitive phrase that is used as a noun.

40. To learn a foreign language is rewarding.
41. In Mr. Roper's class, I learned to answer questions quickly and concisely.
42. Over a period of months, Billy managed to meet everybody in his school.
43. To restore that car may not be possible.
44. To be honest is very important.

16i. Infinitive Phrases Used as Adjectives

From each of the following sentences, write only the infinitive phrase that is used as an adjective.

45. Attempts to climb this mountain are hazardous.
46. There should be a law to prevent fraud.
47. The plot to kidnap the ambassador was thwarted.
48. That magician has the power to cloud people's minds.
49. Her decision to take the class was wise.

16j. Infinitive Phrases Used as Adverbs

From each of the following sentences, write only the infinitive phrase that is used as an adverb.

50. Donna's cousin from Cleveland was eager to visit San Francisco.
51. Donna was very happy to have her as a guest.
52. She hurried to meet the plane.
53. Donna was anxious to see her cousin.
54. They turned on the radio to hear the news.

16k. Diagraming Infinitive Phrases Used as Nouns

The following sentences have infinitive phrases used as subjects or as direct objects. Diagram each sentence.

55. To defend our rights is important.
56. I may decide to work in the warehouse.
57. I will be forced to choose between them.
58. To play volleyball would be fun.
59. To save money should be easy.

16l. Diagraming Infinitive Phrases Used as Adjectives and as Adverbs

The following sentences have infinitive phrases used as adjectives or as adverbs. Diagram each sentence.

60. Helen stood up to see the sunset.
61. Elaine signed a petition to reopen the park.
62. Jimmy has a license to sing on the street.
63. The children were glad to see you.
64. Saul was the first one to laugh at it.

16m. Appositive Phrases

Combine each of the following pairs of sentences to make a new sentence. Use part of the second sentence as an appositive phrase. Write the new sentences.

65. Aunt Etta came to visit us.
    Aunt Etta is my father's sister.
66. The 1956 Thunderbird is a classic.
    The 1956 Thunderbird is a small, sporty car.
67. Ramon broke his ankle last week.
    Ramon is the best pitcher on the team.

17 Clauses

17a. Identifying and Using Independent Clauses

> The Golden Gate Bridge was built in the 1930's.
> It cost 35 million dollars.
>
> Today we are used to huge engineering projects.
> The Panama Canal is still an extraordinary achievement
>
> Massive locks had to be designed for the canal.
> Ships could not move from ocean to ocean.

Read the pairs of sentences in the box.

- What is the subject of each sentence?
- What is the predicate of each sentence?

Combine the two sentences in each pair. Use one of these words to join the sentences: **and, but, or.**

Two sentences can be joined to make a new sentence. Both sentences should be about the same action or idea. They can be joined with a comma and the coordinating conjunction and **,** but **,** or **,** nor **,** for **, or** yet **. They can also be joined by correlative conjunctions. The new sentence is called a** compound sentence **.**

In a compound sentence, each of the shorter sentences is called an independent clause **. A** clause **is a group of words that contains a subject and a predicate. An independent clause is a clause that can stand alone as a separate sentence.**

PRACTICING LANGUAGE SKILLS

■ Read each of the following sentences. If the sentence is a compound sentence, write it. Then underline the two independent clauses and circle the coordinating conjunction. If the sentence is not a compound sentence, write **not a compound sentence.**

1. The Empire State Building was once the world's tallest building, but now there are taller ones.
2. This structure is 1,250 feet high, and it is topped by a 220-foot television antenna.
3. Each year, thousands of people visit the building and enjoy the view.
4. The building houses a small city, and over 58,000 people work there.
5. It has its own fire department and small, elevator-sized trucks.
6. At first, no one believed the building would be occupied, nor did anyone foresee its usefulness.
7. Hoover Dam spans the Colorado River and creates Lake Mead.
8. It was the largest dam of its time, but bigger dams have been built since then.
9. Engineers built the dam in pieces, and each section had air spaces for cooling.
10. Today, people can visit higher dams, or they can read about larger ones.

17b. Diagraming Compound Sentences

Compound sentences can be diagramed to show their structure. For example, the following sentence is a compound sentence.

> The ancient Greeks worshiped many powerful gods, but their gods usually ignored mortals.

To diagram a compound sentence, begin by diagraming the two independent clauses on separate horizontal lines, one above the other. Then write the coordinating conjunction on a short horizontal line between the two independent clauses. Join this short line to the main diagram lines by broken vertical lines. To complete the diagram of the example sentence, write the adjectives, the possessive pronoun, and the adverb on slanted lines below the words they modify.

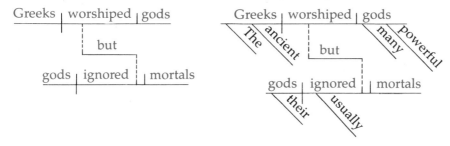

PRACTICING COMPOSITION SKILLS

■ The following sentences are compound sentences. Diagram each sentence.

1. Every nation has myths, and mythology is always fascinating.
2. Gods might rule mortals, or they might control nature.
3. Some gods are aloof, but others appear friendly.
4. Myths explain natural events, or they teach moral lessons.
5. The Greeks created myths, and many stories are still famous.
6. The Greeks admired heroes, but heroes often had flaws.
7. Some famous heroes were brutal, and others were treacherous.
8. The gods often disagreed, and sometimes they quarreled violently.
9. The important Greek gods were a family, and they lived richly.
10. Mount Olympus was their home, but no mortal could visit it.
11. The Olympians ignored lesser gods, and they usually disliked mortals.
12. Zeus was the king, and Hera was the queen.
13. King Zeus was brave, but he was a violent, conceited god.
14. Queen Hera could be motherly, or she could be jealous.
15. Zeus would deceive Hera, or Hera would thwart Zeus.
16. Zeus ruled the heavens, but his brothers ruled the rest of the world.
17. Poseidon ruled the oceans, and Hades ruled the underworld.
18. Athena was the goddess of wisdom, and Hermes was the god of trade.

17c. Adverb Clauses

> We listen to folk tales.
> We hear many exaggerations.
> **When we listen to folk tales,** we hear many exaggerations.
> We hear many exaggerations **when we listen to folk tales.**

Read the sentences in the box.

- How were the first two sentences combined to make the third and fourth sentences?

The third and fourth sentences each have the same two clauses. The clause **we hear many exaggerations** is an independent clause. It can stand alone as a separate sentence. The clause **when we listen to folk tales** is a subordinate clause. **A subordinate clause is a clause that cannot stand alone as a separate sentence.**

The subordinate clause **when we listen to folk tales** is an adverb clause. **An adverb clause is a subordinate clause that modifies a verb or verb phrase.** The adverb clause **when we listen to folk tales** modifies the verb **listen.**

An adverb clause begins with a **subordinating conjunction.** The words in the box below are all subordinating conjunctions.

after	because	since	until	where
although	before	though	when	wherever
as	if	unless	whenever	while

When a subordinate clause comes at the beginning of a sentence, it is followed by a comma.

PRACTICING LANGUAGE SKILLS

- Write only the adverb clause from each of the following sentences.

1. Because America has had an exciting history, its folk tales are very colorful.
2. Though some stories are about animals, others are about people.
3. While folk tales are usually told, they may also be sung.
4. Although they are all entertaining, many also teach us lessons.
5. If the heroes were real people, storytellers exaggerated their qualities.
6. Storytellers invented myths if the facts were too dull.
7. Americans can catch a glimpse of history whenever they read folk tales.
8. Stories about Daniel Boone were popular after he explored the frontier wilderness.
9. As the whaling industry grew, great whalers became heroes.
10. The Paul Bunyan tales sprang up when lumbermen began clearing vast forests.
11. A folk tale is incomplete unless it contains exaggeration.
12. It must be told many times before its heroes are unbelievable enough.

304

17d. Diagraming Adverb Clauses

Sentences with adverb clauses can be diagramed to show their structure. For example, the following sentences have adverb clauses.

> People listen **when meteorologists predict weather.**
> **After scientists have carefully made their predictions,** the weather patterns may suddenly change.

To diagram a sentence with an adverb clause, begin by diagraming the independent clause and the adverb clause on separate horizontal lines, one above the other. Then write the subordinating conjunction that begins the adverb clause on a broken slanted line connecting the verb or verb phrase in the independent clause with the verb or verb phrase in the adverb clause.

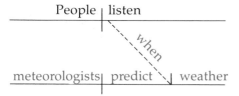

The second sentence is diagramed like the first. To complete the diagram, write the adjectives, the possessive pronoun, and the adverbs of both clauses on slanted lines below the words they modify.

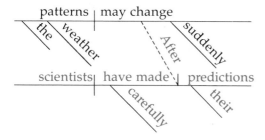

PRACTICING LANGUAGE SKILLS

■ The following sentences have adverb clauses. Diagram each sentence.

1. Skies brightened after it rained.
2. Snow fell before they skied.
3. Leaves turn when autumn arrives.
4. Temperatures soared while he played tennis.
5. Bulbs bloom wherever people plant them.
6. Thunderclouds gathered as she took pictures.
7. The snow has melted since you bought your skis.
8. The wind blew until the sun set.
9. Long icicles form whenever water drips slowly.
10. Wet sidewalks froze because nighttime temperatures dropped.
11. A baseball game will continue unless it is raining heavily.

17e. Adjective Clauses with Relative Pronouns as Subjects

> In the 1930's, millions of Americans listened to the programs.
> The programs were broadcast on the radio.
> In the 1930's, millions of Americans listened to the programs **that were broadcast on the radio.**

Read the sentences in the box above.

- How have the first two sentences been joined to make the third sentence?
- In the third sentence, what word has replaced the subject of the second sentence?
- What word does **that were broadcast on the radio** modify?

> The broadcast was presented by Orson Welles.
> The broadcast terrified many people.
> The broadcast **that terrified many people** was presented by Orson Welles.

Read the sentences in the box above.

- How have the first two sentences been joined to make the third sentence?
- In the third sentence, what word has replaced the subject of the second sentence?
- What word does **that terrified many people** modify?

A subordinate clause that modifies a noun in a sentence is called an adjective clause. Most adjective clauses begin with relative pronouns. The relative pronouns **who, which,** and **that** may be the subjects of adjective clauses. **Who** is used as a subject that refers to one or more persons. **Which** is used as a subject that refers to one or more animals or things. **That** may be used as a subject that refers to one or more animals, things, or persons.

PRACTICING LANGUAGE SKILLS

- Write only the adjective clause from each of the following sentences.

1. The radio station that first transmitted publicly was in Pittsburgh.
2. This was the station which announced the election results in 1920.
3. The number of stations that broadcast programs quickly grew.
4. Most broadcasts were paid for by manufacturers who sold radios.
5. The first commercial that was broadcast advertised real estate.
6. In 1926, NBC aired a concert that was heard from coast to coast.
7. The radio that is popular today developed in the 1930's.
8. Newspeople who feared the rise of radio tried to stop its growth.

9. News agencies which supplied stories cut off their services.
10. Radio networks soon developed special departments which gathered news.
11. People listened to announcers who did on-the-spot coverage.
12. One problem in the early years was amateurs who crowded the wavelengths.
13. Congress passed laws that regulated broadcasts.
14. People still depend on radios for information that is current.
15. The changes in American life that followed the invention of the radio can be felt to this day.
16. Radio was the first form of mass communication that could be heard by millions at the same time.
17. Television was the competition that forced radio to change its programming.
18. Radio stations adopted the music-and-news format that we hear today.
19. Actors who had been stars on radio moved to television.
20. Many programs that had been popular on radio were even more successful on television.
21. People who criticize television sometimes look back nostalgically to the great days of radio.

APPLYING LANGUAGE SKILLS TO COMPOSITION

■ Combine the sentences in each of the following pairs to make a new sentence that has an adjective clause. Make the second sentence an adjective clause in your new sentence. Write each new sentence.

1. Early radio shows were dramas or musicals.
   Early radio shows quickly became popular.
2. Many stars acted in radio dramas.
   Many stars appeared in movies.
3. Rudy Vallee presented a variety show.
   His variety show was very popular with women.
4. The Shadow was an exciting show.
   This show often scared its listeners.
5. Major Bowes' Amateur Hour was a weekly program.
   The program featured amateur performers.
6. One program was Let's Pretend.
   One program thrilled young audiences.
7. The Columbia Workshop presented plays.
   Its plays were very experimental.
8. Lights Out was a suspenseful show of the 1940's.
   The show was devised by Arch Oboler.
9. During World War II, radio reporters developed a style of reporting.
   Their style of reporting is still used today.
10. After the war, radio shared in the economic growth.
    The economic growth was occurring throughout the country.
11. After television became popular, many programmers switched to musical presentations.
    Many programmers were anxious to regain their audiences.
12. Many people feel that radio drama was more exciting than television.
    Radio drama forced listeners to use their imaginations.
13. The revival of radio drama is promising.
    The revival of radio drama began during the 1970's.
14. Mystery and science fiction are two kinds of programs.
    These programs are effective on radio.

17f. Adjective Clauses with Relative Pronouns as Direct Objects

> Billie Jean King is an athlete.
> The world admires this athlete.
> Billie Jean King is an athlete **whom the world admires.**

Read the sentences in the box.

- How have the first two sentences been joined to make the third sentence?
- In the third sentence, what word has replaced the direct object noun of the second sentence?
- What word does **whom the world admires** modify?

A subordinate clause that modifies a noun in a sentence is called an adjective clause. Most adjective clauses begin with relative pronouns. The relative pronouns **whom, which,** and **that** may be the direct objects of adjective clauses. **Whom** is used as a direct object that refers to one or more persons. **Which** is used as a direct object that refers to one or more animals or things. **That** may be used as a direct object that refers to one or more animals, things, or persons.

PRACTICING LANGUAGE SKILLS

- Write only the adjective clause from each of the following sentences.

1. Many athletes that fans have admired have experienced personal hardships.
2. Lou Gehrig was one player whom the New York Yankees hired.
3. Gehrig suffered many injuries which he often ignored.
4. He was often overshadowed by other players whom fans adored.
5. Lou Gehrig was stricken by a mysterious disease that he never overcame.
6. It quickly ended the career which he had built.
7. Wilma Rudolph became an athlete whom Olympic spectators applauded.
8. At four, she developed partial paralysis which she conquered with therapy.

APPLYING LANGUAGE SKILLS TO COMPOSITION

- Combine the sentences in each of the following pairs, making the second sentence an adjective clause in your new sentence. Write each new sentence.

1. A baseball contract launched Jackie Robinson on his career.
   The Kansas City Monarchs offered a baseball contract.
2. The Dodgers' Branch Rickey was determined to eliminate discrimination.
   All major league clubs practiced discrimination.
3. Robinson was a good athlete.
   The fans respected a good athlete.
4. Robinson starred in every position.
   The manager assigned every position.
5. Jackie Robinson suffered threats.
   He handled threats with dignity.
6. He helped make baseball a great sport.
   All Americans enjoy this great sport.

17g. Adjective Clauses Beginning with When, Where or Whose

> The Ice Age was an era.
> Great changes in the earth's surface occurred then.
> The Ice Age was an era **when great changes in the earth's surface occurred.**

Read the sentences in the box.

- How have the first two sentences been joined to make the third sentence?
- In the third sentence, what word has replaced the word **then** from the second sentence?
- What word does **when great changes in the earth's surface occurred** modify?

A subordinate clause that modifies a noun in a sentence is called an adjective clause. An adjective clause may begin with the word **when, where,** or **whose.**

PRACTICING LANGUAGE SKILLS

■ Write only the adjective clause from each of the following sentences.

1. The Ice Age was a time when sheets of ice crawled across the land.
2. Glaciers whose depths reached thousands of feet carved mountains.
3. Melted water covered great areas where glaciers had withdrawn.
4. The land where ice sheets had once been eventually supported life again.
5. Scientists are studying Ice Age people whose traces have been found.
6. These people often lived in caves where they sought shelter.
7. The Ice Age was a period when humans could not yet write.
8. They drew pictures on the walls of caves where they lived.
9. Pictures of long-extinct animals were found in places where they had lived.
10. The Ice Age was an era when people migrated frequently.

APPLYING LANGUAGE SKILLS TO COMPOSITION

■ Complete each of the following sentences by adding an adjective clause that modifies the word in dark type. Begin your adjective clause with the word in parentheses. Write the sentences.

1. The Ice Age was a **period** (when) ||||||||||||||| .
2. Glaciers moved to **regions** (where) ||||||||||||||| .
3. Early humans lived in **caves** (where) ||||||||||||||| .
4. They were **hunters** (whose) ||||||||||||||| .
5. Our prehistoric ancestors were **artists** (whose) ||||||||||||||| .
6. Mammoths and saber-toothed tigers lived in an **era** (when) ||||||||||||||| .
7. During this time, animals moved to **areas** (where) ||||||||||||||| .
8. Plant life died in **places** (where) ||||||||||||||| .

17h. Restrictive and Nonrestrictive Adjective Clauses

> Presidents **who made difficult decisions** are respected by historians.
> Lincoln, **who made difficult decisions,** is respected by historians.

Read the sentences in the box.

- What is the adjective clause in each sentence?
- What noun does each adjective clause modify?
- In which sentence is the adjective clause needed to make clear the meaning of the noun it modifies?
- In which sentence is the meaning of the modified noun clear without the adjective clause?

If an adjective clause is needed to make clear the meaning of the noun it modifies, it is called a restrictive adjective clause. In the first sentence in the box, the subject, **presidents,** is made smaller and more specific by the clause **who made difficult decisions.**

If an adjective clause merely adds information about the noun it modifies, it is called a nonrestrictive adjective clause. A nonrestrictive adjective clause is separated by commas from the rest of the sentence.

In the second sentence in the box, the subject, **Lincoln,** is already very specific. The clause **who made difficult decisions** does not change the meaning of **Lincoln.**

PRACTICING LANGUAGE SKILLS

■ Write only the adjective clause from each of the following sentences. Then write **restrictive** or **nonrestrictive** to identify the kind of adjective clause.

1. Presidents frequently face situations which affect the entire world.
2. Harry S. Truman, who often created controversy, became president in 1945.
3. He took over after Roosevelt's death, which shocked the nation.
4. Many people lacked faith in the man who had been a store clerk.
5. World War II, which threatened the free world, was raging.
6. In August 1945 Truman made a decision that changed the course of the war.
7. He authorized the bombing of Hiroshima, which led to Japan's surrender.
8. One man who brought a new vigor and enthusiasm to the presidency was John F. Kennedy.
9. Supporters admired him for his handling of the Cuban missile crisis, which occurred in 1962.
10. Ships that carried Soviet missiles to Cuba returned to Russia.
11. Kennedy negotiated a treaty which ended aboveground nuclear testing.
12. He recognized the needs of nations that are beginning to develop.
13. Kennedy organized the Peace Corps, which recruited thousands of volunteers.

15. Peace Corps volunteers, who work throughout the world, are helping people build better lives.
16. Those who become president must realize their influence on world affairs.
17. Historians who evaluate past presidents help us see them in a new light.
18. George Washington, who once seemed like an infallible hero, now appears more human.
19. Washington had to struggle with dozens of political factions that existed in the first years of the United States.
20. He was like other presidents who have had to make compromises.
21. There were people who wanted to make Washington a king.
22. Washington, who detested that idea, wanted to be a symbol of unity.
23. There were members of Congress who resented the president's power.
24. They would not approve the treaties which Washington arranged with foreign countries.
25. Washington's cabinet disagreed over the revolution which was taking place in France.
26. Washington, who believed in neutrality, had to keep peace among his feuding cabinet members.

APPLYING LANGUAGE SKILLS TO COMPOSITION

■ Complete each of the following sentences by adding a restrictive adjective clause. Write the sentences.

1. My brother always wanted a bicycle |||||||||||||| .
2. Instead, he was given a bike |||||||||||||| .
3. A present |||||||||||||| would have been more to his liking.
4. The class I enjoyed the most was the one |||||||||||||| .
5. It was taught by an unusual man |||||||||||||| .
6. He told us about the experiences |||||||||||||| .
7. The people and places |||||||||||||| seemed almost incredible.
8. In India he had climbed a mountain |||||||||||||| .
9. My sister Rose did not believe that there was a lake |||||||||||||| .
10. It had to be true, because we had a teacher |||||||||||||| .
11. My uncle Bill is the one |||||||||||||| .
12. The piano |||||||||||||| has been in our family for generations.

■■ Complete each of the following sentences by adding a nonrestrictive adjective clause. Write the sentences.

1. Joey Amodio, |||||||||||||| , loves to tell tall stories.
2. My father, |||||||||||||| , says Joey is a liar.
3. I think his stories, |||||||||||||| , are just exaggerations.
4. Joey once told us he had found a diamond ring, |||||||||||||| .
5. This story, |||||||||||||| , interested us greatly.
6. Raul, |||||||||||||| , asked to see the ring.
7. Joey, |||||||||||||| , said he had lost it again.
8. A sinister bearded man, |||||||||||||| , had taken it from him.
9. Joey, |||||||||||||| , admitted later that he had been exaggerating.
10. The ring, |||||||||||||| , had really been almost worthless.
11. That story, |||||||||||||| , made me feel rather embarrassed.
12. Joey, |||||||||||||| , wants to reform.
13. My little sister, |||||||||||||| , has trouble telling truth from fiction.

17i. Diagraming Adjective Clauses

Sentences with adjective clauses can be diagramed to show their structure. For example, the following sentences have adjective clauses.

National parks, which conserve wildlife, provide much enjoyment.
We visited the park which Congress established.

To diagram the first sentence, begin by diagraming the independent clause and the adjective clause on separate horizontal lines, one above the other. Then connect the two clauses with a broken slanted line from the subject noun in the independent clause to the relative pronoun in the adjective clause. To complete the diagram, write each adjective on a slanted line below the noun it modifies.

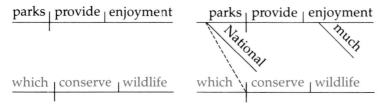

To diagram the second sentence, again diagram the independent clause and the adjective clause on separate horizontal lines. This time, connect the two clauses with a broken slanted line from the direct object noun in the independent clause to the relative pronoun in the adjective clause. Complete the diagram by writing the adjective on a slanted line below the noun it modifies.

PRACTICING LANGUAGE SKILLS

■ Each of the following sentences has an adjective clause in which the relative pronoun is used as a subject or as a direct object. Diagram each sentence.

1. Parks that have many visitors employ rangers.
2. Rangers who give speeches inform the campers.
3. Lectures that stress conservation protect the environment.
4. People who appreciate wildlife enjoy national parks.
5. Animals who must hunt food are often hungry.
6. Old Faithful, which tourists visit, is a spectacular geyser.
7. Its eruption, which visitors photograph, is predictable.
8. Guides, whom everyone may use, lead many tours.

312

17j.   Noun Clauses Used as Subjects

> **That a canal should be built** was agreed.
> **Who could design it** was the question.
> **Which route was best** was studied.

Read the sentences in the box. The subject of each sentence is in dark type.

- What clause is used as the subject of each sentence?
- With what word does each clause begin?

A subordinate clause that is used as a noun is called a noun clause. A noun clause can begin with one of the words in the box below.

how	whatever	which	whose
that	when	who	why
what	where	whoever	

A noun clause can be used as the subject of a sentence.

PRACTICING LANGUAGE SKILLS

- Write only the noun clause from each of the following sentences.

1. That the Suez Canal is important has been recognized.
2. Who first excavated it is not known.
3. That a canal has existed for centuries has been determined.
4. Whoever controlled the canal would rule Egypt.
5. That a modern canal was necessary was understood.
6. That the cost would be high was an accepted fact.
7. Who would finance it was the concern of many people.
8. Whose plan was best was investigated.
9. When it could open was predicted.
10. Which company would build it was debated.
11. What countries the canal would border was arranged.
12. How everyone could use it was the subject of much discussion.
13. That the British leave the canal was demanded by the Egyptians.
14. Who would maintain it was not decided.
15. Which countries can now use the Suez Canal is questioned.

APPLYING LANGUAGE SKILLS TO COMPOSITION

- Complete each of the following sentences by adding a noun clause. Write the sentences.

1. ||||||||||||||||| was debated.
2. ||||||||||||||||| is not clear.
3. ||||||||||||||||| was arranged.
4. ||||||||||||||||| will be the winner.
5. ||||||||||||||||| should explain it to me.
6. ||||||||||||||||| was agreed.
7. ||||||||||||||||| was accepted.
8. ||||||||||||||||| will be considered.
9. ||||||||||||||||| may tell us about it.
10. ||||||||||||||||| was argued.

313

17k. Noun Clauses Used as Predicate Nominatives

> Fun is **what everyone wants.**
> The truth is **that we all enjoy picnics.**
> The question is **when to have one.**

Read the sentences in the box. The predicate nominative of each sentence is in dark type.

- What is the verb in each sentence?
- What clause is used as the predicate nominative of each sentence?
- With what word does each clause begin?

A subordinate clause that is used as a noun is called a noun clause. **A noun clause can begin with one of the words in the box below.**

how	whatever	which	whose
that	when	who	why
what	where	whoever	

A noun clause can be used as the predicate nominative of a sentence.

PRACTICING LANGUAGE SKILLS

■ From each of the following sentences, write only the noun clause that is used as a predicate nominative.

1. A race is what excites picnickers.
2. The entrants are whoever signs up.
3. This is how the team must run.
4. Prizes are whatever merchants donate.
5. Good sportsmanship is why races are enjoyable.
6. Comradeship is what team members feel.
7. The good news is that we won.
8. The question is where we will have dinner.
9. One problem is who should pay.
10. The answer is whoever has the money.
11. A good meal is what I need.
12. This is how you play the game.
13. The theater is where we are going next.

APPLYING LANGUAGE SKILLS TO COMPOSITION

■ Complete each of the following sentences by adding a noun clause used as a predicate nominative. Write the sentences.

1. Ample food for everyone is ||||||||||||||| .
2. The barbecue chef is ||||||||||||| .
3. Hot dogs and hamburgers are ||||||||||||||| .
4. A hot fire is ||||||||||||| .
5. The cook must remain ||||||||||||| .
6. Cold drinks are ||||||||||||| .
7. A pleasant meal is ||||||||||||| .
8. Trash cans are ||||||||||||| .
9. The unlucky dishwasher is ||||||||||||||| .
10. A day in the sun is ||||||||||||| .
11. The problem is ||||||||||||| .
12. The good weather was ||||||||||||| .
13. Enjoyable company is ||||||||||||| .
14. The park was ||||||||||||| .

171. Noun Clauses Used as Direct Objects, as Indirect Objects, and as Objects of Prepositions

> I took **what I could carry.**
> She told **whoever would listen** the truth.
> He wrote about **what he knew.**

Read the first sentence in the box.

- Which clause is used as the direct object of the sentence?

Read the second sentence in the box.

- Which clause is used as the indirect object of the sentence?

Read the third sentence in the box.

- Which clause is used as the object of a preposition?

A subordinate clause that is used as a noun is called a noun clause. **A noun clause can be used as a direct object, an indirect object, or the object of a preposition.** A noun clause can begin with one of the words in the box below.

how	whatever	which	whose
that	when	who	why
what	where	whoever	

PRACTICING LANGUAGE SKILLS

■ From each of the following sentences, write only the noun clause. Then write **direct object, indirect object,** or **object of a preposition** to show how the clause is used in the sentence.

1. People communicate by whatever is available.
2. Drum signals have sent whoever listens messages.
3. Smoke signals told about what Indian tribes planned.
4. Generals knew whose pigeons carried military secrets.
5. Samuel Morse discovered how long-distance communication can work.
6. We know when Bell invented the telephone.
7. Bees watch how other bees dance.
8. Bees tell where nectar exists.
9. Bird calls give whoever is near warning.
10. Dolphins whistle for whoever can come.
11. Communication affects what we think about the world around us.
12. Modern science is predicting how we will communicate in the future.
13. Portable videophones will show us what is happening at the other end of the line.
14. People will be amazed by how the world has grown smaller.
15. Rockets will send whoever is interested information about space.
16. Scientists will learn whatever they can about the planets.
17. Astronomers will be excited by what satellite telescopes reveal.

17m. Diagraming Noun Clauses

Sentences with noun clauses can be diagramed to show their structure. For example, the following sentences contain noun clauses.

> **What an actor wants** is a good play.
> Critics applaud **whomever they like.**
> **Whoever attends plays** has a favorite star.

The sentences above are diagramed in almost the same way. Only the position of the line connecting the noun clause to the remaining part of the sentence is changed. This connecting line is drawn to show the use of the noun clause in the sentence.

To diagram the first sentence, begin by writing the verb and the predicate nominative of the independent clause on a horizontal line. Write the subject, verb, and direct object of the noun clause on a horizontal line. Draw this horizontal line above the subject position for the independent clause.

Connect the noun clause to the rest of the sentence with this line (λ). Add the adjectives on slanting lines.

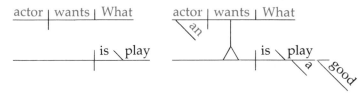

The second sentence is diagramed in the same way. Only the position of the noun clause is changed.

The third sentence is diagramed like the first sentence. In this sentence, however, the relative pronoun is the subject of the noun clause.

PRACTICING LANGUAGE SKILLS

■ The following sentences have noun clauses used as subjects and direct objects. Diagram each sentence.

1. What Shakespeare wrote is classic.
2. Whomever Barrymore played became real.
3. Whatever critics wrote was favorable.
4. Whomever fans choose become stars.
5. What audiences enjoy is entertainment.
6. What playwrights need is money.
7. What actors want is eternal youth.
8. Whatever he produces becomes a hit.
9. Whoever stars in it will become rich.

17n. Simple, Compound, Complex, and Compound-Complex Sentences

> America has produced outstanding musicians.
> Geniuses have written moving songs, and talented artists have sung them.
> Louis Armstrong, whom many considered the world's greatest trumpet player, did much to promote jazz.
> Beverly Sills, who began singing at the age of five, was a star of the New York City Opera for over twenty years, and in 1978 she became the general manager of the company.

Read the sentences in the box.

- Which sentence has one independent clause and no subordinate clause?
- Which sentence has two independent clauses but no subordinate clause?
- Which sentence has one independent clause and one subordinate clause?
- Which sentence has two independent clauses and one subordinate clause?

A **simple sentence** **is a sentence that has one independent clause and no subordinate clause.** A simple sentence may have a compound subject or compound predicate.

A **compound sentence** **is a sentence that has two independent clauses but no subordinate clauses.**

A **complex sentence** **is a sentence that has one independent clause and at least one subordinate clause.**

A **compound-complex sentence** **is a sentence that has at least two independent clauses and at least one subordinate clause.**

PRACTICING LANGUAGE SKILLS

■ Read the following sentences. Write **simple, compound, complex,** or **compound-complex** to identify each type of sentence.

1. Music brightens and enriches our lives.
2. It is a source of pleasure, and it provides us with entertainment.
3. Most musicians are ordinary people, but they have a talent that is very special.
4. Irving Berlin, who couldn't even read music, composed thousands of songs.
5. His first successful song, "Alexander's Ragtime Band," was written in 1911 and is still popular.
6. He also composed several musical comedies.
7. Both talent and hard work made him successful.
8. Marian Anderson, whose singing career began at age eight, delighted audiences for many years.
9. She began to sing at many church-sponsored events, where she received much praise.
10. A friend who knew a singing teacher arranged lessons for her, and Anderson began her operatic training.
11. Her reputation, which grew rapidly, was established in Europe, and she made her debut at the Metropolitan in 1955.
12. She was the Metropolitan Opera Company's first black singer.

Reviewing 17 Clauses

17a. Identifying and Using Independent Clauses

Read each of the following sentences. If the sentence is a compound sentence, write it. Then underline the two independent clauses and circle the coordinating conjunction. If it is not a compound sentence, write **not a compound sentence.**

1. Jeannie wrote the play, and David wrote the music.
2. Thor discovered the island, and he wrote a book about his voyage.
3. Julie built the window and the frame.
4. Megan won the election, but she won it honestly.
5. Cesar sanded and polished the floor.

17b. Diagraming Compound Sentences

Diagram each of the following sentences.

6. Harold left, but nobody missed him.
7. Marie read the story, and Julie listened.
8. He spoke only Greek, but I knew French.
9. The pants are too short, or my legs are too long.

17c. Adverb Clauses

Write only the adverb clause from each of the following sentences.

10. I will wait until my brother arrives.
11. Margo left because she was ill.
12. No one came in while I was speaking.
13. Mr. Harris will go wherever he is sent.
14. Eve will not join unless we ask her.

17d. Diagraming Adverb Clauses

Diagram each of the following sentences.

15. Tom saw the movie before he read the book.

16. The car stalls whenever I start it.
17. The day grew hot after the sun rose.
18. Although I took the trip, I did not see the Grand Canyon.
19. The trees will bear fruit after you fertilize them.

17e. Adjective Clauses with Relative Pronouns as Subjects

Write only the adjective clause from each of the following sentences.

20. The costume that caused so much trouble is in the attic.
21. The play that opens next week is good.
22. The rehearsals which take place every night are necessary.
23. The girl who sings has the best role.

17f. Adjective Clauses with Relative Pronouns as Direct Objects

Write only the adjective clause from each of the following sentences.

24. That is one story which I cannot believe.
25. He was one person whom Ed trusted.
26. Larry did everything that she asked.
27. She was a teacher whom everyone respected.

17g. Adjective Clauses Beginning with When, Where, or Whose

Write only the adjective clause from each of the following sentences.

28. This is a time when we must save fuel.
29. Work, home, and school are places where we can save electricity.
30. Many of us use appliances whose energy consumption is too high.
31. You should not use an air conditioner on days when it is not necessary.

32. Open the windows at times when breezes will cool the house.

17h. Restrictive and Nonrestrictive Adjective Clauses

Write only the adjective clause from each of the following sentences. Then write **restrictive** or **nonrestrictive** to identify the kind of adjective clause.

33. Stan Herrera, who attends our school, has an unusual talent.
34. He can memorize a list of names or numbers which is read to him once.
35. Carol Myers, who is in my English class, also has a great memory.
36. She can memorize any poem which appears in print.

17i. Diagraming Adjective Clauses

Diagram each of the following sentences.

37. People who enjoy pie are common.
38. Our cat, which is a Manx, likes lemons.
39. People who smoke pollute the air.
40. Adele is the girl who swims best.

17j. Noun Clauses Used as Subjects

Write only the noun clause from each of the following sentences.

41. That she is intelligent is very clear.
42. How much she knows is open to question.
43. Where to go is still being debated.
44. Why the principal had imposed the rule was not clear to us.

17k. Noun Clauses Used as Predicate Nominatives

From each of the following sentences, write only the noun clause that is used as a predicate nominative.

45. A good time is what we want.

46. The first question is whose car this is.
47. Our problem is how we can get home.
48. The leader is whoever wants the job.

17l. Noun Clauses Used as Direct Objects, as Indirect Objects, and as Objects of Prepositions

From each of the following sentences, write only the noun clause. Then write **direct object, indirect object,** or **object of a preposition** to show how the clause is used in the sentence.

49. I will agree to whatever you say.
50. Lisa will tell whoever listens about her troubles.
51. That movie shows what money can do.
52. Tony knows when his paper is due.

17m. Diagraming Noun Clauses

Diagram each of the following sentences.

53. What you have said makes sense.
54. I admire whoever can walk that tightrope.
55. Maria will say what she thinks.
56. Whatever you want you will get.
57. What he selected is expensive.

17n. Simple, Compound, Complex, and Compound-Complex Sentences

Read the following sentences. Write **simple, compound, complex,** or **compound-complex** to identify each type of sentence.

58. Jules Verne was a popular writer, and he is called the father of science fiction.
59. Five Weeks in a Balloon and Journey to the Center of the Earth first made him famous.
60. From the Earth to the Moon, which was published in 1865, predicted space travel.
61. Verne's astronauts, who were fired from a huge cannon, orbited the moon.

18 Sentence Problems

18a. Correcting Sentence Fragments

A word, a phrase, or a dependent clause that has been incorrectly written as a sentence is called a sentence fragment. **When you find a sentence fragment in your writing, rewrite it as part of another sentence.**

> **Sentence:** Stephen talks too much.
> **Sentence Fragment:** When he is nervous.
> **Rewritten Sentence:** Stephen talks too much when he is nervous.
>
> **Sentence Fragment:** Singing in the shower.
> **Sentence:** My father woke me.
> **Rewritten Sentence:** Singing in the shower, my father woke me.

PRACTICING YOUR SKILLS

■ Read each sentence and sentence fragment. Rewrite the sentence fragment as part of the sentence.

1. Julia went home early. To study for her science test.
2. Merv lives on Collins Street. Near a large park.
3. Surrounded by tall trees. The lake looked inviting.
4. Carla introduced us to two of her friends. Andrea and Martine.
5. My uncle is coming to visit us. For the first time in several years.
6. Baffled by the lack of even one clue. The police didn't know where to start their investigation.
7. Yelling at Daniel. David ran into the house.
8. Gary had no time. To play.

■■ Read each pair of word groups. If one of the groups of words is a sentence fragment, rewrite the fragment as part of the sentence. If both groups of words are sentences, write the phrase **two sentences.**

1. When she enters college. Carol will study Italian.
2. Laughing quietly. Vincent read the card to himself.
3. Florence gave me a record for my birthday. I play it all the time.
4. The garden looks beautiful. In the sunlight.
5. Startled by the sudden noise. Larry jumped.
6. Sarah stayed up late last night. To read a novel.
7. I think the radio is too loud. We should turn it down.
8. They'll begin construction of the new office building. After the ground is prepared.
9. Nancy watched only two programs on television last night. An old movie and the news.
10. Gerald can hardly wait. To visit his aunt.
11. Sonja and Elena are like twins. They go everywhere together.
12. Richard and Phil have formed a band. Called the Post-Bohemians.
13. Marcia constructed this kaleidoscope. With plexiglass, cardboard, and aluminum.

18b. Correcting Run-on Sentences

Two independent clauses that have been incorrectly written together, without a conjunction or a semicolon, form a run-on sentence. **When you find a run-on sentence in your writing, rewrite it as two sentences.**

Run-on Sentence: Christie called from school, can she stay for the basketball game?

Two Sentences: Christie called from school. Can she stay for the basketball game?

Run-on Sentence: Has Christie called from school, she's later than usual.

Two Sentences: Has Christie called from school? She's later than usual.

PRACTICING YOUR SKILLS

■ Rewrite each run-on sentence as two sentences. Use the correct punctuation mark at the end of each sentence.

1. Sunlight streamed through the windows, Tom woke up feeling wonderful.
2. Then he remembered he had a biology test, he wanted to stay in bed.
3. There was a knock at the door, his mother had come to wake him for school.
4. Could he pretend to be sick, Tom coughed a few times.
5. The coughs sounded fake, Tom knew his mother would be suspicious.
6. Tom got out of bed, he put on jeans and a T-shirt.
7. He drank some orange juice and ate a bowl of cereal, it was getting late.

■■ Read each word group. If the word group is a run-on sentence, rewrite it as two sentences. If the group is one complete sentence, write the word **sentence.**

1. English class finally ended, biology was Tom's next course.
2. Tom felt very nervous about the test, biology is a difficult subject.
3. He knew that he had studied for a long time, would it do him any good.
4. There were so many details to remember, and Tom was sure he'd forget them.
5. He finally got to the classroom, everyone looked tense.
6. The teacher entered the room, holding the tests in his hand.
7. He finally handed out the tests, they looked long.
8. Tom looked at the first question, he was surprised that he knew the answer.
9. He settled down to work, the test wasn't as difficult as he had feared.
10. He answered most of the questions easily, and there were only a few that he wasn't sure of.
11. Tom was one of the first people to finish, there were ten minutes remaining in the class period.
12. Tom went over his answers carefully.
13. He turned in the test happily, the torture had ended.
14. He wondered why he had been so upset, biology isn't that difficult after all.

18c. Correcting Rambling Sentences

A rambling sentence is too long to be clearly understood. When you find a rambling sentence in your writing, rewrite it as two or more sentences.

Rambling Sentence: Ella T. Grasso was elected to the Connecticut House of Representatives in 1955, and later she became the secretary of state of Connecticut, and then in 1970 Grasso was elected to the United States House of Representatives, and so she served there until she was elected governor of Connecticut in 1975.

Rewritten Sentences: Ella T. Grasso was elected to the Connecticut House of Representatives in 1955. Later she became the secretary of state of Connecticut. In 1970, Grasso was elected to the United States House of Representatives. She served there until she was elected governor of Connecticut in 1975.

PRACTICING YOUR SKILLS

■ Rewrite each of the following rambling sentences as two or more sentences.

1. Cassie was walking down the street when she decided to visit Alicia, and so she turned on Drummond Place, but then she couldn't remember which house Alicia lived in, so she looked for a phone booth so she could call Alicia and ask her for the address.

2. The dogs started barking last night, and they woke everyone up, and we all went to see what was bothering them, but we couldn't find anything that could be making them bark.

3. It was the last of the ninth, and the bases were loaded, and there were two outs, and the count was three and two, and the crowd was yelling, but then the batter swung and missed, and we lost, and everyone was depressed.

4. No one understood the lesson, and so we all asked questions, but then the teacher became confused, and she had to stop and think, and then she explained it to us clearly.

5. We were walking to the market, and then we saw someone giving away puppies, and so we went over to look at them, and there was a black and white one that I fell in love with, and I wanted to take it home even though we have two dogs, so I called home and my grandmother said I could have the puppy.

6. Debra loves animals, and she has two dogs and three cats, and she has trained them herself, and she takes complete care of them, and she'd like to be a veterinarian when she grows up.

7. Colette goes to summer school in the morning, and then she baby-sits in the afternoon except on Friday when she has a piano lesson, and so Roger fills in for her.

8. Carrie is going to Camp Sunrise this summer, and she went there last year, and then she made many new friends, and so she is looking forward to seeing them again.

9. After school, I usually do something with my friends, and then I come home and help with dinner, and then we eat dinner, and then I have to do my homework, and if it isn't too late, I might read a story or watch television.

10. Lydia doesn't know if she can get a job this summer, but she hopes so because she needs the money, so I was wondering if you know of anyone who might be able to hire her, because she's my best friend, and I'd like to help her if I can.

11. Henry and I were getting bored, and so we decided to just walk around, but then we spotted a carnival that looked interesting, and so we walked over there and spent the rest of the day there, and we weren't bored at all.

12. Mike's parents took us to Disneyland, and there were twelve of us, that is, my two sisters and my brother and I, and Mike and his brother and sister, and Mike's little cousins Jamey and Joey, and Mike's parents, and one of their friends, and the first thing we did was take a train ride around the park, and then some of us wanted to go to Tomorrowland, except that Mike's parents wanted to go to Main Street, and the vote was ten to two against Main Street, and so then we went to Main Street first, and then we saw the Pirates of the Caribbean, and Jamey was very frightened of the Pirates, but he's only four years old, and I had to take him outside, and later we went on the Matterhorn, and Jamey ate too much taffy, and he felt sick, and we all had a wonderful time.

13. Raul told me he'd sell me his old bike for thirty dollars, and I wanted to buy it, but I didn't have thirty dollars, and so I counted my money, and I had five dollars my parents had given me for my birthday, and I had two dollars the Feldmans had paid me for watching their cat for a week, and that was while they were in Hawaii, and so I had seven dollars, and I looked all over my room and found a dollar in change, and so I gave Raul the eight dollars, and I owed him twenty-two, and I asked him if I could pay him two dollars a month for eleven months, because I can save that from mowing lawns, and he said, "Sure," and then he said, "And you can take the bike now."

14. Last week Uncle Allan came to visit, and he's my mother's older brother, and he's a fascinating man, because he was in the merchant marine, and he has thick gray hair and several tattoos, and he told us about when his ship sailed from Singapore, and then it sailed down the coast of Sumatra, south of Borneo, and into the Macassar Strait, and he said the water was very warm, and then he told us he had seen flying fish on many occasions, and I have to admit I found that hard to believe, and I asked, "Are you sure you saw them?" but then my mother said, "Allan has never told a lie in his life."

15. The body of a grasshopper has three sections, and the front section is called the head, and the head has the antennae of the grasshopper, and the grasshopper uses its antennae to examine food, and the grasshopper's five eyes are also located on its head, and then the middle section is called the thorax, and the grasshopper's wings and legs are attached to the thorax, and then the last part is called the abdomen, and this part has ten tiny holes, and the grasshopper uses the holes to breathe.

18d. Avoiding Unnecessary Repetition in Sentences

Avoid unnecessary repetition in sentences. Take out any words, phrases, or clauses used to express ideas that have already been expressed.

Repetitive Sentence: My French friend Monique, who is from France, will stay with us all summer.

Rewritten Sentence: My French friend Monique will stay with us all summer.

Repetitive Sentence: The huge, big monster had appeared unexpectedly and without warning.

Rewritten Sentence: The huge monster had appeared unexpectedly.

PRACTICING YOUR SKILLS

- Rewrite the following sentences to avoid unnecessary repetition.

1. The lost children who could not find their way found a house made of gingerbread.
2. The second, newer version of your report is better than the first, older version.
3. The pink clouds looked rosy as the setting sun went down.
4. Tonight's guest speaker, Ms. Takeda, who will be speaking tonight, is an editor of textbooks.
5. My friend has a beach house at the beach.
6. The important information in this notice is significant.
7. The spinning top twirled endlessly for a long time.
8. Their successful business is thriving.
9. The painter especially liked rural areas in the country.
10. Living in an urban area of a city can be very exciting.
11. Many slim, slender people diet almost constantly nearly all the time.
12. The tired travelers were weary in the evening at the end of the day.
13. Everyone enjoyed the funny, laughable antics of the clowns.
14. The television program that I watched on television last night was quite interesting.
15. Janelle worked all summer last summer.
16. The closet door to the closet won't close.
17. JoAnn's story about the canine dogs is totally and completely false.
18. The scent from the aromatic fragrance of the jasmine filled the garden.
19. The mimes moved silently and noiselessly across the dim, dark stage.
20. Everyone noticed the similarity between the two reports that were almost exactly like one another.
21. The strong workers, who had great strength, lifted the truck easily and with little effort.
22. In most cases, you should usually ask for the teacher's permission and authorization.
23. Hermione requested and asked for advice repeatedly over and over again.
24. Our guest, who is a visitor here, should be treated politely and with courtesy.
25. The intelligent students, who were all quite bright, were surprised and astounded by the simplicity of the solution.

19 Subject-Verb Agreement

19a. Present Tense Verb Forms

A present tense verb form agrees with the subject noun or pronoun of the sentence. Use a singular form verb with singular noun subjects and with the pronoun subjects he, she, and it.

> Bernice **bakes** cakes.
> She **sells** them to restaurants.

Use a plural form verb with plural noun subjects and with the pronoun subjects I, you, we, and they.

> Her friends **bake** cakes.
> They **sell** them to restaurants.

PRACTICING YOUR SKILLS

■ Choose from each set of parentheses the verb form that agrees with the subject noun or pronoun of the sentence. Write the sentences.

1. The hamsters (stay, stays) in their cage all day long.
2. My brothers (drink, drinks) milk at every meal.
3. She (know, knows) the people across the street.
4. My brother (plant, plants) new flowers every spring.
5. The buses (arrive, arrives) every thirty minutes.
6. He always (tell, tells) the truth.
7. Cars (line, lines) the streets during rush hour.
8. Marcelo (visit, visits) his grandparents once a month.
9. They (sew, sews) many of their own clothes.
10. Water (boil, boils) at 100° C.
11. It often (rain, rains) in the spring.
12. Meats (spoil, spoils) in hot weather.
13. Birds (fly, flies) south for the winter.
14. Lisa (find, finds) interesting shells on the beach.
15. Monica (love, loves) swimming.
16. The musicians (practice, practices) nightly.
17. We (enjoy, enjoys) each other's company.
18. Snow (fall, falls) in winter.
19. You often (play, plays) loud music.
20. Mr. Simmons (import, imports) goods from Germany.
21. Erica (sing, sings) in the shower.
22. Bees (live, lives) in hives.
23. I (study, studies) Chinese.
24. Paul (crack, cracks) the eggs into the bowl.
25. Ms. Paredes (travel, travels) all over the world on business.
26. Maria (read, reads) everything she can.
27. Those dogs (eat, eats) everything in sight.
28. Ranchers (breed, breeds) cattle.
29. Carrinne (jog, jogs) a mile every day.
30. Tulips (thrive, thrives) in Holland.
31. Clemente (run, runs) extremely fast.
32. Stephanie (live, lives) in the suburbs.
33. Balloons (soar, soars) upward.
34. Crayons (melt, melts) in the sun.
35. Many people (enjoy, enjoys) traveling.
36. This cottage cheese (taste, tastes) sour.
37. Marva Dawn (prefer, prefers) yogurt.

19b. Indefinite Pronoun Subjects

The indefinite pronouns in the box below are singular. When one of these indefinite pronouns is the subject of a sentence, use a singular form verb.

another	either	nobody	other
anybody	everybody	no one	somebody
anyone	everyone	nothing	someone
anything	everything	one	something
each	neither		

Each **walks** to the platform.
Everyone **is** on the platform.

The indefinite pronouns in the box below are plural. When one of these indefinite pronouns is the subject of a sentence, use a plural form verb.

both	few	many	several

Both **walk** to the platform.
Several **are** on the platform.

The indefinite pronouns in the box below may be singular or plural. Use a singular form verb if the indefinite pronoun refers to a singular noun. Use a plural form verb if the indefinite pronoun refers to a plural noun.

all	any	most	some	none	such

Most of that speech **was** dull.
Most of the speeches **were** dull.

PRACTICING YOUR SKILLS

■ Choose from each set of parentheses the verb form that agrees with the subject of the sentence. Write the sentences.

1. Anything (taste, tastes) good on a picnic.
2. All of the pie (is, are) gone.
3. Many (try, tries) hard.
4. Neither (was, were) home.
5. Some of the students (work, works).
6. Some of the pie (is, are) still here.
7. Nobody (was, were) hungry.
8. Nothing (fit, fits) this lock.
9. Few (understand, understands) it.
10. One (seem, seems) clear.
11. Everyone (have, has) certain duties.
12. Something (seem, seems) wrong.
13. Everybody (know, knows) that song.
14. Both (speak, speaks) convincingly.

19c. Collective Noun Subjects

A noun that names a group of people or things, such as team or fleet is called a collective noun. Collective nouns may be used either as singular nouns or as plural nouns.

Usually a collective noun is used as a singular noun. It refers to a group as a single unit. When a collective noun with this meaning is the subject of a sentence, use a singular form verb.

> The jury **listens** to the evidence.
> The orchestra **is** on the stage.

Sometimes a collective noun is used as a plural noun. It refers to the individual members of a group. When a collective noun with this meaning is the subject of a sentence, use a plural form verb.

> The jury **disagree** about the evidence.
> The orchestra **are** in their seats.

PRACTICING YOUR SKILLS

■ Assume that the collective nouns in the following sentences refer to the group as a single unit. Choose from each set of parentheses the correct verb form. Write the sentences.

1. The herd (move, moves) slowly across the plain.
2. Our team (is, are) the winner of the trophy.
3. The band (play, plays) at each game.
4. The army (is, are) on maneuvers.
5. The flock (graze, grazes) in the meadow.
6. The audience (seem, seems) restless.
7. The crowd (was, were) unruly.
8. The chorus (rehearse, rehearses) three afternoons a week.
9. Our club (schedule, schedules) guest lecturers every month.
10. My class (enjoy, enjoys) that subject.
11. The troop (go, goes) on several hikes each year.
12. The committee (meet, meets) today.
13. The group (ask, asks) for donations.
14. The public (is, are) apathetic.
15. The mob (sound, sounds) angry.
16. My family (vacation, vacations) at the beach.
17. The jury (is, are) in seclusion.
18. The panel (ask, asks) for questions from the audience.
19. The battalion (was, were) under attack.
20. Our team (want, wants) to win the championship.
21. My family always (believe, believes) in me.
22. The orchestra (play, plays) better with the regular conductor.
23. The pride (wait, waits) for the last lion to join the kill.
24. The club (accept, accepts) anybody as a member.
25. The combo (sound, sounds) fantastic tonight!
26. The choir (hold, holds) auditions three times a year.
27. The fleet (is, are) gathering off the coast for maneuvers.
28. The entire regiment (was, were) promoted after the battle.
29. The whole company always (go, goes) to the New Year's party.

19d. Subject Noun or Pronoun Modified by a Prepositional Phrase

The present tense verb form agrees with the subject noun or pronoun of the sentence. When a prepositional phrase modifies the subject noun or pronoun, the form of the verb does not change.

Everyone **wants** to win.
Everyone on both teams **wants** to win.

The lemons **look** ripe.
The lemons on the tree **look** ripe.

PRACTICING YOUR SKILLS

■ Choose from each set of parentheses the verb form that agrees with the subject noun or pronoun of the sentence. Write the sentences.

1. The man with the skis (is, are) my instructor.
2. The houses on the hill (have, has) a breathtaking view.
3. No one in the room (know, knows) the answer.
4. The flowers in the vase (need, needs) water.
5. The author of these books (admire, admires) Dickens.
6. Everything on these shelves (is, are) free.
7. The trunk under the stairs (belong, belongs) to the previous tenant.
8. The suitcases in the cellar (is, are) empty.
9. Somebody in the chorus (sing, sings) off key.
10. Cities on the coast (attract, attracts) tourists.
11. The woman with the packages (have, has) two daughters.
12. Everybody at camp (write, writes) letters home.
13. The painter of those portraits (use, uses) soft colors.
14. The members of the cast (practice, practices) every day.
15. Students in the senior class (tutor, tutors) freshmen.
16. My friend from Des Moines (visit, visits) me every summer.
17. The player on the sidelines (is, are) hurt.
18. The cheerleaders for our team (encourage, encourages) the players.
19. The birds in the nest (chirp, chirps) in ·the morning.
20. The designer of the dresses (give, gives) a fashion show each year.
21. The owner of the planes (rent, rents) them to the public.
22. The clocks in this store (is, are) antiques.
23. Several booths at the crafts fair (display, displays) handmade jewelry.
24. The manager of the Buckos (is, are) confident they will win.
25. The cocker spaniels in the window (is, are) for sale.
26. Some comedians on television (tell, tells) corny jokes.
27. The car with the new tires (belong, belongs) to Jose's dad.
28. The building beyond those trees (is, are) the Hartman Building.
29. The keys in my coat pocket (fit, fits) the lock on the cellar door.
30. The black cat with four white paws (is, are) the one I've told you about.

19e. Compound Subject

Two or more subject nouns or pronouns may be joined in the compound subject of a sentence. When two or more subjects are joined by and, use a plural form verb.

> Martha, George, Terry, and Pete **study** in the library.
> The boys and girls **are** in the cafeteria.

When two plural subjects are joined by or or nor, use a plural form verb.

> Either the boys or the girls **study** in the library.
> Either the boys or the girls **were** in the cafeteria.

When two singular subjects are joined by or or nor, use a singular form verb.

> Either he or she **studies** in the library.
> Either Martha or George **is** in the cafeteria.

PRACTICING YOUR SKILLS

■ Choose from each set of parentheses the verb form that agrees with the compound subject of the sentence. Write the sentences.

1. Rob or Josefa (know, knows) the answer.
2. Both roses and daisies (bloom, blooms) in my garden.
3. Radishes, zucchini, or cucumbers (taste, tastes) good in a salad.
4. Carrots and potatoes (is, are) in the stew.
5. Both Felipe and Noel (like, likes) your idea.
6. Christa and I (need, needs) help!
7. Either Ramon or Rod (was, were) late for school.
8. A singer or a pianist (perform, performs) every evening.
9. My aunts, uncles, and cousins (visit, visits) us during the summer.
10. You and she never (listen, listens) to me!
11. Neither the toast nor the bacon (is, are) ready.
12. John, Frank, and Brian (collect, collects) coins.
13. Either soccer or football (is, are) her favorite sport.
14. Both Joey and Geraldine (complain, complains) endlessly.
15. Maria and I (have, has) fun together.
16. Bill and Luis (ride, rides) their bikes to school.
17. Either Gordon or Chip (tutor, tutors) two freshmen.
18. The atlases and the almanacs (is, are) in that section.
19. Neither she nor Lina (is, are) asleep.
20. Both the Stillwells and the Lees (invite, invites) us to their parties.
21. Either Francesco or Gabriela (work, works) at the store in the afternoon.
22. Terence and Gina always (get, gets) the leading roles.
23. He and she (work, works) together on the project.
24. Neither Kevin nor Katie (is, are) at home.
25. Dad or Elena (is, are) going to have to clean up this mess.
26. Russ and Jay seldom (agree, agrees) about anything.

19f.   Sentences Beginning with Here and There

Use a singular form verb after here or there when the subject noun or pronoun of the sentence is singular.

Here **is** the assignment for tomorrow.
There **was** a fly on the windowpane.
Here **comes** Cynthia now.

Use a plural form verb after here or there when the subject noun or pronoun of the sentence is plural.

Here **are** the assignments for tomorrow.
There **were** several flies on the windowpane.
Here **come** Cynthia and Jan.

PRACTICING YOUR SKILLS

■ Choose from each set of parentheses the verb form that agrees with the subject noun or pronoun of the sentence. Write the sentences.

1. There (was, were) three people in the market.
2. Here (is, are) your test paper.
3. There (was, were) a parade yesterday.
4. Here (is, are) the groceries.
5. There (is, are) a meeting tonight.
6. There (is, are) a new student in our class.
7. Here (stand, stands) the counseling center.
8. Here (is, are) my keys!
9. There (is, are) nothing edible in the refrigerator!
10. There (was, were) some beautiful jackets on sale.
11. Here (is, are) the present I made for you.
12. Here (is, are) the instructions.
13. There (was, were) no reason for the delay.
14. There (go, goes) Joey!
15. Here (is, are) my old neighborhood.
16. There (is, are) some cookies in the freezer.
17. Here (is, are) the record you lent me.
18. Here (is, are) Julann and David.
19. There (was, were) two frogs in the swimming pool!
20. There (is, are) a laundromat across the street.
21. Here (is, are) the site of the proposed library.
22. There (was, were) a soccer game last week.
23. Here (is, are) the notes from yesterday's lesson.
24. There (was, were) too many people in the elevator.
25. There (was, were) no vacancies at the motel.
26. Here (is, are) the morning paper.
27. There (is, are) a person I'd like you to meet.
28. Here (is, are) the lemons for the lemonade.
29. Here (is, are) the three people I told you about.
30. Here (is, are) First Up Everest, The Life of Michelangelo, and One Small Step.
31. There (go, goes) Eddie, Vince, and Ron.
32. Here (come, comes) one of my best friends.
33. There (is, are) three eggs, two ounces of cheese, and a green pepper in the refrigerator.

19g. Titles, Names of Organizations, and Names of Countries as Subjects

When the subject of a sentence is a title or the name of an organization or country, use a singular form verb.

Water Lilies **is** a beautiful painting by Claude Monet.
The United Nations **has** its headquarters in New York City.
The Netherlands **is** often called Holland.

PRACTICING YOUR SKILLS

■ Choose from each set of parentheses the verb form that agrees with the subject of the sentence. Write the sentences.

1. Dangerous Creatures (tell, tells) about octopi, squid, killer whales, and sea snakes.
2. Nighthawks (depict, depicts) lonely people in a diner very late at night.
3. The Camp Fire Girls (have, has) groups throughout the United States.
4. Some Things Weird and Wicked (contain, contains) twelve suspenseful stories.
5. Circular Forms (show, shows) circular forms.
6. The United Arab Emirates (produce, produces) and (export, exports) petroleum.
7. "The Red Shoes" (is, are) in Andersen's Fairy Tales.
8. Pro Football's Rag Days (describe, describes) the early days of football in America.
9. The United States (have, has) a population of over 200 million people.
10. Secrets with Ciphers and Codes (provide, provides) hours of fun on a rainy day.
11. The United Mine Workers (represent, represents) workers in the coal industry.
12. Three Women (is, are) by the painter Léger.
13. Gulliver's Travels (relate, relates) Gulliver's fantastic adventures in strange lands.
14. The Seychelles, an African country, (consist, consists) of coral islands and granite islands in the Indian Ocean.
15. The Three Musketeers (recount, recounts) the adventures of Athos, Porthos, Aramis, and D'Artagnan.
16. The United Automobile Workers (have, has) local unions in Canada and the United States.
17. Sports Illustrated (arrive, arrives) at my home each week.
18. Andersen's Fairy Tales (include, includes) "The Ugly Duckling" and "The Fir Tree," two of my favorites.
19. The Philippines (export, exports) sugar and coconuts.
20. Twelve Views from a Thatched Cottage, an ink painting by Hsia Kuei, (date, dates) from the thirteenth century.
21. Oarsmen at Chaton (is, are) a French impressionist painting.
22. The United Service Organizations (organize, organizes) entertainment for members of the armed forces.
23. Great American Athletes of the Twentieth Century (contain, contains) profiles of forty-nine athletes.
24. The Maids of Honor (is, are) an oil painting by Velázquez.
25. The Great Chiefs (tell, tells) about the Old West.

19h. Expressions of Amount as Subjects

An expression of amount may be the subject of a sentence. When the amount is considered as a single unit, use a singular form verb.

Eight dollars **is** an excellent price for that blouse.
Two thirds of the test **was** easy.

When the amount is considered as individual units, use a plural form verb.

Eight dollars **are** scattered on the floor.
Two thirds of the test questions **were** easy.

PRACTICING YOUR SKILLS

■ Consider each of the following expressions of amount as a single unit. Choose from each set of parentheses the correct verb form. Write the sentences.

1. Three yards of this fabric (is, are) enough to make the dress.
2. Ten pounds of anything (weigh, weighs) as much as ten pounds of anything else.
3. Seven hundred forty francs (buy, buys) a lovely blouse in Belgium.
4. Thirteen kilograms (is, are) the approximate weight of my dog.
5. Six kilometers (is, are) the distance between your house and mine.
6. In Spain, sixty pesetas (was, were) the hourly fee we paid the baby-sitter.
7. To an ant, thirty centimeters (look, looks) like an enormous height.
8. Twenty-four degrees Celsius (is, are) a pleasant temperature.
9. One liter of milk daily (supply, supplies) sufficient calcium for a growing youngster.
10. Forty Turkish lire (buy, buys) more than forty Italian lire.
11. Four German marks (was, were) all the money the tourist had left.
12. Two dollars (is, are) too much to pay.

■■ Consider each of the following expressions of amount as individual units. Choose from each set of parentheses the correct verb form. Write the sentences.

1. Two meters of this fabric (have, has) flaws.
2. Fourteen days (equal, equals) two weeks.
3. Three fourths of my class (take, takes) Spanish.
4. The last two weeks of school (pass, passes) too slowly!
5. Two hours of tennis (fly, flies) by!
6. Two gallons of milk (is, are) in the refrigerator.
7. Five kilograms (is, are) sometimes unbelievably difficult to shed.
8. Five Irish pounds (was, were) on the dresser.
9. Sixty cubic centimeters (fill, fills) this tiny jar.
10. Three yards of material (is, are) necessary.
11. More than half of the school soccer team (is, are) graduating this spring.
12. Two kilometers (is, are) much harder to jog than one.

19i. Do **and** Does; Don't **and** Doesn't

Do is a plural form verb. Use do and don't with noun and pronoun subjects that agree with plural form verbs.

> The boys **do** the dinner dishes every other night.
> They **don't** fix dinner on those evenings.

Does is a singular form verb. Use does and doesn't with noun and pronoun subjects that agree with singular form verbs.

> Kelley **does** her homework after her piano lesson.
> She **doesn't** take violin lessons anymore.

PRACTICING YOUR SKILLS

■ Choose from each set of parentheses the verb form that agrees with the subject noun or pronoun of the sentence. Write the sentences.

1. Mr. Ramirez (don't, doesn't) drive to work.
2. I (do, does) like your idea.
3. They (do, does) work after school.
4. My dogs (don't, doesn't) like strangers.
5. He (don't, doesn't) need any help.
6. Matthew (do, does) sing well.
7. Amy (don't, doesn't) read many books.
8. She (don't, doesn't) watch television, either.
9. We (do, does) enjoy riding our bikes.
10. A box of candy (do, does) make a delicious gift.
11. You (do, does) that trick superbly.
12. You (don't, doesn't) listen to me!
13. I (don't, doesn't) want any dinner.
14. Saul (do, does) feel better today.
15. It (don't, doesn't) make any sense.
16. The twins (don't, doesn't) look alike.
17. The sun (do, does) shine brightly.
18. Luke (do, does) write poems.
19. Sally (do, does) understand the question.
20. She (don't, doesn't) know the answer.
21. Everybody (do, does) some kind of work.
22. The clowns in the circus (do, does) make me laugh.
23. The woman in the black cape (do, does) magic tricks.
24. Naomi and Bettina (do, does) handstands.
25. Either Carol or Bill (do, does) the dishes each night.
26. Our dog and our cat (do, does) compete for our attention.
27. I (don't, doesn't) see why you're so angry.
28. A large car (do, does) have some advantages, but I (don't, doesn't) think economy is one of them.
29. Both Tom and Melissa (do, does) the wash on weekends.
30. Either Eric or Elaine (do, does) something for Grandma Wilkes every Thanksgiving.
31. Our dog (do, does) the funniest things with his dish.
32. Uncle Vincent (do, does) hope you'll drop by one evening.
33. You (don't, doesn't) believe everything you read, (do, does) you?
34. I (don't, doesn't) like mustard in my tuna sandwiches.
35. (Do, Does) your cousins read the sports section of the paper every morning?

Reviewing 18 Sentence Problems and 19 Subject-Verb Agreement

18a. Correcting Sentence Fragments

Read each sentence and sentence fragment. Rewrite the sentence fragment as part of the sentence.

1. Alice will play the piano. At the school concert next week.
2. Standing in the rain. We waited for the bus.
3. Leslie gave a party. To celebrate the Fourth of July.
4. Eleanor is taking riding lessons. And ballet lessons.

18b. Correcting Run-on Sentences

Rewrite each of the following run-on sentences as two sentences. Use the correct punctuation mark at the end of each sentence.

5. Can we catch that bus, let's hurry.
6. Donna's more than an hour late, where do you suppose she is?
7. Don't you want to eat at Original Joe's, I really love Italian food.
8. Please wait, I can't keep up with you.

18c. Correcting Rambling Sentences

Rewrite each of the following rambling sentences as two or more sentences.

9. Moira dashed out of the house, realizing she'd have to run for the bus, but then she noticed that she'd forgotten her books, and so she ran back home for them.
10. The teacher asked for our homework papers, and almost everyone said they hadn't done the assignment because it was too hard, but then Melinda turned her paper in without any excuse, and so everyone glared at her.

11. My father called me and asked me where I'd been, and I told him that Sheila and I had gone to the beach, and I asked him if he'd like to join us when we go again, and he said he would when he got the car running again, so I asked, "What's the matter with it?" and he said, "What isn't?"
12. A gnu is a large African antelope, and it has high shoulders and a thick neck, and then on its head the gnu has a pair of long, curved horns.

18d. Avoiding Unnecessary Repetition in Sentences

Rewrite the following sentences to avoid unnecessary repetition.

13. The dull movie that we saw when we went to the movies was boring.
14. The tired children were exhausted and ready for bed.
15. I telephoned my friend Herman and talked to him on the phone after I called him up.
16. Barry bought a pair of two shoes which he purchased at the store.
17. Some geologists who study geology are concerned with the changes and alterations in the surface of the earth.

Choose from each set of parentheses the verb form that agrees with the subject noun or pronoun of the sentence. Write the sentences.

19a. Present Tense Verb Forms

18. Marc (play, plays) the cello.
19. Several students (dance, dances).
20. She (perform, performs) with her sister.

19b. Indefinite Pronoun Subjects

21. Everyone (study, studies) current events, but not everyone (like, likes) them.
22. Many (read, reads) a newspaper daily, but few (read, reads) one all the way through.
23. Some (prepare, prepares) reports for class, and all (listen, listens) to them.
24. Nobody (understand, understands) it.

19c. Collective Noun Subjects

Assume that the collective nouns in the following sentences refer to the group as a single unit.

25. The football team (play, plays) better at home than away.
26. The audience (clap, claps) enthusiastically at the end of the play.
27. The mime troupe (display, displays) extraordinary skill.

19d. Subject Noun or Pronoun Modified by a Prepositional Phrase

28. The scientists at this laboratory (investigate, investigates) the causes of many diseases.
29. The house with the shuttered windows (is, are) for sale, and the cottages in the garden (is, are) for rent.
30. The members of the Forensic Club (debate, debates) each weekend.
31. Two students from each school (participate, participates) in the discussion.

19e. Compound Subject

32. Neither the Dodgers nor the Yankees (deserve, deserves) the pennant this year.
33. Either Barry or Phil (play, plays) the leading role in the musical.
34. Seiji and his brother Endo (look, looks) alike.

19f. Sentences Beginning with Here and There

35. There (was, were) several problems in our first plan, and there (was, were) still more problems in the second.
36. There (go, goes) the seniors, and here (come, comes) the juniors.
37. Here (is, are) your allowance, and there (is, are) the car keys.
38. Here (is, are) the other puzzle pieces.
39. There (was, were) one piece on the floor.

19g. Titles, Names of Organizations, and Names of Countries as Subjects

40. The Netherlands (have, has) a fascinating history.
41. The Red and the Black (is, are) by the French author Stendhal.
42. The United Nations (establish, establishes) many international agencies.
43. The Friends of the Library (has, have) 153 members.

19h. Expressions of Amount as Subjects

Consider each of the following expressions of amount as a single unit.

44. Forty seconds (was, were) the time limit for the first race.
45. One thousand Italian lire (is, are) worth little more than a dollar.
46. Five dollars (seem, seems) like a fortune to me right now.

19i. Do and Does; Don't and Doesn't

47. Ronnie (do, does) his exercises every morning, but I (don't, doesn't).
48. My sister (don't, doesn't) like to play with dolls, but Gene's sisters (do, does).
49. The paintings (don't, doesn't) look quite right there.
50. That table (don't, doesn't) need any more shellac, but these chairs (do, does).

20 Verb Usage

20a. Irregular Verb Forms I

The following irregular verbs have past tense forms and past participle forms that follow the same pattern.

Present	Past	Present Participle	Past Participle
drive, drives	drove	(is) driving	(has) driven
ride, rides	rode	(is) riding	(has) ridden
rise, rises	rose	(is) rising	(has) risen
write, writes	wrote	(is) writing	(has) written

PRACTICING YOUR SKILLS

■ Use either the past tense form or the past participle form of the verb in parentheses to finish each sentence. Write sentences.

1. Last summer, the Bergermanns (drive) to British Columbia.
2. They had never (drive) that far before.
3. Lorene (drive) part of the way.
4. Otis (drive) the new van.
5. Blake had (drive) the Model T to the car show.
6. Yolanda has (drive) us to school every day this week.
7. Rosa and Kiyoko have (drive) out to the ruins.
8. Ms. Frazier (drive) to the airport to meet a friend.
9. They (drive) the cattle across the plains.
10. Have you ever (drive) the truck?
11. She should have (drive) the truck.
12. Kaye (drive) straight to the hospital.
13. Gaby had never (ride) in a horse show.
14. She (ride) for several hours every day.
15. They have always (ride) bareback.
16. Chuck (ride) Sundance in the horse show.
17. Ruby has (ride) an elephant and a llama.
18. Have you ever (ride) in an old-fashioned buggy?
19. Yon Tu (ride) with us to the exhibition.
20. Olga has not (ride) her bike for days.
21. We (ride) the roller coaster fifteen times.
22. Indian Summer is the best horse that I have ever (ride).
23. Duane had never (ride) a horse before.
24. Lupe and Elaine (ride) their bikes to the lake.
25. They had never (ride) that far before.
26. We should have (ride) with them.
27. During the storm, the river (rise) to flood level.
28. Everyone had (rise) to the occasion.
29. We (rise) late the next day.
30. A full moon (rise) over the quiet desert.
31. The soufflé had (rise) beautifully.
32. Antonia had (rise) early to go fishing.
33. The river had (rise) to a dangerous level.
34. By the time the sun had (rise), we were ready to go.
35. The delegates (rise).
36. Has the bread (rise) enough yet?
37. The temperature has (rise) dramatically.
38. Everyone in the courtroom (rise).
39. Marcus has (write) a new script for the school play.
40. He (write) the script for the play last year too.
41. Dora (write) an introduction to the play.
42. Robin has already (write) her essay.
43. She (write) it in one day.

20b. Irregular Verb Forms II

The following irregular verbs have past tense forms and past participle forms that follow the same pattern.

Present	Past	Present Participle	Past Participle
bring, brings	brought	(is) bringing	(has) brought
buy, buys	bought	(is) buying	(has) bought
seek, seeks	sought	(is) seeking	(has) sought
teach, teaches	taught	(is) teaching	(has) taught
think, thinks	thought	(is) thinking	(has) thought

PRACTICING YOUR SKILLS

■ Use either the past tense form or the past participle form of the verb in parentheses to finish each sentence. Write the sentences.

1. That disaster (bring) out the best in everyone.
2. Volunteers had (bring) food and water.
3. They have (bring) good news.
4. Gabriel has (bring) his dogs with him.
5. Nobody had (bring) the groceries in from the car.
6. Linda has (bring) a solar cell to class.
7. We should have (bring) something to eat.
8. Marcus (bring) two newspapers, a book, and four magazines.
9. The messenger (bring) news from a neighboring kingdom.
10. I have not (buy) my brother's birthday present yet.
11. Leon (buy) all of us lunch yesterday.
12. Sondra (buy) a pound of apples.
13. Guadalupe and Elettra have (buy) the supplies for our project.
14. Who (buy) these pastries?
15. A land speculator had (buy) all the available property near the lake.
16. The Sellins have just (buy) a new couch.
17. They (buy) two chairs last week.
18. They had (buy) the chairs to match the rug.
19. Columbus (seek) a new route to the East.
20. Lila has (seek) the information in every newspaper.
21. Miners (seek) gold in the mountains of Colorado.
22. For years, scientists have (seek) alternative energy sources.
23. Explorers had (seek) the Fountain of Youth.
24. They (seek) a new solution to an old problem.
25. They have (seek) the answer everywhere.
26. They had only (seek) to help us.
27. Ms. Martinez (teach) English last year.
28. She had (teach) history in previous years.
29. She has also (teach) French.
30. Olivia Brooks (teach) us to ski.
31. She has (teach) skiing since 1973.
32. Yoonja (teach) her brother to read.
33. Neil had (teach) English in Indonesia.
34. No one has ever (teach) me to cook.
35. Has anyone (think) of a theme yet?
36. We had never (think) of you as an actress!
37. Luis (think) about how to spend his summer vacation.
38. He had (think) about going to camp.
39. He had also (think) about finding a job.
40. Joey (think) of a solution.

20c. Irregular Verb Forms III

The following irregular verbs have past tense forms and past participle forms that follow the same pattern.

Present	Past	Present Participle	Past Participle
eat, eats	ate	(is) eating	(has) eaten
give, gives	gave	(is) giving	(has) given
lie, lies	lay	(is) lying	(has) lain

PRACTICING YOUR SKILLS

▪ Use either the past tense form or the past participle form of the verb in parentheses to finish each sentence. Write the sentences.

1. The hikers hadn't (eat) for hours.
2. They (eat) an early lunch.
3. Somebody must have (eat) the snake we had prepared.
4. Seth (eat) most of it last night.
5. Cathy's pet rat has (eat) part of the telephone cord.
6. Who (eat) all the grapes?
7. Haven't you ever (eat) snails?
8. Has Paul (eat) all the tuna?
9. We (eat) too much during our vacation.
10. Our dog Shana once (eat) an entire box of Brillo.
11. Terry has already (eat) three hamburgers.
12. Kurt (eat) very little during his illness.
13. The travelers (eat) a variety of unusual foods.
14. That goat must have (eat) everything.
15. April (eat) dinner at her friend's house last night.
16. Has somebody (eat) the rest of the fruit salad?
17. The cats may have (eat) the dog's food.
18. Everyone had (eat) at home.
19. Nakita (give) an excellent speech.
20. Has Oscar (give) his opinion yet?
21. Manuela (give) us our instructions.
22. Mr. LaRosa has (give) the question careful consideration.
23. You have (give) me an idea!
24. Ms. Cheatham (give) him the message.
25. Frances had already (give) a reasonable excuse.
26. That noise (give) me a terrible shock!
27. Evelyn had almost (give) up.
28. Tony (give) a carefully worded answer to the question.
29. Have all the members (give) Mr. Martinez their permission slips?
30. Dennis had (give) me the recipe for that pie.
31. You should have (give) me your answer earlier.
32. The fans (give) the pitcher a standing ovation.
33. Has Dr. Delgado already (give) you the test?
34. Karl (give) a party last weekend.
35. He has (give) several parties before.
36. He (give) every guest a small gift.
37. Each guest (give) Karl a gift.
38. Tony (lie) down to rest.
39. He had (lie) awake for hours.
40. His cat (lie) on the pillow beside him.
41. Sonny has (lie) in the hammock all day.
42. The cat (lie) close to the fire.
43. I could have (lie) in bed all day!
44. The bicycle (lie) on its side in the yard.
45. Those books have (lie) on that table for weeks!
46. Juan's birthday presents (lie) on the floor of the closet.

20d. Irregular Verb Forms IV

The following irregular verbs have past tense forms and past participle forms that follow the same pattern.

Present	Past	Present Participle	Past Participle
begin, begins	began	(is) beginning	(has) begun
drink, drinks	drank	(is) drinking	(has) drunk
ring, rings	rang	(is) ringing	(has) rung
shrink, shrinks	shrank	(is) shrinking	(has) shrunk
swim, swims	swam	(is) swimming	(has) swum

PRACTICING YOUR SKILLS

■ Use either the past tense form or the past participle form of the verb in parentheses to finish each sentence. Write the sentences.

1. The tournament had (begin) at nine o'clock.
2. The second round (begin) at noon.
3. The players had (begin) to feel tired by evening.
4. The crowd (begin) to drift away.
5. The movie had already (begin).
6. At the signal, everyone (begin) to chant.
7. Julian has not yet (begin) his campaign.
8. In the middle of her speech, Alison (begin) to laugh.
9. Jesse and Will (begin) this project months ago.
10. Mae-Su has already (begin) to write her research report.
11. Alan has already (drink) nearly two quarts of milk.
12. When we were in the desert, we (drink) a special sage tea.
13. The horses (drink) at the stream.
14. Lee has (drink) all the tomato juice.
15. Bonnie and I ate popcorn and (drink) fruit punch all afternoon.
16. Some of the players had (drink) too much water before the game.
17. After the game, everyone (drink) lemonade.
18. Have you ever (drink) it before?
19. Lonny (ring) the door bell three times.
20. Somebody had (ring) the bell in the tower.
21. The alarm (ring) at six o'clock.
22. It must have (ring) for five minutes.
23. The chimes (ring) out over the countryside.
24. The phone (ring) suddenly, startling everyone.
25. Has the timer (ring) yet?
26. The last bell had already (ring).
27. Those bells have (ring) every Sunday for the past three hundred years.
28. The phone has (ring) six times already.
29. Neville's sweater (shrink) in the wash.
30. The politician's following had (shrink).
31. The meat (shrink) while it was being cooked.
32. Those pants have (shrink).
33. Your appetite may have (shrink).
34. Perhaps all these clothes have (shrink).
35. He (shrink) the material before he cut it.
36. I think my waist has (shrink).
37. Everyone (swim) slowly at first.
38. Delilah had never (swim) in a race before.
39. She (swim) very well.
40. What is the farthest you've ever (swim)?
41. Sergio (swim) in the Aegean Sea.
42. Have you ever (swim) at Little Lakes?

20e. Irregular Verb Forms V

The following irregular verbs have past tense forms and past participle forms that follow the same pattern.

Present	Past	Present Participle	Past Participle
break, breaks	broke	(is) breaking	(has) broken
steal, steals	stole	(is) stealing	(has) stolen
tear, tears	tore	(is) tearing	(has) torn
wear, wears	wore	(is) wearing	(has) worn

PRACTICING YOUR SKILLS

■ Use either the past tense form or the past participle form of the verb in parentheses to finish each sentence. Write the sentences.

1. Someone has (break) my favorite glass.
2. Who (break) it?
3. Lonny (break) the fall with her wrist.
4. She has (break) her wrist.
5. The people in that group may have (break) a world record.
6. Who could have (break) that vase?
7. Danielle (break) her leg while she was skiing.
8. Rafael may have (break) his promise.
9. Marlita (break) her watch yesterday.
10. You have (break) the last piece of chalk.
11. Phyllis tried to explain how she had (break) her arm.
12. They may have (break) the law.
13. The burglar (steal) all the fine china.
14. Somebody has (steal) your idea.
15. Teresa (steal) first base while Tennie was up at bat.
16. Perhaps someone (steal) our lunches.
17. Who could have (steal) your notebook?
18. Margie claimed that Fred had (steal) her recipe for pecan pie.
19. Ms. Machado identified the person who had (steal) her purse.
20. Why would anyone have (steal) that box?
21. Marga (steal) away from the crowd.
22. Has somebody (steal) the equipment?
23. They (steal) a look at the gifts in the closet.
24. Paula impatiently (tear) the letter open.
25. The wind has (tear) the leaves from that young tree.
26. Mick had already (tear) the paper into pieces when he realized he still needed it.
27. The dog (tear) in one door and out the other.
28. That rock has (tear) a hole in my jeans.
29. Your cat has (tear) that plastic mouse to shreds.
30. Bobbi has (tear) several ligaments in her leg.
31. Jane (tear) a hole in the bag.
32. Peter (tear) the loaf of bread into pieces.
33. Everyone (wear) extraordinary outfits to the costume party.
34. Tanya (wear) a refrigerator box decorated to look like a computer.
35. Sandro had (wear) his costume in a play.
36. Have you (wear) your new boots yet?
37. All this walking has (wear) a hole in my shoes.
38. Armando (wear) a suit to the meeting.
39. Sherm has never (wear) the sweater that you made for him.
40. Clint (wear) the cast for three months.
41. Melanie and Jessie (wear) the same outfit to the party.
42. Eddie (wear) his black cape to the Halloween party.

20f. Irregular Verb Forms VI

The following irregular verbs have past tense forms and past participle forms that follow the same pattern.

Present	Past	Present Participle	Past Participle
blow, blows	blew	(is) blowing	(has) blown
fly, flies	flew	(is) flying	(has) flown
grow, grows	grew	(is) growing	(has) grown
know, knows	knew	(is) knowing	(has) known
throw, throws	threw	(is) throwing	(has) thrown

PRACTICING YOUR SKILLS

■ Use either the past tense form or the past participle form of the verb
in parentheses to finish each sentence. Write the sentences.

1. The message might have (blow) away.
2. It may have (blow) out the window.
3. The breeze (blow) gently through the trees.
4. Could the wind have (blow) the newspapers away?
5. The dragon (blow) great puffs of blue and green smoke.
6. The most important papers have (blow) away.
7. Lissa (blow) out all the candles on her cake.
8. The wind must have (blow) that branch off the tree.
9. A flock of birds (fly) overhead.
10. Has another bird (fly) into the window?
11. They (fly) to Amsterdam last night.
12. Have you ever (fly) in a small plane?
13. The birds (fly) many miles to reach their destination.
14. We (fly) to Chicago and took the train home from there.
15. The plane (fly) over the Grand Canyon.
16. Pat has (fly) around the world.
17. The kite (fly) into the tree.
18. How many butterflies have (fly) by your window this morning?
19. These vegetables (grow) without much help from us.
20. The town's population has not (grow) much since 1900.
21. Grandpa has always (grow) prize-winning roses.
22. The corn has already (grow) to its full height.
23. The sapling has (grow) into a magnificent tree.
24. Several rosebushes (grow) near the fence last year.
25. The people in the crowd have (grow) angry.
26. Carla had (know) about the test for days.
27. She (know) more than she could tell us.
28. How long have they (know) about this?
29. Dan had (know) about the plan all along.
30. Only Mr. Espinosa (know) the truth.
31. Ken (know) who would win the award.
32. I never (know) what his real name was.
33. Who else could have (know) about it?
34. How long have you (know) the secret?
35. Demetrius has (throw) the discus in competition for several years.
36. He (throw) especially well today.
37. Guy (throw) the ball over the fence.
38. What else had they (throw) out?
39. Why have you (throw) your books away?
40. Sheila (throw) the ball, and the dog ran after it.

20g. Irregular Verb Forms VII

The following irregular verbs have past tense forms and past participle forms that follow the same pattern.

Present	Past	Present Participle	Past Participle
choose, chooses	chose	(is) choosing	(has) chosen
freeze, freezes	froze	(is) freezing	(has) frozen
speak, speaks	spoke	(is) speaking	(has) spoken

PRACTICING YOUR SKILLS

■ Use either the past tense form or the past participle form of the verb in parentheses to finish each sentence. Write the sentences.

1. Have you (choose) the subject for your report yet?
2. I (choose) mine last week.
3. Bob has (choose) a parakeet instead of a cat.
4. Raleigh (choose) to wait there for the other members of the team.
5. Have you (choose) your favorite flavor of ice cream yet?
6. Conrad (choose) chocolate mint.
7. Catherine has (choose) a career in accounting.
8. Marta (choose) the calico kitten.
9. The class has already (choose) a new president.
10. Have you (choose) your advisor yet?
11. Linda should have (choose) a different topic for her report.
12. Several people have (choose) to walk rather than drive.
13. Joni has (choose) to ride the bus.
14. Bryjid (choose) a very nice gift for her mother.
15. You could have (choose) your own assignment.
16. Ezra (choose) the red jacket.
17. Everything (freeze) during the long winter storm.
18. Even the lake had completely (freeze).
19. Have they (freeze) the rest of that meat?
20. You might have (freeze) out there!
21. The water in the birdbath (freeze) several times last winter.
22. The refrigerator is so cold that the milk has (freeze).
23. Is it true that the pipes have (freeze)?
24. Has the fruit on the trees (freeze)?
25. I feel as if my hands have (freeze).
26. Reggy baked an extra pie and (freeze) it.
27. Perhaps we should have (freeze) some of the peaches.
28. As soon as the pond had (freeze), Nick organized a skating party.
29. Hasn't Armando (speak) to Lee yet?
30. Drake (speak) to the whole group.
31. I have not (speak) to her in weeks.
32. Nobody has (speak) to me about this problem.
33. I (speak) to her yesterday.
34. Bob has often (speak) of you, Mr. Manuel.
35. Brenda (speak) about the plans for the trip.
36. Have the other candidates (speak) already?
37. After Kathy has (speak), we will go to lunch.
38. I wish I had (speak) with him sooner.
39. Since the principal has already (speak) on that matter, there is little we can do.
40. The editor (speak) with the author about the progress of the manuscript.

20h. Irregular Verb Forms VIII

The following irregular verbs have unusual past tense forms and past participle forms.

Present	Past	Present Participle	Past Participle
burst, bursts	burst	(is) bursting	(has) burst
come, comes	came	(is) coming	(has) come
do, does	did	(is) doing	(has) done
fall, falls	fell	(is) falling	(has) fallen
go, goes	went	(is) going	(has) gone
run, runs	ran	(is) running	(has) run
see, sees	saw	(is) seeing	(has) seen
take, takes	took	(is) taking	(has) taken

PRACTICING YOUR SKILLS

■ Use either the past tense form or the past participle form of the verb in parentheses to finish each sentence. Write the sentences.

1. Hilary (burst) into the room, laughing excitedly.
2. The dam could have (burst) during the storm.
3. The fireworks (burst) into showers of color.
4. The piñata had (burst) and scattered candies onto the floor.
5. The meeting had still not (come) to order.
6. The pianist (come) onto the stage.
7. Have you (come) to see the kittens?
8. Ms. Lightfoot (come) to our meeting last week.
9. He should have (come) to class on time.
10. The bus (come) to a sudden stop.
11. Who could have (do) it?
12. Elsie has already (do) all her work.
13. Len should have (do) the work more carefully.
14. Vera has (do) everything she could to help you.
15. Reggie (do) the dishes last night.
16. No one had (do) them for several days.
17. You should have (do) it yourself.
18. Several books had (fall) from the shelf.
19. I tripped and (fall) over one of them.
20. You might have (fall)!
21. The huge oak tree had (fall) across their driveway.
22. Most of the fruit has already (fall) from the trees.
23. Anders has (go) to Hawaii for the summer.
24. He (go) to Mexico last year.
25. Somebody should have (go) to the store.
26. Chris and Elena (go) to camp last summer.
27. Have you ever (go) to a summer camp?
28. Carlos (run) up to me, nearly out of breath.
29. He had (run) all the way from school.
30. We had all (run) out of ideas.
31. Thea has (run) around the track eight times.
32. They (run) a mile every day.
33. How many times have you (see) that movie?
34. You should have (see) those acrobats!
35. Raoul (see) Michael at the beach yesterday.
36. Erin (see) <u>The Gold Rush</u> last week.

20i. Lie **and** Lay

Use a form of lie to mean "to get into or be in a reclining position."
Many sunbathers **lie** on the beach now.
Many sunbathers **lay** on the beach yesterday.
Many sunbathers are **lying** on the beach.
Many sunbathers have **lain** on the beach.

Use a form of lay to mean "to put or place something."
The children will **lay** the plates on the table.
The children **laid** the plates on the table.
The children are **laying** the plates on the table.
The children have **laid** the plates on the table.

PRACTICING YOUR SKILLS

- Use a form of **lie** or **lay** to finish each sentence. Write the sentences.

1. Why don't you ‖‖‖‖‖‖‖ down for a nap?
2. The paper napkins are ‖‖‖‖‖‖‖ in the kitchen drawer.
3. The students had ‖‖‖‖‖‖‖ down their pencils.
4. He ‖‖‖‖‖‖‖ his tools on the workbench.
5. We have ‖‖‖‖‖‖‖ on the grass.
6. She is ‖‖‖‖‖‖‖ squares of tile flooring.
7. They ‖‖‖‖‖‖‖ in the sun yesterday.
8. Ms. Perkins ‖‖‖‖‖‖‖ her purse on her desk.
9. All the books were ‖‖‖‖‖‖‖ on the table.
10. The puppies are ‖‖‖‖‖‖‖ in the basket.
11. ‖‖‖‖‖‖‖ all the ingredients on the counter before you begin to cook.
12. I'd like to ‖‖‖‖‖‖‖ in the hammock now.
13. She had ‖‖‖‖‖‖‖ down to rest earlier in the day.
14. They are ‖‖‖‖‖‖‖ the utensils on the buffet table.
15. He ‖‖‖‖‖‖‖ his head on my shoulder.
16. They ‖‖‖‖‖‖‖ on the floor in front of the television all yesterday afternoon.
17. She has ‖‖‖‖‖‖‖ the scissors somewhere, and she can't find them.
18. She ‖‖‖‖‖‖‖ down the letter with a sigh.
19. He ‖‖‖‖‖‖‖ awake for an hour before he fell asleep.
20. ‖‖‖‖‖‖‖ your head on the pillow.
21. Michael ‖‖‖‖‖‖‖ down the dictionary so that it was ‖‖‖‖‖‖‖ on the edge of the desk.
22. It's past time for your nap, Junior; you should be ‖‖‖‖‖‖‖ down.
23. Will you ‖‖‖‖‖‖‖ out on paper exactly what you want me to do?
24. The ship ‖‖‖‖‖‖‖ in harbor for a week before sailing away.
25. I've ‖‖‖‖‖‖‖ out all the reports in order; they're ‖‖‖‖‖‖‖ on the conference table.
26. After listening to both stories, I feel that the truth ‖‖‖‖‖‖‖ somewhere in between.
27. I've ‖‖‖‖‖‖‖ down every afternoon for a month: while ‖‖‖‖‖‖‖ there, I've thought of many things.
28. Tessa's been ‖‖‖‖‖‖‖ on the couch, trying to remember where she ‖‖‖‖‖‖‖ down the groceries.
29. I don't know who ‖‖‖‖‖‖‖ it there, but that pile of mail has been ‖‖‖‖‖‖‖ on the bookcase for three days.

20j. Rise and Raise

Use a form of rise to mean "to move upward" or "to assume an upright position."

> The balloons **rise** in the air.
> The balloons **rose** in the air.
> The balloons are **rising** in the air.
> The balloons had **risen** in the air.

Use a form of raise to mean "to move something upward."

> He **raises** the window shade.
> He **raised** the window shade.
> He is **raising** the window shade.
> He had **raised** the window shade.

PRACTICING YOUR SKILLS

- Use a form of **rise** or **raise** to finish each sentence. Write the sentences.

1. The water in the reservoir |||||||||||||||| five inches during the storm.
2. Peter |||||||||||||| at seven o'clock each morning.
3. The landlord has |||||||||||||||| our rent.
4. My employer is |||||||||||||||| my salary.
5. Why are prices |||||||||||||| ?
6. Are you |||||||||||||| early tomorrow?
7. I |||||||||||||| my head and opened my eyes when the scary part of the movie was over.
8. Please |||||||||||||| that painting another few inches.
9. I |||||||||||||| later today than usual.
10. The tide had |||||||||||||| drastically.
11. Robert had |||||||||||||| earlier than the rest of us.
12. The sun will |||||||||||||| at six A.M. tomorrow.
13. I |||||||||||||| my hand and hoped the teacher would call on me.
14. Sarah has |||||||||||||| her biology grade from a B to an A.
15. Can you |||||||||||||| your arm, or does it still hurt?
16. In certain situations, it is a mark of respect to |||||||||||||| from one's seat.
17. Which river |||||||||||||| most during the rainy season?
18. The markets are |||||||||||||| the prices of canned goods.
19. I will |||||||||||||| your allowance if you take on more responsibilities.
20. The jet is |||||||||||||| into the sky.
21. The paper reports that prices |||||||||||||| fifteen percent last year, and they're still |||||||||||||| .
22. I |||||||||||||| my hand to answer the teacher's question.
23. The protester |||||||||||||| at the end of the meeting and |||||||||||||| his sign.
24. I |||||||||||||| at five o'clock this morning, and this afternoon I can hardly |||||||||||||| my head from my desk.
25. Meg usually |||||||||||||| earlier than Melinda does, but all this week Melinda has |||||||||||||| earlier than Meg.
26. The oil dipstick now reads full; the level must have |||||||||||||| since I |||||||||||||| the hood.
27. If you |||||||||||||| the curtain, you can watch the moon |||||||||||||| .
28. The sound from the auditorium |||||||||||||| in volume.

20k. Sit and Set

Use a form of sit to mean "to rest in a seated position."

I **sit** in the front row today.
I **sat** in the front row yesterday.
I am **sitting** in the front row.
I have **sat** in the front row.

Use a form of set to mean "to put something."

She **sets** the ladder against the wall.
She **set** the ladder against the wall.
She is **setting** the ladder against the wall.
She has **set** the ladder against the wall.

20l. Teach and Learn

Use a form of teach when you mean "to instruct a person or animal."

Harry **teaches** magic tricks to his friends.
Harry **taught** magic tricks to his friends.
Harry is **teaching** magic tricks to his friends.
Harry has **taught** magic tricks to his friends.

Use a form of learn when you mean "to gain a skill or knowledge."

Benny **learns** some magic tricks.
Benny **learned** some magic tricks.
Benny is **learning** some magic tricks.
Benny has **learned** some magic tricks.

PRACTICING YOUR SKILLS

■ Use a form of **sit** or **set** to finish each sentence. Write the sentences.

1. Please ‖‖‖‖‖‖‖‖ in your chairs.
2. It's your turn to ‖‖‖‖‖‖‖‖ the table.
3. We ‖‖‖‖‖‖‖‖ in the first row.
4. Edward ‖‖‖‖‖‖‖‖ the clock there.
5. She is ‖‖‖‖‖‖‖‖ down the knife carefully.
6. She has ‖‖‖‖‖‖‖‖ in the chair for hours.
7. The guests were ‖‖‖‖‖‖‖‖ in the den.
8. She had ‖‖‖‖‖‖‖‖ them on the counter.
9. He was ‖‖‖‖‖‖‖‖ on the rocking horse.
10. We all ‖‖‖‖‖‖‖‖ quietly until the end.

■■ Use a form of **teach** or **learn** to finish each sentence. Write the sentences.

1. Ms. Berman ‖‖‖‖‖‖‖‖ skiing to me.
2. I am ‖‖‖‖‖‖‖‖ Greek from him.
3. We have ‖‖‖‖‖‖‖‖ from our parents how to cook nourishing meals.
4. She ‖‖‖‖‖‖‖‖ English to adults.
5. Are you still ‖‖‖‖‖‖‖‖ them to cook?
6. I try to ‖‖‖‖‖‖‖‖ from my mistakes.
7. Please ‖‖‖‖‖‖‖‖ me that song.
8. She has ‖‖‖‖‖‖‖‖ her brother to sail.
9. Heidi ‖‖‖‖‖‖‖‖ new skills quickly.
10. They were ‖‖‖‖‖‖‖‖ to dive.
11. The children had ‖‖‖‖‖‖‖‖ to read.

20m. Avoiding Unnecessary Changes in Verb Tense

Verbs of the same tense usually indicate the same time. Except to show a change in time, use verbs of the same tense throughout a sentence.

> **Sentence with Unnecessary Change:** Jasmine **walks** the dog and **took** out the garbage.
>
> **Rewritten Sentence:** Jasmine **walks** the dog and **takes** out the garbage.
>
> **Rewritten Sentence:** Jasmine **walked** the dog and **took** out the garbage.

PRACTICING YOUR SKILLS

- Read each sentence. Find the sentences with verbs that have unnecessary changes of verb tense. Rewrite those sentences correctly.

1. The world changes dramatically when the barbarians invaded Rome.
2. David sings at the concert and played the guitar.
3. When the wolf entered, he surprises the grandmother.
4. Julia told us a joke, and we all laughed.
5. Before my mother leaves for work, she helped us get ready for school.
6. Kate was in the park when she sees Felipe.
7. The music was so loud that we can't hear each other.
8. She reads the newspaper and drank juice every morning.
9. My hands were shaking as I open the telegram.
10. When Simon gets home from school, he usually starts dinner.
11. I'm looking everywhere, but I couldn't find the phone number.
12. When he finished speaking, everyone claps excitedly.
13. We were just talking about you when you come in.
14. Fiona goes to lunch, and she ordered a small health salad.
15. The dogs bark menacingly whenever they saw a stranger.
16. I tried to open the suitcase, but it was locked.
17. I turn on the television and watched my favorite program.
18. We walked to the movie theater and meet our teacher on the way.
19. Cheryll tries on the hat, and it looked pretty.
20. The merry-go-round stopped, and I jump off the horse.
21. We boarded the plane and sit in our seats.
22. He says goodbye to us and rode off on his horse.
23. Bert changes the sheets while Abby vacuumed.
24. I made dinner last night and surprise my family with it.
25. He walks upstairs and turned on the hall light.
26. The elevator finally arrived, and I get into it.
27. I got up at seven, drink my juice, brushed my teeth, and run out of the house.
28. Last night Alberta catches the plane and flew to Denver.
29. I talked to Peter right after class, and he tells me about his new bike.

Reviewing 20 Verb Usage

Use either the past tense form or the past participle form of the verb in parentheses to finish each sentence. Write the sentences.

20a. Irregular Verb Forms I

1. My cousin (drive) a moving van from Philadelphia to Astoria, while her brother (ride) in the cab with her.
2. Maryellen has (ride) her bicycle to school every day this week; today she (write) a report about her experiences.
3. John had (rise) early the day of the hike and had (write) a letter to his grandmother.
4. The dough for the bread has already (rise) twice.

20b. Irregular Verb Forms II

5. When I arrived at the picnic grounds, I (think) I had (bring) the apples I (buy) last Thursday.
6. Socrates (teach) Plato, who in turn (teach) Aristotle.
7. Scientists have (seek) solutions to environmental problems.
8. I had (think) about that clock for two weeks before I finally (buy) it.
9. Reilly should have (bring) the records that she (buy) last week.

20c. Irregular Verb Forms III

10. Sheila has (give) away our secret; I've (lie) awake all night worrying about it.
11. David (eat) an entire pizza last night; then he said, "I feel sick," and (lie) down.
12. I (give) you a pound of cheese last night; I can't believe you've (eat) it all.
13. The unpaid bills had (lie) on his desk for more than two months.
14. You have (give) me an idea.

20d. Irregular Verb Forms IV

15. The actors (begin) rehearsals last week, but the cast (shrink) rapidly.
16. The telephone (ring) when I had (drink) only half the glass of milk.
17. Jeannie has (swim) for years; she (begin) when she was only two.
18. Cindy Nicholas (swim) from England to France and back again in less than twenty hours.

20e. Irregular Verb Forms V

19. Ms. Oviatt has (break) her leg and has (wear) a cast for months.
20. He had (steal) another person's idea; he had (break) his promise.
21. I (tear) my shirt on a nail; fortunately, I had almost (wear) it out.
22. Somebody has (steal) her bicycle.

20f. Irregular Verb Forms VI

23. They have (fly) to Montreal several times this year.
24. Only Sabrina (know) the entire truth last week.
25. The wind (blow) savagely along the coast and destroyed the few trees that had (grow) there.
26. The other students should have (know) about the test.

20g. Irregular Verb Forms VII

27. Haven't the players (choose) their captain yet?
28. This river (freeze) last winter; everyone (speak) about it.
29. Ms. Monturo had (speak) to our group once, but she (choose) not to speak again.
30. Monty may have (freeze) the rest of that boysenberry pie.

20h. Irregular Verb Forms VIII

31. We (burst) into laughter when Arnold (come) into the room.
32. Katya (run) faster than Hank.
33. I (fall) down the stairs the night I (take) Ilsa to the movies.
34. They should not have (go) into that cave by themselves.
35. Mrs. Toganaka (see) that we had already (do) most of the work.

Finish each sentence by choosing the correct verb form in parentheses. Write the sentences.

20i. Lie and Lay

36. Toby (lay, laid) his books on the desk and (lay, laid) down on the couch.
37. Anita had (lain, laid) in bed for several days after the operation when she noticed that the flowers were (lying, laying) nearby.
38. The newspaper is (lying, laying) on the table; I (lay, laid) it there this morning.
39. Nobody has (lain, laid) the dinner dishes on the table yet.
40. Ms. Kirkwood (lay, laid) a new floor in the kitchen last week.

20j. Rise and Raise

41. The temperature (rose, raised) suddenly this afternoon and may (rise, raise) again tomorrow.
42. Ron (rose, raised) his arm in a gesture of farewell and (rose, raised) to go.
43. She had (risen, raised) from her seat before I had (risen, raised) from mine.
44. Many prices have (risen, raised) drastically during the past year.
45. The merchants have (risen, raised) so many of their prices that now I check prices for large items in at least two stores.

20k. Sit and Set

46. Monty was (sitting, setting) in the front row, where he had (sat, set) for weeks.
47. I (sat, set) through the entire lecture, then (sat, set) the important parts down in my notes.
48. Eric carefully (sat, set) the figurine on the table and (sat, set) down opposite it.
49. Ramona (sat, set) the package down and then (sat, set) down on the couch.
50. You could have heard better if you had (sat, set) in the front.

20l. Teach and Learn

51. My cousin (taught, learned) me to play checkers, and I (taught, learned) fast.
52. She had (taught, learned) to play from her mother, who had also (taught, learned) her two sisters.
53. This has certainly (taught, learned) me a lesson; I'll never forget what I've (taught, learned).
54. After Rikki (teaches, learns) how to play backgammon, she will (teach, learn) us.
55. We (taught, learned) quickly because she (taught, learned) us well.

20m. Avoiding Unnecessary Changes in Verb Tense

Rewrite the following sentences to avoid unnecessary changes of tense.

56. I was in the middle of a sentence when the phone rings.
57. He walks into the classroom and looked for a friendly face.
58. We were watching television, and suddenly the sound goes off and the lights go out.
59. When the class ended, he submits a report to the principal.
60. As soon as Walt smelled the smoke, he gets up from his desk and hurried down the hall to the kitchen.

21 Modifiers

21a. Distinguishing between Adjectives and Adverbs

Use adjectives to modify nouns or pronouns.

> The **hungry** dogs stared at my dinner.
> They looked **hungry**.

Use adverbs to modify verbs or verb phrases.

> The dog stared **hungrily** at my dinner.

PRACTICING YOUR SKILLS

■ Finish each sentence by choosing the correct word from the parentheses. Write the whole sentence. Then write **adjective** or **adverb** to identify the kind of word you chose.

1. Meg has a very (soft, softly) voice.
2. Bernard read the newspaper (quick, quickly).
3. The room was very (quiet, quietly).
4. Vivien paced (impatient, impatiently).
5. The (playful, playfully) kitten peeked out from behind the piano.
6. That (ferocious, ferociously) dog frightens us.
7. It growls (menacing, menacingly) at everyone.
8. Inge (angry, angrily) threw the book onto the floor.
9. He greeted us (cold, coldly).
10. His dinners are always (delicious, deliciously).
11. The sun shone (bright, brightly) overhead.
12. Work (slow, slowly) and (careful, carefully).
13. The (restless, restlessly) audience stirred in their seats.
14. Your new dress is very (pretty, prettily).
15. The bird sang (happy, happily) from the branch.
16. His cap was set (jaunty, jauntily) on his head.
17. What a (perky, perkily) child he is!
18. Laurie (excited, excitedly) planned her vacation.
19. I want you to be (honest, honestly) with me.
20. They worked (steady, steadily) from noon until four-thirty.
21. Donald answered the question (flippant, flippantly).
22. Gordon exercises (faithful, faithfully) each morning and evening.
23. She has a (serene, serenely) smile.
24. Can you answer this question (correct, correctly)?
25. David was crying (loud, loudly).
26. What a (courageous, courageously) young woman she is!
27. We were (eager, eagerly) to see the sequel to the movie.
28. That jacket fits you (loose, loosely).
29. Eduardo spoke quite (soft, softly).
30. Livorna walked (confident, confidently) to the front of the room.
31. Desmond always has a (cheerful, cheerfully) attitude.
32. Each member of the club has a (secret, secretly) nickname.
33. The director paced (nervous, nervously) across the stage.

21b. Distinguishing between Good and Well

Good is an adjective. Use good to modify a noun or pronoun.

> They are proud of their **good** work.
> They feel **good** about their work.

Well can be an adverb. The adverb well means "expertly," "capably," or "satisfactorily." Use the adverb well to modify a verb or a verb phrase.

> He plays the cello **well.**

Well can also be an adjective. The adjective well means "healthy" or "satisfactory." Use the adjective well to modify a noun or pronoun.

> The patient feels **well** now.
> Even a **well** person may have some complaints.

PRACTICING YOUR SKILLS

■ Use either **good** or **well** to finish each sentence. Write the sentences.

1. They played a |||||||||||||| game of tennis.
2. Both girls play very |||||||||||||| .
3. Lucille is a |||||||||||||| server.
4. You returned that serve |||||||||||||| .
5. Does Craig feel |||||||||||||| enough to go on the field trip?
6. That cake looks |||||||||||||| .
7. Ramon frosted it |||||||||||||| .
8. While she was camping, Sonja slept |||||||||||||| every night.
9. My mother knows Ms. Contreras quite |||||||||||||| .
10. We felt |||||||||||||| about our accomplishments.
11. Each contestant performed the task |||||||||||||| .
12. If you concentrate, you will do |||||||||||||| .
13. Michael was quite sick last week, but he is |||||||||||||| now.
14. Every member of the orchestra played |||||||||||||| last night.
15. It was an exceptionally |||||||||||||| concert.
16. Roxanne sings very |||||||||||||| .

17. She is also a |||||||||||||| dancer.
18. Stewart presented a |||||||||||||| report.
19. He had prepared his report |||||||||||||| .
20. Luis is a |||||||||||||| soccer player; he also throws the javelin |||||||||||||| .
21. I think the party went very |||||||||||||| ; I certainly had a |||||||||||||| time.
22. Listen |||||||||||||| to what Mr. Koenig says!
23. She is a very |||||||||||||| doctor; there is no reason you shouldn't get |||||||||||||| soon.
24. The car was in the shop for a week, and now it runs |||||||||||||| .
25. Avery works |||||||||||||| without supervision.
26. Ever since I got chilled in the rain, I haven't been feeling |||||||||||||| .
27. My health is |||||||||||||| ; I feel |||||||||||||| .
28. Huckleberry Finn is a very |||||||||||||| book.
29. Joan has three dogs, and she takes |||||||||||||| care of them.
30. My grandmother always says, "Get a |||||||||||||| night's sleep if you want to get |||||||||||||| ."

21c. Comparisons with Adjectives

Use the comparative form of an adjective to compare two people or things. To make the comparative form **of most adjectives with one syllable and of some adjectives with two syllables, add -er. Use** more **before some adjectives with two syllables and most adjectives with more than two syllables.**

> Caroline is a **smoother** swimmer than Debby.
> Caroline is a **more energetic** swimmer than Debby.

Use the superlative form **of an adjective to compare more than two people or things. To make the superlative form of most adjectives with one syllable and of some adjectives with two syllables, add -est. Use** most **before some adjectives with two syllables and most adjectives with more than two syllables.**

> Caroline is the **smoothest** swimmer on the team.
> Caroline is the **most energetic** swimmer on the team.

21d. Comparisons with Good and Bad

The adjectives good **and** bad **have unusual comparative and superlative forms. The comparative and superlative forms of** good **are** better **and** best. **The comparative and superlative forms of** bad **are** worse **and** worst.

> This pen is **better** than that one.
> That pen is the **worst** one I've ever used.

PRACTICING YOUR SKILLS

■ Write each sentence. Use a comparative or superlative form of the adjective in parentheses.

1. Madrid is (old) than Los Angeles.
2. Jory chose the (long) book in the library.
3. My cold is (bad) today than it was yesterday.
4. This is the (good) ice cream I've ever tasted.
5. The (interesting) suggestions of all were made by Otis.
6. My new shoes are (comfortable) than my old ones.
7. Do you think tonight's stew was (good) than last night's pot roast?
8. Harlan owns the (mean) dog in the neighborhood.
9. Tanya is the (artistic) student in our class.
10. The barrel is even (heavy) than the crate.
11. I sometimes think that I'm the (clumsy) person in the world.
12. Lorraine is probably (active) than you.
13. That was the (bad) movie I've ever seen.
14. The colors in the painting are (vivid) than the colors in the reproduction.
15. Sven's story was even (boring) than Sheila's.
16. Sally is the (good) ice skater in the class.
17. It was the (bad) storm of the decade.
18. The soup tasted much (good) than the salad.

21e. Comparisons with Adverbs

Use the comparative form **of an adverb to compare two people or things. To make the comparative form of most adverbs with one syllable, add -er. Use** more **before adverbs that end in** ly.

Caroline swims **faster** than Debby.
Caroline swims **more gracefully** than Debby.

Use the superlative form **of an adverb to compare more than two people or things. To make the superlative form of most adverbs with one syllable, add -est. Use** most **before adverbs that end in** ly.

Caroline swims **fastest** of all.
Caroline swims **most gracefully** of all.

21f. Comparisons with Well

The adverb well **has unusual comparative and superlative forms. The comparative and superlative forms of** well **are** better **and** best.

The second machine works **better** than the first one.
The third machine works **best** of all.

PRACTICING YOUR SKILLS

■ Write each sentence. Use a comparative or superlative form of the adverb in parentheses.

1. Les dances (energetically) than Stewart.
2. Grace eats (slowly) of all.
3. The boat arrived (late) than the train.
4. The bus arrived (late) of all.
5. Sylvia arrived (early) than Charmian.
6. Cedric answered (kindly) than Kip did.
7. Reginald answered (kindly) of all.
8. Alma plays the piano (well) than her sister does.
9. Naomi can jump (high) than Rolf.
10. Chuck behaves (cautiously) than his brother.
11. Lissy visits Grandmother (frequently) than I.
12. Norman performs (well) of all.
13. Today, I played (well) than my sister.
14. August goes to the gym (regularly) than Dennis does.
15. The affirmative team spoke (convincingly) than the negative team.
16. Joelle skis (well) of all the skiers on the team.
17. She even skis (well) than Dorothy!
18. The hare was running (fast) than the tortoise.
19. The tortoise moved (steadily) than the hare.
20. Seth works (thoroughly) of all the students in the class.
21. Ms. Choi teaches American Literature I (well) than any other member of the faculty.
22. Ming Han acts the part (convincingly) than Beth does.
23. The small plane landed (noisily) than the large plane.

21g. Other and Else in Comparisons

A sentence may express a comparison between one person or thing and the other members of a group to which that person or thing belongs. In such a sentence, include the word other **or** else.

Colin is a member of the swim team:
Colin swims faster than any **other** member of the team.
Colin swims faster than anyone **else** on the team.

If a sentence expresses a comparison between one person or thing and other people, things, or groups, the word other **or** else **is not needed.**

Colin is not a member of the swim team:
Colin swims faster than any member of the team.
Colin swims faster than anyone on the team.

PRACTICING YOUR SKILLS

■ Read each sentence. Find the sentences to which **other** or **else** should be added. Rewrite those sentences correctly.

1. Stuart is smarter than anyone in his class.
2. This coin of mine is more valuable than any coin in my collection.
3. Jeff's hair is longer than Cullen's is.
4. My friend Patti is more loyal than any friend of mine.
5. The shortstop steals more bases than anybody on her team.
6. This red rose is more fragrant than that yellow one.
7. Sometimes I think I'm more awkward than anyone in my gym class.
8. This fabric is prettier than any fabric we've seen so far.
9. These boots are more comfortable than any boots I've tried on.
10. My sister is more graceful than anybody in my family.
11. December is usually colder than November.
12. This meal you prepared is better than any meal you've made.
13. My classmate Joan works harder than anyone in our class.
14. Star Wars is better than any movie about space.
15. The host seemed to have more fun than anybody at the party.
16. You always take longer to finish dinner than anyone at the table.
17. Giving can be more rewarding than receiving.
18. The senator from my state has a better attendance record than any senator.
19. Clarice made more suggestions at the meeting than anyone there.
20. I find backgammon more interesting than checkers.
21. Tom likes chocolate ice cream better than any flavor.
22. My friend Betty is more helpful than anybody I know.
23. I've been more bored this morning than at any time in my life.
24. I think pansies are prettier than any flower.
25. The book I just finished reading was funnier than any book I've read.
26. Your grades in math are better than mine.

21h. Avoiding Misplaced Adjectives

Place adjectives, adjective phrases, and adjective clauses as near as possible to the nouns they modify.

Misplaced Adjective: A **French** group of tourists looked in the window.

Correctly Placed Adjective: A group of **French** tourists looked in the window.

Misplaced Adjective Phrase: The actress bowed to the audience **holding her bouquet.**

Correctly Placed Adjective Phrase: The actress, **holding her bouquet,** bowed to the audience.

Misplaced Adjective Clause: I saw a girl in the park **that I know.**

Correctly Placed Adjective Clause: In the park, I saw a girl **that I know.**

PRACTICING YOUR SKILLS

■ Read each sentence. Find the sentences with misplaced adjectives, adjective phrases, or adjective clauses. Rewrite those sentences correctly.

1. Sarah made the skirt from a new pattern that she's wearing.
2. The woman congratulated each winner presenting the awards.
3. He emptied the sour bottle of milk into the sink.
4. We like amusement parks that have exciting rides.
5. A group of large people had gathered in front of the building.
6. The captain selected the people to be on the team that she wanted.
7. Joey saw the puppy in the pet store window that he wants.
8. Jacey, celebrating her graduation, went to dinner at a restaurant.
9. A delicious bowl of fruit was on the table.
10. The children played with the animals laughing happily.
11. We listened to the bird on our windowsill that chirped merrily.
12. Hugh has a foreign collection of stamps.
13. I gave the money to the police that I found on the sidewalk.
14. Ursula recited a poem that she had written.
15. Dr. Aaron examined the patient using a stethoscope.
16. The painting depicted a sunrise that won first place in the art show.
17. The reporter held a camera wearing a long overcoat.
18. The man is my father in the overalls.
19. The group of students went to the movies that had been excused from school.
20. My sister is the girl carrying the gray suitcase.
21. The book actually belongs to Janice that I lent you.
22. Risha has a pink collection of shells.
23. The woman is the president of the company who spoke to you.

21i.   Avoiding Dangling Modifiers

An introductory participial phrase should modify the first noun or pronoun that follows it. When the participial phrase does not modify that noun or pronoun, or does not modify any noun or pronoun in the sentence, it is called a dangling modifier **When you find a dangling modifier in your writing, rewrite the sentence. (See Participial Phrases,** pages 290–292.)

> **Dangling Modifier: Looking in the pet store window,** the **puppies** charmed us.
> **Rewritten Sentence: Looking in the pet store window, we** were charmed by the puppies.

> **Dangling Modifier: Sailing on the lake,** the **wind** blew gently.
> **Rewritten Sentence: Sailing on the lake, we** felt a gentle breeze.

PRACTICING YOUR SKILLS

■ Read each sentence. Find the sentences that have dangling modifiers. Rewrite those sentences correctly.

1. Watching the late movie on television, too many commercials interrupted it.
2. Typing my term paper for English, the typewriter keys jammed.
3. Jogging along the road, someone honked at us.
4. Crossing her fingers, Marta made a wish.
5. Having danced all night, Eliza's feet ached.
6. Holding his finger to his lips, we watched Gerald tiptoe into the kitchen.
7. Driving down the dark road, it was lonely and scary.
8. Preparing my animals' food, they watched me intently.
9. Dialing Sylvia's number, the last digit escaped my memory.
10. Gathering flowers from the garden, I thought how pretty they would look at the dinner table.
11. Having entertained the audience for over two hours, we watched the band take its final bow.
12. Looking at Hugh's book of stamps, each page represented a different country.
13. Eating dinner, the phone rang.
14. Baking a chocolate souffle, its aroma filled the kitchen.
15. Working every summer, the money helped Terry pay for college.
16. Watching the movie, I ate some popcorn.
17. Inquiring about the refrigerator on display, the salesperson told us it was on sale.
18. Running up the steps, I stubbed my toe.
19. Diving into the pool, the dog barked at the noise we made.
20. Reading the book, it was quite interesting.
21. Walking down the hall, the carpet tripped me.
22. Driving his new car, Greg's cat got carsick.
23. Lying quietly on the sofa, the loud noise surprised Gena.
24. Waiting on the corner, I grew impatient.

21j. Avoiding Misplaced Adverbs

In sentences, place adverbs, adverb phrases, and adverb clauses to avoid any possible confusion.

Misplaced Adverb: The safety committee will meet to discuss the traffic accident that occurred outside the school **tomorrow.**

Correctly Placed Adverb: The safety committee will meet **tomorrow** to discuss the traffic accident that occurred outside the school.

Misplaced Adverb Phrase: Loretta won the prize for being the fastest sprinter **at the awards ceremony.**

Correctly Placed Adverb Phrase: **At the awards ceremony,** Loretta won the prize for being the fastest sprinter.

Misplaced Adverb Clause: Our dog hides **whenever he hears thunder** under the bed.

Correctly Placed Adverb Clause: Our dog hides under the bed **whenever he hears thunder.**

PRACTICING YOUR SKILLS

■ Read each sentence. Find the sentences with misplaced adverbs, adverb phrases, or adverb clauses. Rewrite those sentences correctly.

1. We asked Mrs. Long if she would show slides during her speech before the meeting began.
2. I called the school office to find out when summer school opens yesterday.
3. George and Judy were awarded first place for creating the best vegetable casserole by the judges.
4. Shelley is doing research on Marie Curie in the library.
5. During summer vacation, Bob is working at a restaurant.
6. We were discussing the benefits of jogging in class.
7. They talked about taking a vacation whenever they saw each other.
8. I asked her if I could go to the matinee last night.
9. They decided to meet after school during lunch hour.
10. Cynthia told me to watch for a rainbow as the rainstorm began.
11. We read our programs before the play started.
12. When I visit you, we can talk about what we each did on our summer vacations next time.
13. My brother told me to stop playing the drums in an angry voice.
14. She warned me not to reveal her secret in a whisper.
15. No one answered when I called your home last night.
16. She looked at the tennis court they were building out the window.
17. Put the puppy in the box with your free hand.
18. The dean of admissions said how happy she was that Keo would be a student in her letter.
19. Hang your clean clothes in your closet.
20. The emcee asked the contestants to guess the number of beans in the jar on the program.

21k. Avoiding Double Negatives

Words such as no, not, none, never, nobody, no one, nothing, **and** hardly **are called** negative words. **A negative word may change the whole meaning of a sentence. Use only one negative word to change the sentence meaning.**

> I did **nothing.**
> I did**n't** do anything.
> I **never** did anything.
> **No one** did anything.

PRACTICING YOUR SKILLS

■ Each of the following sentences has two negative words. Rewrite each sentence, using only one negative word.

1. I can't hardly hear you.
2. We don't have no money.
3. You didn't give us no instructions!
4. He doesn't like no one.
5. You don't make no sense.
6. I don't want to have nothing to do with this activity.
7. I couldn't hardly understand the directions they gave me.
8. Ed didn't see nobody.
9. I couldn't see nothing when the lights went out.
10. Don't tell nobody!
11. We can't go nowhere today.
12. Tomas doesn't never believe me.
13. Cherie didn't know no one at the party.
14. I'm not doing no dishes!
15. They don't have no idea where he is.
16. They can't get nobody to help them.
17. She wouldn't let no one explain.
18. Don't do nothing foolish!
19. I can't hardly believe it.
20. There isn't nobody home today.
21. I don't want none of that candy.
22. Marilou doesn't have no time to study today.
23. There isn't no more bread.
24. He won't wait for nobody.
25. She can't think of nothing to say.
26. The pie wasn't no good.
27. He doesn't hardly talk much.
28. She doesn't have no problems.
29. We didn't go nowhere on our vacation.
30. I don't know nobody named Ben.
31. I can't find no flour to make the cake.
32. He didn't say nothing to me about it.
33. We can't find the scissors nowhere.
34. Don't never say that again!
35. That doesn't hardly sound like Penny.
36. I don't believe nothing I read in the newspapers.
37. Nobody never told me about the special school holiday today.
38. I don't think there's nothing wrong with your car.
39. I'm not going to no graduation!
40. None of these colors doesn't look good on me.
41. Craig hadn't hardly awakened before he knew he was late for school.
42. Nobody never stayed after school to help with the project.
43. It had gotten so dark that the players couldn't hardly see the ball anymore.
44. Shelly hardly never has time to visit his grandmother.
45. The pieces of a jigsaw puzzle don't never fit together easily.
46. The hikers hadn't had nothing else to eat all day.

211. Less and Fewer

Use less before a singular noun. Use fewer before a plural noun.

There is **less** candy in the dish.
There are **fewer** candies in the dish.

PRACTICING YOUR SKILLS

- Use **less** or **fewer** to finish each sentence. Write the sentences.

1. We need |||||||||||||| sugar for the cake than for the cookies.
2. |||||||||||||| people enrolled in the course this year.
3. There are |||||||||||||| nuts in the coffee cake than usual.
4. We have |||||||||||||| homework on Tuesdays than on Wednesdays.
5. It takes |||||||||||||| time to do these problems when you have already done some.
6. |||||||||||||| students are absent today than yesterday.
7. Terry has |||||||||||||| lines in the play than he had expected.
8. Lately, I seem to have |||||||||||||| money than ever.
9. Make |||||||||||||| noise!
10. The pattern for the skirt requires |||||||||||||| material than the pattern for the jacket.
11. |||||||||||||| oranges have been harvested this year than last.
12. In this class, there are |||||||||||||| boys than girls.
13. Toni has |||||||||||||| interest in this subject than she used to.
14. If you invite |||||||||||||| guests, you will need |||||||||||||| food for dinner.
15. Jonathan made |||||||||||||| mistakes on the exam than anyone else.
16. I slept |||||||||||||| hours last night than I did the night before.
17. There are |||||||||||||| pictures in this book than in the other one.
18. We are trying to eat |||||||||||||| sweets.
19. We are also trying to eat |||||||||||||| salt.
20. Our tree is yielding |||||||||||||| nectarines than it used to.
21. There is |||||||||||||| dust on the piano than on the bookshelves.
22. Sometimes I have |||||||||||||| confidence than at other times.
23. Marie exhibits |||||||||||||| skill at painting than Maggie does.
24. Paul has |||||||||||||| coins in his collection since he sold some.
25. |||||||||||||| waste would result in |||||||||||||| want.
26. Next time Brad makes this dessert, he will use |||||||||||||| sugar.
27. The tree has |||||||||||||| lemons this year than it did last year.
28. We sold |||||||||||||| tickets to the fair than we had hoped.
29. Put |||||||||||||| cucumbers in the salad.
30. There seem to be |||||||||||||| ants at this picnic.
31. Did you make |||||||||||||| potato salad than you usually do?
32. Is there |||||||||||||| mayonnaise in the cole slaw?
33. There are |||||||||||||| books in the branch library than in the main library.
34. |||||||||||||| people ride horses than drive cars.
35. Why are there now |||||||||||||| good movies than there used to be?
36. There are |||||||||||||| pages in this book than I thought there were.
37. Jory always has |||||||||||||| energy in the evening than she has in the morning.

Reviewing 21 Modifiers

21a. Distinguishing between Adjectives and Adverbs

Finish each sentence by choosing the correct word from the parentheses. Write the whole sentence. Then write **adjective** or **adverb** to identify the kind of word you chose.

1. Rose speaks very (loud, loudly) when she's nervous.
2. This salad is (excellent, excellently) and tastes (delicious, deliciously).
3. They drove (careful, carefully) and reached their destination (safe, safely).

21b. Distinguishing between Good and Well

Use either **good** or **well** to finish each sentence. Write the sentences.

4. Louis is a |||||||||||||| class president; he serves our class |||||||||||||| .
5. Elaine did a |||||||||||||| job repairing the car; it runs |||||||||||||| now.
6. You may leave the hospital as soon as you are |||||||||||||| .

Write each sentence. Use a comparative or superlative form of the adjective in parentheses.

21c. Comparisons with Adjectives

7. This watch is (expensive) than that one, but it is also (handsome).
8. Danny is the (skillful) player we've seen today, although Ramon may be (strong) than Danny.
9. This new method is (simple) than the old one, and I believe it is also (precise).
10. This must be the (long) submarine sandwich in the whole world!

21d. Comparisons with Good and Bad

11. That was the (bad) speech I've ever heard; it was even (bad) than Mr. Allen's.
12. Katie has a (good) voice than Monica, but Judy's is the (good) of all.
13. These are the (good) seats in the theater; the (bad) are in the last row.
14. Fronë is probably the (good) athlete in the school.
15. Manley has the (bad) handwriting that I have ever seen.

Write each sentence. Use a comparative or superlative form of the adverb in parentheses.

21e. Comparisons with Adverbs

16. Tabatha finished the exam (fast) than Ted did, and she left the room (early) than I did.
17. Ted answered the questions (carefully) than Tabatha, and he wrote (slowly) than she did.
18. Penny laughed (loudly) of all, and she danced (enthusiastically) than Lexie.
19. Tonio finished the sack race (quickly) of all.
20. Sonja works (diligently) now than she used to.

21f. Comparisons with Well

21. Tess fields the ball (well) than Eva does, but Eva catches (well) than Tess does.
22. Todd plays the guitar (well) of all my students; Carmen plays (well) than Judd.
23. Kelly sings (well) than she dances.
24. Fortunately, Ernest can catch a football (well) than he can throw one.

21g. Other **and** Else **in Comparisons**

Write each sentence. Add **other** or **else** wherever necessary.

25. Our teacher has taught longer at our school than any teacher.
26. Eric likes chocolate ice cream better than any dessert.
27. David has earned more Cub Scout merit badges than anyone in his den.
28. My brother thinks he knows more than anyone in our family.
29. Swimming is better than any form of exercise.

Rewrite each sentence to avoid a misplaced adjective, adjective phrase, adjective clause, or dangling modifier.

21h. Avoiding Misplaced Adjectives

30. Mr. Ramirez has taken our well-done order for two steaks.
31. The blues singer sang an old ballad dressed in red.
32. The letter is still sitting on the desk that Sven wrote yesterday.
33. Beatrice and her brother have a round collection of stones.
34. A messenger delivered this note wearing a dark purple cloak.

21i. Avoiding Dangling Modifiers

35. Hiking in the woods, a huge tree blocked our path.
36. Walking home in the dark, every shadow frightened me.
37. Mewing plaintively, Barbara picked up the tiny kitten.
38. Hurrying into class, Ken's notebook fell to the floor.
39. Echoing loudly in every corner of the room, my brother and I were awakened by the noise of the alarm clock.

21j. Avoiding Misplaced Adverbs

Rewrite each sentence to avoid a misplaced adverb, adverb phrase, or adverb clause.

40. Vikki Carr agreed to sing at our next benefit yesterday.
41. We decided to give a party while we were shopping.
42. They discussed the possibility of interplanetary travel at the meeting.
43. The members agreed that they would participate more regularly at the last club meeting.
44. Angelina told us all about her adventures in a letter.

21k. Avoiding Double Negatives

Each of the following sentences has two negative words. Rewrite each sentence, using only one negative word.

45. You shouldn't have said nothing about our plans.
46. Rachel couldn't hardly hear over the roar of the machinery.
47. Dave doesn't never think before he acts.
48. The town council meetings don't hardly ever start on time.
49. Nobody even tried to do nothing to solve that problem.

21l. Less **and** Fewer

Use **less** or **fewer** to finish each sentence. Write the sentences.

50. Helen earned |||||||||||||||| money washing cars than she did mowing lawns.
51. There are |||||||||||||||| cars on the street tonight than I've ever seen before.
52. You'll have |||||||||||||||| problems putting the bike together if you read the directions first.
53. Next year there will be |||||||||||||||| students in this math class.
54. Next time, use |||||||||||||||| salt.

22 Pronouns

22a. Subject and Object Form Pronouns

The form of a personal pronoun depends upon how the pronoun is used in a sentence. Subject form pronouns, listed in the box below, are used as sentence subjects and predicate nominatives.

I	you	he	she	it	we	they

He and **she** are going to the market.
The next shoppers will be Arturo and **I.**

Object form pronouns, listed in the box below, are used as direct objects, indirect objects, and objects of prepositions.

me	you	him	her	it	us	them

Stephen called **you** and Hildy yesterday.
Stephen gave **us** a message.
Please give Stephen's message to **me.**

PRACTICING YOUR SKILLS

■ Choose from each set of parentheses the correct pronoun form. Write the sentences.

1. How did you know it was (I, me)?
2. (He, Him) and (she, her) are going to the football game.
3. Call (they, them) after five o'clock this evening.
4. My friend and (I, me) will meet you at the record store.
5. Grandma brought (she, her) and (I, me) presents.
6. I talked with Mary and (he, him) last week.
7. (They, Them) went to a play last night.
8. Can you give (I, me) a ride to town?
9. The audience clapped for (we, us).
10. This is a secret between you and (I, me).
11. You and (I, me) have been friends for three years.
12. It's (I, me)!
13. Please wait for (she, her) and (I, me).
14. The teacher read (he, him) and (she, her) a story.
15. Can it really be (they, them)?
16. Yes, it really is (he, him) and (she, her).
17. Barry invited Sharon and (I, me) to the party.
18. Send (they, them) a postcard from Iowa.
19. Please visit (we, us) next weekend.
20. The Lucases invited (they, them) and (I, me) to swim.
21. You've met (he, him) and (she, her) before.
22. Can Eric go with you and (she, her) to the movie?
23. Eduardo gave Tonio and (I, me) the tickets.
24. (We, Us) and (they, them) played on opposite teams.

22b. Avoiding Unclear Antecedents

A personal pronoun should refer clearly to its antecedent, the noun it replaces. If there is more than one possible antecedent for a personal pronoun, the reference is unclear. When you find such an unclear reference in your writing, rewrite the sentence.

> **Unclear Reference:** Tony, John, and Paul agreed that **he** should make the presentation.
>
> **Rewritten Sentence:** Tony, John, and Paul agreed that **Paul** should make the presentation.

PRACTICING YOUR SKILLS

■ Rewrite each sentence to correct the unclear pronoun reference.

1. Sheldon and Terry got lost because he had misunderstood the directions.
2. The Amatos were worried that the Ameers had forgotten what time they had promised to be at the theater.
3. Tanya told Denise that she would win the award.
4. When Dana and Shirley brought the twins home, their mother scolded them.
5. Mark told Tony that he was wrong about Cleo.
6. Melissa told Helen to leave so that she could think about the problem alone.
7. Kurt told Tom that he would have to go shopping.
8. Donna jogged with Diane until she became tired.
9. Cindy asked Julie to come to dinner because she was lonely.
10. Margaret's mother told her she had a dental appointment in the morning.
11. The race between Pamela and Wendy ended when she crossed the finish line.
12. The teachers reminded the students that they would be busy all afternoon.
13. Janna and Thalia agreed that she should go first.
14. Ned and Marcus rehearsed the line he would say in the play.
15. Michael and James had trouble with his car.
16. There is no doubt that in the last Kings-Canadiens game they won because they made an extra effort.
17. When the Harrises and the Wilcoxes had dinner together, they were very impressed with their house.
18. Melissa and Marie disagreed, but finally she admitted that she was wrong.
19. When we went out with the Elfmans, the Smiths, and the Durans, I thought they were the happiest family I'd ever seen.
20. After Ken read "The Gold Bug" and "The Purloined Letter," he declared it was the most exciting story he'd ever read.
21. Less than a year after Jose and Mark joined the track team, he had already won three medals.
22. After Sonny's brother broke his bike and his skateboard, he took it in to be repaired.
23. Jack told me to see The Slithering Terror and The Frog That Ate Yonkers, but I thought it was an awful movie.
24. Jennifer waved to Cassandra as she was walking onto the stage.
25. Arne has a fountain pen and a ball-point pen, so you can probably borrow it.
26. The adults played softball with the children until they became tired.

22c. Avoiding Missing Antecedents

A personal pronoun should refer clearly to its antecedent, the noun it replaces. If there is no antecedent for a personal pronoun, the reference is missing. When you find such a missing reference in your writing, rewrite the sentence.

Missing Reference: The police worked hard to solve the crime, but they never caught **them.**

Rewritten Sentence: The police worked hard to solve the crime, but they never caught the **thieves.**

PRACTICING YOUR SKILLS

■ Rewrite each sentence to correct the missing pronoun reference.

1. After we finished dinner, we washed all of them.
2. Lawrence enjoys gardening, but few of them grow very well.
3. We went to the market and brought all of them home.
4. Ronald is a good songwriter, but none of them have ever been recorded.
5. Amanda won't get involved in politics because she thinks they're all dishonest.
6. The car salesman tried to convince us that it was a good buy.
7. Valerie likes to drive, but it keeps breaking down.
8. Luis spoke for fifteen minutes, but we couldn't hear it too well because the acoustics were poor.
9. Ms. Ito advised me to take algebra this semester, but I didn't follow it.
10. Marie enjoyed the music very much, but she thought they should have played longer.
11. We wrote our friends while we were on vacation, but we forgot to mail them.
12. Jill followed the directions carefully, but she couldn't find it.
13. The students looked on every shelf, but someone must have checked it out.
14. Jerome checked all the television channels, but it wasn't on yet.
15. I have to go to the library because it is due today.
16. Vanessa regretted forgetting her key because it was locked.
17. I wanted to mail this letter, but she had already come and gone.
18. Art tried to wash the clothes last night, but it was too crowded.
19. Alicia looked through the newspaper, and then she cut it out.
20. Renaldo wants to go shopping now, but it isn't open this late.
21. Amelia read the entire list of flavors, but they didn't have it.
22. Maura's hobby is photography, and it is going to be printed in the newspaper.
23. Henny has learned to speak Japanese, but she has never visited it.
24. When Jessica arrived at the airport, the attendant told her that it had been delayed.
25. Everyone heard the siren, but nobody could see it.
26. The necklace broke, and they scattered all over the floor.
27. Buddy enjoys playing tennis, but his dog prefers chasing them.
28. Before you go out onto the ice, lace them as tightly as possible.

22d. Pronouns and Compound Antecedents

When two or more singular or plural antecedents are joined by and, **use a plural pronoun to refer to them.**

Both Glen and Phil were playing **their** instruments.
The violinists and the cellists were rehearsing **their** parts.

When two or more plural antecedents are joined by or **or** nor, **use a plural pronoun to refer to them.**

Either the violinists or the cellists were rehearsing **their** parts.

When two or more singular antecedents are joined by or **or** nor, **use a singular pronoun to refer to them.**

Neither Glen nor Phil was rehearsing **his** part.

PRACTICING YOUR SKILLS

■ Finish each sentence. Add a plural pronoun or a singular pronoun.
Write the sentences.

1. Carol or Mary will star in |||||||||||||| own show next season.
2. Have Gordon and Albert found |||||||||||||| way home?
3. Neither Blake nor Robert enjoys |||||||||||||| work.
4. Both the Dodgers and the Giants have won |||||||||||||| last five games.
5. Either the Lees or the Zacutos have dropped |||||||||||||| keys on the grass.
6. Regular exercise and proper nutrition are recommended for |||||||||||||| good effects on health.
7. Either the biology teacher or the algebra teacher just went to |||||||||||||| office.
8. Charley, Leo, and Kevin brought |||||||||||||| essays to class a day early.
9. Neither the Raineys nor the Robothams are using |||||||||||||| lawnmowers today.
10. The coaches and the players don't like being away from |||||||||||||| families so much.
11. Is Edna or Emily going to read |||||||||||||| poem next?
12. Either Marie, Claire, or Patsy will display |||||||||||||| hobbies in this section of the room.
13. Both Belinda and Katherine are putting on |||||||||||||| stage makeup for the performance.
14. Either the ninth graders or the tenth graders will make |||||||||||||| own costumes.
15. Neither this book nor that one is in |||||||||||||| proper place in the bookcase.
16. The Yankees, the Expos, and the Twins give |||||||||||||| fans free jackets at one game during the season.
17. Neither Conrad nor Brad will answer |||||||||||||| telephone after ten o'clock in the evening.
18. Both Greg and Robin have presented |||||||||||||| reports to the committee.
19. Either Mom or Aunt Celia must have left |||||||||||||| keys on the kitchen counter.

22e. Who and Whom as Interrogative Pronouns

The interrogative pronoun who is used as the subject of an interrogative sentence. The interrogative pronoun whom is used as the direct object or the object of a preposition in an interrogative sentence.

> **Who** is knocking at the door?
> **Whom** have you invited?
> To **whom** is the visitor speaking?

PRACTICING YOUR SKILLS

■ Choose from each set of parentheses the correct interrogative pronoun. Write the sentences.

1. With (who, whom) is Dennis going to the party?
2. (Who, Whom) gave you that locket?
3. (Who, Whom) will Angie visit in Arizona?
4. (Who, Whom) stars in the play?
5. By (who, whom) was it written?
6. For (who, whom) did you vote?
7. (Who, Whom) ate all the cake?
8. (Who, Whom) did Katie invite for dinner?
9. (Who, Whom) correctly predicted the outcome of the football game?
10. (Who, Whom) fed the cat?
11. About (who, whom) was the poem written?
12. Near (who, whom) does Harold sit in class?
13. (Who, Whom) is it?
14. (Who, Whom) wrote this essay?
15. To (who, whom) did you tell my secret?
16. From (who, whom) is this package?
17. (Who, Whom) is on the swimming team?
18. (Who, Whom) knows the answer?
19. (Who, Whom) said that?
20. (Who, Whom) are you calling?
21. For (who, whom) is this message?
22. With (who, whom) do you ride to school?
23. (Who, Whom) is in the shower?
24. (Who, Whom) made this mess?
25. (Who, Whom) did he photograph?
26. To (who, whom) shall I deliver these flowers?
27. At (who, whom) are you shouting?
28. By (who, whom) was the movie directed?
29. (Who, Whom) can guess the number of freckles on my nose?
30. (Who, Whom) are you calling a liar?
31. (Who, Whom) is playing such loud music?
32. From (who, whom) is this donation?
33. (Who, Whom) do you trust?
34. (Who, Whom) taught you to drive?
35. (Who, Whom) asked, "Is it time to go home?"
36. I don't know (who, whom) you are talking about.
37. (Who, Whom) called this afternoon, and (who, whom) did he ask for?
38. (Who, Whom) should Marcelle ask for the directions to Camp Conklin?
39. With (who, whom) had you been speaking?
40. (Who, Whom) taught you to serve a tennis ball like that?
41. From (who, whom) have you been taking piano lessons?
42. (Who, Whom) could have sent us a package from London?

22f. Who and Whom as Relative Pronouns

The relative pronoun who is used as the subject of an adjective clause.
The relative pronoun whom is used as the direct object or the object of a preposition in an adjective clause. (See **Adjective Clauses,** pages 306–311.)

I know the man **who** called Frank.
I know the woman **whom** Frank called.
I know the people with **whom** Frank spoke.

PRACTICING YOUR SKILLS

■ Choose from each set of parentheses the correct relative pronoun.
Write the sentences.

1. The person (who, whom) answered the phone hung up on me!
2. This is Erica, with (who, whom) I jog each morning.
3. Tim Campbell, (who, whom) I met in Cleveland, is in town for a visit.
4. I admire Ms. Richland, (who, whom) is a fine architect.
5. Rita Mae, (who, whom) is a country singer, has had seven gold records.
6. The boy with (who, whom) I went to the soccer game is Aubrey.
7. Mr. Twain, with (who, whom) my grandfather founded the repertory company, presented the awards.
8. I've always enjoyed the performances of Suzy Sabovich, (who, whom) the students voted Best Actress.
9. The dentist (who, whom) you recommended no longer practices dentistry.
10. She doesn't know (who, whom) she should believe.
11. The driver (who, whom) was speeding got a ticket.
12. There is Mr. Hsu, with (who, whom) I studied painting.
13. We knew all the people (who, whom) were guests at the party.
14. The man (who, whom) you met last night is my uncle.
15. I am pleased to introduce Mrs. Scott, (who, whom) will answer your questions.
16. Geraldine, (who, whom) sent me this postcard, won't be home until next month.
17. You didn't seem to recognize the woman with (who, whom) I was speaking.
18. The man to (who, whom) Jack sold his cow gave him some beans.
19. Here comes Mr. Yost, (who, whom) we have asked to join our staff.
20. Dr. Marks, (who, whom) the school is honoring, will retire at the end of the semester.
21. Joseph Strom, (who, whom) is a dealer in rare coins, studies gourmet cooking.
22. The girl (who, whom) I invited to the picnic has chicken pox.
23. Rick is a person (who, whom) others ask for advice.
24. I have never forgotten Mrs. Weeks, (who, whom) was my first piano teacher.
25. I don't know the students (who, whom) you tutor.
26. Those students (who, whom) have finished the exam may leave the room.
27. You should ask somebody (who, whom) you know well to write a letter of reference.

22g. Pronouns in Comparisons

In a comparison with the word than or as, the second clause in the comparison may not be completely stated. If the predicate of that clause is omitted, only the subject noun or pronoun is left. In such a sentence, use a subject form pronoun after the word than or as.

> We can run faster than **they can run.**
> We can run faster than **they.**
> He plays tennis as well as **she plays tennis.**
> He plays tennis as well as **she.**

22h. Possessive Pronouns before Gerunds

Use a possessive pronoun form before a gerund or gerund phrase.

> **Their singing** is delightful.
> I can't stand **your talking** with your mouth full!

PRACTICING YOUR SKILLS

■ Choose from each set of parentheses the correct pronoun form. Write the sentences.

1. Tommy cooks better than (I, me).
2. You can do it as quickly as (they, them).
3. Imogene plays tennis as often as (he, him).
4. Are you taller than (she, her)?
5. The Zanes stayed later than (we, us).
6. Alexei is a stronger swimmer than (I, me).
7. Did you eat as much dinner as (she, her)?
8. I can stand on my head longer than (he, him).
9. We leave for school as early as (they, them).
10. Jerry can answer that question as well as (I, me).
11. The Stones go camping more often than (we, us).
12. Have you ever met anyone as vain as (he, him)?

■ ■ Finish each sentence by adding a possessive pronoun before the gerund. Write the sentences.

1. |||||||||||||| whining annoys me.
2. I enjoy |||||||||||||| singing in the shower.
3. |||||||||||||| leaving dirty clothes on the floor makes me angry.
4. How do you like |||||||||||||| cooking?
5. |||||||||||||| typing has improved over the summer.
6. |||||||||||||| sending me a single rose each day while I was ill was very thoughtful.
7. I like |||||||||||||| bringing me breakfast in bed.
8. |||||||||||||| taking notes in class will be helpful.
9. |||||||||||||| constant lying is destroying our friendship.
10. I can't take |||||||||||||| nagging any longer.
11. |||||||||||||| giggling all the time is very annoying.
12. Can't you stop |||||||||||||| complaining?
13. I appreciate |||||||||||||| confiding in me.
14. |||||||||||||| dancing is very graceful.

23 Prepositions

23a. Between and Among

Use the preposition between to refer to two people or things. Use the preposition among to refer to more than two people or things.

> Alice sat **between** two oak trees.
> Alice sat **among** the oak trees in the orchard.

23b. Beside and Besides

Use the preposition beside to mean "next to." Use the preposition besides to mean "in addition to."

> Alice sat **beside** an oak tree.
> **Besides** oak trees, there were pine trees and maple trees.

PRACTICING YOUR SKILLS

■ Use **between** or **among** to finish each sentence. Write the sentences.

1. We may choose |||||||||||||||| chocolate eclairs and chocolate chip cookies.
2. Dorothy stood |||||||||||||||| Marita and Josette.
3. The rabbit was hiding |||||||||||||||| the flowers.
4. I circulated a petition |||||||||||||||| my friends.
5. My math homework is stuck |||||||||||||||| the piano and the wall.
6. What is the difference |||||||||||||||| algebra and geometry?
7. |||||||||||||||| the two of us, we should finish this job in half the time.
8. Can you tell the difference |||||||||||||||| Grace and her twin?
9. Sometimes it's difficult to distinguish |||||||||||||||| flowers and weeds.
10. List the similarities |||||||||||||||| France and England.
11. We spotted Randy sitting |||||||||||||||| the stalks of corn.
12. Who |||||||||||||||| you will help me?

■■ Use **beside** or **besides** to finish each sentence. Write the sentences.

1. Your keys are |||||||||||||||| your wallet in the dining room.
2. The dog lay contentedly |||||||||||||||| the little boy.
3. |||||||||||||||| being an excellent source of vitamins, fresh vegetables taste delicious.
4. |||||||||||||||| the old farm house is a pond.
5. |||||||||||||||| having to study English, I also have to study algebra and history.
6. |||||||||||||||| The Buckles, is any other band peforming at tomorrow's concert?
7. |||||||||||||||| the fireplace is an old rocking chair.
8. We planted the tomatoes |||||||||||||||| the carrots.
9. |||||||||||||||| roast beef, we also had roast potatoes and broccoli.
10. May I sit |||||||||||||||| you?
11. Who is that woman standing |||||||||||||||| the gate?
12. You will get a ticket if you park |||||||||||||||| a curb that is painted red.

23c. In and Into

Use the preposition in to mean "inside" or "within." Use the preposition into to suggest movement toward the inside of a building or area.

> They were **in** the kitchen.
> They walked **into** the kitchen.

23d. Of

Do not use the preposition of after off.

> **Incorrect:** Take the pan **off of** the stove.
> **Correct:** Take the pan **off** the stove.

23e. At

Do not use the preposition at after where.

> **Incorrect: Where's** the kitchen **at**?
> **Correct: Where's** the kitchen?

PRACTICING YOUR SKILLS

■ Use **in** or **into** to finish each sentence. Write the sentences.

1. Don't let the dog go |||||||||||||| the house.
2. I was |||||||||||||| the den when the doorbell rang.
3. There is some fruit |||||||||||||| the refrigerator.
4. Please come |||||||||||||| my office.
5. The fox crept sneakily |||||||||||||| the hen house.
6. The farmer ran |||||||||||||| the hen house after the fox.
7. We had to stay |||||||||||||| the house all day.
8. Is the doctor |||||||||||||| her office?
9. There is too much salt |||||||||||||| the soup.
10. Please drive the car |||||||||||||| the garage.
11. A truck, a lawn mower, two bicycles, and three tricycles are already |||||||||||||| the garage.
12. Rodney closed his eyes, made a wish, and threw the coin |||||||||||||| the well.

■■ Read each sentence. Find the sentences in which **of** or **at** should be omitted. Rewrite those sentences correctly.

1. The cat jumped off of the table.
2. Is Jaime at school?
3. Where is your brother at now?
4. We each dived off of the diving board.
5. Do you know where the scissors are at?
6. He is one of my three best friends.
7. Take the dirty dishes off of the table.
8. Is he at home?
9. Where shall I put them at?
10. You told me where Charlie is at, but I can't remember what you said.
11. Somebody should have taken the newspapers off of the dining room table.
12. Where did you find this book at?
13. I can't remember where I left it at.
14. Rollie fell off of the sofa.

24 Parallel Structure

24a. Parallel Structure: Nouns, Adjectives, and Adverbs

Ideas of equal importance are parallel ideas. Parallel ideas may be expressed in a series or a comparison. They may also be joined by a coordinating conjunction or a correlative conjunction.

Use the same grammatical form to express parallel ideas in a sentence. Using the same grammatical form to express parallel ideas is called using parallel structure. To be sure of using parallel structure, use nouns with nouns, adjectives with adjectives, and adverbs with adverbs.

Not Parallel: The size of a pet may be as important as what kind of personality it has.

Parallel: The **size** of a pet may be as important as its **personality.**

Not Parallel: We chose this cat because it was friendly, quiet, and had fluffy fur.

Parallel: We chose this cat because it was **friendly, quiet,** and **fluffy.**

Not Parallel: You should approach a new pet quietly and with gentleness.

Parallel: You should approach a new pet **quietly** and **gently.**

PRACTICING YOUR SKILLS

■ Rewrite each sentence, using parallel structure to express parallel ideas.

1. Everyone appreciates a person who is friendly, loyal, and practices honesty.
2. Many people actually prefer rain to sunny days.
3. We will need either a new floor or to buy a rug for this area.
4. They enjoyed both the interesting choreography and how talented the dancers were.
5. Your name is not as important as what kind of character you have.
6. Noisily and at a very slow speed, the train pulled out of the station.
7. Jeff chose this vase because of its color, its shape, and how beautiful it is.
8. The peaches were fresh, ripe, and had a lot of juice.
9. Squash, racketball, and that game you play with your hand are Patrice's favorite sports.
10. You may choose either blueberry pie or the pie made with pumpkins.
11. The basement was dark, dusty, and in a mess.
12. We pried the lid from the crate slowly, deliberately, and did it with great care.
13. We were impressed by the dancer's agility, grace, and how strong she was.
14. The speech was long, dull, and had many complications.
15. Aline read the instructions slowly, carefully, and in a clear manner.
16. The teacher promised us few homework assignments and that she would give interesting lectures.

24b. Parallel Structure: Gerunds and Infinitives

Use parallel structure within a sentence. Use gerunds with gerunds and gerund phrases. Use infinitives with infinitives and infinitive phrases. Do not combine gerunds and infinitives to express parallel ideas within a sentence.

Not Parallel: Sulla likes diving, swimming, and to surf.
Parallel: Sulla likes **diving, swimming,** and **surfing.**
Parallel: Sulla likes **to dive, to swim,** and **to surf.**

Not Parallel: Directing a play may be more difficult than to act in one.
Parallel: **Directing a play** may be more difficult than **acting in one.**
Parallel: **To direct a play** may be more difficult than **to act in one.**

PRACTICING YOUR SKILLS

■ Rewrite each sentence, using parallel structure to express parallel ideas.

1. Resting for a few moments or to take a few sips of water may help you.
2. Juan likes to read books and going to plays.
3. Jogging, skating, and to swim are Dena's favorite activities.
4. Listening carefully is as important as to read carefully.
5. Each student will develop skills in both weaving and to spin.
6. Ben prefers discussing the problem rather than to work on a solution.
7. Mopping the floors and to clean the bathtub are two household chores I especially dislike.
8. The secretary's duties include writing letters and to take notes.
9. You may choose between taking a final exam and to write a term paper.
10. Nora will choose either singing or to dance.
11. Frederick will be in charge of planning the meeting, inviting the guest speakers, and to send invitations.
12. To decorate the gym might be as expensive as renting a room for the dance.
13. They are planning on working for a month and then to go on a short vacation.
14. Cecil enjoys making films, watching films, and to read about films.
15. Each camper must choose between taking a nature hike and to gather firewood.
16. To complete the project yourself would probably be easier than explaining the instructions.
17. Everyone on the team will practice running, jumping, and to throw.
18. Monica's household chores include washing the dishes and to take out the garbage.
19. The girls spent an hour running around the track, riding their bicycles, and to roller-skate.
20. Do you prefer cooking special foods or to eat them?
21. Thinking about your work may be more difficult than to do your work.
22. Sandy enjoys rebuilding cars, repairing cars, and to drive cars.
23. Watching that race was more tiring than to run in it.

24c. Parallel Structure with Correlative Conjunctions

Use parallel structure with correlative conjunctions. Place the parts of a correlative conjunction directly before parallel expressions.

> **Not Parallel:** Theodora **not only** swims for exercise **but also** for fun.
> **Parallel:** Theodora swims **not only** for exercise **but also** for fun.
> **Not Parallel:** Rob **both** owns a bull terrier **and** a mastiff.
> **Parallel:** Rob owns **both** a bull terrier **and** a mastiff.

PRACTICING YOUR SKILLS

■ Read each sentence. Find the sentences that do not use parallel structure with correlative conjunctions. Rewrite those sentences, using parallel structure.

1. Jean-Marc not only plays the piano but also the violin.
2. Kristen will either call you this evening or tomorrow morning.
3. The basket of fresh fruit included both papayas and guavas.
4. We neither saw George in the library nor in the bookstore.
5. We can either have tuna or salmon for dinner.
6. Stella neither understands Spanish nor Portuguese.
7. The players have to both practice their dribbling and their shooting before the next game.
8. Miss Preciado either goes to work at eight o'clock or at nine o'clock.
9. Carlo has neither written to me nor to Steve.
10. Shelly both paints portraits and landscapes.
11. We can either take the bus or the subway.
12. The puppy is not only friendly but playful.
13. Melissa both enjoyed the book and the movie.
14. Each tutor works either with a student in another school or a member of the class.
15. The creature not only had a fierce expression but also a very mean growl.
16. We can either meet you at the park or at Alvin's house.
17. Every student will be expected to both read the poem and to memorize part of it.
18. After the play, everyone felt not only exhausted but also felt elated.
19. They had been given permission neither to use the laboratory nor the gym.
20. There was still no sign of either Harris or of Antonia.
21. Ms. Salisbury's comments were not only correct but also were helpful.
22. The actress who played the lead was both talented and enthusiastic.
23. I felt encouraged about neither my Latin homework nor about my math homework.
24. Most students will be allowed to enroll either in dance classes or music classes.
25. Edwin will be allowed to enroll in both the dance class and the music class.
26. Simca may be either in the library or the park.
27. We have looked both in the kitchen and the dining room for the missing plates.
28. Perhaps someone left them in either the living room or in the bedroom.
29. Some of the players felt discouraged not only after the game but also discouraged before the game.

Reviewing 22 Pronouns 23 Prepositions and 24 Parallel Structure

22a. Subject and Object Form Pronouns

Choose from each set of parentheses the correct pronoun form. Write the sentences.

1. (He, Him) and (she, her) met Ricki at the bus station.
2. Can Ms. Coppola give (they, them) and (I, me) a ride home?
3. (She, Her) and (I, me) are best friends.

Rewrite each sentence to correct the unclear or missing pronoun reference.

22b. Avoiding Unclear Antecedents

4. Mary and Juliana were discussing her career plans.
5. Brian and Dave will practice the scene he has chosen.
6. Elaine and Martha wondered what part she would play.

22c. Avoiding Missing Antecedents

7. Steve studied hard, but he didn't pass it.
8. Norm and Betty cooked for us, and it was delicious.
9. Katerina is a poet, but none of them have ever been published.

22d. Pronouns and Compound Antecedents

Finish each sentence. Add either a plural pronoun or a singular pronoun. Write the sentences.

10. Either Rob or Tim will bring ||||||||||||| tape recorder.
11. Neither the Dodgers nor the Expos could depend upon ||||||||||||| relief pitchers.
12. The lions and the tigers ate all ||||||||||||| food.

Choose from each set of parentheses the correct interrogative or relative pronoun. Write the sentences.

22e. Who and Whom as Interrogative Pronouns

13. (Who, Whom) is in charge of the project?
14. About (who, whom) are you writing your report?
15. (Who, Whom) did you notify?

22f. Who and Whom as Relative Pronouns

16. The applicant (who, whom) they chose was unable to accept the position.
17. There is the man to (who, whom) I gave your message.
18. The girl (who, whom) just entered is my sister.

22g. Pronouns in Comparisons

Choose from each set of parentheses the correct pronoun form. Write the sentences.

19. Mrs. Alonso is as excited as (we, us).
20. Those people have been waiting longer than (I, me).
21. You can do it better than (she, her).

22h. Possessive Pronouns before Gerunds

Finish each sentence by adding a possessive pronoun before the gerund. Write the sentences.

22. I appreciate ||||||||||||| explaining the assignment to me.
23. ||||||||||||| singing is delightful.
24. They don't like ||||||||||||| teasing.

23a. Between and Among

Use **between** or **among** to finish each sentence. Write the sentences.

25. We found an arrowhead |||||||||||||||| the pebbles.
26. Lynn sat |||||||||||||| Neil and Janine.
27. I have to decide |||||||||||||| physics and chemistry for my next science course.
28. The responsibilities should be divided equally |||||||||||||| those four students.

23b. Beside and Besides

Use **beside** or **besides** to finish each sentence. Write the sentences.

29. We picnicked |||||||||||||||| a lake.
30. |||||||||||||| sandwiches and cole slaw, we had a special dessert.
31. |||||||||||||| the easy chair is an antique table.
32. The puppy sat down |||||||||||||| me.

23c. In and Into

Use **in** or **into** to finish each sentence. Write the sentences.

33. Anita walked |||||||||||||| the old house.
34. She met her new employer |||||||||||||| the library.
35. There was a dog |||||||||||||| the middle of the room.
36. Ken may have left it |||||||||||||| the closet.

Find the sentences in which **of** or **at** should be omitted. Rewrite those sentences correctly.

23d. Of

37. Please take the record off of the stereo.
38. The ball bounced off of the fence.
39. Do you know the name of our new coach?
40. Four pencils rolled off of the desk.

23e. At

41. Is your mother at work?
42. I don't know where my keys are at.
43. Where's the movie theater at?

Rewrite each sentence, using parallel structure to express parallel ideas.

24a. Parallel Structure: Nouns, Adjectives, and Adverbs

44. The film was well written, well directed, and the actors were good.
45. Charles approaches problems alertly, intelligently, and with confidence.
46. Everyone admires Nora's thoughtfulness and what a friendly person she is.

24b. Parallel Structure: Gerunds and Infinitives

47. Heidi likes playing baseball, listening to music, and to go to the movies.
48. To stay at home can be more restful than going on vacation.
49. Many artists have found that making one hit record is easier than to stay popular.
50. To be a member of the chorus is not as difficult as singing a solo.

24c. Parallel Structure with Correlative Conjunctions

Find the sentences that do not use parallel structure with correlative conjunctions. Rewrite those sentences, using parallel structure.

51. They will either give their reports tomorrow or next week.
52. Rosa has both studied algebra and geometry.
53. Artie not only likes Italian food but also Japanese food.

25 Capital Letters

25a. Capital Letters at the Beginning of Sentences

Capitalize the first word in a sentence.

> **Every** plant needs special care.
> **Which** plants require direct sunlight?
> **Water** the plants.

25b. Capital Letters in Direct Quotations

Capitalize the first word in a direct quotation. Capitalize the first word in the second part of a direct quotation only if that word is the first word of a new sentence.

> Bev asked, "**Have** you watered the plants today?"
> "**No,** I watered them yesterday," answered Phil.
> "**I** think," said Anne, "they need water only every three days."
> "**This** plant looks dry," added Paul. "**What** do you think?"

PRACTICING YOUR SKILLS

■ Write the following sentences. Use capital letters wherever they are needed.

1. some people talk to their plants.
2. other people claim that plants like music.
3. "the thing to remember," said Danita, "is that plants should not be neglected."
4. "pansies need water," she explained, "or they will wilt."
5. which plants are easy to grow?
6. "palms are fairly simple," Andy replied. "they require only fresh air and water."
7. every neighborhood has its own special plants.
8. do you know which trees grow on your street?
9. "sometimes," responded Donna, "trees have been brought from other areas."
10. "where did palm trees originate?" asked Brian.
11. our teacher explained, "they came from South America and Asia."
12. "it's fascinating," remarked Alexander, "that every area has its own vegetation."
13. "we went hiking last week," said Juan.
14. "we saw twenty different kinds of plants," he added.
15. "we tried to identify them," Paul said, "but we could recognize only two plants."
16. "this morning I had the most annoying experience!" said Janet.
17. "there was a concert advertised in the paper," she added. "of course I wanted to go."
18. "when you called the number in the paper," asked Jack, "what happened?"
19. "it was ridiculous," said Janet. "all I could get was a recording."
20. "what did it say?" asked Lorene. "did it tell you where to get tickets?"
21. "no," said Janet, "it didn't. all it said," she added, "was that all their lines were busy. then I was put on hold for two hours."

25c. Capital Letters in Names of People

Capitalize each word in a proper noun that names a person. Capitalize an initial that stands for a name. Capitalize the abbreviation Jr. or Sr. that follows a name.

> We have been reading about **Susan B. Anthony.**
> That famous speech was made by **Martin Luther King, Jr.**

25d. Capitalizing the Personal Pronoun I

Capitalize the personal pronoun I.

> Carol and **I** are sisters.

PRACTICING YOUR SKILLS

■ Write the following phrases. Use capital letters wherever they are needed.

1. eric p. tilman
2. harry rotolo, sr.
3. my sisters and i
4. my friend rico and i
5. arthur m. schlesinger, jr.
6. barbara c. jordan
7. lynn elizabeth barber
8. doris rainey mills
9. patricia roberts harris
10. scott j. bornstein
11. sheryl, nina, you, and i
12. erlinda r. hassenpfeffer
13. patrice and augie
14. helena and her friend celia
15. lynette c. eschevaria
16. w. eugene houston, sr.
17. manollo, harry, link, and i
18. lyndon b. johnson

■■ Write the following sentences. Use capital letters wherever they are needed.

1. My sister emily has gone to the park with her friends antonia and marty.
2. Isn't justine preparing a report about elizabeth cady stanton?
3. Mail for timothy smith, sr., often reaches timothy smith, jr.
4. May i introduce you and rodolfo to leona furushiro?
5. The speaker tonight will be arletta n. goldberg.
6. Doesn't the library have a book about anna e. dickinson?
7. The party was held in honor of letticia u. brown.
8. Junior's real name is claude augustus washington, jr.
9. The members of the committee include paolo, risha, sue ellen, and tomas.
10. You and i will work with juanita and marilyn.
11. The principal of the new school will be donna t. varga.
12. How many Wimbledon titles did billie jean king win?
13. Their favorite boxer is still muhammad ali.
14. In 1917, jeanette rankin became a member of the United States House of Representatives.
15. The nominees for treasurer are bette bastione, luis seminario, and dana chan.

25e. Capital Letters in Titles of People

Capitalize each word in a title that comes before a noun. Capitalize the abbreviation of a title. Do not capitalize a title that is used without a name.

> The appointment of **Mrs.** Oveta Culp Hobby was announced by **President** Eisenhower.
> The judge and **Dr.** Clarence are sisters.

25f. Capital Letters in Titles of Relatives

Capitalize the title of a relative when it is used with the relative's name. Capitalize a title such as Mother, Father, or Grandpa when it is used alone as a name.

> We will visit **Aunt** Kay and **Uncle** Leo this summer.
> They have also invited **Grandma** and my cousin.

PRACTICING YOUR SKILLS

■ Write the following phrases. Use capital letters wherever they are needed.

1. professor Virginia Stannet
2. uncle Carl
3. grandmother Alma
4. dean Margaret Howard
5. dr. Shaw
6. mrs. Evelyn Crais
7. captain R. K. Franklin
8. a captain and two sergeants
9. mr. Hugh Ward
10. governor Ella T. Grasso
11. ms. G. Page
12. aunt Bea
13. your aunt
14. grandpa Al
15. president Jimmy Carter
16. senator Margaret Chase Smith

■■ Write the following sentences. Use capital letters wherever they are needed.

1. Don't you have an appointment with dean Harris this afternoon?
2. My friends and I saw professor Williams yesterday.
3. The criminal was apprehended by officer Feldman.
4. Has judge Hamilton arrived yet?
5. Two of our favorite people are grandma Carrie and grandpa Bob.
6. Will governor Hunt do something about the situation?
7. When is your next appointment with dr. Yee?
8. Tomorrow, grandpa and I will go fishing.
9. The professor spoke with dean Holmes.
10. I'm sure mom and mrs. Hinojosa will be at the meeting.
11. Where are aunt Millie and uncle Harry?
12. Haven't you called grandma Edna yet?
13. If ms. Kim is not available, I will speak with dr. Reynosa.
14. My parents have already met mr. and mrs. Santiago.
15. Will senator Schnitz be having a press conference this afternoon?

25g. Capital Letters in Names of Days, Months, and Holidays

Capitalize each important word in a proper noun that names a day, month, or holiday. Articles, conjunctions, and prepositions are not considered important words and are not capitalized. Do not capitalize the name of a season.

> Cheryll will arrive the third **Monday** in **June.**
> She will definitely visit until the **Fourth of July.**
> Perhaps she will stay the entire summer.

25h. Capital Letters in Abbreviations of Days and Months

Capitalize the abbreviation of the name of a day or month. Avoid these abbreviations in formal writing.

Sunday	Sun.	Tuesday	Tues.	Friday	Fri.
Monday	Mon.	Wednesday	Wed.	Saturday	Sat.
		Thursday	Thurs.		

January	Jan.	May	——	September	Sept.
February	Feb.	June	——	October	Oct.
March	Mar.	July	——	November	Nov.
April	Apr.	August	Aug.	December	Dec.

PRACTICING YOUR SKILLS

■ Write the following phrases. Use capital letters wherever they are needed.

1. the day before halloween
2. spring fever
3. independence day
4. the first monday in may
5. one week in july
6. new year's eve
7. saturday and sunday
8. washington's birthday
9. april fools' day

■■ Write the abbreviations for the names of the following days and months.

1. December
2. January
3. April
4. Friday
5. Saturday
6. September
7. Monday
8. November
9. August
10. Thursday

■■■ Write the following sentences. Use capital letters wherever they are needed.

1. Our summer vacation will begin on june 15.
2. The last monday in may is memorial day.
3. In Great Britain, boxing day is a legal holiday.
4. In may, many Canadians celebrate victoria day.
5. In Maine and Massachusetts, patriots' day is celebrated on the third monday in april.
6. We enjoy sending and receiving valentines on valentine's day.
7. Many people make resolutions on new year's day.

25i. Capital Letters in Names of Streets and Highways

Capitalize each important word in a proper noun that names a street or highway. Articles, conjunctions, and prepositions are not considered important words and are not capitalized. Do not capitalize common nouns.

> Our office is at 88 **Avenue of the Stars.**
> This road intersects **Highway 61.**
> The theater is on **Second Street.**

25j. Capital Letters in Place Names

Capitalize each important word in a proper noun that names a city, state, country, or continent. Do not capitalize common nouns.

> Our friends moved to **Raleigh, North Carolina.**
> They toured **Italy** while they were in **Europe.**
> We will visit the country where our ancestors were born.

PRACTICING YOUR SKILLS

■ Write the following phrases. Use capital letters wherever they are needed.

1. 3032 ewing avenue
2. glendale, california
3. highway 101
4. naples, italy
5. sixth street
6. 19 rose avenue
7. 11733 calahan street
8. the capital of sweden
9. two countries in africa
10. city streets
11. georgia and alabama
12. route 99
13. new york, new york
14. new mexico
15. mexico city
16. a small town near tulsa

■■ Write the following sentences. Use capital letters wherever they are needed.

1. While she was in brazil, she spent a week in fortaleza.
2. Sean O'Casey, a famous playwright, was born in dublin, ireland.
3. Dorothy Parker was born in new jersey, but she spent most of her life in new york.
4. We took a plane from kansas city to baltimore.
5. Keith lives in la mirada, california.
6. We stay on interstate 98 until we reach santa clara.
7. He lives at 1212 robertson boulevard.
8. Tom was born in arkansas and later moved to montana.
9. Vivian was born in south america.
10. Many people from great britain settled in canada.
11. Randy has decided to visit australia and new zealand.
12. My favorite country in europe is spain.
13. For many years I lived on spinnaker way, just outside the city limits of venice, california.

25k. Capital Letters in ZIP Code Abbreviations

Capitalize both letters of a ZIP code abbreviation. Do not use periods with these special abbreviations.

Alabama AL	Idaho ID	Missouri MO	Pennsylvania PA
Alaska AK	Illinois IL	Montana MT	Rhode Island RI
Arizona AZ	Indiana IN	Nebraska NE	South Carolina SC
Arkansas AR	Iowa IA	Nevada NV	South Dakota SD
California CA	Kansas KS	New Hampshire NH	Tennessee TN
Colorado CO	Kentucky KY	New Jersey NJ	Texas TX
Connecticut CT	Louisiana LA	New Mexico NM	Utah UT
Delaware DE	Maine ME	New York NY	Vermont VT
District of	Maryland MD	North Carolina NC	Virginia VA
Columbia DC	Massachusetts MA	North Dakota ND	Washington WA
Florida FL	Michigan MI	Ohio OH	West Virginia WV
Georgia GA	Minnesota MN	Oklahoma OK	Wisconsin WI
Hawaii HA	Mississippi MS	Oregon OR	Wyoming WY

25l. Capital Letters in Abbreviations of Academic Degrees

Capitalize each part of the abbreviation of an academic degree.

> We met Dorothy Lu, **Ph.D.**
> She earned her **M.A.** at Hunter College.

25m. Capital Letters in Abbreviations of Time

Capitalize each part of an abbreviation of time.

> Augustus reigned as emperor of Rome from 27 **B.C.** to **A.D.** 14.
> Your plane will leave at 10:15 **A.M.**

PRACTICING YOUR SKILLS

■ Write the ZIP code abbreviations for the following states.

1. Florida
2. Washington
3. Maine
4. California
5. Idaho
6. South Carolina
7. Delaware
8. Nebraska
9. Utah
10. Alabama
11. Vermont
12. Ohio
13. Georgia
14. Pennsylvania
15. Alaska

■■ Write the following sentences. Use capital letters wherever they are needed.

1. Sam Domani, d.d.s., will attend the conference.
2. I usually go to sleep about 11 p.m. and wake up at 6:30 a.m.
3. Does that college award the b.s. degree in biology?
4. Agrippina the Elder lived from about 13 b.c. to a.d. 33.
5. Carline Kraus, m.d., arrived at her office and waited for her first patient.
6. William Fox received his r.n. from Brooklyn College.

25n. Capital Letters in Names of Geographical Features

Capitalize each important word in a proper noun that names a geographical feature. Words such as the before a proper noun are usually not considered part of the proper noun. Do not capitalize common nouns.

> She had never visited the **Grand Canyon.**
> We went fishing in the **Gulf of Mexico.**
> There are many lakes in the northern part of the state.

PRACTICING YOUR SKILLS

■ Write the following phrases. Use capital letters wherever they are needed.

1. the gobi desert
2. the aleutian islands
3. lake tahoe
4. the yangtze river
5. the mediterranean sea
6. mount hood
7. the bay of naples
8. the pacific ocean
9. the bay of biscay
10. marvel cave
11. chesapeake bay
12. the colorado river
13. the rocky mountains
14. lake erie
15. the potomac river
16. upper red lake
17. the baltic sea
18. the gulf of bothnia
19. lake placid
20. the cape of good hope
21. mount diablo
22. lake cumberland
23. the ohio river
24. fort peck lake
25. tokyo bay
26. the north sea

■■ Write the following sentences. Use capital letters wherever they are needed.

1. The danube river inspired a waltz.
2. Have you ever visited carlsbad caverns?
3. The highest peak in the world is mount everest.
4. Which bridges cross the hudson river?
5. We stood at the top of mount tamalpais and watched the sailboats on san francisco bay.
6. Ithaca is at the south end of lake cayuga.
7. Are sailboats allowed on lake armington?
8. Highway 93 runs through the white mountains.
9. Olivia still talks about her trip to the bernese alps.
10. Huckleberry Finn floated down the mississippi river on a raft.
11. Next year, we'll go camping in death valley national monument in California.
12. The strait of magellan is the only strait between the atlantic ocean and the pacific ocean.
13. Sarita is planning to cruise in the caribbean sea.
14. Perhaps they will visit the bahama islands.
15. A traditional spot for honeymooners is niagara falls.
16. The philippine sea is actually part of the pacific ocean.
17. The andes mountains extend from cape horn to Panama.
18. The surface of lake chad is covered with tangled weeds.

25o. Capital Letters in Names of Buildings and Other Structures

Capitalize each important word in a proper noun that names a building, bridge, or other structure. Words such as the before a proper noun are usually not considered part of the proper noun. Do not capitalize common nouns.

> You must travel to Arizona to see **London Bridge.**
> Does the **Leaning Tower of Pisa** really lean?
> We took photographs of the hotel.

PRACTICING YOUR SKILLS

■ Write the following phrases. Use capital letters wherever they are needed.

1. the transamerica building
2. buckingham palace
3. the severn bridge
4. the new river gorge bridge
5. the empire state building
6. the museum of modern art
7. museums in New York
8. central park
9. the bronx zoo
10. columbia university
11. three colleges in Maine
12. amherst college
13. the oceanside hotel
14. the pasadena civic auditorium
15. the park theater
16. the theater on Oxnard Street
17. the george washington bridge
18. the towers of that bridge
19. the smithsonian institution
20. the conway building
21. the clift hotel
22. the arco towers

■■ Write the following sentences. Use capital letters wherever they are needed.

1. We attended a concert at the shrine auditorium.
2. My favorite museum is the american museum of natural history in New York.
3. The exhibits at the hayden planetarium have always fascinated me.
4. While we were in San Francisco, we took pictures of the golden gate bridge.
5. The chrysler building is in Manhattan.
6. Do you know what movies are showing at the nuart theater?
7. The students spent the entire day at the museum of science and industry.
8. Her office is on the seventeenth floor of the coast building.
9. They met on the steps of the continental building at noon.
10. The ticket agency is located in the monroe building.
11. Visitors enjoy a view of the city from tokyo tower.
12. The eiffel tower is in Paris.
13. Both the holland tunnel and the lincoln tunnel connect New York with New Jersey.
14. The space needle is an important Seattle landmark.
15. The terminal tower building in Cleveland is one of the country's tallest buildings.
16. The oldest museum in Canada is the montreal museum of fine arts.
17. The brooklyn bridge was completed in 1883.
18. The verrazano-narrows bridge is a famous suspension bridge.

25p. Capital Letters in Titles

Capitalize the first word and each important word in the title of a work of art. Such works include stories, books, poems, essays, periodicals, articles, chapters, movies, plays, television programs, paintings, and musical compositions. Articles, conjunctions, and prepositions are not considered important words and are not capitalized.

Elinor Wylie wrote **"The Eagle and the Mole."**
Many people have enjoyed reading **A Wrinkle in Time**.

PRACTICING YOUR SKILLS

■ Write the following titles. Use capital letters wherever they are needed.

1. san francisco chronicle
2. mona lisa
3. the raven
4. grease
5. moonlight sonata
6. the glass menagerie
7. sports illustrated
8. then again, maybe i won't
9. little house on the prairie
10. hit and run
11. the lifeguard
12. wonderful town
13. mork and mindy
14. younger than springtime
15. psychology today
16. los angeles times
17. the turning point
18. whistler's mother
19. farmer boy
20. i know why the caged bird sings

■■ Write the following sentences. Use capital letters wherever they are needed.

1. The novel ivanhoe was written by Sir Walter Scott.
2. Most people enjoy the rhythm of the poem "annabel lee."
3. Who has seen close encounters of the third kind?
4. A famous painting by Picasso is guernica.
5. Scott Joplin wrote "maple leaf rag," a popular tune.
6. Anna Guest's story "beauty is truth" first appeared in seventeen magazine.
7. The musical my fair lady is based on the play pygmalion.
8. Did you stay up to watch the tonight show?
9. Many people enjoy doing the crossword puzzle in the los angeles times.
10. Tolstoy's most famous novel is war and peace.
11. The class is studying Charles Dickens' a tale of two cities.
12. A short story by Edgar Allan Poe is "the tell-tale heart."
13. Pat's favorite poem is "stopping by the woods on a snowy evening."
14. The Drama Club is rehearsing you can't take it with you.
15. The most popular opera written by an American is porgy and bess.
16. My favorite song from the king and i is "hello, young lovers."
17. Carol enjoyed reading the last of the really great whangdoodles.
18. Sondra has submitted an article to cosmopolitan.

25q. Capital Letters in Names of Organizations

Capitalize each important word in a proper noun that names an organization, business firm, institution, or government body. Words such as the before a proper noun are usually not considered part of the proper noun. Do not capitalize common nouns.

> In 1977, the **Department of Energy** was established.
> My father attended **San Francisco State College.**
> I belong to three clubs which meet after school.

25r. Capital Letters in Names of Historical References

Capitalize each important word in a proper noun that names a historical event, period, or document. Words such as the before a proper noun are usually not considered part of the proper noun. Do not capitalize common nouns.

> The **Middle Ages** lasted a thousand years.
> In 1791, the **Bill of Rights** was ratified.
> Three nations have decided to sign a treaty.

PRACTICING YOUR SKILLS

■ Write the following phrases. Use capital letters wherever they are needed.

1. the national aeronautics and space administration
2. the american dental association
3. williams college
4. three different fan clubs
5. the Vincent Price fan club
6. the ford motor company
7. the stamp collectors club of america
8. world war I
9. the national education association
10. the united states naval academy
11. attending a college
12. the interstate commerce commission
13. the united states olympic committee

■■ Write the following sentences. Use capital letters wherever they are needed.

1. The civil aeronautics board promotes safety in aviation.
2. Will has decided to attend amherst college.
3. The interstate commerce commission was established in 1887.
4. Mary and her friends have formed the computer club.
5. The chrysler corporation manufactures automobiles.
6. The declaration of independence was adopted in 1776.
7. Many people vividly remember the great depression.
8. The red cross was founded in Switzerland in 1863.
9. Please explain the effects of the missouri compromise.
10. David joined the peace corps in 1964.
11. The louisiana purchase doubled the size of the United States.
12. The battle of bunker hill was fought in 1775.

25s. Capital Letters in Brand Names

Capitalize each important word in a proper noun that names a particular product. Do not capitalize a common noun that follows a brand name.

> Our family uses **Crest** toothpaste.
> Buy some toothpaste while you're at the store.

25t. Capital Letters in Names of Ships, Planes, and Trains

Capitalize each important word in a proper noun that names a ship, plane, or train. Words such as the before a proper noun are usually not considered part of the proper noun. Do not capitalize common nouns.

> Charles Lindbergh made his most famous flight in the Spirit of St. Louis.
> Have you ever flown a plane?

PRACTICING YOUR SKILLS

■ Write the following phrases. Use capital letters wherever they are needed.

1. using an olivetti typewriter
2. sailing on the pinta
3. drinking lipton tea
4. sealing a package with scotch tape
5. riding the zephyr
6. buying alpo dog food
7. eating dannon yogurt
8. cruising on the S.S. bremen
9. drinking perrier mineral water
10. traveling on the city of new orleans
11. using ivory soap
12. looking for gallo salami

■■ Write the following sentences. Use capital letters wherever they are needed.

1. My father prefers best foods mayonnaise.
2. One of Columbus' ships was the santa maria.
3. The stourbridge lion was the first full-sized locomotive in North America.
4. This sandwich is made with smucker's preserves, peter pan peanut butter, and pepperidge farm bread.
5. Chuck and Anne first met on the S.S. seven seas.
6. Sean was eating a burger king hamburger.
7. Charmaine brought home a gallon of dreyer's ice cream.
8. One of Magellan's ships, the santiago, was wrecked in a storm.
9. The san antonio , another of Magellan's ships, returned in secret to Spain.
10. Only the victoria completed the voyage around the world.
11. The dancers were wearing danskin leotards and capezio shoes.
12. Aunt Inez told us about her trip on the super chief.
13. For many years the great eastern was the largest ship afloat.
14. The U.S.S. constitution is also known as old ironsides.

25u.   Capital Letters in Names of Monuments and Awards

Capitalize each important word in a proper noun that names a monument or award. Words such as the before a proper noun are usually not considered part of the proper noun. Do not capitalize common nouns.

Newcomers to America are welcomed by the **Statue of Liberty.**
Bill has won a **National Merit Scholarship.**
Has anyone else won a scholarship?

25v.   Capital Letters in Names of School Subjects

Capitalize the name of a school subject only if it is the name of a language or a course name followed by a number.

Stella will study **Spanish** this year.
Did you pass **Chemistry I**?
My favorite subject is not mathematics.

PRACTICING YOUR SKILLS

■ Write the following phrases. Use capital letters wherever they are needed.

1. awarding the purple heart
2. visiting the lincoln memorial
3. studying french and biology
4. taking physics II
5. winning the nobel prize
6. photographing the washington monument
7. enrolling in auto mechanics I
8. receiving the spingarn medal
9. choosing between mechanical drawing I and history
10. awarding the caldecott medal
11. visiting the tomb of the unknown soldier
12. walking toward the jefferson memorial

■■ Write the following sentences. Use capital letters wherever they are needed.

1. Next year, Lexie will take english, geology, geometry, and latin.
2. Stan is taking swimming I, italian, and history.
3. Willie Mays won the rookie of the year award in 1951.
4. The Montreal Canadiens won the stanley cup in 1978.
5. Which cartoonist won the pulitzer prize last year?
6. Mr. Garvey teaches german and russian at Acalanes High School.
7. Susan Cooper won the newbery medal for her book The Grey King.
8. Lois Lenski won the regina medal in 1969.
9. Would you rather take modern dance II or field hockey I?
10. The heisman memorial trophy is presented each year to the country's outstanding college football player.
11. I was very pleased when Superman won an academy award for special effects.

25w.   Capital Letters in Proper Adjectives

Capitalize each important word in a proper adjective. (See **Proper Adjectives,** page 233.)

Karen is learning some **Spanish** songs.
A **South American** restaurant is opening this evening.
Do you think a **French** person would understand it?

PRACTICING YOUR SKILLS

■ Write the following phrases. Use capital letters wherever they are needed.

1. the new york skyline
2. indian silk
3. texas oil
4. japanese poetry
5. african history
6. the california coastline
7. a canadian coin
8. irish linen
9. an italian sailor
10. roman roads
11. greek philosophy
12. belgian waffles
13. israeli folk dances
14. a swiss watch
15. a russian diplomat
16. some idaho potatoes
17. florida grapefruit
18. washington apples
19. hawaiian beaches
20. bermuda onions

■■ Write the following sentences. Use capital letters wherever they are needed.

1. Last summer we visited several european countries.
2. We enjoyed eating french food.
3. Kevin especially enjoyed the parisian bakeries.
4. Sarah argued that we spent too much time in italian restaurants.
5. Everyone wanted to see the swiss alps.
6. Alexander decided to visit the egyptian pyramids.
7. Did you go through customs at the mexican border?
8. We all learned a lot about american history.
9. Kevin and Wendy will meet us at the brazilian exhibit.
10. Last year I bought a rug at the persian booth.
11. Linda bought a canadian doll for her nephew.
12. Everyone learned to do some russian folk dances.
13. After dinner we sang indian songs.
14. Laura and Genie were wearing peruvian dresses.
15. Pedro played several chilean songs on his guitar.
16. Almost everyone understood the portuguese lyrics.
17. Monica and Juan baked some romanian pastries.
18. Nguyen read us a vietnamese poem.
19. The welsh legends are very interesting.
20. The favorite sport of the nigerian people is soccer.
21. I wonder whether venetian houses are all built along canals.
22. Their favorite japanese dish is sashimi.
23. Several australian tennis players have become famous throughout the world.

25x. Capital Letters in Names of Languages and Nationalities

Capitalize each important word in a proper noun that names a language. Capitalize each important word in a proper noun that names a nationality or other group of people.

> Sarit speaks **Dutch, German,** and **English.**
> Earl is a **New Zealander.**
> Katherine is a **Bostonian.**

25y. Capital Letters in Names Related to Religions

Capitalize the name of a specific deity. Capitalize the name of a religion or religious group. Capitalize the names of sacred writings. Do not underline such names. Do not capitalize common nouns.

> The **Muslims** worship **Allah.**
> One of the sacred books of **Judaism** is the **Torah.**
> The Pilgrims thanked **God** for the good harvest.
> The ancient Greeks believed in many gods.

PRACTICING YOUR SKILLS

■ Write the following phrases. Use capital letters wherever they are needed.

1. speaking portuguese
2. a visiting australian
3. worshiping jehovah
4. reading the bhagavad-gita
5. believing in buddhism
6. becoming a catholic
7. learning italian
8. a native californian
9. praising god
10. a book in the new testament
11. belief in judaism
12. become a taoist
13. studying greek
14. some touring canadians

■■ Write the following sentences. Use capital letters wherever they are needed.

1. Our high school offers classes in french, spanish, and russian.
2. A person born in the United States is called an american.
3. Did you know that Caroline is a chicagoan?
4. The ancient persians worshiped mithras.
5. The mahabharata, a collection of writings sacred to the hindus, illustrates the futility of war.
6. An important religion of the japanese is shinto.
7. A language of ancient India is sanskrit.
8. George speaks korean, italian, and swedish.
9. Jon is an armenian.
10. Corinne and Josette are parisians.
11. The god of zoroastrianism is ahura mazda, and the sacred book is the avesta.
12. One language which is now rarely spoken is latin.
13. The hungarians and the chinese are holding a series of meetings.

Reviewing 25 Capital Letters

Write the following sentences. Use capital letters wherever they are needed.

25a. Capital Letters at the Beginning of Sentences

1. can you roller-skate?
2. many people enjoy swimming.

25b. Capital Letters in Direct Quotation

3. Jaime asked, "does anyone want pizza?"
4. "salads," replied Tony, "would be more nutritious."

25c. Capital Letters in Names of People

5. The man signing autographs is gilbert raleigh owens, jr.
6. Our teacher is margaret a. tufts.

25d. Capitalizing the Personal Pronoun I

7. The meal i prepared was delicious.
8. She is an author whose books i enjoy.

25e. Capital Letters in Titles of People

9. Would you like to leave a message for ms. Kremer?
10. Where is professor Andersen?

25f. Capital Letters in Titles of Relatives

11. We will soon celebrate grandpa's eightieth birthday.
12. Is daddy with uncle murray?

25g. Capital Letters in Names of Days, Months, and Holidays

13. School begins on the second tuesday in september.
14. He was born on april fools' day.

25h. Capital Letters in Abbreviations of Days and Months

Write the abbreviation for each of the following names.
15. tuesday   16. september   17. june

Write the following sentences and phrases. Use capital letters wherever they are needed.

25i. Capital Letters in Names of Streets and Highways

18. We ran out of gas on route 10.
19. Our new apartment is on gleane street.

25j. Capital Letters in Place Names

20. Ms. Rodriguez is on a business trip in atlanta, georgia.
21. They visited several countries in asia.

25k. Capital Letters in ZIP Code Abbreviations

22. Stone Mountain, ga
23. Petaluma, ca
24. Luckenbach, tx

25l. Capital Letters in Abbreviations of Academic Degrees

25. Kate Chu, d.d.s., is our dentist.
26. I'm studying for my m.a. in psychology.

25m. Capital Letters in Abbreviations of Time

27. Your flight leaves Atlanta at 9:20 p.m.
28. Claudius I lived from 10 b.c. to a.d. 54.
29. Jerry rises each morning at 6:00 a.m.

25n. Capital Letters in Names of Geographical Features

30. We watched boat races at lake wheeler.
31. How long is the mississippi river?
32. The sahara desert is in Africa.

25o. Capital Letters in Names of Buildings and Other Structures

33. Donald will work as a guide this summer at the san diego zoo.
34. The sears tower is the tallest building in the United States.

25p. Capital Letters in Titles

35. My brother is reading <u>the wind in the willows</u>.
36. We sang "michael, row the boat ashore."

25q. Capital Letters in Names of Organizations

37. Stan is attending the fashion institute of technology.
38. Anna has a summer job with the environmental protection agency.

25r. Capital Letters in Names of Historical References

39. The magna carta granted certain rights to the nobles of England.
40. The battle of waterloo led to Napoleon's downfall and exile.

25s. Capital Letters in Brand Names

41. My cat prefers meow mix cat food. .
42. Buy some kleenex tissues while you're at the market.

25t. Capital Letters in Names of Ships, Planes, and Trains

43. Columbus commanded <u>la capitana</u> on his fourth trip to America.
44. The Wright brothers' first plane was called the <u>flyer</u>.

25u. Capital Letters in Names of Monuments and Awards

45. In San Francisco, we visited coit tower.
46. Each year, the record industry gives out grammy awards.
47. <u>Bridge to Terabitha</u> won the newbery medal.

25v. Capital Letters in Names of School Subjects

48. Regan can't decide between algebra II and trigonometry.
49. Mr. Amato teaches russian, spanish, french, and latin.

25w. Capital Letters in Proper Adjectives

50. Nasreen made a salad with greek olives and italian cheese.
51. Ronit taught us some israeli folk songs.

25x. Capital Letters in Names of Languages and Nationalities

52. Olga is a hungarian.
53. I'm learning chinese.
54. My uncle is a texan.

25y. Capital Letters in Names Related to Religions

55. The sacred book of islam is the koran.
56. Meditation is emphasized in zen buddhism.
57. Some people in China follow the tao.

26 Periods, Question Marks, and Exclamation Marks

26a. End Punctuation

Use a period at the end of a declarative sentence or an imperative sentence. Use a question mark at the end of an interrogative sentence. Use an exclamation mark at the end of a declarative sentence or an imperative sentence that shows strong feeling.

> Someone is knocking at the door.
> Wash your hands before dinner.
> Is Carlyn at home?
> I can't wait to see you!
> Watch out!

26b. Periods in Abbreviations

Use a period at the end of each part of an abbreviation.

> We voted for **Mrs.** DuBois.
> The polls opened at 7:00 **A.M.** yesterday.

PRACTICING YOUR SKILLS

■ Write the abbreviations for the following words and word groups.

1. August
2. Thursday
3. Webster Drive
4. December
5. Saturday
6. Hampton Street
7. April
8. Monday
9. Venice Boulevard
10. September
11. Friday
12. Lania Road
13. January
14. Sunday
15. Allan Avenue

■■ Write the following sentences. Add periods, question marks, and exclamation marks wherever they are needed.

1. Ms Adams is learning karate
2. English class ends at 2:55 PM today
3. Are you tired
4. Help
5. The Greeks lost their independence in 338 BC and regained it in AD 1829
6. Have you met George Sloane
7. Dr Mills is attending a conference
8. In 776 BC, the first Olympic Games were held
9. Please don't slam the door
10. Be quiet
11. Mrs Danton is here to see you
12. I always wake up at 6:45 AM, but I stay in bed half an hour longer
13. He announced the arrival of Albert Barber, Sr
14. Our coach is Mr Goodman
15. Will everyone be ready by noon
16. Either Mr Ditomaso or Mrs Inguito will accompany the group
17. That's fantastic
18. The meeting that had been scheduled for 4:00 PM today has been postponed until 10:00 AM tomorrow
19. I still can't believe it
20. Dr Lovalhati is not in her office yet

27 Commas

27a. Commas in Dates

Use a comma after the number of the day in a date. If the date does not come at the end of a sentence, use a comma after the number of the year.

Carol was born on **April 15, 1967.**
On **September 3, 1980,** we moved to New Orleans.

27b. Commas in Place Names and Addresses

In the name of a place, use a comma between the name of the city or town and the name of the state or country. If the place name does not come at the end of a sentence, use a comma after the name of the state or country. Use a comma between the name of a street and the name of a city in an address.

Paul spent a year in **Tokyo, Japan.**
San Francisco, California, is an exciting city.
The address is **21-B Huston Street, Old Bridge, New Jersey.**

PRACTICING YOUR SKILLS

■ Write the following sentences. Add commas wherever they are needed.

1. The last day of the twentieth century will be December 31 1999.
2. On January 1 2000 there will be a huge celebration.
3. Is there really a place named Walla Walla Washington?
4. The romantic atmosphere of Paris France has inspired many artists.
5. Send me a postcard at 203 Commonwealth Avenue Middletown New York.
6. In Buenos Aires Argentina December 25 falls in the middle of summer.
7. Nashville Tennessee is considered the home of country and western music.
8. You won't be able to reach me between December 26 1980 and January 13 1981.
9. My new address will be 14757 White Oak Lane Sherman Oaks California.
10. Irene found a copy of the April 2 1919 issue of The New York Times.
11. John Milton was born on December 9 1608.
12. October 24 1961 is William's birth date.
13. The new transportation system will begin service on March 2 1981.
14. Jaime is from San Juan Puerto Rico.
15. The haunted house is located at 54 Rose Lane Cleveland Ohio.
16. Lee and Gabriel bicycled from Amsterdam Holland to Rome Italy last summer.
17. Casablanca Morocco has a very hot climate.
18. The film Gloria produced will be released on June 7 1980.
19. Peking China is a place I have always wanted to visit.

27c. Commas in Series

Use a comma to separate words or phrases in a series.

> **Sue, Stan,** and **Sal** are on the soccer team.
> He **sat down, closed his eyes,** and **fell asleep.**

27d. Commas between Adjectives

In most cases, use a comma to separate two adjectives before a noun. Do not use a comma after an adjective that is an article or determiner.

> A **loud, shrill** siren pierced the silence.
> I feel lazy in **hot, muggy** weather.

If the adjective before the noun is very closely related to the noun, do not use a comma.

> Juana was waiting beside a high brick wall.

PRACTICING YOUR SKILLS

- Write the following sentences. Add commas wherever they are needed.

1. Running swimming and dancing are excellent forms of exercise.
2. A tall thin woman entered the room.
3. The recipe calls for meat noodles tomatoes and spices.
4. The ad attracted several bright creative people.
5. The candidate walked to the podium looked at the audience and began to speak.
6. The dark stormy sea is fascinating in the moonlight.
7. Everyone felt cheerful in the warm festive atmosphere.
8. Caroline Felipe and Nan will meet us this afternoon.
9. It was a bleak gray morning.
10. They needed protection from the hot bright sun.
11. Grace owns three dogs a parakeet and two rabbits.
12. He is a charming delightful person.
13. Julio is visiting his aunt his uncle and his cousins.
14. Our new puppy chewed holes in a slipper a sock and my favorite sweater.
15. Their loud raucous laughter kept me awake.
16. His harsh angry words hurt me.
17. Taos Santa Fe and Albuquerque are three cities in New Mexico.
18. This weekend I have to read a book write an essay and study for an exam.
19. The hikers slowly made their way down the steep rocky hill.
20. June July and August are my favorite months of the year.
21. Please bring a notebook a pen a sketch pad and some pencils.
22. The large clumsy dog has already knocked three plates a bowl and two glasses off the table.
23. Arturo Tanya Millie and I were sitting in the front row.
24. They spotted a wren two robins a jay and several pigeons.

27e. Commas with Nouns of Address

Use one or two commas to separate a noun of address from the other words in a sentence.

> **Jerry,** is your homework done?
> Please finish your homework, **Jerry.**
> Your homework, **Jerry,** is correct.

27f. Commas with Interrupters

Use commas to separate an interrupter from the other words in a sentence.

> This movie, **in my opinion,** is the worst of the year.
> It has, **however,** attracted large audiences.

27g. Commas with Introductory Yes and No

Use a comma after yes or no when it is the first word in a sentence.

> **Yes,** dinner is ready.
> **No,** we didn't make a salad.

27h. Commas with Interjections

Use a comma after an interjection when it is the first word in a sentence.

> **Well,** I've finally finished painting.
> **Oh,** the room looks wonderful!

PRACTICING YOUR SKILLS

■ Write the following sentences. Add commas wherever they are needed.

1. Erica may I speak with you?
2. Yes I'll meet you after class.
3. We have unfortunately only one day to rehearse.
4. Well do you like the new house?
5. Really you tell the most amazing stories!
6. His arrival I was told coincided with my departure.
7. No Casablanca is not in Spain.
8. Have you heard the news Roger?
9. I know Clara that you were here first.
10. Yes I understand the question.
11. No I don't know the answer.
12. The answer if you care is on page 41.
13. Honestly I did study last night.
14. Oh that's a surprise!
15. Don't be sarcastic George.
16. No it still doesn't make sense to me.
17. Andre can you explain it?
18. Do you agree with all these statements Connie?
19. The class unfortunately is almost over.
20. No we cannot wait until tomorrow.

27i. Commas in Compound Sentences

Use a comma before the coordinating conjunction that joins the two independent clauses in a compound sentence.

> Sherman ordered a hamburger, **and** Molly asked for a ham sandwich.
> Justine wanted a glass of milk, **but** the milk was not cold.
> Roy might have cottage cheese, **or** he might prefer yogurt.
> There were no napkins on the table, **nor** could our waiter find any.

PRACTICING YOUR SKILLS

■ Write the following sentences. Add commas wherever they are needed.

1. I can drive you to school or you can ride your bike.
2. Bertrand is an excellent athlete but he never learned how to roller-skate.
3. It was a warm day and we decided to go to the beach.
4. Stella hardly ever smiles nor have I ever heard her laugh.
5. Rochelle plays the tuba and Dennis plays the flute.
6. Joan should have arrived by now but I don't see her.
7. I haven't seen Tommy today nor do I know where he might be.
8. We should begin work today or the project will never be finished.
9. Marilyn received a new album for her birthday and she's invited us to hear it.
10. Quentin has never visited Hawaii but he plans to go there next year.
11. Stella never cheats nor does she lie.
12. We can play backgammon or we can do a puzzle together.
13. Mr. Lee is quite handsome but he doesn't seem vain.
14. Catherine loves to travel and she is taking flying lessons.
15. Carl doesn't like physics nor is he interested in chemistry.
16. We can have dinner at home or we can go to a restaurant.
17. Allan has two tickets to the ballet and he wants me to go with him.
18. The instructions sounded easy but assembling the gym set was quite difficult.
19. You could write her or you could phone her.
20. I don't like to write letters nor do I enjoy talking on the telephone.
21. Sally will join us but Christy needs to study.
22. The wind blew and leaves rustled in the trees.
23. I don't play chess nor do I want to learn.
24. I can do my algebra homework first or I can begin my English essay.
25. Agnes read each question aloud and Vanessa called on volunteers.
26. Ms. Jameson can give us the directions or we can find the route on a map.
27. Maura has not received any letters from Andy nor has she talked with him.
28. Diane complained to the manager but no adjustment was made.
29. Wilton has not eaten tripe nor does he care to try it.
30. Aurelia checked every reference book but she could not find the correct date.
31. Simca drew the chart and Cora filled in the numbers.
32. We will have to hurry or the train will leave without us.

27j. Commas with Appositive Phrases

Use one or two commas to separate an appositive phrase from the rest of a sentence.

Alfred Hitchcock, **the famous director,** appears in all his own films.
There is Woody Allen, **the director of <u>Manhattan</u>.**

PRACTICING YOUR SKILLS

■ Write the following sentences. Add commas wherever they are needed.

1. Tallulah Bankhead an American actress was the daughter of a United States senator.
2. I'd like you to meet Dr. Anne Lane my dog's veterinarian.
3. Cliff the new secretary types 102 words per minute.
4. Ms. Finnell a friend of the family is a mechanical engineer.
5. Raul an avid sailor is moving to Tahiti.
6. Ask Emily the treasurer of our club.
7. Give your ticket to Mr. Greene the man at the door.
8. The lecture will be given by Dr. Estolano a noted psychologist.
9. Thomas Wolfe the author of <u>Look Homeward, Angel</u> also wrote <u>You Can't Go Home Again</u>.
10. Jennifer a singer in the chorus has developed laryngitis.
11. David plays the guitar my favorite instrument.
12. Yesterday I saw Mr. Martinez my former employer.
13. Marguerite a delightful young woman has offered to give me piano lessons.
14. Lasagna a layered casserole is not difficult to prepare.
15. Jonathan the man with the snake is a herpetologist.
16. His sister a college student has a part-time job.
17. Have you met Dmitri and Alyosha our new neighbors?
18. Maureen an exchange student from Ireland has made many friends here.
19. Stan the winner of the election gave an acceptance speech in the auditorium.
20. We bought a new car a four-door Volvo.
21. This ballet has been written especially for Ilise our prima ballerina.
22. Murph and Vic friends of mine are angry with each other.
23. Mr. Goodman the camp director hired another counselor yesterday.
24. Ms. Biederman the school principal will give the graduation speech.
25. Neil the blond guitar player is also the singer for the band.
26. We spoke to Angela the person in charge of the committee about the meeting on Friday.
27. It seems that Jeremy the recreation advisor spent all the money on our last party.
28. We will meet with Pat the president of the group to try to decide what should be done.
29. Peter the man in the brown suit has been talking to Mr. Gomez for more than an hour.
30. Sammy the playful kitten attacked several garbage bags.
31. Many members of the press were at the airport to greet Todd the famous rock star.
32. She refused to give interviews to anyone except Miss Wilson a writer for a local magazine.

27k. Commas with Introductory Adverbial Prepositional Phrases

A prepositional phrase that is used as an adverb may come at the beginning of a sentence. When it does, use a comma after the prepositional phrase. If two or more prepositional phrases are used as adverbs at the beginning of a sentence, use a comma after the last prepositional phrase.

> **Without a word,** Lisa stormed out of the room.
> **From the top of the mountain,** Karl surveyed the valley.

PRACTICING YOUR SKILLS

■ Write the following sentences. Add commas wherever they are needed.

1. After the storm the animals emerged from their places of shelter.
2. With a quick glance at his watch Antonio rushed out of the house.
3. After the fall of the Roman Empire Europe was in a chaotic state.
4. Before dinner we were all extremely irritable.
5. During the performance I couldn't take my eyes from Nureyev.
6. In the midst of the crowd one person stood out.
7. In the middle of the road a large oak tree was growing.
8. Throughout the night the snow had continued to fall.
9. From fans around the world letters and postcards arrived daily.
10. Without your valuable assistance we could never have completed the project.
11. To Sandor the instructions seemed quite logical.
12. To the other students the instructions were very confusing.
13. During the intermission Loretta met her friends in the lobby.
14. With luck we will reach the summit before noon.
15. After dark the park is usually deserted.
16. On the top shelf you will find an extra jar of honey.

■■ Rewrite the following sentences. Move the prepositional phrase that is used as an adverb to the beginning of the sentence. Use a comma in each new sentence.

1. Everyone participated in those activities at camp.
2. Nola enjoys skiing and skating during the winter.
3. The members of the committee will meet here again at noon.
4. Ludda found this old crate under the oak tree.
5. The students always do their best work in that class.
6. They had less than a dollar between them.
7. My friends and I were sure of our theory until last night.
8. Someone had left a strange message on the dining room table.
9. A new cabin had been built beside the river.
10. We can have dinner together after the movie.
11. Randall could see everything from his window.
12. The party was not much fun without you.

271. Commas with Participial Phrases

Use a comma after a participial phrase at the beginning of a sentence.

    Crossing her fingers, Elena made a wish.

Use one or two commas to separate a nonrestrictive participial phrase from the other words in a sentence. A nonrestrictive participial phrase adds information about the noun it modifies, but is not needed to make clear the meaning of that noun.

    Elena, **crossing her fingers,** made a wish.

Do not use commas with a restrictive participial phrase.

    The girl crossing her fingers was Elena.

PRACTICING YOUR SKILLS

■ Write the following sentences. Add commas wherever they are needed.

1. Leaning out the window Mona waved goodbye one last time.
2. Alonzo hoping for a good response announced his decision immediately.
3. Dozing in her seat Ada missed the end of the movie.
4. Ms. Delgado confused by the various reports decided to conduct her own investigation.
5. Having slept for eight hours Helen woke up feeling refreshed.
6. Engrossed in the television movie Miguel didn't hear the ring of the telephone.
7. Looking out the window Wendy watched a bird build its nest.
8. Jason daydreaming in class missed the lecture on how to deal with boredom.
9. Elated by the news Marian ran home eagerly.
10. Glancing at the envelope in the stranger's hand I immediately noticed the familiar handwriting.
11. Aubrey having waited for more than an hour finally grew impatient.
12. Shouting excitedly the children ran into the yard.
13. Exhausted by our long hike we sat quietly around the camp fire.
14. Mr. Jeffers worried by the unusual engine noise took the car to a mechanic.
15. Holding the hood up with one hand the mechanic glanced at the engine.
16. Waving proudly to her friends Alexis walked toward the stage.
17. Left alone in the strange house Bonita explored every room.
18. Sasha sitting alone near the window seemed lost in thought.
19. Hurrying up the steps Adam tripped and twisted his ankle.
20. Carlotta watching everyone carefully formed her own opinions.
21. Pacing nervously across the room Lola accidentally stepped on the cat's tail.
22. Lifting the carton carefully Reggie checked the contents.
23. Our dog sleeping in a pool of sunlight looked content with the world.
24. George trying to be helpful dropped two bags of groceries.
25. Shaking her head sadly Alanna left the room.

27m. Commas with Introductory Adverb Clauses

An adverb clause may come at the beginning of a sentence. When it does, use a comma at the end of the adverb clause.

> **Although the sun is shining,** the air is cold.
> **When the movie ended,** the audience applauded.

PRACTICING YOUR SKILLS

■ Write the following sentences. Add commas wherever they are needed.

1. While we waited we each ate an apple and some crackers.
2. Until I received your postcard I didn't know you had left town.
3. Since Gloria got a job she has no time to see me.
4. After the plane reached cruising altitude I unbuckled my seat belt.
5. If I go to the beach Marion will come with me.
6. Unless the rain stops soon our game will be canceled.
7. Though we had worked for hours we still weren't finished.
8. Wherever we go we take pictures.
9. Whenever I sing my dog howls.
10. Because she felt chilly Leonore went indoors.
11. As I shivered in my bed a mournful cry pierced the night air.
12. When the alarm rang Anton groaned.
13. After the party guests had departed we began to wash the dishes.
14. Before I had finished the first chapter I had puzzled out the mystery.
15. If Mary's not home I'll call Verna.
16. Since you moved away our old neighborhood just isn't the same.
17. Whenever Maura is embarrassed she giggles.
18. Because you asked me nicely I'll do this favor for you.
19. While you're in the kitchen would you bring me a glass of water?
20. Unless you put the snake back in its cage I will not open this door!
21. Although Toni was not old enough to vote she participated in the campaign.
22. Until I turned on the television I was unaware of the terrible news.
23. Wherever you go please remember me.
24. Though we are apart we can still be friends.
25. As I was dialing the telephone the doorbell rang.
26. Before we have dessert let's take a walk.
27. Since I have been exercising each day I feel much healthier.
28. Until the lecture begins we can wait in the corridor.
29. If Kara calls please tell her I've gone to the library.
30. Unless Maggie arrives by noon we'll have to leave without her.
31. When Justin gets home from school he sets the table for dinner.
32. Whenever you are in town please call us.
33. While you were out Mr. Bloch called.
34. After we finish the kitchen the entire apartment will be freshly painted.
35. Although we hadn't seen each other in three years we had corresponded regularly.
36. Because you have been such a help to us we'd like to do something for you.
37. Though Marty was favored to win he came in second.

27n. Commas with Nonrestrictive Adjective Clauses

Use one or two commas to separate a nonrestrictive adjective clause from the other words in a sentence.

Stefanie, **who likes children,** may become a pediatrician.
Ms. Coulter, **whom I admire,** is running for mayor.
We are reading Gulliver's Travels, **which was written by Jonathan Swift.**

PRACTICING YOUR SKILLS

■ Write the following sentences. Add commas wherever they are needed.

1. The Cabinet of Dr. Caligari which was first shown in the United States in 1921 is a fascinating German film.
2. Michael Berlyn whom I met last week just sold his first novel.
3. I finally spoke with Lisa who is a hard person to reach.
4. Mr. Gould who taught me to swim coaches at the university.
5. Zena whom the class elected vice-president hopes to be the first woman on the moon.
6. Lon enjoyed the movie Star Wars which won an Academy Award for special effects.
7. My father's car which is a 1964 model runs better than many newer cars.
8. Ms. Jurgens whom the children always badger for cookies won a prize at the county fair.
9. We spent yesterday with Larry who just returned from a year abroad.
10. Tony who wants to be a deep-sea diver is saving his money for lessons.
11. Mrs. Beatty whom the company will honor this evening is retiring after thirty years as personnel manager.
12. We spent the summer on Catalina which is an island off Los Angeles.
13. San Diego which attracts many tourists has a mild climate throughout the year.
14. Mr. Burns whom I always visit after school was once a mountain climber.
15. We have been reading about Amelia Earhart who was the first woman pilot to cross the Atlantic.
16. Elaine who introduced me to Robert sculpts miniature unicorns.
17. Marcia whom we visited in Washington will stay with us next summer.
18. I am reading The Woman in White which is Wilkie Collins' most famous novel.
19. Starry Night which was painted by Van Gogh imparts a mood of solitude.
20. Archie whom you met yesterday was once a circus acrobat.
21. We bought this watch for Kelly who is graduating this month.
22. Travis who appears in television commercials will endorse only products he believes in.
23. Libby whom the audience liked best of all took three curtain calls.
24. We subscribe to Consumer Reports which contains useful information about many products.
25. Texas which was once the largest state in the union now ranks second in size to Alaska.
26. Maureen who once hoped to become a famous violinist has decided to become an actress.
27. The other members of the club were waiting for Hal who was supposed to chair the meeting.

27o. Commas with Transitional Words and Phrases

Use one or two commas to separate a transitional word or phrase from the other words in a sentence. Some examples of transitional words and phrases are however, therefore, **and** for example.

> There are ways to cope with the gasoline shortage. **For example,** we can use public transportation more often.
>
> Lana hopes to become an oceanographer. She will, **therefore,** have to work hard in school.
>
> Barry had to cancel his appointment for today. He will call tomorrow to make a new appointment, **however.**

PRACTICING YOUR SKILLS

- Write the following sentences. Add commas wherever they are needed.

1. It was a beautiful day. Nevertheless Marissa felt depressed.
2. Brian is talented, intelligent, and attractive. Furthermore he has a wonderful personality.
3. Many of our traditional energy sources are becoming depleted. Consequently we must find new ways to generate power.
4. Janine doesn't speak German. She had a wonderful time in Munich nevertheless.
5. Camille sprained her ankle yesterday. Therefore she won't be able to go hiking with us this weekend.
6. I usually avoid foods which contain refined sugar. Yesterday however I had ice cream and cake at my sister's birthday party.
7. We are moving on Friday, and I spent all weekend packing. Consequently I haven't finished the assignment.
8. I've spent all my allowance. Therefore I can't go to the movies tonight.
9. I've helped you with the garden many times. For instance last year I mowed the lawn, and the year before that I raked the leaves.
10. Maureen wants to visit Italy because she has relatives there. Furthermore she loves Italian food!
11. I've invited Charles for dinner several times. Each time however he's had other plans.
12. No one has been Teddy's friend longer than I have. Consequently he trusts me more than he trusts anyone else.
13. Becky had an earache yesterday. She felt better today however.
14. The encyclopedia contains many interesting facts. However it is difficult to read more than a few entries at a single sitting.
15. Terry went shopping on Saturday, but all the shops were closed. Furthermore she was irritated because she couldn't find a parking place.
16. Meg was pleased to have caught the early bus. Nevertheless she was late to school because of a traffic jam on the freeway.
17. Many people attended the concert. My friend Rob for example was sitting in the first row.
18. Many joggers wear brightly colored clothes to avoid being hit by unsuspecting motorists. Nevertheless they must still contend with barking dogs and rude spectators.
19. Ibi thought he'd never get the part. However he decided to try anyway.

27p. Commas with Abbreviations

Use a comma after a proper noun when it is followed by the abbreviation Jr. or Sr. or by the abbreviation of an academic degree.

The letter was addressed to **Carl Furlong, Jr.**
The guest speaker will be **Miranda Myles, M.D.**

PRACTICING YOUR SKILLS

■ Write the following phrases. Add commas wherever they are needed.

1. Philip Martin D.D.S.
2. Joy Allen C.P.A.
3. Fred L. Bergen Jr.
4. Paul Archer M.A.
5. Margaret Archer M.S.
6. Donald Collins Sr.
7. Barbara K. Dodge Ph.D.
8. George O'Brien M.D.
9. Melanie Brill R.N.
10. Barbara Ruth Dietz J.D.
11. Charles S. Parker D.V.M.
12. Doris K. Feld Litt.D.
13. Elliott Baum B.A.
14. Henry H. Hall Esq.
15. Amanda Hay LL.B.
16. Laura V. Dent B.S.
17. Reuben Connolly J.P.
18. Morgan D. Hunt L.H.D.
19. Rinaldo Cortez LL.D.
20. Leif Huston Ph.B.
21. Margaret M. May Ph.G.
22. Conrad F. Contino Sr.
23. Nancy Flanders J.P.
24. Norman Strick M.D.

■■ Write the following sentences. Add commas wherever they are needed.

1. We were introduced to Nathan Popkin Jr.
2. The injured dog was rushed to the office of Jane Harmon D.V.M.
3. The last guest to arrive was Audrey Elliott M.D.
4. Our next speaker will be Bettina Kates D.D.S.
5. On the door were the following words: Peter Gath Ph.D.
6. You may now call me Fred Holman Sr.!
7. The person who helps us with our taxes is Jerry Presson C.P.A.
8. I was impressed with the talk given by Steven McCarthy R.N.
9. The staff therapist is Kitty Sauber M.A.
10. The attorney for the defense is Richard Fuller J.D.
11. Yesterday we met Paul Sloane M.S.
12. Please send the letter to Harold Lavet D.D.S.
13. The wedding will be conducted by Richard Haley J.P.
14. The party honored our new pharmacist, Scott Mirman Ph.G.
15. He prefers to be addressed as Paul Bellasario Esq.
16. The president of the Alumnae Club is Vera K. Landon B.A.
17. Send any inquiries to Frank S. Godfrey Jr.
18. The nurse on duty is Betty Yates R.N.
19. The president of the firm is Erin Moore LL.D.
20. You were recommended by Charlotte Nakagawa C.P.A.
21. I can't find the office of Jay Wohlstadter D.D.S.
22. The head of the department is Marilyn Frankel Ph.D.
23. The person you are thinking of is Catherine Hunt Litt.D.

Reviewing 26 Periods, Question Marks, Exclamation Marks and 27 Commas

Write the following sentences. Add periods, question marks, and exclamation marks wherever they are needed.

26a. End Punctuation

1. May I speak with Amelia
2. Our new teacher is Ms. Davis
3. Leave him alone

26b. Periods in Abbreviations

4. We are waiting for Ms Barnes and Mr Dominguez.
5. The baby was born at 10:13 AM yesterday to Mr and Mrs Martin H Greenberg.
6. Mr and Mrs Povich are coming for dinner at 6:30 PM next Thursday.

Write the following sentences. Add commas wherever they are needed.

27a. Commas in Dates

7. On June 20 1980 we left for Canada, where we had not been since January 1 1968.
8. The new shopping center will open on February 12 1982.
9. On November 14 1986 she will be ten years old.

27b. Commas in Place Names and Addresses

10. Belgrade Yugoslavia is my grandfather's birthplace, and Genoa Italy is my grandmother's.
11. We're moving from Bellingham Washington to Fort Lauderdale Florida.
12. Send the package to 24 Concord Place Maspeth New York.

27c. Commas in Series

13. Carla washed her car swept out the inside touched up the paint waxed the surface and polished the chrome.
14. Philippe Yolanda and Sergei are coming to join Noriko Stan my parents and me for lunch.
15. I'm making the salad with radishes mushrooms tomatoes onions and lettuce.

27d. Commas between Adjectives

16. Sometimes I enjoy wet gloomy days more than bright sunny ones.
17. We peered into the dark dusty cave, listening for the faint distant echo.
18. The sound of happy laughing voices could be heard.

27e. Commas with Nouns of Address

19. Virginia I wish you would answer the telephone this time.
20. I am very sorry Mr. Brown that your package has not arrived.
21. Can't you remember where you left the car keys Hughie?

27f. Commas with Interrupters

22. My last name strangely enough is the same as yours.
23. Our plans have unfortunately been canceled, and we won't be going after all.
24. These figurines on the other hand are quite fragile and should in my opinion be packed with special care.

27g. Commas with Introductory Yes and No

25. No school does not end early today.
26. Yes you may go to the beach with us if you can be ready in five minutes.
27. No I haven't finished practicing.

27h. Commas with Interjections

28. Oh what a lovely surprise!
29. Really you are so thoughtful!
30. Well I guess it's time to go home.

27i. Commas in Compound Sentences

31. Martha hasn't called me today but I heard from her yesterday.
32. Colette barbecued the ribs and Noel prepared a bean salad.
33. We can take a picnic lunch to the beach or we can buy some food there.

27j. Commas with Appositive Phrases

34. Ms. Sanchez the program administrator was out to lunch.
35. We had dinner with Mr. Chung the director of the play and with Ms. Concetti the principal dancer.
36. Alexis my best friend is moving from Arizona her present home to Ohio.

27k. Commas with Introductory Adverbial Prepositional Phrases

37. Before the curtain rose the actors were nervous.
38. From our kitchen window we watched the children at play.
39. With great enthusiasm the audience applauded the dancers.

27l. Commas with Participial Phrases

40. Kim seeing that Henry was in danger swam to his rescue.

41. Waiting for the bell to ring Emil found it difficult to concentrate.
42. Waving goodbye Nathan rounded the corner.

27m. Commas with Introductory Adverb Clauses

43. Until the official results were announced no one knew who had won the election.
44. Because the weather was so delightful we decided to do our homework outside.
45. After classes had ended for the day we all went to the basketball game.

27n. Commas with Nonrestrictive Adjective Clauses

46. Ms. Kline who speaks seven languages is a translator for the United Nations.
47. Mr. Delgado whom everyone likes is an animal trainer.
48. We saw Rocky which won an Academy Award for best picture.

27o. Commas with Transitional Words and Phrases

49. Toni is busy Friday evening. She can however babysit for you on Saturday.
50. It was raining this morning. I rode my bike to school nevertheless.
51. You may have one extra week to complete your projects. Therefore any project which is turned in late will be given a failing grade.

27p. Commas with Abbreviations

52. The nurse on duty this evening is Linda Williams R.N.
53. First place was won by Alfredo Espinoza Jr.
54. He was posing as Samuel Peters M.S.

28 Other Punctuation Marks

28a. Quotation Marks with Titles

Use quotation marks at the beginning and at the end of the title of a story, a poem, an essay, an article, a chapter, or a song.

The poem **"Winter Sunset"** contains vivid images.
Chapter 9, **"The French Revolution,"** was the most interesting part of the book.

28b. Underlines with Titles

Underline the title of a book, periodical, movie, play, television program, painting, or long musical composition. In books and magazines, such titles are usually printed in a special kind of type, called *italics*.

He has a subscription to **Newsweek.**
The first musical comedy to win a Pulitzer Prize was **Of Thee I Sing.**

PRACTICING YOUR SKILLS

■ Write the following phrases. Add quotation marks and underlines wherever they are needed.

1. the story The Gift of the Magi
2. the book From Here to Eternity
3. People magazine
4. the poem Fog
5. the movie Close Encounters of the Third Kind
6. the play A Chorus Line
7. the television program Quincy
8. an article entitled How to Get the Most out of Jogging
9. the chapter entitled Magnetism
10. the song Yesterday

■■ Write the following sentences. Add quotation marks and underlines wherever they are needed.

1. The essay Self-Reliance is by Ralph Waldo Emerson.
2. The television program I Love Lucy was first seen in 1951.
3. Rembrandt's most famous painting is The Night Watch.
4. You Light Up My Life was Debbie Boone's first hit song.
5. Casey at the Bat is a delightful poem which is fun to read aloud.
6. The poem To Autumn was recited by David.
7. Alice has been chosen editor of Argus, our literary magazine.
8. My uncle started as a cub reporter on the Middletown Crier.
9. Bonanza is a television program I always enjoyed watching.
10. James Michener's novel Centennial has been adapted for television.
11. There are many interesting characters in Truman Capote's story The Silver Jug.
12. One of my favorite movies is Julia.

28c. Punctuation Marks with Direct Quotations

Use quotation marks at the beginning and at the end of each part of a direct quotation. Use a comma, a question mark, or an exclamation mark to separate a direct quotation from the other words in a sentence.

> Monty said, "The cookies are all gone."
> "Did you look in the cookie jar?" asked Nora.

Always place a period or a comma inside the closing quotation marks. Place a question mark or an exclamation mark inside the closing quotation marks only if the direct quotation is an interrogative sentence or an imperative sentence. Use only one punctuation mark at the end of each part of a direct quotation.

> "Yes," answered Monty, "but it's empty."
> "Let's bake some fresh cookies!" suggested Pam.
> Why did Monty say, "The cookies are all gone"?

PRACTICING YOUR SKILLS

■ Write the following sentences. Add quotation marks, commas, question marks, and exclamation marks wherever they are needed.

1. What are we having for dinner asked John.
2. That depends replied Laurel on what you feel like cooking.
3. I think I'll fry some chicken he suggested.
4. Paul exclaimed That's my favorite dinner!
5. The only problem said Laurel is that we didn't defrost the chicken.
6. John sighed I guess we could have hamburgers.
7. I want a cheeseburger Gail shouted from the next room.
8. If we have any lettuce said Laurel I'll make a salad.
9. Timmy jumped up and down and said Let's have a picnic!
10. It's too dark and cold outside answered Gail from the doorway.
11. Timmy asked Can we have a picnic tomorrow?
12. We'll see said John.
13. Little brothers murmured Paul should be seen and not heard.
14. That's not fair pouted Timmy.
15. Stop squabbling ordered John and set the table.
16. Why can't Gail set the table demanded Paul.
17. Gail snapped I'm making the potatoes!
18. I'll set the table sulked Timmy but I won't wash the dishes.
19. John asked Can't we ever have a peaceful evening around here?
20. I'm hungry complained Paul.
21. Then why don't you do something useful instead of complaining said Gail.
22. Where do you keep the lettuce asked Laurel.
23. It's in the refrigerator said Paul. Where else would it be?
24. This is amazing exclaimed Laurel. There are five heads of lettuce in here.
25. Don't you remember said John. We have rabbits.
26. I'm afraid of rabbits wailed Timmy.
27. Stop complaining about everything ordered Gail.

28d. Quotation Marks within Quotations

Use single quotation marks at the beginning and at the end of each part of a direct quotation within another direct quotation. When a title which would ordinarily need quotation marks is within a direct quotation, use single quotation marks at the beginning and at the end of the title.

> "That sign says, 'No left turn,'" she warned.
> "Today," the teacher said, "we will study the poem 'Eldorado.'"

PRACTICING YOUR SKILLS

■ Write the following sentences. Add single quotation marks wherever they are needed.

1. "This label says, Wash by hand," said Angela.
2. Christie remarked, "I think Marcia said, Meet me at ten."
3. "I know," said Frank, "that Ms. Zoller said, Your essays are due next Friday."
4. "Have you read The Highwayman yet?" asked Mira.
5. "No," answered Mark, "I'm still reading The Rime of the Ancient Mariner."
6. "When you were absent," Paul told Peter, "Mr. Reynolds announced, There will be no class on Tuesday."
7. "I'd like one of you to recite Trees for the rest of the class," said Mr. Hailey.
8. "No one seems to remember all the words to America the Beautiful," Jane said.
9. "My report will be on Washington Irving's story Rip Van Winkle," Jeff told Mrs. Strom.
10. "Mine," added Jeremy, "will be on T. S. Eliot's poem The Love Song of J. Alfred Prufrock."
11. "At ten o'clock every night," sighed Mary, "my mother always calls out, Bedtime!"
12. "When I was little," she reminisced, "she sang Rockabye Baby to me."
13. "Did Dad say, Take out the garbage?" asked John.
14. "I think," answered Cliff, "that he said, I'll take out the garbage."
15. Aunt Sophie said, "I have told you time and time again, Don't track dirt in here!"
16. "Does the label say, Boil for ten minutes?" Ginny asked.
17. "No," replied Jesse, "it says, Simmer for ten minutes."
18. "We will now sing the Star-Spangled Banner," Mr. Morkar told the class.
19. "Please tell us the moral of The Tortoise and the Hare," the teacher said to Julie.
20. "When Hamlet said, O! that this too too solid flesh would melt," asked Bill, "was he trying to diet?"
21. "I read The Masque of the Red Death last night," said Enrique. "It frightened me even more than The Fall of the House of Usher."
22. "When my father yelled, Richard, come inside and lock the door right now!" said Ricky, "I didn't think he meant it. Now I know that when he shouts Richard! like that, I'd better pay attention.
23. "Susan's written three poems, Flowers, Grass, and Butterflies," said Cheryl. "I asked her why she didn't call them Dandelions, Crabgrass, and Aphids."
24. "The first time my little sister watched television," said Amy, "she asked, How do all those people fit in that little box?"

28e.   Apostrophes in Possessive Nouns

**Add an apostrophe and an s or only an apostrophe to a noun to make
its possessive form. Add an apostrophe and an s if the noun does not
end with s. Add only an apostrophe if the noun ends with s.**

> The **rabbit's** nose is twitching.
> All the **rabbits'** noses are twitching.
> **James'** rabbits are twitching their noses.

28f.   Apostrophes in Contractions

**Use an apostrophe in place of the missing letter or letters in a
contraction.**

> Cora is = Cora's   they would = they'd
> who is = who's   should not = shouldn't

Notice these special contractions.

> will not = won't   cannot = can't

PRACTICING YOUR SKILLS

■ Write the following sentences. Add apostrophes wherever they are
needed.

1. Ill call you at eight o'clock if that isnt too late.
2. Have you seen Philips book?
3. Who has seen the dogs leash?
4. Im surprised that you dont remember me.
5. Theres no doubt that theyre fibbing.
6. Are all the horses saddles in place?
7. Were going to the Andersons party in the Morettis car.
8. The design of the girls uniforms will be changed next year.
9. She wouldnt tell me why shes crying.
10. It isnt raining, and you wont need your umbrella.
11. Whats bothering Jeannie?
12. The Hutchinsons fence is broken.
13. The teachers record book is missing.
14. Sallys worrying about the exam.
15. Theyll ask you why you didnt write.
16. Wheres Donalds briefcase?
17. Randys report card is on the table next to Mickys.
18. The secretarys desk is cluttered.
19. Wheres the movie theater?
20. Its on Westwood Boulevard next to Juniors delicatessen.
21. We cant tell you whos playing.
22. All the ships crews are working hard.
23. The Browns dog is barking at the Mortons cat.
24. Cindys sister is visiting Nepal.
25. He shouldnt have visitors until theres no danger of contagion.
26. You arent going in the right direction.
27. Id like to vacation where its warm.
28. Which of Fitzgeralds stories did you enjoy the most?
29. Have you finished reading Hemingways novel?
30. They werent aware that the faucet wasnt leaking any more.

28g. Colons before Lists

Use a colon to draw attention to a list of items. Do not use a colon when a list comes immediately after a verb or preposition.

The following books are on my desk: Roget's Thesaurus, the Guinness Book of World Records, and Webster's New Collegiate Dictionary.

The books on my desk are Roget's Thesaurus, the Guinness Book of World Records, and Webster's New Collegiate Dictionary.

28h. Colons in Expressions of Time

Use a colon between the hours and the minutes when writing the time in numerals.

Our flight leaves Los Angeles at **1:00** P.M.
We'll arrive in Dallas at **4:15** P.M.

PRACTICING YOUR SKILLS

■ Write the following sentences. Add colons wherever they are needed.

1. The following students will receive awards Steve, Linda, Philip, Colleen, and Marjorie.
2. My classes begin at 900, and my first free period is at 100.
3. Did Caitlin say to meet her at 500 or 530?
4. We are growing four kinds of vegetables in our garden green peppers, lettuce, carrots, and corn.
5. The room was furnished with objects which differed greatly in style an ornate clock, a starkly modern couch, and a Persian rug.
6. Is midnight 1200 A.M. or 1200 P.M.?
7. I'll be serving dinner promptly at 700 this evening.
8. Please inform the following people that the meeting date has been changed George, John, Deborah, and Patty.
9. We are out of the following flavors of ice cream chocolate, vanilla, and strawberry.
10. Coffee breaks for our department are at 1020 A.M. and 320 P.M.
11. Our office is open from 900 A.M. to 500 P.M.
12. The concert is sold out on the following dates May 5, May 8, and May 9.
13. Orchestra seats are available only on the following dates September 1, October 15, and December 29.
14. I usually go to lunch at 1230 P.M.
15. The movie will begin at 840 P.M. and will end at 1017 P.M.
16. The doctor can see you tomorrow at 315 or Wednesday at 200.
17. We saw three different breeds of cats at the show Persian, Siamese, and Maltese.
18. The cat could be hiding in one of these places under the bed, behind the washing machine, or in my sewing basket.
19. I can meet you at one of these three times 1030 A.M., 115 P.M., or 245 P.M.

28i. Semicolons in Lists

Use a semicolon to separate the items in a list when the items contain commas.

> Three people had excuses for being late to school: John, who lives across the street from the school, said he had been delayed by traffic; Mindy, who lives at the foot of the mountain, said that the sun had risen late in her area; and Vera, who lives in a ground-floor apartment, said she had been stuck in the elevator.

PRACTICING YOUR SKILLS

- Write the following sentences. Add semicolons wherever they are needed.

1. I present to you the following slate of candidates: Becky Pedrini, a twelfth-grader Floyd Akrens, an eleventh-grader Conrad Tyler, a tenth-grader and Allison Pickering, a ninth-grader.

2. The following people will receive special awards: Katherine Baum, for her special work in science Kevin Ward, for his service to the school and Darlene Ganz, for her volunteer work at the hospital.

3. I read four books during my vacation: Pride and Prejudice, which I enjoyed Emma, which I have now read twice Jane Eyre, which I plan to read again, and Wuthering Heights, which is my favorite.

4. When I wasn't reading, I did some traveling: to San Francisco, where I rode a cable car to Los Angeles, where I visited a movie studio and to San Diego, where I spent a day at the zoo.

5. Four people were absent Thursday: Karen, who had a cold Jaime, who still has the flu Ilona, who is recovering from an appendectomy and Andrew, who hasn't been heard from in three days.

6. The Piersons owned some strange animals: two kangaroos, one of which hopped over their fence frequently three roosters, all of which crowed every morning and a baby tiger, which they eventually gave to a friend with a larger yard.

7. Our committee had made the following recommendations to the chairperson: our meetings, which are normally held on Fridays, should be held on Thursdays our elections, which usually take place in June, should take place in May and our dues, which are now a dollar a year, should be reduced to fifty cents.

8. Bring these items on the camping trip: warm clothes, which you will need for the cold nights cool clothes, which you will need for the hot days and insect repellent, which you will need all the time.

9. I hereby excuse the following people from the final exam: Phillip, who has an A average Sheri, who has written two reports for extra credit and Odette, who has attended every class session.

10. The principal introduced three new teachers at the September assembly: Ms. Simmons, who previously taught English at Fairfax High School Mr. Gendron, who has just received his M.A. in French and Mrs. Mancinelli, who is an exchange teacher from Italy.

28j. Semicolons in Compound Sentences

Use a semicolon to join two closely related independent clauses that are not joined by a conjunction.

> Manuel is trying very hard for the track team; he's not sure he'll qualify.
>
> Laura is saving her money; she wants to go to college.

PRACTICING YOUR SKILLS

■ Write the following sentences. Add semicolons wherever they are needed.

1. Donald went to the market he wanted something special for dinner.
2. Everyone watched the movie they thought it was excellent.
3. Rafael did the dishes Barbara washed a load of clothes.
4. Set the alarm for 6:30 we have to be at school early.
5. I never heard the alarm luckily, the noise of the garbage truck woke me in time.
6. The concert has been canceled not enough tickets were sold.
7. We'll have to postpone the meeting no one can get here in this storm.
8. The final exam was extremely difficult some people will have to repeat the course.
9. No one knew the correct answer we all looked frantically through our notes.
10. There was a landslide yesterday the road is closed until further notice.
11. My father is a marvelous cook he creates new dishes all the time.
12. My mother also cooks well she prefers to use old family recipes.
13. My brother and I each cook dinner one night a week this helps our parents, who both work until five o'clock.
14. The auditorium was absolutely silent we all waited to hear who had been chosen for the play.
15. I watched <u>Casablanca</u> on television last night it is a movie I never tire of seeing.
16. Marty looks exhausted he was up all night finishing his report.
17. The wind and rain caused a power failure we had to use candles for light.
18. My car wouldn't start the battery was dead.
19. The camp advertised for twelve counselors sixteen people applied for the jobs.
20. The camp directors were very impressed with all the applicants it was hard to decide which ones should be hired.
21. Finally, a compromise was reached twelve people were hired as counselors and four people as assistant counselors.
22. The curtain fell the play was over.
23. The alarm rang I pulled the blanket up over my head and pretended I hadn't heard it.
24. I could hardly believe the job was done I was completely exhausted.
25. I'm not sure Dan's ready for college he doesn't know how to type.
26. You should speak a little more loudly not everyone can hear you.
27. Marvin smiled proudly his presentation had been a success.
28. Lester B. Pearson became the prime minister of Canada in 1963 he resigned in 1968.
29. Trudy competes in several field events the javelin throw is her favorite.

28k. Hyphens

Use a hyphen in a compound number from twenty-one to ninety-nine. Use a hyphen in a fraction that is used as an adjective.

We baked seventy-two cookies.
There was a two-thirds reduction in the price.

28l. Parentheses

Use parentheses to enclose words or phrases which add information to a sentence but which are not essential to the meaning of the sentence.

The city's population increased dramatically in 1978 (see figure 2).
Senator Cranston (D-California) conferred with President Carter.

PRACTICING YOUR SKILLS

■ Write the following phrases. Add hyphens wherever they are needed.

1. ninety nine students in the senior class
2. seventy three spectators at the game
3. a four fifths majority
4. twenty four questions on the exam
5. forty eight books on the shelf
6. a one fifth share
7. fifty five dishes to wash
8. sixty seven paintings in the exhibit
9. a one third reduction
10. thirty six flavors of ice cream
11. eighty two tickets to sell
12. a one sixth interest in the company
13. forty one of the fifty states
14. twenty eight counties
15. only twenty four more sentences
16. thirty two students
17. a two thirds majority
18. seventy eight different colors
19. twenty two stars in the constellation
20. eighty eight athletes
21. fifty six years old
22. a one third increase

■■ Write the following sentences. Add hyphens and parentheses wherever they are needed.

1. There are thirty five students in the class.
2. This bill requires a three fourths majority to pass.
3. Thread the wire through the loop see figure 1.
4. Jackson never returned home again see Chapter 3.
5. A one sixth share of the profits will earn you three dollars a day.
6. My grandfather will be sixty one years old on August 19.
7. Only ninety four signatures are needed.
8. A one quarter reduction in my cost means I can sell this item at a one quarter reduction in price.
9. Senator Goldwater R-Arizona will speak at our next meeting.
10. The large number of new members eighty nine requires us to find a larger meeting place.
11. Queen Victoria 1819–1901 ruled England for sixty three years 1837–1901.
12. During her reign, the Crimean War 1854–1856 and the South African War 1899–1902 were fought by the British.

Reviewing 28 Other Punctuation Marks

Write the following sentences. Add quotation marks and underlines wherever they are needed.

28a. Quotation Marks with Titles

1. The Beatles' first hit song was I Want to Hold Your Hand.
2. Ivan's essay is entitled The Greatest American Automobile.
3. The story The Green Hills of Earth is set in the future.
4. Vi has memorized Dust of Snow, a short poem by Robert Frost.
5. Night Drive is a frightening short story.

28b. Underlines with Titles

6. One Flew Over the Cuckoo's Nest was a novel, a play, and a movie.
7. We subscribe to the National Geographic and to Smithsonian.
8. Have you read either Huckleberry Finn or Tom Sawyer?
9. You might find that information in The Book of Lists.

Write the following sentences. Add quotation marks, single quotation marks, commas, question marks, and exclamation marks wherever they are needed.

28c. Punctuation Marks with Direct Quotations

10. When will the audience begin to arrive Lesley inquired.
11. I believe answered Chris that the doors open at eight o'clock.
12. Oh, I'm so nervous exclaimed Wally. Do you think they'll like the play he added.
13. Why doesn't everybody just try to act calm asked the director.

28d. Quotation Marks within Quotations

14. The recipe says, Bring to a full boil, said Norm.
15. Your father said, Be home by eleven, said Susan, and he added, Or else.
16. Sally said, Fog is a famous poem by Carl Sandburg.
17. My next poem, announced Cedric, will be Nursery Rhyme for the Tender-Hearted, by Christopher Morley.
18. Who asked, Why can't we do it tomorrow, Mr. Walrath demanded sternly.

Write the following sentences. Add apostrophes wherever they are needed.

28e. Apostrophes in Possessive Nouns

19. The babys rattle is in the playpen next to Dads old slipper.
20. All the players lockers are downstairs to the right of the coachs office.
21. Marcias film will be released in March, two months after Charles film comes out.
22. The womens coats are in the department just past the childrens shoes.
23. Lauras aunt is my sisters friend.
24. Has anybody seen Dennis new tennis racket?

28f. Apostrophes in Contractions

25. Youre talking too loudly.
26. Im sure weve met before. Werent you in The Sound of Music?
27. He cant find the car keys, and Im sure Sheilas waiting impatiently.
28. Why isnt anybody paying attention to the musicians?
29. Havent the other players arrived yet?
30. We wont enjoy the concert if you arent there with us.

Write the following sentences. Add colons wherever they are needed.

28g. Colons before Lists

31. I have visited each of these cities Los Angeles, Santa Barbara, Sacramento, and San Francisco.
32. Put the following items on your shopping list cheese, eggs, milk, margarine, tomato sauce, and lettuce.
33. These are the people I have chosen for my team Karyn, Bobby, Peter, Ernie, Raul, and Jane.

28h. Colons in Expressions of Time

34. You can meet me at the entrance at 815 A.M., or you can meet me inside at 825.
35. Shall we see the movie at 700 P.M. or 930 P.M.?
36. Set the alarm for 645 A.M., and call me if I'm not up by 715.

Write the following sentences. Add semicolons wherever they are needed.

28i. Semicolons in Lists

37. Some interesting people attended the meeting: Carlos, who was born in Brazil Sarit, who is an exchange student from India and Heidi, who hopes to study in Germany next year.
38. Bring the following to the picnic: hot dogs, which we will barbecue fruit, which we will have for dessert and potato salad, which we have to keep cold.
39. Three people phoned while you were out: Jacey, who asked if you had finished your script Paul, who wants you to call him back immediately and Penny, who needs a ride to tonight's rehearsal.

28j. Semicolons in Compound Sentences

40. Patrick's car stalled on the hill it was out of gas.
41. Andrea washed the windows Shaun scrubbed the floors.
42. Cindy leaves for college tomorrow we have to drive her to the airport.
43. This machine is entirely unpredictable we never know what it will produce next.
44. The test was surprisingly difficult nobody in the class answered more than half the questions correctly.

Write the following sentences. Add hyphens and parentheses wherever they are needed.

28k. Hyphens

45. There are only twenty seven more school days until summer vacation.
46. Tomorrow my uncle will be thirty one years old, and next week my aunt will be twenty nine.
47. Does this bill require a two thirds majority or a three fourths majority to pass?
48. Did she ask for thirty four balloons and fifty five paper plates or fifty four balloons and thirty five paper plates?

28l. Parentheses

49. Profits declined in the first quarter of the year see figure 3.
50. Senator Dirksen R-Illinois was minority leader of the Senate for ten years 1959–1969.
51. Grover Cleveland 1837–1908 served one term as president 1885–1889, left office, then was elected for a second term 1893–1897.
52. The population of the western states see figure 12 increased rapidly.

29 Plural Forms of Nouns

29a. Nouns That Add -s

Form the plural of most nouns by adding -s.

one book—several books   one idea—several ideas

29b. Nouns That Add -es

Form the plural of nouns that end with the letters s, x, z, ch, or sh by adding -es.

one glass—several glasses   one bush—several bushes

PRACTICING YOUR SKILLS

■ Write the plural form of each noun.

1. knob	15. trip	29. branch
2. suffix	16. gas	30. marsh
3. friend	17. propeller	31. bench
4. waltz	18. complex	32. address
5. knee	19. hall	33. wish
6. trench	20. perch	34. fox
7. ring	21. locket	35. brush
8. business	22. equinox	36. class
9. back	23. window	37. bulb
10. prefix	24. hex	38. box
11. coin	25. dream	39. grape
12. bunch	26. annex	40. painter
13. myth	27. bus	41. guess
14. paradox	28. inch	42. blouse

■■ Complete each of the following sentences by adding the plural form of the noun in parentheses. Write the sentences.

1. We listened to the (speech) of all the candidates at the assembly.
2. Put those (dish) on the second shelf in the dining room cabinet.
3. All the (watch) in this display case will be on sale until Wednesday.
4. Do we have enough (brick) to pave both the patio and the path?
5. The (flash) of lightning brilliantly illuminated the sky.
6. Those (sandwich) are for the picnic.
7. How many (street) do you have to cross on the way to school?
8. The (wrench) on this table are separated by size.
9. The (dress) on the rack near the door are all your size.
10. Shall I serve the cottage cheese with (peach) or with (pear)?
11. This rat has found its way through three different (maze).
12. His (lunch) are always nutritious.

29c. Nouns That End in a Consonant and y

Form the plural of nouns that end in a consonant and y by changing the y to i and adding -es.

one spy—several spies   one party—several parties

29d. Nouns That End in a Vowel and y

Form the plural of nouns that end in a vowel and y by adding -s.

one toy—several toys   one essay—several essays

PRACTICING YOUR SKILLS

■ Write the plural form of each noun.

1. library	15. boy	29. guy
2. day	16. jetty	30. enemy
3. key	17. stairway	31. subway
4. lullaby	18. ploy	32. duty
5. pottery	19. pony	33. display
6. bluejay	20. entity	34. city
7. body	21. stray	35. tray
8. berry	22. elegy	36. putty
9. alley	23. donkey	37. holiday
10. sky	24. joy	38. passkey
11. railway	25. alloy	39. guppy
12. copy	26. baby	40. ray
13. gypsy	27. ally	41. melody
14. covey	28. spray	42. rhapsody

■■ Complete each of the following sentences by adding the plural form of the noun in parentheses. Write the sentences.

1. The (butterfly) I like best are the ones whose wings look like velvet.
2. Robin has written seven (play), none of which have been produced.
3. Pick enough (strawberry) so that we can make jam as well as a pie.
4. What are the most important (quality) you look for in a friend?
5. The book contains so many delightful (story) that I can't pick a favorite.
6. If there are any more (delay) on this project, we'll have to cancel it.
7. On this map, the (valley) are indicated by dark green.
8. The (army) of toy soldiers faced each other across the bedspread.
9. Last month there were three (vacancy), but the apartments are all rented now.
10. These six (monkey) will be the control group for the experiment.
11. I have fond (memory) of my vacation two years ago in Scotland.
12. The (history) of those two families were entwined for nearly seven generations.
13. Last summer, Jill read two (biography) of Golda Meir.
14. Huge (quantity) of dirt had been deposited in the yard overnight.

29e. Nouns That End in f or fe

Form the plural of many nouns that end in f or fe by adding -s. Form the plural of some nouns that end in f or fe by changing the f to v and adding -es or -s. Refer to a dictionary for the correct spelling of the plural form.

> one roof—several roofs
> one knife—several knives

Some nouns that end in f have alternative plural forms. Refer to a dictionary for the preferred spelling of the plural form. The preferred spelling of the plural form appears first.

> one calf—several calves or calfs
> one kerchief—several kerchiefs or kerchieves

PRACTICING YOUR SKILLS

■ Write the plural form of each noun.

1. rebuff	12. clef	23. beef
2. cuff	13. fief	24. wife
3. wolf	14. gaff	25. oaf
4. mastiff	15. ruff	26. reproof
5. elf	16. waif	27. bluff
6. whiff	17. gaffe	28. serf
7. fluff	18. skiff	29. turf
8. carafe	19. staff	30. grief
9. gulf	20. dwarf	31. hoof
10. sheaf	21. puff	32. leaf
11. muff	22. proof	33. scarf

■■ Complete each of the following sentences by adding the plural form of the noun in parentheses. Write the sentences.

1. Ada found three new (kerchief) on the floor of her closet.
2. How many (loaf) of bread does that bakery bake each day?
3. All the (wharf) in our city need extensive repairs.
4. The robbers blew open two hotel (safe) yesterday and escaped with over four thousand dollars in cash and jewelry.
5. The (chief) of police of six counties will meet today.
6. Those (reef) look hazardous.
7. All the (roof) in this area must be fire-resistant.
8. Yesterday, we lined all the (shelf) in the kitchen and dining room.
9. (Knife) must be handled carefully.
10. What (belief) does that group hold?
11. First, cut your apple into two (half).
12. The (cliff) of Dover have been immortalized in a poem.
13. The (thief) might return to the scene of the crime.
14. Do cats really have nine (life)?
15. The greatest (chef) in the world will be at the hotel next week.
16. Have any (giraffe) been born at the local zoo this year?

29f.   Nouns That End in a Consonant and o

Form the plural of many nouns that end in a consonant and o by adding -s. Form the plural of some nouns that end in a consonant and o by adding -es. Refer to a dictionary for the correct spelling of the plural form.

> one dynamo—several dynamos
> one hero—several heroes

Some nouns that end in a consonant and o refer to music. Form the plural of most of these nouns by adding -s.

> one piano—several pianos
> one alto—several altos

Some nouns that end in a consonant and o have alternate plural forms. Refer to a dictionary for the preferred spelling of the plural form.

> one avocado—several avocados or avocadoes
> one tornado—several tornadoes or tornados

29g.   Nouns That End in a Vowel and o

Form the plural of nouns that end in a vowel and o by adding -s.

> one stereo—several stereos
> one tattoo—several tattoos

PRACTICING YOUR SKILLS

■ Write the plural form of each noun.

1. gyro	16. folio	31. veto
2. mosquito	17. magneto	32. hobo
3. curio	18. arpeggio	33. oratorio
4. soprano	19. torpedo	34. rondo
5. zero	20. zoo	35. tomato
6. rodeo	21. piccolo	36. radio
7. domino	22. stiletto	37. voodoo
8. grotto	23. ratio	38. scherzando
9. patio	24. cargo	39. motto
10. trio	25. calico	40. studio
11. bravo	26. oleo	41. desperado
12. cello	27. cuckoo	42. potato
13. kangaroo	28. olio	43. duo
14. echo	29. contralto	44. bravado
15. ego	30. cameo	45. palomino

29h. Compound Nouns

Some compound nouns contain a noun and one or more words that modify the main noun. Some of these compound nouns are hyphenated. To form the plural of many of these nouns, make the main noun plural.

> one attorney at law—two attorneys at law
> one secretary-general—two secretaries-general

29i. Irregular Nouns

A few nouns do not change to the plural form by adding -s or -es. They change in irregular ways.

> one ox—several oxen
> one child—several children
> one man—several men
> one woman—several women

> one tooth—several teeth
> one foot—several feet
> one goose—several geese
> one mouse—several mice

29j. Nouns That Do Not Change

No change is made to form the plurals of a very few nouns. These nouns have the same singular and plural forms.

> one sheep—several sheep
> one moose—several moose
> one swine—several swine
> one species—several species
> one series—several series

PRACTICING YOUR SKILLS

- Write the plural form of each noun.

1. mother-in-law
2. mouse
3. justice of the peace
4. woman
5. attorney at law
6. tooth
7. sergeant–at–arms
8. swine
9. son-in-law
10. ox
11. hanger-on
12. goose
13. secretary-general
14. series
15. postmaster-general
16. sheep
17. daughter-in-law
18. child
19. editor in chief
20. foot
21. brother-in-law
22. moose
23. stick-in-the-mud
24. species
25. man
26. sister-in-law

29k. Greek and Latin Nouns

Form the plural of some nouns from Greek and Latin as they are formed in the original language. Refer to a dictionary for the correct spelling of the plural form.

  alumna—alumnae
  alumnus—alumni
  crisis—crises
  genus—genera
  corpus—corpora
  bacterium—bacteria

Some nouns from Greek and Latin have alternate plural forms: one as in the original language, and one as formed in English. Refer to a dictionary for the preferred spelling of the plural form.

  formula—formulas or formulae
  vertebra—vertebrae or vertebras
  index—indexes or indices
  cortex—cortices or cortexes
  aquarium—aquariums or aquaria
  terrarium—terraria or terrariums
  nucleus—nuclei or nucleuses
  opus—opera or opuses
  phenomenon—phenomena or phenomenons
  philodendron—philodendrons or philodendra

PRACTICING YOUR SKILLS

■ Write the plural form of each noun.

1. alumna	15. analysis	29. parenthesis
2. amoeba	16. phenomenon	30. index
3. diagnosis	17. bacterium	31. minutia
4. alga	18. formula	32. criterion
5. phylum	19. oasis	33. matrix
6. appendix	20. vertebra	34. ellipsis
7. stimulus	21. stratum	35. medium
8. cortex	22. apex	36. addendum
9. genus	23. fungus	37. opus
10. cerebrum	24. hypothesis	38. equilibrium
11. thesis	25. aquarium	39. gymnasium
12. terrarium	26. nova	40. stadium
13. alumnus	27. nucleus	41. philodendron
14. thesaurus	28. crisis	42. corpus

■■ Choose five of the nouns in the preceding exercise, and write a sentence for each, using the plural form.

30 Prefixes

30a. The Prefixes in-, il-, im-, and ir-

A prefix is one or more syllables added to the beginning of a word to make a new word. Adding a prefix does not change the spelling of the original word. The prefixes in-, il-, im-, and ir- add the meaning "not" to a word. Use il- before l; im- before m or p; ir- before r; and in- before other sounds.

il + literate = illiterate   ir + responsible = irresponsible
im + practical = impractical   in + active = inactive

30b. The Prefixes non-, un-, and dis-

The prefixes non-, un-, and dis- also add the meaning "not" to a word.

non + magnetic = nonmagnetic
un + necessary = unnecessary
dis + agreeable = disagreeable

PRACTICING YOUR SKILLS

■ Add a prefix from the box to change the meaning of each word. Write the new words you make. Then write sentences for five of the words you made.

| in-   il-   im-   ir- |

1. exact	7. regular	13. resistible	19. mature
2. probable	8. legible	14. liberal	20. patient
3. logical	9. tolerable	15. tangible	21. limitable
4. rational	10. mortal	16. polite	22. replaceable
5. moral	11. legal	17. mobile	23. operable
6. capable	12. relevant	18. accurate	24. partial

■■ Add a prefix from the box to change the meaning of each word. Write the new words you make. Then write sentences for five of the words you made.

| non-   un-   dis- |

1. even	6. similar	11. aware	16. loyal	21. imaginable
2. honest	7. honorable	12. violent	17. breakable	22. productive
3. toxic	8. fattening	13. taxable	18. verbal	23. technical
4. able	9. ethical	14. educated	19. existent	24. reputable
5. profit	10. pleasing	15. obedient	20. respectful	25. satisfied

30c. The Prefixes mis-, over-, under-, and re-

The prefix mis-adds the meaning "badly" or "poorly" to a word. The prefix over-adds the meaning "too much." The prefix under-adds the meaning "too little." The prefix re-adds the meaning "again."

mis + spell = misspell   under + paid = underpaid
over + worked = overworked   re + count = recount

30d. The Prefixes pre-, post-, and anti-

The prefix pre-adds the meaning "earlier" or "before" to a word. The prefix post-adds the meaning "after." The prefix anti-adds the meaning "against."

pre + shrunk = preshrunk
post + graduate = postgraduate
anti + freeze = antifreeze

PRACTICING YOUR SKILLS

■ Add a prefix from the box to change the meaning of each word. Write the new words you make. Then write sentences for five of the words you made.

mis- over- under- re-

1. estimate	7. examine	13. consider	19. inform
2. elect	8. weight	14. behave	20. affirm
3. value	9. pronounce	15. charge	21. connect
4. judge	10. appear	16. rate	22. represent
5. act	11. interpret	17. nourished	23. copy
6. calculate	12. possess	18. active	24. treat

■■ Add a prefix from the box to change the meaning of each word. Write the new words you make. Then write sentences for five of the words you made.

pre- post- anti-

1. soak	7. static	13. trust	19. treat
2. date	8. school	14. war	20. nasal
3. social	9. natal	15. bacterial	21. smog
4. operative	10. paid	16. verbal	22. cook
5. toxin	11. doctoral	17. septic	23. poverty
6. heat	12. pollution	18. hypnotic	24. classical

31 Suffixes

31a. Spelling That Does Not Change

A **suffix** is one or more syllables added to the end of a word to make a new word or another form of a word. Do not change the spelling of most words that end in a consonant when adding a suffix that begins with a consonant.

cup + ful = cupful   quiet + ness = quietness

31b. Dropping Final e

Adding a suffix sometimes changes the spelling of the original word. Drop the final **e** from most base words when adding a suffix that begins with a vowel.

dispose + able = disposable   amuse + ing = amusing

Keep the final **e** in words that end in **ce** or **ge** when adding a suffix that begins with **a** or **o**.

courage + ous = courageous   peace + able = peaceable

31c. Keeping Final e

Keep the final **e** in most base words before a suffix that begins with a consonant.

sure + ly = surely   amuse + ment = amusement

Drop the final **e** in the following words.

true + ly = truly   judge + ment = judgment
due + ly = duly   argue + ment = argument
whole + ly = wholly   nine + th = ninth

PRACTICING YOUR SKILLS

■ Combine the following pairs of words and suffixes to make new words. Write the new words you make.

1. friend + ship	8. change + able	15. nine + ty	22. aspire + ing
2. imagine + ary	9. advantage + ous	16. care + ful	23. fame + ous
3. raise + ing	10. argue + ment	17. glad + ly	24. judge + ment
4. true + ly	11. wipe + ed	18. admire + able	25. due + ly
5. notice + able	12. state + ment	19. peace + ful	26. confuse + ion
6. erase + er	13. child + like	20. whole + ly	27. escape + ed
7. observe + ation	14. nine + th	21. child + hood	28. sore + ness

31d. Changing Final y to i

Some words end in y preceded by a consonant. In most of these words, change the y to i before a suffix that does not begin with i

worry + some = worrisome
dignify + ed = dignified
spy + ing = spying

Keep the y preceded by a consonant in most one-syllable words before a suffix beginning with a consonant.

shy + ly = shyly   sly + ness = slyness

31e. Keeping Final y

Some base words end in y preceded by a vowel. Keep the y before most suffixes.

joy + ous = joyous   enjoy + ment = enjoyment

Change the final y to i in the following words.

gay + ly = gaily   day + ly = daily

PRACTICING YOUR SKILLS

■ Combine the following pairs of words and suffixes to make new words. Write the new words you make.

1. empty + ness
2. hurry + ed
3. spray + ing
4. play + ful
5. spry + ly
6. curtsy + ing
7. duty + ful
8. day + ly
9. stay + ed
10. wry + ness
11. likely + hood
12. thirty + eth
13. buy + ing
14. coy + ly
15. dry + ly
16. bury + al
17. pity + ful
18. joy + less
19. gay + ly
20. shy + ness
21. merry + ment
22. relay + ed
23. employ + er
24. sky + ward
25. joy + ful
26. dry + ness
27. sly + ly
28. empty + ing
29. copy + ed
30. ally + ance
31. spray + er
32. replay + ed
33. rely + able
34. stray + ing
35. happy + ness
36. twenty + eth
37. bray + ed
38. rely + ance
39. signify + ing
40. happy + ly
41. beauty + ful
42. early + er
43. tally + ed
44. volley + ing
45. pretty + er
46. beauty + fy
47. boy + hood
48. plenty + ful
49. sturdy + ness
50. funny + er
51. play + er

■■ Choose five of the words you made in the preceding exercise. Write a sentence for each.

31f.   Doubling the Final Consonant in One-Syllable Words

A base word that ends in a single consonant preceded by a single vowel letter may have only one syllable. When it does, double the final consonant before a suffix beginning with a vowel.

stop + ed = stopped
hit + ing = hitting

31g.   Doubling the Final Consonant in Words of More Than One Syllable

A base word that ends in a single consonant preceded by a single vowel may be accented on the last syllable. When it is, you usually double the final consonant before a suffix beginning with a vowel.

confer + ing = conferring
prefer + ed = preferred

You usually do not double the final consonant if the accent shifts to a different syllable in the new word.

confer + ence = conference
prefer + able = preferable

PRACTICING YOUR SKILLS

■ Combine the following pairs of base words and suffixes to make new words. Write the new words you make.

1. wed + ing	18. upset + ing	35. jog + er
2. propel + er	19. confer + ence	36. cram + ed
3. prefer + ence	20. read + ing	37. refer + able
4. weed + ing	21. snap + ing	38. retail + er
5. stop + er	22. compel + ed	39. spin + ing
6. control + ed	23. occur + ence	40. defer + ment
7. refer + ence	24. hinder + ing	41. infer + able
8. travel + er	25. slip + er	42. follow + ing
9. ship + ed	26. incur + ing	43. permit + ed
10. omit + ing	27. excel + ent	44. inter + ment
11. defer + ence	28. propel + ed	45. confer + ing
12. wind + ing	29. clap + ing	46. impel + ed
13. clip + ing	30. propel + ant	47. prefer + able
14. admit + ance	31. control + able	48. compel + ing
15. infer + ence	32. hamper + ed	49. defer + able
16. limit + ed	33. fib + ing	50. prefer + ed
17. plan + er	34. repel + ent	51. steam + er

■■ Choose five of the words you made in the preceding exercise. Write a sentence for each.

32 Spelling Rules

32a. Words That Are Spelled with ie or ei

When choosing between ie and ei, listen to the vowel sound. When you hear the sound of long e, choose ie in most words. When you hear the sound of long e after c, the sound of long a, or any other vowel sound, choose ei in most words.

    relieve   receive   freight   height   foreign

32b. Words That End in -cede, -ceed, or -sede

A very few words end in -cede. Three words end in -ceed. One word ends in -sede.

accede	exceed	supersede
concede	proceed	
intercede	succeed	
precede		
recede		
secede		

PRACTICING YOUR SKILLS

■ Fill in each box with **ie** or **ei** to make a word. Write the words you make.

1. f ▯ ld
2. perc ▯ ve
3. h ▯ r
4. sh ▯ ld
5. r ▯ n
6. n ▯ ghbor
7. dec ▯ ve
8. forf ▯ t
9. conc ▯ t
10. w ▯ ght
11. c ▯ ling
12. y ▯ ld
13. n ▯ ce
14. v ▯ l

15. counterf ▯ t
16. gr ▯ ve
17. rec ▯ pt
18. ach ▯ ve
19. p ▯ ce
20. f ▯ nd
21. bel ▯ ve
22. dec ▯ t
23. sl ▯ gh
24. rel ▯ f
25. r ▯ gn
26. w ▯ gh
27. w ▯ ld
28. ap ▯ ce

29. fr ▯ ghter
30. f ▯ lder
31. bel ▯ f
32. th ▯ f
33. ch ▯ f
34. rel ▯ ve
35. h ▯ ress
36. rec ▯ ve
37. af ▯ ld
38. f ▯ ndish
39. for ▯ gn
40. h ▯ ght
41. fr ▯ ght
42. gr ▯ f

■■ Fill in each box with **-cede, -ceed,** or **-sede** to make a word. Write the words you make.

1. se ▯
2. super ▯
3. ac ▯
4. ex ▯
5. re ▯
6. suc ▯
7. con ▯
8. pro ▯
9. pre ▯

33 Spelling Words Correctly

33a. Dividing Words into Syllables

Divide a word into syllables to help spell the word correctly. Refer to a dictionary for the correct division of a word into syllables.

di - vide   dic - tio - nar - y
syl - la - bles   cor - rect

33b. Pronouncing Words Distinctly

Pronounce a word correctly and distinctly to help spell the word correctly. Pronounce each syllable of a word. Do not leave out any syllables or parts of syllables. Do not add any extra sounds or syllables. Do not substitute one sound for another. Refer to a dictionary for the correct pronunciation of a word.

prob - a - bly   ath - lete
Feb - ru - ar - y   es - cape

PRACTICING YOUR SKILLS

■ Say each of the following words to yourself, pronouncing each syllable distinctly. Then look up the word in a dictionary. Write the word, dividing it into syllables. Pronounce the word again. Did your first pronunciation differ from that given in the dictionary? If so, try to give a reason why.

1. library	17. laboratory	33. generally
2. usually	18. ninety	34. sandwich
3. surprise	19. nuclear	35. handkerchief
4. perhaps	20. miniature	36. difference
5. recognize	21. government	37. sophomore
6. separate	22. clothes	38. hindrance
7. height	23. arctic	39. interfere
8. perspire	24. quantity	40. especially
9. temperature	25. irrelevant	41. length
10. incidentally	26. conference	42. interesting
11. jewel	27. accidentally	43. maintenance
12. realtor	28. temperament	44. practically
13. everybody	29. strictly	45. mathematics
14. lightning	30. representative	46. veterinarian
15. umbrella	31. specifically	47. naturally
16. identity	32. desperate	48. designate

■■ Choose five of the words you made in the preceding exercise. Write a sentence for each.

33c. Words That May Be Confused with Other Words

Certain words may be misspelled because they are similar to other words in spelling or pronunciation. Read and study the following list of words that are often confused and therefore misspelled. Refer to a dictionary for the meaning of any word you are unsure of.

advice—advise	moral—morale
accept—except	passed—past
affect—effect	peace—piece
bare—bear	plain—plane
board—bored	principal—principle
brake—break	scene—seen
calendar—colander	shone—shown
capital—capitol	some—sum
coarse—course	stationary—stationery
council—counsel	than—then
councilor—counselor	their—there—they're
dear—deer	threw—through
dual—duel	to—too—two
formally—formerly	waist—waste
hear—here	weak—week
lessen—lesson	weather—whether
loose—lose	whose—who's
miner—minor	your—you're

PRACTICING YOUR SKILLS

■ Finish each sentence by choosing the correct word from each pair in parentheses. Write the sentences.

1. May I have another (peace, piece) of pie?
2. Baton Rouge is the (capital, capitol) of Louisiana.
3. They both (passed, past) the exam.
4. We were (shone, shown) around the new school.
5. Who is the (principal, principle) of your school?
6. He quickly stepped on the (brake, break).
7. We'll have another exam next (weak, week).
8. What (advice, advise) did you give her?
9. Please (accept, except) my apology.
10. (Your, You're) mother is calling you.
11. The campers were startled by the appearance of a (bare, bear).
12. (Who's, Whose) books are these?
13. The tune was written in the key of C (miner, minor).
14. Did you (loose, lose) your homework again?
15. I don't know (weather, whether) the (weather, whether) will be warm enough for our picnic.
16. How many (councilors, counselors) are on the (council, counsel)?
17. The medicine had no (affect, effect).
18. Is that (their, there, they're) boat over (their, there, they're)?

33d.   A List of Commonly Misspelled Words

Use the following list of words for reference and for study. These words are often misspelled.

abbreviation	biscuit	curiosity	financial
absence	bookkeeper	cylinder	financier
acceptance	bulletin	decision	foreign
accidentally	bureau	definitely	
accommodate		descent	forfeit
accomplish	business	description	fourth
accurate	cafeteria	desperate	fragile
across	calendar	diameter	frequent
acquaintance	campaign	difference	further
address	candidate		generally
	category	disagree	genius
affectionate	cemetery	disappearance	glorious
agriculture	certain	disappointment	government
all right	certificate	discipline	gracious
already	characteristic	economical	
always		efficiency	grammar
amateur	colonel	eighth	guarantee
analyze	colossal	eligible	guard
answer	column	eliminate	gymnasium
apologize	commissioner	embarrass	handkerchief
apology	committee		heavily
	comparative	emphasize	height
appearance	comparison	enthusiastic	hindrance
appreciate	compel	environment	horizon
approach	competition	especially	humorous
approval	complexion	exaggerate	
arctic		excellent	hungrily
ascend	compulsory	exceptional	icy
assassinate	conscience	exercise	ignorance
associate	conscious	exhaust	imaginary
attendance	consensus	existence	imagination
audience	constitution		immediately
	convenience	expense	incidentally
available	cooperate	experience	inconvenience
awkward	correspondence	familiar	incredible
balance	courteous	fascinating	indefinitely
bargain	criticism	fatigue	
believe		February	indicate
bicycle	criticize	feminine	indispensable

inevitable
infinite
influence
innocence
inoculation
insurance
intelligence
interfere

interpretation
irresistible
knowledge
laboratory
leisure
lengthen
lieutenant
lightning
literacy
literature

loneliness
magazine
maintenance
maneuver
marriage
mathematics
mechanical
medicine
medieval
merchandise

microphone
miniature
minimum
mischievous
missile
misspell
mortgage
municipal
muscle
naturally

necessary
nickel
niece

ninety
noticeable
nuclear
nuisance
obstacle
occasionally
occur

occurrence
offense
opinion
outrageous
opportunity
optimistic
originally
pamphlet
parallel
parliament

particularly
percentage
permanent
permissible
perseverance
personal
perspiration
persuade
picnic
picnicking

pleasant
pneumonia
politician
politics
possess
possibility
practically
practice
precede
preference

preferred
prejudice
preparation
privilege

probably
proceed
professor
pronunciation
propeller
prophecy

psychology
pursue
pursuit
qualities
quantity
questionnaire
realize
receipt
recognize
recommendation

reference
referring
rehearse
reign
relieve
repetition
representative
restaurant
rhythm
ridiculous

sandwich
schedule
scissors
secretary
separate
sergeant
similar
sincerely
solemn
sophomore

source
souvenir
specifically
specimen
straighten

strictly
substitute
subtle
succeed
successful

sufficient
summary
superior
surprise
syllable
sympathy
symptom
tariff
temperament
temperature

thorough
throughout
together
tomorrow
traffic
tragedy
transferred
truly
tyranny
twelfth

unanimous
undoubtedly
unnecessary
urgent
vacuum
vengeance
vicinity
villain
weird
wholly

34 Defining Words

34a. Learning New Words

Define an unfamiliar word from its verbal context, or from the other words in the sentence.

Read the sentence in the box. Think about the meaning of the word in dark type.

> I do not doubt the **veracity** of his statement, because he has never told me a lie.

- Why does the speaker not doubt "the veracity of his statement"?
- What does the speaker not doubt?
- What does "veracity" probably mean?

34b. Words That Have Multiple Meanings

Most words have more than one meaning. When you use a dictionary to find the definition of a word, be sure the meaning you choose fits the context in which you found the word.

Read the sentences in the box. Think about the meanings of the words in dark type.

> The speaker **addressed** the audience.
> She **addressed** the envelope.

- In the first sentence, what is the meaning of "addressed"?
- In the second sentence, what is the meaning of "addressed"?

34c. Words That Can Be Used as Different Parts of Speech

Many words can be used as more than one part of speech. Decide how a particular word is being used in a sentence. Then look up in a dictionary the definition of the word when it is used as that part of speech.

Read the sentences in the box. Think about the meanings of the words in dark type.

> The bells **toll** solemnly every hour.
> One must pay a **toll** to cross that bridge.

- In the first sentence, what part of speech is "toll"?
- What does the verb "toll" mean?
- In the second sentence, what part of speech is "toll"?
- What does the noun "toll" mean?

PRACTICING YOUR SKILLS

■ Read each sentence. Use the other words in the sentence to define the word in dark type. Write a brief definition of the word.

1. The ship, seeking **refuge** from the approaching storm, headed towards the harbor.
2. The pirates **plundered** the defenseless ship, leaving nothing of value.
3. They were so **ravenous** that they gulped down their food and still wanted more.
4. The air was delightfully **redolent** with the sweet smell of jasmine.
5. Jonathan had not expected to be called upon; therefore, his speech to the audience was **extemporaneous.**
6. She sought **redress** for the wrong that had been done to her family.
7. The child tried to **placate** the bully, doing everything the bully told him to do.
8. The grieving woman sought **solace** from her family and friends.
9. She **repented** her decision, but it was too late to change it.
10. The ancient Greeks **hypothesized** that the world was round, even though they could not prove it.

■■ Read each sentence. Use a dictionary to find the definition of the word in dark type. Write a brief definition of the word as it is used in the sentence.

1. They invested most of their **capital** in a new business.
2. The kidney **transplant** seems to have been successful.
3. The location of the fort made it **vulnerable** only from the front.
4. The members of the studio audience saw themselves on the **monitor.**
5. Uncle Arnie is the most **rotund** member of the family.
6. They're not interested in making a large profit; they charge only a **nominal** fee.
7. They were arrested last Saturday for **poaching.**
8. Alan wears glasses because he is **shortsighted.**
9. The committee voted to **dissolve** the corporation.
10. Barbara sent money by **cable** to her friend in New Jersey.

■■■ Read each sentence. Determine what part of speech the word in dark type is being used as. Write its part of speech. Look up in a dictionary the definition of the word when it is used as that part of speech. Write a brief definition of the word.

1. Some people season their poultry dressing with **sage.**
2. The old woman was consulted often because she always gave **sage** advice.
3. He designed an **implement** for eating which made forks obsolete.
4. The committee agreed to **implement** the new plan immediately.
5. The traveler had to **compress** the contents of the suitcase.
6. A cold **compress** was placed upon her swollen eyelid.
7. My new shirt has a **ruffle** on each cuff.
8. Sometimes I **ruffle** through the pages of a magazine before I buy it.
9. A delightful **brook** wound its way through the meadow.
10. She insisted that she would **brook** no dissent.
11. The **skate,** gliding through the water, was swallowed by a larger fish.
12. If you know how to **skate,** please join us at the rink tomorrow.

34d. Latin Prefixes and Roots

The following prefixes and roots came into the English language from Latin. Learn the meanings of the prefixes and roots. Knowing the meanings of these word elements will help to define many unfamiliar words.

Prefix	Meaning	Example
ab-, abs-	from, away, off	abnormal, absent
ad-	to, toward, near	adventure, adjoin
bi-	two, twice	bicycle
circum-	around	circumnavigate
com-, con-	with, together	compatriot, conjoin
contra-	against	contraindicate
de-	from, away	defrost, depart
ex-	out of	export
in-	not, into	invisible, indent
inter-	between, among	interstate, intermingle
intra-	within	intrastate
per-	through	perchance
pro-	for, forward	pronoun, prolong
re-	again, back	reheat, return
retro-	backward	retroactive
semi-	half, partly	semicircle, semiconscious
sub-	under	subcommittee
super-	above, beyond	superstructure, superhuman
trans-	across	transatlantic

PRACTICING YOUR SKILLS

- Write the following words. Underline each Latin prefix.

1. propel
2. transmit
3. companion
4. involuntary
5. conjecture
6. circumlocution
7. interjection
8. superstructure
9. adhere
10. conductor
11. producer
12. interrupt
13. inaudible
14. abduct
15. submarine
16. biweekly
17. rejuvenate
18. international
19. semisweet
20. abrupt
21. perambulator
22. intramural
23. adhesion
24. injection
25. retroflex
26. circumflex
27. commiserate
28. perennial
29. perforate
30. aboral
31. rehire
32. contravene

INDEX

Abbreviations
  commas with, 403; reviewing, 405
  of academic degrees, capital letters
    in, 381; reviewing, 390
  of days, capital letters in, 379;
    reviewing, 390
  of months, capital letters in, 379;
    reviewing, 390
  of time, capital letters in, 381;
    reviewing, 390
  periods with, 392; reviewing, 404
Active voice, 212–213
Addresses
  commas in, 393; reviewing, 404
Adjective clauses, 306–311; reviewing,
  318–319
  beginning with relative pronouns,
    217, 306–307; reviewing, 318
  beginning with *when*, 309;
    reviewing, 318–319
  beginning with *where*, 309;
    reviewing, 318–319
  beginning with *whose*, 309;
    reviewing, 318–319
  combining sentences to form, 104
  commas with nonrestrictive,
    310–311, 401; reviewing, 405
  diagraming, 312; reviewing, 319
  misplaced, avoiding, 355; reviewing,
    361
  nonrestrictive, 310–311; reviewing,
    319
  restrictive, 310–311; reviewing, 319
  within sentences, 306–311;
    reviewing, 318–319
  with relative pronoun direct objects,
    308; reviewing, 318
  with relative pronoun subjects,
    306–307; reviewing, 318
Adjective phrases
  misplaced, avoiding, 355; reviewing,
    361
Adjectives
  after noun modified, 234; reviewing,
    246
  after pronoun modified, 234;
    reviewing, 246
  articles as, 230–231
  as object complements, 271;
    reviewing, 275
  capital letters with proper, 388;
    reviewing, 391
  commas between, 394; reviewing,
    404
  comparative form, 352
  comparisons with, 352; reviewing,
    360
  determiners as, 230–231; reviewing,
    246

diagraming, 253; reviewing, 259
infinitive phrases as, 295; reviewing,
  301
less, vs. *fewer*, 359; reviewing, 361
misplaced, avoiding, 355; reviewing,
  361
modified by infinitives, 239;
  reviewing, 247
modified by qualifying adverbs, 237;
  reviewing, 247
modifying nouns, 231–232;
  reviewing, 246
modifying pronouns, 234;
  reviewing, 246
other, vs. *else*, 354; reviewing, 361
parallel structure with, 371;
  reviewing, 375
participial phrases as, 290–291;
  reviewing, 300
participles as, 235; reviewing, 246
phrases as, 286
predicate, 276–277; reviewing, 284
prepositional phrases as, 242, 286;
  reviewing, 247, 300
proper, 233; reviewing, 246
proper, vs. proper nouns, 233
recognizing and using, 230–231;
  reviewing, 246
superlative form, 352
vs. adverbs, 350; reviewing, 359
vs. demonstrative pronouns, 232;
  reviewing, 246
vs. indefinite pronouns, 232;
  reviewing, 246
Adverb clauses, 304; reviewing, 318
  combining sentences to form, 104
  diagraming, 305; reviewing, 318
  introductory, commas after, 400;
    reviewing, 405
  misplaced, avoiding, 357; reviewing,
    361
  with subjunctive form of *be*, 214
Adverb phrases
  misplaced, avoiding, 357; reviewing,
    361
Adverbs
  after linking verbs, 281; reviewing,
    285
  as qualifiers, 237–238
  comparative form, 353
  comparisons with, 353; reviewing,
    360
  diagraming, 253; reviewing, 259
  diagraming qualifying, 254;
    reviewing, 259
  infinitive phrases as, 295; reviewing,
    301
  infinitives as, 239; reviewing, 247
  misplaced, avoiding, 357; reviewing,
    361

modified by qualifying adverbs, 238;
  reviewing, 247
modifying adjectives, 237;
  reviewing, 247
modifying verbs and verb phrases,
  236; reviewing, 246
not as a special, 236
parallel structure with, 371;
  reviewing, 375
phrases as, 286
prepositional phrases as, 242, 286;
  reviewing, 247, 300
qualifying, 237–238; reviewing, 247
recognizing and using, 236;
  reviewing, 247
superlative forms, 353
vs. adjectives, 350; reviewing, 360
Amount
  verb forms with expressions of, 332;
    reviewing, 335
Antecedents of pronouns, 222–223;
  reviewing, 228
  avoiding missing, 364; reviewing,
    374
  avoiding unclear, 363; reviewing,
    374
  compound, 365; reviewing, 374
Apostrophes
  in contractions, 409; reviewing, 414
  in possessive nouns, 409; reviewing,
    414
Application forms
  completing, 97–98
Appositive nouns, 299
Appositive phrases, 299; reviewing,
  301
  combining sentences to form, 350
  commas with, 299, 397; reviewing,
    301, 405
Articles, 230–231
Attitudes, in speaking, 170–171
  evaluating, 188
Auxiliary verbs
  be with present participles, 199;
    reviewing, 216
  do with plural form verbs, 204;
    reviewing, 217
  have with *be* and present participles,
    206–207; reviewing, 217
  have with past participles, 200;
    reviewing, 216

Bad/worse/worst, 352; reviewing, 360
Be
  after *here* and *there*, 330; reviewing,
    335
  as a main verb, 10; reviewing, 216
  forms of, 215; reviewing, 216
  in passive verb phrases, 212–213;
    reviewing, 217

predicate adjectives after, 276–277; reviewing, 284

predicate nominatives after, 276–277; reviewing, 284

subjunctive form of, 214–215; reviewing, 217

Beside, vs. *besides,* 369; reviewing, 375

Between, vs. *among,* 369; reviewing, 375

Bibliographies, 108

Bibliography cards, 69–71, 107

Body language, 166–167
  communicating through, 166
  evaluating use of, 187
  understanding, 167

Book reports
  oral, 178

Business letters, 91–93, 113

Capital letters
  at the beginning of sentences, 376; reviewing, 390
  in abbreviations of academic degrees, 381; reviewing, 390
  in abbreviations of days, 379; reviewing, 390
  in abbreviations of months, 379; reviewing, 390
  in abbreviations of time, 381; reviewing, 390
  in brand names, 386; reviewing, 381
  in direct quotations, 376; reviewing, 390
  in names of awards, 387; reviewing, 381
  in names of buildings and other structures, 383; reviewing, 381
  in names of days, 379; reviewing, 390
  in names of geographical features, 382; reviewing, 391
  in names of highways, 380; reviewing, 390
  in names of historical references, 385; reviewing, 391
  in names of holidays, 379; reviewing, 390
  in names of languages, 389; reviewing, 391
  in names of months, 379; reviewing, 390
  in names of monuments, 387; reviewing, 391
  in names of nationalities, 389; reviewing, 391
  in names of organizations, 385; reviewing, 391
  in names of people, 377; reviewing, 390
  in names of planes, 386; reviewing, 391
  in names of school subjects, 387; reviewing, 391
  in names of ships, 386; reviewing, 391
  in names of trains, 386; reviewing, 391
  in names related to religions, 389; reviewing, 391
  in place names, 380; reviewing, 390
  in proper adjectives, 388; reviewing, 391
  in proper nouns, 377–389; reviewing, 390–391
  in street names, 380; reviewing, 390
  in titles, 384; reviewing, 391
  in titles of people, 378; reviewing, 390
  in titles of relatives, 378; reviewing, 390
  in ZIP code abbreviations, 381; reviewing, 390
  personal pronoun I, 377; reviewing, 390

Characters
  using actions to develop, 39–42
  using descriptions to develop, 35–38
  using dialogue to develop, 43–46

Chronological organization, 50–52
  in narrative speeches, 172
  in paragraphs, 121
  in paragraphs of directions, 55–57
  in summary speeches, 134–135

Clauses, 302–317; reviewing, 318–319
  adjective, 306–311; reviewing, 318–319
  adverb, 304; reviewing, 318
  after subordinating conjunctions, 244, 304
  independent, 302, 317; reviewing, 318–319
  noun, 313–315; reviewing, 319
  subordinate, 304, 306–308, 313–315, 317; reviewing, 318–319

Collective nouns
  verb forms with, 347; reviewing, 355

Colons
  before lists, 410; reviewing, 415
  in expressions of time, 410; reviewing, 415

Commands. *See* Imperative sentences

Commas
  after interjections, 395; reviewing, 405
  after introductory adverb clauses, 400; reviewing, 405
  after introductory adverbial prepositional phrases, 398; reviewing, 405
  after introductory *yes* and *no,* 395; reviewing, 405
  between adjectives, 394; reviewing, 404
  in addresses, 393; reviewing, 404
  in compound sentences, 302, 396; reviewing, 405
  in dates, 205; reviewing, 404
  in place names, 205; reviewing, 404
  in series, 394; reviewing, 404
  with abbreviations, 393; reviewing, 405
  with appositive phrases, 309, 397; reviewing, 301, 405
  with direct quotations, 407; reviewing, 404
  with interrupters, 395; reviewing, 405
  with introductory participial phrases, 399; reviewing, 405
  with nonrestrictive adjective clauses 310–311, 401; reviewing, 405
  with nonrestrictive participial phrases, 290, 399; reviewing, 405
  with nouns of address, 395; reviewing, 404
  with transitional words and phrases, 402; reviewing, 405

Common nouns, 219; reviewing, 228

Communications, 157–171
  analyzing, 158–159
  nonverbal, 166–167
  reasons for breakdown of, 158–159

Comparative form
  of adjectives, 352
  of adverbs, 353

Comparison, paragraphs of, 58–60, 120

Comparisons
  other and *else* in, 354; reviewing, 361
  personal pronouns in, 368
  reviewing, 374
  with adjectives, 352; reviewing, 360
  with adverbs, 352; reviewing, 360
  with *good* or *bad,* 352; reviewing, 360
  with *less* and *fewer,* 359; reviewing, 361
  with *well,* 353; reviewing, 360

Complex sentences, 317; reviewing, 319

Composing
  guidelines for, 10–12

Compound-complex sentences, 317; reviewing, 319

Compound direct objects; 263; reviewing, 274

Compound indirect objects; 268; reviewing, 275

Compound nouns
  plural forms of, 420

Compound predicate adjectives, 279; reviewing, 284

Compound predicate nominatives, 280; eviewing, 284–285

Compound predicates, 250; reviewing, 258
  combining sentences to form, 104
  diagraming, 257; reviewing, 259

Compound sentences, 302, 317; reviewing, 318–319
  commas in, 62, 302; reviewing, 405
  diagraming, 313; reviewing, 318

semicolons in, 313; reviewing, 415
Compound subjects, 250; reviewing, 250
   combining sentences to form, 104
   diagraming, 256; reviewing, 259
   verb forms with, 256; reviewing, 335
Conjunctions, 243–244; reviewing, 247
   coordinating, 243; reviewing, 247
   correlative, parallel structure with, 373; reviewing, 375
   subordinating, 244; reviewing, 247
Connotation, 81
Contractions
   apostrophes in, 409; reviewing, 414
Contrast, paragraphs of, 61–63, 120
Conversations
   listening in, 147–148, 163
   participating in, 147–149, 163
   presenting information in, 131–133
Countries
   verb forms with names of, 331; reviewing, 335

Dangling modifiers
   avoiding, 356; reviewing, 361
Dates
   commas in, 393; reviewing, 404
Debates, 184–185
Declarative sentences, 190; reviewing, 194
   predicates in most, 191; reviewing, 194
   separated verb phrase words in, 202; reviewing, 216
   subjects in most, 191; reviewing, 194
   with inverted order, 192; reviewing, 195
Defining words
   from verbal context, 432–433
   that can be used as different parts of speech, 432–433
   that have multiple meanings, 432–433
   with Latin prefixes and roots, 434
Demonstrative pronouns, 227; reviewing, 29
   vs. adjectives, 232; reviewing, 246
Denotation, 81
Descriptive essays, 32–33
Descriptive paragraphs, 21–31
   sensory details in, 24–26
   spatial organization in, 29–31
   supporting details in, 21–23
   topic sentences in, 21–23
   unusual comparisons in, 27–28
Descriptive writing, 20–33
Details
   in paragraphs, 116
   sensory, in descriptive paragraphs, 24–26
   supporting, in descriptive paragraphs, 21–23

Determiners, 230–231; reviewing, 246
   articles as, 230
Diagnostic checklists, 186–188
Diagrams, sentence. See Sentence diagrams
Dialogue
   writing, 43–46
Direct objects, 260–264; reviewing, 274
   compound, 263; reviewing, 274
   diagraming, 265; reviewing, 274
   gerund phrases as, diagraming, 289; reviewing, 300
   infinitive phrases as, 294
   infinitive phrases as, diagraming, 294; reviewing, 301
   modifiers with, 261; reviewing, 274
   noun clauses as, 315; reviewing, 319
   noun clauses as, diagraming, 316; reviewing, 319
   nouns as, 260; reviewing, 274
   passive verb phrases from sentences with, 264; reviewing, 274
   pronouns as, 260, 262; reviewing, 274
Direct quotations
   capital letters in, 376; reviewing, 390
   commas in, 407; reviewing, 414
   exclamation marks with, 407; reviewing, 414
   periods in, 407; reviewing, 414
   question marks with, 407; reviewing, 414
   quotation marks with, 407; reviewing, 414
   within direct quotations, 408; reviewing, 414
Directions
   giving, 131–133
   writing, 55–57
Discussions
   group, 179
   panel, 180–182
Do
   as an auxiliary with plural form verbs, 204; reviewing, 217
   forms of, 333, 343; reviewing, 335, 349
Double negatives
   avoiding, 358; reviewing, 361
Drafting
   guidelines for, 7–9

End punctuation. See Exclamation marks; Periods; Question marks
Envelopes, addressing, 114
Essays
   descriptive, 32–33
   expository, 67
   persuasive, 88–89
Examples
   in paragraphs, 64–66, 119
Exclamation marks
   at the end of sentences, 392; reviewing, 404

with direct quotations, 407; reviewing, 414
Expository essays, 67
Expository paragraphs, 55–66
   comparisons in, 58–60
   contrast in, 61–63
   examples in, 64–66
Expository speaking, 130–139
   guidelines for, 173
Expository writing, 54–67

Footnotes, 110
Formal language, 168
Fractions
   hyphens in, 413; reviewing, 415
Fragments. See Sentence fragments
Friendly letters, 112

Gerund phrases, 287; reviewing, 300
   as direct objects, diagraming, 299; reviewing, 300
   as subjects, diagraming, 288; reviewing, 300
   parallel structure with, 372; reviewing, 375
Gerunds, 220, 287; reviewing, 228, 300
   parallel structure with, 372; reviewing, 375
   possessive pronouns before, 368; reviewing, 374
Good/better/best, 352; reviewing, 360
Good, vs. well, 353; reviewing, 360
Greek nouns
   plural forms of, 420
Group discussions, 179
Group speaking, 179–185
   evaluating, 188
   group discussions, 179
   panel discussions, 180–181

Have
   as an auxiliary with past participles, 200; reviewing, 216
   in passive verb phrases, 212–213
   with the auxiliary be and present participles, 206–207; reviewing, 217
Here and there
   verb forms with, 330; reviewing, 335
Hyphens, 413; reviewing, 415

Imperative sentences, 190; reviewing, 194
   predicates in, 192; reviewing, 195
   subjects in, 192; reviewing, 195
In, vs. into; reviewing, 375
Incidents
   in paragraphs, 117
Indefinite pronouns, 225; reviewing, 229
   verb forms with, 346; reviewing, 335
   vs. adjectives, 421; reviewing, 246

Independent clauses, 302, 317; reviewing, 318–319
Indirect objects, 266–269; reviewing, 274–275
  compound, 268; reviewing, 273
  modifiers with, 267; reviewing, 275
  noun clauses as, 315; reviewing, 319
  nouns as, 266; reviewing, 274
  passive verb phrases from sentences with, 269; reviewing, 275
  pronouns as, 266, 362; reviewing, 274
Infinitive phrases, 294–298; reviewing, 301
  as adjectives, 295; reviewing, 301
  as adjectives, diagraming, 298; reviewing, 301
  as adverbs, 296; reviewing, 301
  as adverbs, diagraming, 298; reviewing, 301
  as direct objects, 294
  as direct objects, diagraming, 297; reviewing, 301
  as nouns, 294; reviewing, 301
  as nouns, diagraming, 297; reviewing, 301
  as subjects, 294
  as subjects, diagraming, 297; reviewing, 301
  diagraming, 298–299; reviewing, 301
  parallel structure with, 372; reviewing, 375
  verb form in, 291
Infinitives
  as adverbs, 239; reviewing, 247
  as nouns, 221; reviewing, 228
  infinitive phrases, 294–296
  parallel structure with, 372; reviewing, 375
Informal language, 168
Instructions
  giving, 131–133
Interjections, 245; reviewing, 247
Interrogative pronouns, 226; reviewing, 229
  who and whom as, 366; reviewing, 374
Interrogative sentences, 190; reviewing, 194
  predicates in, 193; reviewing, 195
  separated verb phrase words in, 202; reviewing, 216
  subjects in, 193; reviewing, 195
Interrupters
  commas with, 395; reviewing, 404
Interviews
  asking questions in, 151–156
  guidelines, 175
  listening in, 155–156
  preparing for, 151–154, 175
  questions in, 175
  responding in, 155–156
  taking notes in, 175
Intransitive verbs, 248–251; reviewing, 258

  diagraming sentences with, 252–257; reviewing, 259
  modifiers in sentences with, 249; reviewing, 258
  vs. transitive verbs, 261; reviewing, 274
Introduction
  speeches of, 176
Irregular nouns
  plural forms of, 420
Irregular verbs, 197, 336–345; reviewing, 216, 348–349

Language, in speaking
  appropriate, 168–169
  direct, 168–169
  levels of, 168
  vivid, 168–169
Latin nouns
  plural forms of, 421
Latin prefixes, 434
Latin roots, 434
Less, vs. fewer, 359; reviewing, 361
Letters
  business, 91–93, 113
  friendly, 112
Linking verbs, 276–277; reviewing, 284
  adverbs after, 281; reviewing, 285
  diagraming, 281; reviewing, 285
  predicate adjectives after, 276–277; reviewing, 284
  predicate nominatives after, 276–277; reviewing, 284
  prepositional phrases after, 281; reviewing, 285
Listening, 146–156
  evaluating, 186
  guidelines for, 163–165
  in a conversation, 147–148, 163
  in a formal meeting, 149–150
  in an interview, 155–156
  to speeches, 164–165
Lists
  colons before, 410; reviewing, 415
  semicolons in, 411; reviewing, 415

Missing antecedents
  avoiding, 364; reviewing, 374
Modals, 201; reviewing, 216
  with auxiliary be and present participles, 205; reviewing, 217
  with auxiliary have and past participles,05; reviewing, 217
  with have, be, and present participles, 206–207; reviewing, 217
Modifiers
  dangling, avoid, 356; reviewing, 361
  in sentences with direct objects, 261; reviewing, 274
  in sentences with indirect objects, 267; reviewing, 275
  in sentences with intransitive verbs, 249; reviewing, 258
  in sentences with object complements, 272; reviewing, 275

  in sentences with predicate adjectives, 278; reviewing, 284
  in sentences with predicate nominatives, 278; reviewing, 284

Narrative paragraphs, 35–49
Narrative speaking, 125–129
Narrative speeches, 128–129, 172
  guidelines for, 172
  preparing for, 128–129, 172
Narrative writing, 34–53
  describing characters in, 35–38
  using actions in, 36–38
  using dialogue in, 43–46
Negatives
  avoiding double, 350; reviewing, 161
No
  commas after introductory, 395; reviewing, 405
Nomination
  speeches of, 176
Nonrestrictive adjective clauses, 310–311; reviewing, 319
  commas with, 310–311, 401; reviewing, 405
Nonrestrictive participial phrases, 290–291; reviewing, 300
  commas with, 290, 399; reviewing, 405
Nonverbal communication, 166–167
Note cards, 109
  for research reports, 72–73
  organizing, 74–76
Note-taking, 106–108
  bibliographies, 110
  bibliography cards, 69–71, 107
  footnotes, 108
  for summary speeches, 134–135
  in formal meetings, 149–150
  in interviews, 151–152, 175
  in speeches, 164–165
  note cards, 72–73, 109
  summary sentences, 106
Noun clauses, 313–315, reviewing, 319
  as direct objects, 315; reviewing, 319
  as indirect objects, 315; reviewing, 319
  as objects of prepositions, 315; reviewing, 319
  as predicate nominatives, 311; reviewing, 319
  as subjects, 313; reviewing, 319
  diagraming, 316; reviewing, 319
Nouns
  apostrophes with possessive, 409; reviewing, 414
  appositive, 299
  as direct objects, 260; reviewing, 274
  as indirect objects, 266; reviewing, 274
  as object complements, 271; reviewing, 275
  as objects of prepositions, 240–241, 286; reviewing, 247

as predicate nominatives, 276–277; reviewing, 284
common, 219; reviewing, 228
gerund phrases, 287; reviewing, 300
gerunds, 220, 287; reviewing, 228, 300
infinitive phrase as, 294; reviewing, 301
infinitives as, 221; reviewing, 228
of address, 395; reviewing, 404
parallel structure with, 371; reviewing, 375
phrases as, 297
plural forms, 416–421
possessive, 409; reviewing, 414
proper, 219; reviewing, 228
proper vs. proper adjectives, 233
recognizing and using, 218; reviewing, 228
verb forms with collective, 317; reviewing, 335
Numbers
hyphens in, 413; reviewing, 415

Object complements
adjectives as, 271; reviewing, 275
diagraming, 273; reviewing, 275
modifiers with, 274; reviewing, 275
nouns as, 271; reviewing, 275
Object form pronouns, 222–223, 362; reviewing, 374
Objects, direct. See Direct objects
Objects, indirect. See Indirect objects
Objects of prepositions, 240–241; reviewing, 247
noun clauses as, 315; reviewing, 319
nouns as, 240–241, 286; reviewing, 247
pronouns as, 240–241, 286, 362; reviewing, 217
Oral reports
book, 178
research, 138, 139
Organization in paragraphs
chronological, 121
spatial, 29–31, 122
Organizations
capital letters in names of, 385; reviewing, 391
verb forms with names of, 331; reviewing, 335
Other, vs. else, 354; reviewing, 361
Outlines, 111
final, for research reports, 74–76
preliminary, for research reports, 69–71

Panel discussions, 180–181
Paragraphs
chronological organization in, 121
descriptive, 21–31
details in, 116
examples in, 64–65, 119
expository, 55–66
incidents in, 117

narrative, 35–49
of comparison, 27–28, 58–60, 120
of contrast, 61–63, 120
of directions, 55–57
persuasive, 85–87
reasons in, 118
spatial organization in, 29–31, 122
topic sentences in, 115
Parallel structure, 371–373; reviewing, 375
Parentheses, 413; reviewing, 415
Parliamentary procedure, 182–183
Participial phrases as adjectives, 290–291; reviewing, 300
commas with introductory, 399; reviewing, 405
commas with nonrestrictive, 296, 399; reviewing, 405
diagraming, 293; reviewing, 300–301
nonrestrictive, 290–291; reviewing, 300
restrictive, 292; reviewing, 300
Participles
as adjectives, 235; reviewing, 246
in participial phrases, 290–291; reviewing, 300
past, in participial phrases, 290–291; reviewing, 300
past, in passive verb phrases, 212–213; reviewing, 217
past, with have as auxiliary, 200, 205; reviewing, 216–217
present, in participial phrases, 290–291; reviewing, 300
present, with be as auxiliary, 199, 205; reviewing, 216–219
Parts of speech. See individual parts of speech, for example, Nouns; Verbs
Passive verb phrases, 212–213; reviewing, 219
from sentences with direct objects, 264; reviewing, 274
from sentences with indirect objects, 269; reviewing, 275
Passive voice, 212–213
Past participle verb forms, 200, 205; reviewing, 216–217
in participial phrases, 290–291; reviewing, 300
in passive verb phrases, 212–213; reviewing, 217
with have as an auxiliary, 200, 205; reviewing, 216–217
Past tense verb forms, 197, 336–343; reviewing, 348–349
Periods
at the end of sentences, 392; reviewing, 404
with abbreviations, 352; reviewing, 404
with direct quotations, 407; reviewing, 414
Personal pronouns. See Pronouns personal

Persuasive paragraphs, 85–87
Persuasive slogans, 81–84
Persuasive speeches, 143–144
guidelines for, 174
preparing for, 144–145, 174
Persuasive writing, 80–89
slogans, 81–84
Phrases, 278–299; reviewing, 300–301
appositive, 299; reviewing, 301
as sentences fragments, 320; reviewing, 334
gerund, 287–289; reviewing, 300
infinitive, 294–296; reviewing, 301
nonrestrictive participial, 290–291; reviewing, 300
participial, 290–294; reviewing, 300–301
passive verb, 212–213, 264, 270; reviewing, 219, 274–275
prepositional, 240–241, 286; reviewing, 247, 300
restrictive participial, 292; reviewing, 300
verb, 199–207, 212–213; reviewing, 216–217
Plots
of short stories; 47–49
Plural forms of nouns, 420–421
compound, 420
Greek, 421
irregular, 420
Latin, 421
that add -es, 416
that add -s, 416
that do not change, 410
that end in a consonant and o, 419
that end in a consonant and y, 417
that end in a vowel and o, 419
that end in a vowel and y, 417
that end in f, 418
that end in fe, 418
Plural form verbs, 196, 208–209, 325
Possessive nouns, 409; reviewing, 414
Possessive pronouns, 224; reviewing, 229
before gerunds, 368; reviewing, 374
diagraming, 252; reviewing, 259
Practical writing, 90–100
Predicate adjectives, 276–279; reviewing, 284
compound, 279; reviewing, 284
diagraming, 282; reviewing, 285
modifiers with, 278; reviewing, 284
Predicate nominatives, 276–277; reviewing, 284
compound, 280; reviewing, 284–285
diagraming, 282; reviewing, 285
modifiers with, 278; reviewing, 284
noun clauses as, 314; reviewing, 319
nouns as, 276–277; reviewing, 284
pronouns as, 276–277, 362; reviewing, 284
Predicates, 191–193; reviewing, 194–195
compound, 250; reviewing, 258

diagraming, 252; reviewing, 259
diagraming compound, 257;
  reviewing, 259
simple, 283; reviewing, 285
Prefixes, 422–423
Prepositional phrases, 240–241, 296;
  reviewing, 247, 300
  after linking verbs, 281; reviewing,
    285
  as adjectives, 242, 286; reviewing,
    247, 300
  as adverbs, 242, 286; reviewing, 247,
    300
  diagraming, 255; reviewing, 259
  introductory adverbial, commas
    after, 398; reviewing, 405
  recognizing and using, 240–241,
    286; reviewing, 247, 300
Prepositions
  at, 370; reviewing, 375
  beside, vs. besides, 369; reviewing, 375
  between, vs. among, 181; reviewing,
    375
  in, vs. into, 370; reviewing, 375
  of, 370; reviewing, 375
  recognizing and using, 240–241;
    reviewing, 247
Present participle verb forms, 199,
  205–207; reviewing, 216–217
  as gerunds, 287
  in participial phrases, 290–292;
    reviewing, 300
  with be as an auxiliary, 199, 205;
    reviewing, 216–217
Present tense verb forms, 196, 315;
  reviewing, 216, 334
Prewriting activities, 3–9
Pronouns
  demonstrative. See Demonstrative
    pronouns
  indefinite. See Indefinite pronouns
  interrogative. See Interrogative
    pronouns
  personal, 221–223, 226; reviewing,
    228–229
  personal, as direct objects, 260, 362;
    reviewing, 274
  personal, as indirect objects, 266,
    362; reviewing, 274
  personal, as objects of prepositions,
    240–241, 286, 362; reviewing, 247
  personal, as predicate nominatives,
    276–277, 362; reviewing, 284
  personal, in comparisons, 368;
    reviewing, 274
  personal, object form, 222–223, 362;
    reviewing, 274
  personal, possessive forms, 224;
    reviewing, 229
  personal, recognizing and using,
    222–223; reviewing, 229
  personal, reflexive, 226; reviewing,
    229
  personal, subject form, 221–223,
    362; reviewing, 274

personal, with compound
  antecedents, 365; reviewing, 274
relative. See Relative pronouns
Proofreading, 18–19, 105
Proofreading checklist, 105
Proper adjectives, 233; reviewing, 246
  capital letters in, 388; reviewing, 391
  diagraming, 252
Proper nouns, 219; reviewing, 228
  capital letters in, 377–389;
    reviewing, 390–391
Propositions, in debates, 184

Qualifying adverbs, 237–238;
  reviewing, 247
  diagraming, 254; reviewing, 259
  modifying adjectives, 237;
    reviewing, 247
  modifying adverbs; 238; reviewing,
    247
Question marks
  at the end of sentences, 392;
    reviewing, 404
  with direct quotations, 407;
    reviewing, 414
Questions. See Interrogative sentences
  in interviews, 151–156, 175
Quotation marks
  with direct quotations, 407;
    reviewing, 414
  with direct quotations within
    quotations, 408; reviewing, 414
  with titles, 406; reviewing, 414
  with titles within direct quotations,
    408; reviewing, 414

Rambling sentences, avoiding, 322–
  323; reviewing, 334
Reasons
  in paragraphs, 118
Rebuttal speeches
  in debates, 184
Relative pronouns, 227; reviewing,
  229
  as direct objects in adjective clauses,
    308; reviewing, 318
  as subjects in adjective clauses 306–
    307; reviewing, 318
  who and whom as, 367; reviewing, 374
Repetition
  avoiding unnecessary, 324;
    reviewing, 334
  unnecessary, combining sentences
    to avoid, 104
Reports, oral book, 178
Reports, oral research, 138–139
Reports, research. See Research
  reports
Research reports, 68–79
Restrictive adjective clauses, 310–311;
  reviewing, 319
Restrictive participial phrases, 292;
  reviewing, 300
Reviews
  movie, 94–96
Revising
  sentences, in writing, 15–17
  words, in writing, 12–14
Run-on sentences
  avoiding, 321; reviewing, 334

School subjects
  capital letters in names of, 387;
    reviewing, 391
Semicolons
  in compound sentences, 412;
    reviewing, 415
  in lists, 411; reviewing, 415
Sense images, 24–26
Sentence diagrams
  adjective clauses, 312; reviewing,
    319
  adjectives, 253; reviewing, 259
  adverb clauses, 305; reviewing, 318
  adverbs, 253; reviewing, 259
  compound predicates, 257;
    reviewing, 259
  compound sentences, 303;
    reviewing, 318
  compound subjects, 256; reviewing,
    257
  direct objects, 265; reviewing, 274
  gerund phrases, 288–289;
    reviewing, 300
  gerund phrases as direct objects,
    289; reviewing, 300
  gerund phrases as subjects, 288;
    reviewing, 300
  infinitive phrases, 297–298;
    reviewing, 301
  infinitive phrases as adjectives, 298;
    reviewing, 301
  infinitive phrases as adverbs, 298;
    reviewing, 301
  infinitive phrases as direct objects,
    297; reviewing, 301
  infinitive phrases as nouns, 297;
    reviewing, 301
  infinitive phrases as subjects, 297;
    reviewing, 301
  intransitive verbs, 252; reviewing,
    254
  linking verbs, 282; reviewing, 285
  noun clauses, 317; reviewing, 319
  object complements, 273; reviewing,
    275
  participial phrases, 293; reviewing,
    300–301
  possessive pronouns, 252
  predicate adjectives, 282; reviewing,
    285
  predicate nominatives, 282;
    reviewing, 285
  predicates, 252; reviewing, 259
  prepositional phrases, 255;
    reviewing, 259
  proper adjectives, 252
  qualifying adverbs, 254; reviewing,
    259
  subjects, 252; reviewing, 259
Sentence fragments
  avoiding, 320; reviewing, 334
Sentence structure
  proofreading for incorrect, 18–19
Sentence variety, 102–104
Sentences
  avoiding unnecessary repetition in,
    324; reviewing, 336
  capital letters at the beginning of,
    376; reviewing, 390
  commas in compound, 302, 396;
    reviewing, 405

complex, 317; reviewing, 319
compound, 302, 317; reviewing, 318–319
compound-complex, 317; reviewing, 319
declarative, 190; reviewing, 194
declarative, with inverted order, 192; reviewing, 195
imperative, 190; reviewing, 194
interrogative, 190; reviewing, 194
kinds of, 190; reviewing, 194
predicates in, 191–193; reviewing, 194–195
rambling, avoiding, 321–322; reviewing, 336
revising, 15–17
run-on, avoiding, 321; reviewing, 334
semicolons in compound, 412; reviewing, 415
simple, 317; reviewing, 319
subjects in, 191–193; reviewing, 194–195
summary, 106
topic, in paragraphs, 21–23, 115
varying in beginnings of, 103
varying length of, 103
Series
commas in, 394; reviewing, 404
Short stories
chronological order in, 50–52
describing characters in, 35–38
developing plots in, 47–49
dialogue in, 43–46
using actions to develop, 39–42
writing, 53
Simple predicate, 283; reviewing, 385
Simple sentences, 317; reviewing, 319
Simple subject, 283; reviewing, 285
Singular form verbs, 196, 208–209, 346
Slang, 168
Spatial organization
in descriptive paragraphs, 29–31
in paragraphs, 122
Speaking
attitudes in, 170–171
attitudes in, evaluating, 188
audience response, understanding, 167
clearly, 160–161
distinctly, 160–161
expository, 130–139
group, 179–185
guidelines for, 162–164
in debates, 185
kinds of, 172–175
narrative, 124–129
oral book reports, 178
pauses in, 162
persuasive, 140–145
pitch in effective, 162
rate in effective, 162
strongly, 160–161
using vocal variety, 162
volume in effective, 160–162
word choice in, 168–169
Speeches
expository, 173
listening to, 164–165

main, in debates, 184
narrative, 128–129, 172
of acceptance, 177
of introduction, 176
of nomination, 176
of presentation, 177
persuasive, 174
rebuttal, in debates, 184
summary, 134–135
using visual aids in, 136–137
Spelling
commonly misspelled words, 430–431
dividing words into syllables to, 428
pronouncing words distinctly to, 428
with prefixes, 422–423
with suffixes, 424–426
words that are ofen confused, 421
words that end in -cede, -ceed, and -sede, 427
words with ie and ei, 427
Statements. See Declarative sentences
thesis, in research reports, 74–76
Subject form pronouns, 222–223, 362; reviewing, 374
Subjects 191–193, 194–195
collective nouns as, 327; reviewing, 335
compound, 250, 329; reviewing, 258, 335
diagraming, 252; reviewing, 259
diagraming compound, 256; reviewing, 259
expressions of amount as, 332; reviewing, 335
gerund phrases as, diagraming, 288; reviewing, 300
indefinite pronouns as, 346; reviewing, 335
infinitive phrases as, 294
infinitive phrases as, diagraming, 297; reviewing, 301
modified by prepositional phrases, 328; reviewing, 335
names of countries as, 331; reviewing, 335
names of organizations as, 331; reviewing, 335
noun clauses as, 313; reviewing, 319
noun clauses as, diagraming, 316; reviewing, 319
simple, 283; reviewing, 285
titles as, 331; reviewing, 335
writing, choosing for, 3–6
Subjunctive form of be, 214–215; reviewing, 217
Subordinate clauses, 304, 306–311, 313–315, 317; reviewing, 318–319
adjective clauses, 306–311; reviewing, 318
adverb clauses, 304; reviewing, 318
as sentence fragments, 320; reviewing, 334

noun clauses, 313–315; reviewing, 319
Subordinating conjunctions, 244; reviewing, 247
Suffixes
spelling with, 424–426
Summary sentences, 106
Summary speeches, 134–135
preparing for, 134–135
Superlative form
of adjectives, 352
of adverbs, 353

Telling stories, 125–127
Tense, verb, 208–211; reviewing, 219
avoiding shifts in, 347; reviewing, 349
Thesis statements
in research reports, 74–76
Titles
capital letters in, 384; reviewing, 391
quotation marks with, 406; reviewing, 414
underlines with, 406; reviewing, 414
verb forms with, 331; reviewing, 336
within direct quotations, quotation marks with, 408; reviewing, 414
Topic
choosing for research reports, 69–71
guidelines for choosing, 3–6
Topic sentences, 21–23, 115
Transitional words and phrases, 16–17, 50–57
commas with, 402; reviewing, 405
Transitive verbs; 72; reviewing, 274
vs. intransitive verbs, 262; reviewing, 274

Underlines of titles, 406; reviewing, 414

Verb phrases
auxiliaries in, 199–200, 204–207; reviewing, 216–217
in interrogative sentences, 202–203; reviewing, 216
modals in, 201, 205–207; reviewing, 216–217
passive, 212–213; reviewing, 217
passive, from sentences with direct objects, 264; reviewing, 274
passive, from sentences with indirect objects, 269; reviewing, 275
past participles in, 200–205; reviewing, 216–217
plural forms in, 201–204
present participles in, 199, 205–207; reviewing, 216–217
separated parts of, 202–203; reviewing, 216
Verbs
auxiliaries, 199–200, 204–205; reviewing, 216–217

avoiding shifts in tense, 347;
reviewing, 349
be, 198–199, 205–207; reviewing,
216–217
begin/began/begun, 339; reviewing,
348
blow/blew/blown, 341; reviewing, 349
break/broke/broken, reviewing, 348
bring/brought/brought, 337; reviewing,
348
burst/burst/burst, 343; reviewing, 348
choose/chose/chosen, 342; reviewing,
348
come/came/come, 343; reviewing, 349
do, 204, 333, 343; reviewing, 216,
335, 349
drink/drank/drunk, 329; reviewing,
348
drive/drove/driven, 336; reviewing,
348
eat/ate/eaten, 338; reviewing, 348
fall/fell/fallen, 343; reviewing, 349
fly/flew/flown, 341; reviewing, 348
forms after *here* and *there*, 330;
reviewing, 335
forms after prepositional phrases,
338; reviewing, 335
forms in infinitive phrases, 294
forms with collective noun subjects,
337; reviewing, 335
forms with compound subjects, 339;
reviewing, 335
forms with expressions of amount,
332; reviewing, 335
forms with indefinite pronoun
subjects; 326; reviewing, 335
forms with names of countries, 331;
reviewing, 335
forms with names of organizations,
331; reviewing, 335
forms with titles, 331; reviewing,
335
freeze/froze/frozen, 342; reviewing, 348
give/gave/given, 338; reviewing, 348
go/went/gone, 343; reviewing, 349
grow/grew/grown, 341; reviewing, 348
have, 200, 205–207; reviewing, 216–
217
intransitive, 248–251, 262;
reviewing, 258, 274
irregular, 197, 336–353; reviewing,
216, 348–349

know/knew/known, 343; reviewing,
348
lie/lay/lain, 338; reviewing, 348
lie, vs. *lay*, 344; reviewing, 349
linking, 276–277; reviewing, 284
modals, 201, 205–207; reviewing,
216–217
past tense, 197, 336–343; reviewing,
216, 348–349
plural form, 196, 325
present tense forms, 196, 325;
reviewing, 216, 334
recognizing and using, 196;
reviewing, 216
ride/rode/ridden, 336; reviewing, 348
ring/rang/rung, 339, reviewing, 348
rise/rose/risen, 336; reviewing, 348
rise, vs. *raise*, 344; reviewing, 349
run/ran/run, 343; reviewing, 349
see/saw/seen, 343; reviewing, 349
seek/sought/sought, 339; reviewing,
348
shrink/shrank/shrunk, 339; reviewing,
348
singular form, 196, 325
sit, vs. *set*, 346; reviewing, 349
speak/spoke/spoken, 342; reviewing,
348
steal/stole/stolen, 342; reviewing, 348
swim/swam/swum, 339; reviewing,
348
take/took/taken, 343; reviewing, 349
teach/taught/taught, 337; reviewing,
348
teach, vs. *learn*, 346; reviewing, 349
tear/tore/torn, 340; reviewing, 348
think/thought/thought, 337; reviewing,
348
throw/threw/thrown, 341; reviewing,
348
transitive, 260, 262; reviewing, 274
wear/wore/worn, 340; reviewing, 348
write/wrote/written, 336; reviewing,
348
Voice
evaluating use of, 186
guidelines for using effectively,
106–107
Volume
in effective speaking, 106–108

Well
as adjective, 351; reviewing, 360
as adverb, 351; reviewing, 360
Well/better/best, 353; reviewing, 360
Who and *whom*
as interrogative pronouns, 366;
reviewing, 374
as relative pronouns, 367;
reviewing, 374
Word choice in speaking, 168–169
appropriate language, 168–169
direct language, 168–169
evaluating, 187
specific words, 168–169
vivid language, 168–169
Words
as sentence fragments, 320;
reviewing, 334
inappropriate, in writing, 11–14
in writing, revising, 12–14
specific, in speaking, 168–169
specific, in writing, 12–14
Writing
business letters, 91–93, 113
connecting ideas in, 16–17
descriptive, 20–33
directions, 55–57
expository, 54–67
friendly letters, 112
inappropriate words in, 13–14
kinds of, 7
movie reviews, 94–96
narrative, 34–53
outlines, 69–71, 74–76, 111
persuasive, 80–89
practical, 90–100
research reports, 77–79
revising sentences in, 15–17
revising words in, 12–14
sentence variety, 13–15
short stories, 53
specific words in, 12–14
transitional words and phrases in,
16–17
Writing process, 2–19

Yes
commas after introductory, 395;
reviewing, 405